Approaches to Teaching Langland's *Piers Plowman*

The John Louis Haney Fund
provided generous support
for this publication.

Approaches to Teaching Langland's *Piers Plowman*

Edited by

Thomas A. Goodmann

The Modern Language Association of America
New York 2018

Printed in the United States of America

Library of Congress Cataloging-in-Publication Data:

Names: Goodmann, Thomas A., 1956– editor.
Title: Approaches to teaching Langland's Piers Plowman / edited by Thomas A. Goodmann.
Description: New York : The Modern Language Association of America, 2018. |
Series: Approaches to teaching world literature ; 151 | Includes bibliographical references and index.
Identifiers: LCCN 2018026989 (print) | LCCN 2018028514 (ebook) |
ISBN 9781603293396 (cloth : alk. paper) | ISBN 9781603293402 (pbk. : alk. paper)
ISBN 9781603293419 (EPUB) | ISBN 9781603293426 (Kindle) |
Subjects: LCSH: Langland, William, 1330?–1400? Piers Plowman. |
Langland, William, 1330?–1400?—Study and teaching.
Classification: LCC PR2015 (ebook) | LCC PR2015 .A67 2018 (print) | DDC 821/.1—dc23
LC record available at https://lccn.loc.gov/2018026989

Approaches to Teaching World Literature 151
ISSN 1059-1133

Cover illustration of the paperback and electronic editions:
Detail of a miniature of a man plowing with oxen. British Library, Royal MS 12 F XIII, fol. 37v. Public domain image from the British Library's Web site: www.bl.uk/catalogues/illuminatedmanuscripts/ILLUMIN.ASP?Size=mid&IllID=43183.

Published by The Modern Language Association of America
85 Broad Street, suite 500, New York, New York 10004-2434
www.mla.org

CONTENTS

ACKNOWLEDGMENTS

In editing this book I have accumulated many debts, and I offer my thanks for the patience and professionalism of editors throughout this process at the Modern Language Association; to all the accommodating contributors to this volume; and to many colleagues who answered questions and offered advice, especially Frank Grady, Ralph Hanna, Kathryn Kerby-Fulton, Thomas Prendergast, Elizabeth Robertson, Sylvia Tomasch, Stephanie Trigg, and Lawrence Warner. Andrew Cole and Andrew Galloway kindly shared work prior to its publication, as did Michael Calabrese; their generosity helped make introductory material as up-to-date as possible.

I am deeply grateful to my teachers and teaching colleagues with whom I have explored *Piers Plowman* and many other medieval sources. Carter Revard has offered many years of supportive and lively exchange that began when I was an undergraduate at Washington University in St. Louis. In graduate studies at Indiana University, and long afterward, I have benefited greatly from the instruction, advice, and friendship of E. Talbot Donaldson, Alfred David, Paul Strohm, and Sheila Lindenbaum. I owe special thanks to Judith H. Anderson for her initial encouragement and ongoing advice with this project. All these colleagues have shared their pedagogical and scholarly acumen. I was fortunate to be a member of the 1995 National Endowment for the Humanities Chaucer-Langland Summer Institute, led by C. David Benson, Elizabeth Robertson, and James Simpson at the University of Colorado, Boulder; the twenty-six members of that institute formed an ideal educational community, a fair field of folk, indeed. And it has been a privilege to work with my students, undergraduate and graduate, at the University of Miami, many of whom have been models of multilingualism and curiosity.

It is with great sadness that I acknowledge the loss of Mary Clemente Davlin, OP—"Clem"—just as this book neared its final stages late in 2017. She was a great scholar and a champion of Langland's poetry as well as a supportive friend for years to me and to my late wife, Shari. As Langland would surely understand, she lived out all the meanings of the word *kind.*

Above all, I wish to remember the generous example of Lawrence M. Clopper, my mentor at Indiana University and a dear friend too for all the years beyond. I humbly dedicate this book to his memory and so wish he were here to share in its publication.

PREFACE

Will, whose name suggests both desire and willfulness, advances an elemental question—a matter of eternal life or death for the faithful—to Lady Holy Church early on in the poems called *Piers Plowman*: "Teche me to no tresor, but tel me this ilke— / How I may save my soule . . . " (Schmidt, Vision, B.1.83–4). Exploring responses to that question drives the poem from that point to its indeterminate ending as Will, the dreamer, wakes from the sound in his dream of Conscience crying after Grace and embarks on a search for the evanescent figure of Piers Plowman.

"*Piers Plowman* has a good claim to be the greatest poem of the Middle Ages. It was certainly one of the most popular," writes A. V. C. Schmidt in the introduction to his Everyman edition of the B text (Vision xix). David Aers likewise calls it "the greatest English poem of the Middle Ages" (*Beyond* x). My experiences of reading the poem with students, many of whom are arrested by William Langland's urgent, insistent, and colliding voices, bear witness to the enthusiasm of these two leading scholars.

Piers Plowman comes down to us in what most scholars since W. W. Skeat in the nineteenth century identify as three successive versions, named, for modern convenience, the A, B, and C texts, composed between approximately 1369 and 1387. Fifty-two complete manuscripts survive, many of them assembled by scribes in fascinating ways by combining an A manuscript—the shortest and likely the earliest—with the later and longer parts of a B or C text in efforts that imply interest, even urgency, on the part of the copyists to compile a "complete" copy. (There are partial and fragmentary manuscripts too, adding to the sum of surviving texts).

The poem begins with a narrator who tells us he was wandering one summer in the habit of a hermit, "unholy of works" (Donaldson, *Alliterative*, prol. 3), looking for wonders in the world, when he fell asleep by a murmuring stream; it proceeds as a series of eight visionary dreams, two of which are dreams-within-dreams. The dreamer (or Will, as we come later to know his name) sees initially a compelling and comprehensive vision of "a fair field full of folk," "working and wandering as the world requires"—or, alternately, doing their best to do as little as possible (Donaldson, *Alliterative*, prol. 17, 19). He dreams too of figures representing a variety of institutional powers—royal, judicial, manorial, and religious—all of which fail to meet his desire for what he terms a "kind," or natural, inward, and profound knowledge of Christ (Schmidt, Vision, 1.138; Donaldson, *Alliterative*, 1.138).

In the B and C texts, which are much longer than the A text, after these initial, exciting but troubling visions of the world at large; of king, court, and remuneration—or bribery—and of communal, manorial field work frustrated; and of an inadequate "pardon" applying only to some, the poems turn inward as Will searches for what it is, or where it is, to "Do-Well"—a query leading subsequently to a search for "Do-Better" and "Do-Best." Will rejects the confident replies of two friars regarding where "Do-Well" dwells (with themselves, of course). And he meets faculties representing his own self, such as Thought, as well as sources for his development and education, such as Wit and Wit's wife, Dame Study, and Clergie (Learning) and his wife, Scripture, who scorns the dreamer for his intellectual ambitiousness. Following a humbling meeting with the figure of Imaginatif, the power of memory to synthesize varieties of understanding, subsequent dream visions draw with apparent authoritative confidence on Scripture. Beginning with the Good Samaritan, the narrative high point of the B and C versions resides in the dreamer's vision of Jesus jousting in the arms of Piers (B.18, C.20), and the passion and subsequent harrowing of hell, before concluding with a final crisis of institutional instability, seemingly brought on by the presence of friars, whose precise place and finances within the corporate Church deeply troubled Langland and many others in the later Middle Ages.

Dreaming mixed with brief waking experiences suggests the sometimes urgent, often interiorized, and seemingly autobiographical psychology of *Piers Plowman*. This quality makes the poems accessible in broadly imaginative terms for anyone who has ever wondered about the purpose, direction, and destiny of our human lives. The titular character of Piers (modern editors call the poems by his name, but the medieval manuscripts bear no titles) serves as an intermittent and variable guiding figure: often absent, or appearing as a simple plowman, a pilgrim guide, a figure of Christ "jousting" in Piers's human nature, and a referent of abiding spiritual morality. Even in such profoundly medieval and spiritual terms, then, *Piers Plowman* asks questions comprehensible and provocative in the classroom and well beyond.

For all such qualities, these late-fourteenth-century poems attributed to one William Langland and known to modern readers by the title *Piers Plowman* have been much less well represented in the curricula of United States colleges, universities, and secondary schools than other works of medieval English literature, such as *Beowulf* (generally in translation), the *Canterbury Tales*, and *Sir Gawain and the Green Knight* (also typically in translation). And yet, as I hope the essays in this volume will demonstrate, the inquisitive, restive, and multivocal qualities of *Piers Plowman* have the capacity to draw in student readers, just as many of their instructors have been drawn to study the composition, surviving manuscripts, and dream thought of these poems.

A number of aspects, all the same, make reading Langland less easy than reading Chaucer, Langland's much better-known contemporary. First and foremost is the lack of a consistent narrative shaping any of the three versions; reading Langland challenges our habits and expectations of reading itself. Second, the language of *Piers Plowman* is of the author's West Midlands home, not that of Chaucer's London, which is much more closely antecedent to what emerged as present-day English. Third, while aurally and poetically compelling, Langland's verse is not end-rhymed, like that of Chaucer, but alliterative (or front-rhymed, as it is sometimes called), like other late medieval poetic works such as *Sir Gawain and the Green Knight* and *Pearl*, both of which combine alliterative and end-rhymed verse to spectacular effect. Fourth, the poems make frequent, intriguing, and malleable recourse of allegorical figures and episodes whose precise meanings and interrelations repay attentive and recursive reading. Fifth, the deep enmeshments of Langland's poetry with the terms of his culture in a variety of callings, crafts, and discourses make substantial demands on the modern reader.

These qualities notwithstanding, what the essays in this volume collectively advance is that what makes the *Piers Plowman* poems challenging is also what makes them inexhaustibly fascinating—a source for learning about language, literary form, history, and late medieval religious culture at all levels. The procedure of the poems by means of dreams and by manner of inquiry as well as the lack of any single, stable, and doctrinaire answer to the curious question, "Where does Do-Well dwell?" together ask a great deal of responsiveness and responsibility from the reader, opening the poem's abiding question concerning salvation to broader inquiries of how to lead a good life and about the value of work and of human endeavors.

The poems also offer exceptional imagery, figurative language, and passages of sublime poetry. These include the opening vision of the fair field of folk; the figure and trial of Lady Meed regarding a marriage befitting her; the visceral presentation of the seven deadly sins in richly contemporary terms; the plowing of the half acre; the pardon scene; the series of intellective faculties and their various marriages; Will's lapse in the land of longing for what he describes as the better part of his adult life; the banquet of patience in which the dreamer is seated at a side table, listening; Haukyn in his coat stained from living in the world; the polysemous figure of Imaginatif; and the person of Sir Penetrans Domo (Home Invader) who initiates the poem's final crisis within the barn of unity, a figure for the universal Church. And this selection is hardly comprehensive. Langland's poetry comprehends the urban and the agrarian, the political and the spiritual, the individual and the communal, the failures of institutions and of individuals, the messy material and the ineffable sublime.

One important reason for the comparatively low curricular profile of Langland's poems is the lack, until the late twentieth century, of complete and convenient Middle English editions. But a number of widely available translations and recent volumes directed toward students and general readers of Langland's poetry have made this the very best time ever to take up Langland's dream vision allegory. Nevertheless, aside from a few essays in journals, there has been no support for instructors of *Piers Plowman*. This book addresses that absence by offering twenty-four essays and appendixes about how to teach these marvelous poems.

It is hoped that teachers of literary-historical surveys of early English or British literature; of history of religion, including both that of medieval Christianity and of the Protestant Reformation; of ethics; of the Middle Ages, whether in England or elsewhere in Europe; and teachers engaged with modes of literary representation, especially long-lived and diverse modes such as allegory and dream narrative, may draw interest and ideas from these essays in order to take up one of the most substantial, arresting, and urgent literary works that survive from medieval Europe. While we have no evidence that the author of these poems ever traveled outside England (whereas Chaucer did), Langland's poems travel well as companions to reading the *Roman de la Rose*, Dante, Ariosto, *Le pèlerinage de la vie humaine*, Edmund Spenser, John Bunyan, other Middle English alliterative poems, and, of course, Chaucer, as well as a wide array of other documentary sources in medieval culture and discursive sources in medieval spirituality.

The dialect of Langland's poetry bears a less direct relation to our English than that of Chaucer. While some contributors to this volume have more to say on these two poets, here it will suffice to observe that Langland's taste for the complexities of allegory has little in common with the poetry of the *Canterbury Tales*, which is of course the one Chaucerian work that is most often read and taught. Prior to the late 1970s there was no complete, widely available text of the B and C versions of *Piers Plowman* (though selections from both were available). Langland's place in the curriculum was marginal, then, at least in part due to the lack of such materials and to the dearth of instructors who had any experience with the full poem in any of its versions. Since that time the availability of texts, translations, and guides to the poem (and to Middle English literature in general) has increased markedly. At no point since Skeat's parallel-text edition of 1886 has it been easier to access an affordable Middle English edition of the poems and to have recourse to monographs guiding the reader through the B text, which, judging from critical response and publishers' support, enjoys a de facto consensus as the most popular version of the poem.

The general ethic of the essays that follow is to address Langland's poetry directly, neither presuming nor appealing much to prior knowledge of the many discourses to which Langland makes reference. Still, this volume differs from any other available resource in that all the contributors address potential instructors of Langland's poems. It joins a growing literature that aims to support and encourage instructors—nonspecialists and specialists alike—to engage with some of the most intriguing poetry of the European Middle Ages and, as a result, to enlarge the curricular place of *Piers Plowman*.

Part One

MATERIALS

Introduction

The poems called by modern editors *The Vision of Piers Plowman*, *Will's Vision of Piers Plowman*, or, most commonly, *Piers Plowman* survive in three distinct versions preserved in fifty-two (or so) manuscript copies, a black-letter edition of 1550 printed three times, and a number of fragments. The number of manuscripts is variable depending on whether or not the fragments are counted. By comparison, this number is not so far from the eighty-plus manuscripts of *The Canterbury Tales* (only a few of whose contents approximate the contents of modern editions) and surpasses that of another important poem from the period, John Gower's *Confessio amantis*, while *Sir Gawain and the Green Knight* and *Pearl* survive together in a single manuscript copy (Kane, "Text" 175; Schmidt, Vision xix–xx). Based largely on an early fifteenth-century ascription in a manuscript of the C version at Trinity College, Dublin, and the so-called autobiographical passage (C.5), modern consensus is that all versions of the poem are the product of one William Langland, a cleric in minor orders and the son of Eustace Rokayle of Shipton-under-Wychwood, though some dissent from this view (Hanna, *William Langland* 2; Kane, "Langland, William"; Adams, *Langland and the Rokele Family*). The name may well be a pseudonym; for all practical purposes, the author has virtually no known life outside his poem. Since the publication of W. W. Skeat's parallel-text edition in 1886, editors have generally accepted that the surviving manuscripts reveal three successive stages of composition and revision, which Skeat called the A, B, and C texts, or versions. A prologue and eleven *passus* ("steps") make up the A version, running to about 2,550 lines (a twelfth passus is of disputed authenticity in whole or part); B includes a prologue and twenty passus for a total of approximately 7,700 lines; while C shows many substantial revisions of B, and a further division into two more passus—twenty-two in all, then—with about seventy more lines of verse. Evidence for a fourth version, Z, rests in a single manuscript, which some scholars, including A. V. C. Schmidt, view as a draft preceding A. A number of manuscripts represent conjoint texts, bringing together parts of two or even three of the versions. While certainly affirming the necessity of textual editing, George Kane likewise proceeds from the idea of a single author, even as he allows that "there are as many texts of any version of *Piers Plowman* as there are manuscript copies" (Kane, "Text" 198). A summary description is given by Ralph Hanna (*William Langland*), who refers readers to the Athlone Press editions (Kane, Piers [1988]; Kane and Donaldson; Russell and Kane), which have been followed since by Schmidt's parallel-text edition (Piers [1995]; Piers [2008]; Piers [2011]).

Modern classroom editions of the A, B, and C texts; five translations currently in print; and a number of reading and study guides make the present moment the best time in more than a century for teaching *Piers Plowman* in secondary, undergraduate, and graduate courses. The B text—in the form of editions, translations, and excerpts in anthologies—is the most widely available version and consequently the most frequently read and taught, as the essays in this volume suggest. Until recently it has drawn the most critical attention too, but studies of the C text as well as the poem's complex manuscript record have expanded substantially. Anyone interested in becoming familiar with the B text may begin with one of four currently available translations (Donaldson, Piers [1990]; Goodridge; Schmidt, Piers [1992]; Sutton), Schmidt's Everyman edition of B (Vision), and *The Cambridge Companion to* Piers Plowman, edited by Andrew Cole and Andrew Galloway (2014). The reading guides by James Simpson (Piers Plowman*: An Introduction to the B-Text*), by Emily Steiner (*Reading* Piers Plowman), and by Michael Calabrese (*An Introduction to* Piers Plowman), as well as Matthew Boyd Goldie's anthology of historical sources complete a basic introductory library that may be expanded accordingly.

Editions and Facsimiles

Middle English Editions for the Classroom

Míċeál F. Vaughan's 2011 edition of the A text is based on a single manuscript, Bodleian Library MS Rawl. poet. 137 (called "MS R" by editors). The edition includes generous marginal glosses but no glossary; students may be referred to the online *Middle English Dictionary* as needed. A substantial introduction addressed to students includes helpful general sections, a summary of the poem, and literary and historical backgrounds; it also has a general introduction to textual editing and its challenges, which precedes a brief treatment of the A text. Textual notes as well as careful passus-by-passus notes follow the text. There is also a selected bibliography that contains editions, translations, bibliographies, criticism, and background materials. The Middle English text amounts to eighty-six pages, a manageable length that would allow the poem to be included in courses along with other sources in Middle English or in translation. The A version ends with passus 12 (itself of disputed authenticity), in which Will apparently matures into a period of privation, the poem breaking off after Will meets Hunger and then "Fevere-on-the-ferthe-day" (Fever-on-the-fourth-day), a self-described messenger of death (12.79). The final eighteen lines of the passus—or perhaps the entire passus—are claimed to be the work of one Johan But (so named in 12.103), about whom little is known, a situation succinctly addressed in Vaughan's notes (189).

Schmidt's edition of the B text, first published in 1978 and substantially revised in 1995 (Vision), helped to end the nearly century-long drought, extending since

Skeat's work, of full-length editions of the two longer versions of *Piers Plowman* produced for students.[1] Widely available in the Everyman Library from J. M. Dent, Schmidt's edition presents nearly fifty pages of textual and lexical notes and nearly seventy pages of literary and historical commentary and is well suited for graduate students, if potentially overwhelming for undergraduates. The introduction (over eighty pages) offers a fairly technical presentation of textual matters. The text offers some marginal glosses as well as selective linear glosses, including translations from the Latin placed below the text and—below these glosses—a selective critical apparatus on each page. There is also an economical but quite complete glossary. The volume's abundant content introduces readers, with the guidance of instructors, to any number of textual and interpretive matters relating to the B text and to issues of textual editing and commentary.

Derek Pearsall's edition of the C text was also first published in 1978, addressing the dearth of modern editions; a revised edition appeared in 2008. A select bibliography of critical studies precedes the introduction, which offers for student readers a general overview of the poems, the C version, a narrative summary, as well as sections titled "The Church," "Langland's Learning and Reading," and "Allegory and the Dreamer." To the prologue and each passus Pearsall adds a title signaling its thematic focus: passus 1 is called "Holy Church" and passus 6 "The Confession of the Sins," for example. The text itself is supported by fairly light marginal glosses as well as by footnotes, and there is a glossary with each Middle English entry printed in bold type. A section titled "Textual Variants," clarifying editorial interventions based on manuscript evidence, falls near the end of the volume (379–91). The format of this text is the most generous of the three modern editions, incorporating both glosses and explanatory notes on the page (the Vaughan A text similarly presents an uncluttered page for ease of reading and for adding notes, though it uses endnotes). Students may need some initial help to negotiate Pearsall's text, in which thorn and yogh are replaced by their modern equivalents but "medieval use of *i/j* and *u/v* is preserved" (Pearsall, Piers 19). Neither Vaughan nor Schmidt follows this practice.

Elizabeth Robertson and Stephen H. A. Shepherd's complementary edition in the Norton Critical Editions series, first published in 2006, pairs a Middle English text with E. Talbot Donaldson's translation (Piers [1990]) on facing pages. Shepherd chose Bodleian Library MS Laud 581 (given the sigil "L" by editors), emending the text to bring it in line with the edition of Kane and Donaldson (see below). Robertson and Shepherd note that there are more than four hundred points in the translation where Donaldson preferred a reading other than what is recorded in the Kane and Donaldson edition. The adoption of modernized spelling for Middle English *u/v* and *i/j* and of the graphemes thorn and yogh eases reading for students while yielding some of the estrangement of the poem's language. The edition does not include glosses on Middle English words or phrases, as the translation on facing pages is intended to serve this purpose broadly; nor is there a glossary. Footnotes are kept to a minimal and explanatory role, slightly revised from Donaldson's 1990 stand-alone translation; the gloss of key terms and figures are retained from the 1990 translation. Following the format of other volumes in the series, the text is followed by a section titled "Sources and Backgrounds," including relevant selections from the Douai Bible; selections from Julian of Norwich and from Margery Kempe; the Statute of Laborers (1349); the General Prologue to *The Canterbury Tales*; and the Letter of John Ball, among others. The section "Criticism" includes excerpts from C. S. Lewis, Anne Middleton, Elizabeth Kirk, and James Simpson, among many others. Introductory sections titled "Reading Middle English" and "Reading Langland's Alliterative Verse" are followed by a selected bibliography.

Scholarly Editions of Reference

There are two scholarly editions of reference; neither is suitable as a classroom text except at the most advanced level. The first comprises the three volumes of the Athlone Press edition: the A version edited by George Kane (1960; 1988), the B version edited by Kane and Donaldson (1978; 1988), and the C Version edited by George Russell and Kane (1997). Schmidt's four-text parallel edition, Piers Plowman*: A Parallel-Text Edition of the A, B, C, and Z Versions* (2011) corrects and supplants in two volumes Schmidt's earlier four-text edition (Piers [1995]; Piers [2008]). The Athlone Press and the Schmidt editions do not share the same lineation. Rooted in distinctive principles of editing, each presents monumental work on Langland's poems; both are invaluable additions to the library of anyone working on Langland. Scholars frequently cite Schmidt's Everyman edition of the B text (Vision).

A. G. Rigg and Charlotte Brewer's edition of the so-called Z text (1983) is based on Bodleian MS 851. The editors state that this manuscript is a working or draft version of the A text, a view that Schmidt affirms by including it in his parallel-text edition (Piers [1995]; Piers [2008]; Piers [2011]), though others have disputed this view (e.g., Hanna, "Versions" 40).

Electronic Editions

The ongoing efforts of the *Piers Plowman Electronic Archive* (piers.chass.ncsu .edu) intend to present the full textual tradition in digital facsimiles and documentary editions in hyperlinked form, as well as critical editions with textual notes (but not interpretive commentary). Originally brought out as CD-ROMs available from various publishers under the aegis of the Medieval Academy of America and the Society for Early English and Norse Electronic Texts (SEENET), since 2014 the texts have been available as Web editions. To date these include eight documentary editions. Volume 9 is the critical edition of version Bx, *The B-Version Archetype*, edited by John Burrow and Thorlac Turville-Petre.

Early Modern and Modern Printed Editions

While *The Canterbury Tales* were among the first works printed by William Caxton around 1476, Robert Crowley was Langland's first editor. He printed a B text from now lost exemplars three times in 1550, correcting and resetting the text for the third printing; Owen Rogers reprinted this third printing in 1561, adding *Pierce the Ploughman's Crede*, suggesting that Langland was also the author of that poem. In 1813 Thomas Whitaker edited a C text manuscript, now known as Huntington Library MS 137; disputing the quality of Whitaker's work, Thomas Wright produced in 1832 an edition of a B text manuscript, Trinity College Cambridge B.15.17 (Kane, "Text" 176), subsequently reprinted with revisions in 1842 and 1856. Skeat's 1886 parallel-text edition is perhaps of greatest historical importance among the early editions, having subsumed nearly twenty years of its editor's prior research and publication on the poems. Though now superseded both in textual and critical terms, Skeat's edition remains useful for anyone tracing the modern reception of the poems because it first made the case for the three versions and formulated other interpretations about the poems and their author. Other significant editions include Thomas A. Knott and David C. Fowler's edition of the A version (1952), the first academic text since Skeat's; Elizabeth Salter and Pearsall's edition of selections from the C text (1967); and J. A. W. Bennett's edition of the B text's prologue and passus 1–7 (1972). The last two, intended for the classroom, may fairly be termed the first instructor support for the poems, translations aside, for they were the first modern student editions of the B prologue and passus 1–7 since Skeat's edition.

Editorial History and Practices

Charlotte Brewer's *Editing* Piers Plowman*: The Evolution of the Text* offers a history of editing the poems from Crowley's 1550 edition, the editio princeps, through the mid-1990s. Brewer's book preceded the final volume in the Athlone Press edition, Russell and Kane's on the C text, though it is fair to say that Brewer is critical of editorial principles underlying the A and B Athlone editions. For a considered defense of the Kane and Donaldson B text, see Lee Patterson's essay "The Logic of Textual Criticism and the Way of Genius: The Kane-Donaldson *Piers Plowman* in Historical Perspective." Brewer does not address Schmidt's parallel-text edition, Pearsall's revised C text edition, the Norton complementary-text edition, or Vaughan's A text edition, all of which were published after her book. For

Schmidt's account of this editorial history, see "The Editorial Tradition of *Piers Plowman*" in his parallel-text edition (Piers [2008] 10–90).

Facsimiles in Print

Besides the digital facsimiles included in the productions of the *Piers Plowman Electronic Archive*, some print facsimiles of *Piers Plowman* manuscripts have appeared, most recently augmented by Tomonori Matsushita. All offer opportunities to explore aspects of book production and paleography and to introduce students to the variety of scribal hands and practices.

J. A. W. Bennett edited a facsimile edition (*Vision* [1976]) of Crowley's first printing. R. W. Chambers and others edited Piers Plowman*: The Huntington Library Manuscript (HM 143) Reproduced in Photostat* (1936). Tomonori Matsushita offers an updated reproduction of the same manuscript (The Vision of Piers Plowman*: The C Text; A Facsimile of Huntington Library, San Marino, MS Hm 143* [2010]).

Derek Pearsall and Kathleen L. Scott produced a facsimile edition, Piers Plowman*: A Facsimile of Bodleian Library, Oxford, MS Douce 104* (1992). The sole subject of this manuscript, exceptional for its seventy-two marginal illustrations, is the *Piers* C text. Kathryn Kerby-Fulton and Denise L. Despres offer a study of this manuscript and its program of illustration for an Anglo-Hibernian audience in *Iconography and the Professional Reader: The Politics of Book Production in the Douce* Piers Plowman (1998).

A. I. Doyle's *The Vernon Manuscript: A Facsimile of Bodleian Library, Oxford, MS Eng. poet.a.1* (1987) presents one of the most important and compendious manuscripts of the period, almost entirely English in its contents, including an A text of *Piers Plowman.* This manuscript has been the subject of sustained study in two volumes: Derek Brewer's *Studies in the Vernon Manuscript* (1990) and Wendy Scase's *The Making of the Vernon Manuscript: The Production and Contexts of Oxford, Bodleian Library, MS Eng. poet.a.1* (2013).

Charlotte Brewer and A. G. Rigg's Piers Plowman*: A Facsimile of the Z-Text in Bodleian Library, Oxford, MS Bodley 851* presents the controversial Z text, which the editors argue precedes all other versions of Langland's poem; that other scholars have been less sanguine to come to this view makes the manuscript no less valuable.

Tomonori Matsushita offers a full account of A text manuscripts in Piers Plowman*: The A Version, Facsimiles of the Twenty Manuscripts with Their Diplomatic Texts.* Matsushita has also published *William Langland's* The Vision of Piers Plowman*: The B-Text, A Facsimile of Trinity College, Cambridge MS B.15.17*; Piers Plowman: *The A Text, A Facsimile of Trinity College, Cambridge MS R.3.14*; Piers Plowman*: The A Text, A Facsimile of the Society of Antiquaries* *of London MS 687*; and Piers Plowman*: The Z Version, A Facsimile of Bodleian Library, Oxford MS Bodley 851.*

Translations

Instructors who choose to teach a version of Langland's poems in present-day English may select from four available translations of the B text (Goodridge; Donaldson, Piers [1990]; Schmidt, Piers [1992]; Sutton) and one version of the C text (Economou).

The oldest continuously available translation of the B text is the prose version of J. F. Goodridge; in addition, it is the only translation currently available as an e-book (Kindle edition). Goodridge divides and numbers the passus as "books," heading each with a narrative summary. Further, each book bears a title announcing its thematic focus: for example, passus 10, in which the dreamer meets Lady Study and Learning ("Clergy"), is titled "Study and Learning." Latin quotations are retained in the text; translations of these appear in the notes and commentary that run to over fifty pages. Appendix A includes the translator's prose rendition of the so-called autobiographical passage (C.5); Appendix B contains his translation of C text, passus 10, lines 71–97, a pathos-laden passage on the poor. All in all, the Goodridge translation gives the reader a great deal of guidance, though its distance from the form and language of the poem offers a reading experience closer to that of a prose novel.

Donaldson's verse translation has been in print since 1990. A fluent translation with respect to the syntax of present-day English, the style and verse form hew closely to the Middle English, giving the reader a stronger sense of the Middle English in a manner less expansive than that of Goodridge's translation. Economical explanatory notes, including citations for quotations and references, support the text. In addition, asterisked words may be consulted in a gloss that explains key figures, such as Dominic, and terms, such as *consistory* and *pardoner.* An appendix contains Donaldson's translation of the so-called autobiographical passage (C.5). This translation, with some revision to the notes, is also published in facing-page layout in the edition of the B text by Robertson and Shepherd. Its clean presentation foregrounds the translated text, with limited ancillary support for the reader new to Langland.

Schmidt's prose translation, which includes an introduction and explanatory notes, has been in print since 1992. The introduction offers sections addressing the poem's authorship, context, and intellectual and religious background. There is a brief selective bibliography and a chronology. Passus are simply titled and numbered. Explanatory notes follow the text, along with an appendix, "Langland's Alliterative Verse," with an excerpt from the Middle English text, part of the harrowing of hell scene (B.18.314–72). Schmidt's translation is syntactically and stylistically more demanding and technical than those by Donaldson or Goodridge (Goodridge's is the most colloquial of the three).

Peter Sutton's Piers Plowman*: A Modern Verse Translation* (2014) is an approachable translation, written in an English somewhat less Latinate than that of other translators, and echoing Langland's alliterative style while conceding that exact imitation is of course impractical. The volume offers an introduction that outlines the poem, including a synopsis of the passus (which it calls "steps"), along with a summary of the textual sources, the verse form, the translator's approach, the poem's major imagery, and a section on the author's identity. Sutton's interventions intended to aid the modern reader include heading each passus with a brief prose summary in the first person, as if delivered by a narrator. Further, Sutton introduces spaces within verse passages, creating pauses, an interpretive gesture emphasizing his sense of shifts in speaker and thought. His introduction repeats long-held views about the development and order of the poems' three versions; the translation was originally founded on Skeat's parallel-text edition and later revised in consultation with that of Schmidt. The volume also contains a selected bibliography and a list of names and terms.

A verse translation of the C text by George Economou has been available since 1996. Like Donaldson's translation of the B text, it aims to provide sufficient yet concise materials in addition to the translation text. The introduction succinctly presents an overview of the poems and their authorship, a summary of the poem, remarks on the translation, and a bibliography of editions, translations, and critical studies. Brief notes follow the text. An appendix outlines additions, deletions, and transpositions of material between the B and C versions. Economou's translation presents the poem in an idiomatic style; thoroughly modernized yet not overly colloquial, it does not adhere to the varying demands of Langland's alliterative lines for their own sake.

Other verse translations of the B text now out of print include Arthur Burrell's from 1912, D. and R. Attwater's *The Book Concerning Piers the Plowman* (1957), and Margaret Williams's Piers the Plowman *by William Langland* (1971). Francis Dolores Covella's translation of the A text was published in 1992. Terence Tiller's verse translation of the B text was originally created as scripts for broadcast in thirteen episodes in 1980 for a program directed (uncannily) by Piers Plowright. Tiller subsequently completed the translation, including episodes left out from the broadcasts, and it was published in 1981. A short introduction and succinct and informative notes frame the text; each passus has a headnote summarizing the action. The translation stands in strong if somewhat formal lines, though not strictly adherent—by design—to the demands of Middle English alliterative meter. It was republished at least once as an Everyman volume, along with J. R. R. Tolkien's translations of *Sir Gawain and the Green Knight* and *Pearl* (Tiller and Tolkien).

Selections in Anthologies

As with the Middle English of *Sir Gawain and the Green Knight*, anthology editors in the United States usually treat the language of *Piers Plowman* as implicitly too difficult for undergraduates, unlike that of Chaucer, which is nearly always excerpted in the original. And while the documents supporting *Piers Plowman*, offered in text or on publishers' Web sites, are to be appreciated, they sometimes imply an outdated bifurcation in the critical reception of Chaucer and Langland—that is, that Chaucer may be enjoyed more easily and more obviously on literary grounds, while Langland offers more for those interested in the history of the period, as if *Piers Plowman* is more of a historical source than a literary creation. The issue invites investigation with students, as David Lawton's essay in this volume makes clear.

Since its third edition (1974), *The Norton Anthology of English Literature* has included varying selections from the Donaldson translation of *Piers Plowman*, primarily drawn from the B text, sometimes supplemented with the C text's autobiographical passage (Abrams). The ninth edition (Greenblatt [2012]) includes, under William Langland, selections from passus 1, 5, 6, and 7 of the B text as well as passus 5 of the C text; in a section on Christ's humanity it includes the Crucifixion and harrowing of hell (B.18). Comparing the poem's prologue in Donaldson's 1990 translation with those translations by Donaldson published in the third and fourth editions of the *Norton Anthology* reveals substantial differences among the three versions; later editions of the anthology excerpt the published, stand-alone translation. Such differences present productive opportunities for students to analyze the translator's changes as well as the editors' choices of selections.[2]

When first published, *The Longman Anthology of British Literature* (Damrosch) challenged the established place of the Norton by offering a somewhat more culturally comprehensive sense of historical and literary contexts for English-language literature. Its fourth edition draws Langland selections from the Donaldson translation of the B text, including passages from the prologue and passus 6 and all of passus 2, 8, and 20. Following these readings is a section of contemporary documentary and literary sources, "*Piers Plowman* and Its Time," which includes a passage from the *Anonimalle Chronicle* regarding Wat Tyler's meeting with Richard II, John Ball's letter (often said to reference Langland's poem), and a short selection translated from Gower's *Vox clamantis*, among other items. The inclusion of such materials suggests a decidedly historicist approach to understanding Langland. There is no similar set of ancillary materials following the selections from Chaucer.

The Broadview Anthology of British Literature (Black et al.) echoes the British focus of the Longman (as distinct from the somewhat more exclusively English cast of the Norton). Emily Steiner has translated selections, including the B text prologue and passus 18, in the print edition; further selections (part of B.5 and all of B.7) are available to registered users in the substantial online resources. "Contexts: The Crises of the Fourteenth Century" (261–74) supports Langland and other late medieval readings, including selections from the chronicles of Froissart and Knighton, and the Statute of Laborers, among others. Among the online resources is an excerpt from *Wynnere and Wastour*. The anthology is also available as an e-book (Kindle edition).

Chaucer to Spenser: An Anthology of Writings in English, 1375–1575, edited by Derek Pearsall, is available as a print-on-demand publication and contains a number of selections from the C text, including passages from the prologue through passus 10, and from 20 (the Crucifixion and the harrowing of hell) and 22 (the coming of Antichrist and the end of the poem). A more selective anthology drawn from this volume is Pearsall and Duncan Wu's *Poetry from Chaucer to Spenser*. Elaine Treharne's *Old and Middle English, c. 890–c. 1450: An Anthology* contains a brief selection from Langland. *Medieval English Literature*, volume 1 of *The Oxford Anthology of English Literature*, edited by J. B. Trapp et al., offers selections from the B prologue and passus 1 and 18.

Recommended Reading for Undergraduates

Guides to Reading the Poems

As of this writing, four books address themselves to student readers of Langland; many instructors will find them useful too. All but one focus primarily on the B text. James Simpson's Piers Plowman*: An Introduction to the B-Text* was published in 1990 and revised in 2007. Its introduction sets out general characteristics of the poem, including its context and structure. Seven subsequent chapters follow the poem in linear fashion, divided among the eight visions. Each chapter begins with a summary of the passus under discussion. The analysis is close and attentive to Langland's generic and stylistic commitments and to Will's theological peregrinations. Simpson directs his analysis most often toward two issues: the shortcomings of institutions and the competing demands of mercy and justice. The discussion is also usefully recursive, making reference to points previously discussed to help the reader hold the poem together. A generous bibliography of primary and secondary sources, to which reference is made throughout, concludes the volume.

Emily Steiner's *Reading* Piers Plowman (2013) explores the B text in sequence through key terms, synthesizing sections according to thematic concerns. The introduction addresses the prologue, and subsequent chapters take up value

(B.1–4), community (B.5–7; written subsequently to Steiner's essay in this volume), learning (B.8–12), practice (B.13–15), belief (B.16–18), and institutions (B.19–20). An introduction heads each chapter, followed by titled subsections presenting analysis in digestible portions. By this method, too, the author reaches out discursively to many relevant sources outside the poem, historical and textual, such as Boethius's *Consolation of Philosophy* and "Cato," implicitly suggesting further learning in medieval thought. The introduction succinctly sets out what little is known securely about the poet and what constitutes common knowledge about the surviving copies of the poems in formal, metrical, and scribal terms. The author adroitly presents the many-mindedness among Langland's early readers, suggested by variance in scribal subdivisions in the manuscripts and by a rehearsal of the poem's several genres recorded in explicits. The book expertly situates the poem at interpretive crossroads: an author revealing his identity in a "signature" line—"'I have lived in londe,' quod I, 'my name is Longe Wille'" (15.152)—or concealing it in the same conventionalized terms; the inclusive belief that all may be saved versus the anxiety-provoking exclusions of predestination. *Reading* Piers Plowman charts a middle course between communicating deep historical, theological, and textual detail and assuming too little of readers. Similarly, Steiner quotes the B text in Middle English, followed by translations, meeting the needs of many potential readers.

Anna Baldwin's *A Guidebook to* Piers Plowman (2007) offers an analytical, interrogative approach to the B text (with reference to significant differences in C). She devotes a chapter to each passus, further dividing her discussion with subtitles and subsections. Each chapter opens with a summary, followed by a succinct outline analysis of the passus. Several of the subsections bear interrogative titles—for example, "Who is Patience?"—and fifteen text boxes take up historical and cultural topics, with titles such as "Church Courts," "Minstrels and Poets," and "Monks and Friars." Rather than stating what the poem means at any given point, the *Guidebook* clarifies its formal features and figures, engaging readers through questions. The formatting of the volume would seem to address readers at the secondary and beginning university level who may prefer to take in discrete measures of information and analysis. Sections on further reading within the chapters and bibliographies within the text boxes refer readers to items in the concluding bibliography.

Michael Calabrese's comprehensive *An Introduction to* Piers Plowman (2016) offers students a narrative reading guide. The book is unique among guides to (and nearly all discussions of) Langland's poetry in its inclusive treatment of the A, B, and C versions throughout, discussing passus from each version in parallel. Colloquial chapter titles aim to make the poems less forbidding—"Lady Meed Tries Everything" addresses passus 3, while "The Hunger Artists," alluding to Kafka's story, takes up version A, passus 7; B, passus 6; and C, passus 8. To aid the reader, the author selectively adds glosses in brackets to quotations in Middle

English. The book offers a historical chronology, an account of what is known or cautiously surmised about the author's life, the narrative reading guide (the book's centerpiece), and supporting sections on Langland and his contemporaries, along with a list of persons and personifications as well as a pronunciation guide. The book is by far the longest such guide, addressing the development and differences across the three versions.

Claire Marshall provides a useful, brief overview of Langland's work for fairly advanced readers in her *William Langland:* Piers Plowman. In just over one hundred pages, Marshall offers an introduction, a narrative synopsis of the B text, and three topical essays: the first analyzes language and allegory; the second addresses the work's contestatory and subversive potential, including its associations with the Rising of 1381; and the third covers the crises of subject formation presented in the poem. Marshall interweaves reference to contemporary criticism as well as to theory (including postmodern thought), seeming to imply an audience of advanced undergraduates and graduate students. She cites the text in Middle English, providing a select gloss below quotations.

Now out of print, another helpful book-length study of Langland is Joseph S. Wittig's *William Langland Revisited.* An attempt "to approach Langland's poem 'from the inside' or 'on its own terms,'" Wittig's book addresses "the serious reader who is not a specialist in the Middle Ages" (vii) and follows modern critical conventions in its focus on the B version. Its ethos as an introductory book is clear from its blend of glossed Middle English quotations along with frequent paraphrase and translation; line references correspond to the Donaldson translation. The discussion proceeds sequentially so that readers effectively reread the B version. Opening with a brief chronology, the book's first chapter introduces Langland as author and Will as persona, appealing to modern literary sensibilities while providing an overview of what is known of the poems and of their poet, attentive to seeming touches of autobiography while acknowledging what Kane called "the autobiographical fallacy" ("Autobiographical Fallacy"). Wittig devotes over one-third of the volume to the opening sequence of the poem before turning to more compressed accounts of the remaining passus.

Recommended Reading for Advanced Undergraduates and Graduate Students

The Cambridge Companion to Piers Plowman (2014), edited by Andrew Cole and Andrew Galloway, offers twelve topical essays by leading scholar-critics, organized into three sections, and in many ways updates John A. Alford's 1988

Companion to Piers Plowman in the light of scholarly advances over the past twenty-five years, especially in textual studies and critical developments. Typical of such efforts, for example, are the chapters "The Versions and Revisions of *Piers Plowman*" (Ralph Hanna), "The Rokeles: An Index for a 'Langland' Family History" (Robert Adams), and "*Piers Plowman* in Theory" (Nicolette Zeeman). Altogether the book offers a range of summary accounts of literary, historical, and critical currents useful to beginning and advanced students of Langland's poetry as well as to instructors.

Alford's *Companion* continues to offer a strong entry point to the poems for students at any level beyond the most introductory. Anne Middleton's "An Introduction: The Critical Heritage" describes the relatively late and slow entry of the poems to critical and curricular interests, while Ann Hudson's "Epilogue" addresses (among much else) John Ball's letter related to the Rising of 1381, when Langland's poetry appears to have been invoked rhetorically to serve the rebellion. In between are nine topical essays on the poem's design, historical context, theology, allegory, satire, sermons, dialect, and the alliterative style.

The Author, Manuscript, and Editorial History

The essays in *The Cambridge Companion to* Piers Plowman reference previously published work that address what is known of the author's life and matters of manuscript and textual history. Modern assessments of the authorship question begin with Kane's Piers Plowman*: The Evidence for Authorship* (1965). In *William Langland* (1993), Ralph Hanna summarizes the few facts known of Langland as well as the dating of the A, B, and C versions; Robert Adams's *Langland and the Rokele Family: The Gentry Background to* Piers Plowman (2013) is a fuller study of plausible family affiliations. The Athlone Press editions (Kane, Piers [1988]; Kane and Donaldson; Russell and Kane) and the recent parallel-text edition of Schmidt (Piers [2011]) provide advanced students and instructors with the materials for deep study of the complex state of surviving manuscripts.

C. David Benson and Lynne S. Blanchfield in *The Manuscripts of* Piers Plowman*: The B-Version* (1997) describe all of the features of surviving B manuscripts, including annotations, glosses, marginalia, and marks of emphasis. Charlotte Brewer's *Editing* Piers Plowman (1996) covers the textual history from 1550 through the mid-1990s. In the second volume of the four-text edition, Schmidt (Piers [2008]) also advances a thorough account of the editorial history from the sixteenth century forward (10–90). In two recent books, *The Lost History of* Piers Plowman*: The Earliest Transmission of Langland's Work* (2011) and *The Myth of* Piers Plowman*: Constructing a Medieval Literary Archive* (2014), Lawrence Warner radically challenges the conventional narrative concerning the order of composition and content of the A, B, and C versions.

Commentary

When completed, *The Penn Commentary on* Piers Plowman will offer the most comprehensive annotation to date. Addressing the C, B, and A texts in reverse order of their assumed composition, the editors exclude the Z text on the grounds that its differences from A do not derive from Langland. The first and fifth volumes have so far been published (Galloway, *Penn Commentary*; Barney, *Penn Commentary*); the fourth volume is forthcoming in 2018 (Lawler, *Penn Commentary*), and volumes two and three are to follow.

Aids to Teaching and Advanced Study

Summary Critical Introductions and Annotated Bibliographies of Piers Plowman

Annotated bibliographies introduce advanced students and instructors to editions of and critical responses to *Piers Plowman* since Crowley's editions of 1550. For an overview of critical issues, an excellent place to start is Anne Middleton's chapter, "An Introduction: The Critical Heritage" in Alford's *Companion*, which takes readers through the major issues of authorship, form, and history up to the mid-1980s. Also very useful are Schmidt's introductory essays on the manuscripts and the editorial tradition as well as the essay, "The Poem in Time," in the second volume of his parallel-text edition (Piers [2008] 1–90, 269–304). Earlier print bibliographies include A. J. Colaianne's Piers Plowman*: An Annotated Bibliography of Editions and Criticism, 1550–1977* (1978) and Vincent DiMarco's Piers Plowman*: A Reference Guide* (1982), which cites responses to Langland from 1395 to 1979. DiMarco includes some items not in Colaianne; the two may be used together to search earlier work on the poems. Derek Pearsall's *An Annotated Critical Bibliography of Langland* (1990) covers "whole text" (6) editions since Wright's (1842) and addresses selected critical studies since 1900 (that is, following Skeat's parallel-text edition of 1886). Also useful is Middleton's "XVIII. *Piers Plowman*," an adroit overview of the poems and a bibliography. These four bibliographical sources will introduce readers to the full range of work on Langland since 1550 and especially the growing body of work since 1886.

The International *Piers Plowman* Society publishes the *Yearbook of Langland Studies*. Since its inauguration in 1987 it has published, along with new work on Langland, an annual annotated bibliography, available on the society's Web site, of scholarship on the poems, a convenient way to review recent work. The society also organizes sessions for major annual international meetings such as the International Congress on Medieval Studies at Western Michigan University and the International Medieval Congress hosted by the University of Leeds. The society also hosts conferences on Langland every four years at varying locations; sessions devoted to teaching Langland's poetry are frequently featured.

Dictionaries and Glossaries

The *Middle English Dictionary* (*MED*), an invaluable resource for students, was published in print form in 2001; a searchable online version is available. The *Oxford English Dictionary* is also an indispensable starting point for students and may be especially useful for researching "false friends" between Middle and present-day English. It is available in print and online with subscription.

Also useful are Kane's Piers Plowman*: Glossary: Will's Visions of* Piers Plowman*, Do-Well, Do-Better, and Do-Best* (2005) and Schmidt's parallel-text edition (Piers [2008]; Piers [2011]). Schmidt includes an indexical glossary ([2008] 753–928; [2011] 753–928), which is more replete than that of Kane. Wittig's Piers Plowman*: Concordance* (2001) lists concordances of Middle English, Latin, and French words in the poem, following the Athlone editions.

Tomonori Matsushita's *A Glossarial Concordance to William Langland's* The Vision of Piers Plowman*: The B-Text* offers four parts in three volumes, including variant spellings in its listing of Middle English, Latin, and French words, phrases, proper names, and alliterative words. Matsushita has also edited *A Glossarial Concordance to William Langland's* The Vision of Piers Plowman*: The A-Text.*

Journals of Medieval Studies

Besides the *Yearbook of Langland Studies*, journals that often publish articles on Langland, Piers Plowman, and other relevant topics include *The Chaucer Review*, *Studies in the Age of Chaucer*, *Medium Ævum*, *New Medieval Literatures*, and *Speculum*. Journals that occasionally publish essays on teaching Langland include *Studies in Medieval and Renaissance Teaching* (*SMART*) and the online journal *The Once and Future Classroom* (*OFC*), published by the Teaching Association for Medieval Studies (TEAMS).

Introductions to Manuscript Studies

Two excellent textbooks for introducing students to the study of medieval manuscripts have been published recently: Raymond Clemens and Timothy Graham's *Introduction to Manuscript Studies* (2007) and *Opening Up Middle English Manuscripts* (2012) by Kathryn Kerby-Fulton, Maidie Hilmo, and Linda

Olson. The first offers a broad account of the book in the Middle Ages. The second is a more focused study of Middle English manuscripts, including some *Piers Plowman* manuscripts, such as the C text in Douce 104. It instructs readers about many aspects of book production, codicology, and paleography, as well as how to read elements of page design and layout, including illustration and rubrication.

Audio Recordings

To supplement reading aloud in class meetings, complete recordings of the B text with various readers are available from *The Chaucer Studio* Web site. Extended selections from the B text, read in Middle English by eight scholars, as well as selections from Economou's C text translation, read by the translator, are available at the University of Pennsylvania's *PennSound* Web site in MP3 format ("William Langland's *Piers Plowman* at the Kelly Writers House").

Digital Sources

Internet sources devoted to Langland are, not surprisingly, far fewer in number than those devoted to Chaucer and his writings. In addition to a few Web sites relevant to Langland, there are a number of well-established sites useful for the study of the Middle Ages.

Sources on Langland and on *Piers Plowman*

The online *Oxford Dictionary of National Biography* has an important entry for William Langland, written by Kane ("Langland, William"). There are Langland pages at *Luminarium: Anthology of English Literature* as well as pages ancillary to Harvard's *Geoffrey Chaucer Page*. The *Piers Plowman Electronic Archive* includes teaching resources for high school and for university.

Digitized Manuscripts and Manuscript Images

Wendy Scase has edited *A Facsimile Edition of the Vernon Manuscript*, made available on DVD-ROM. The Vernon Manuscript, produced in the last decade of the fourteenth century, contains an A text of *Piers Plowman* (and much else), making it one of the most important surviving miscellanies of the period.

The Web offers many images from manuscripts of *Piers Plowman* and an ever-growing body of other medieval manuscripts. Digitized images from *Piers Plowman* manuscripts can be found at the following sites:

The online *Guide to Medieval and Renaissance Manuscripts in the Huntington Library* includes links to some images from HM 114, a composite manuscript (primarily a B Text, but containing lines and passages from A and C) as well as from HM 137, a C Text ("HM 114"; "HM 137").

The site offers seven images from HM 143, a C text written on parchment ("HM 143").

The International *Piers Plowman* Society's Web site includes a link to images from two Trinity College, Cambridge manuscripts: Cambridge, Trinity College MSS R.3.14 and B.15.17.

Several folios from Corpus Christi College (Oxford) MS. 201, a B text, may be seen online at *Early Manuscripts at Oxford University* ("Corpus Christi"). The resolution is more than sufficient for the classroom or for individuals and small groups to work on small computers and tablet devices.

Searching "William Langland" on the *Oxford Digital Library* site produces over eighty folio images, mostly drawing on the illustrations from Bodleian MS Douce 104.

The *Luminarium* site also offers several images from Douce 104 ("Manuscript Images").

Marginalia from selected manuscripts is accessible at the *Rare Book School* Web site (Schott). Acknowledging debts to the *Piers Plowman Electronic Archive*, also hosted at the University of Virginia, the site states that Benson and Blanchfield's account of the B manuscripts is the "print counterpart" of this site.

General sources for digitized images from medieval manuscripts include the Web site *Manuscripts Online*; the site *Medieval Manuscripts on the Web*, maintained by Siân Echard of the University of British Columbia; *Early Manuscripts at Oxford University*; *Digital Bodleian*; the *British Library* Web site; the collection of medieval and Renaissance manuscript images at *The New York Library Digital Collections*; *Digital Medieval Manuscripts at Houghton Library*, hosted by Harvard College Library; *Illuminated Manuscripts Collection (Princeton University Library)*, hosted by Artstor; *Penn in Hand: Manuscripts* and the *Schoenberg Database of Manuscripts*, both hosted by the University of Pennsylvania; and *Medieval Writing*, an interactive paleography site.

Angela Bennett Sigler explores digital encoding of medieval manuscripts at her site, *A Material Piers Living in a Digital World*, and posts updates on *Twitter*.

The Instructor's Library

Editions

For close study of the texts, access to the Athlone editions (Kane, Piers [1988]; Kane and Donaldson; Russell and Kane) and to Schmidt's parallel-text edition (Piers [1995]; Piers [2008]; Piers [2011]) are requisite. Skeat's parallel-text edition of 1886, particularly its notes, will lend a sense of deep history to critical appreciation of the poems. No one has more insistently queried the textual bases and the long history of scholarly investments in this narrative than Warner in *The Lost History of* Piers Plowman and in *The Myth of* Piers Plowman.

General Guides to Langland's Poems

The reading guides of Baldwin, Calabrese, Marshall, Simpson (Piers), Steiner (*Reading*), and Wittig (*William Langland*), along with Alford's *Companion*, Cole and Galloway's *Cambridge Companion*, and the *Penn Commentary*, will familiarize instructors with the principal issues that have occupied Langland's readers for over a century. The comprehensive notes accompanying Schmidt's B text edition (Vision) or, much more exhaustively, the second edition of his parallel-text edition (Piers [2011]) will also serve this purpose. Matthew Boyd Goldie's anthology, *Middle English Literature: A Historical Sourcebook* (2003), usefully gathers many documentary sources.

Earlier Monographs and Critical Overviews

Important earlier studies of Langland include T. P. Dunning's Piers Plowman*: An Interpretation of the A-Text* (1937); E. Talbot Donaldson's Piers Plowman*: The C-Text and Its Poet* (1949); D. W. Robertson, Jr., and Bernard F. Huppé's Piers Plowman *and Scriptural Tradition* (1951); Piers Plowman *and the Scheme of Salvation* (1957), by Robert W. Frank, Jr.; John Lawlor's Piers Plowman*: An Essay in Criticism* (1962); and Elizabeth Salter's Piers Plowman*: An Introduction* (1962). All offer overviews of the poem, a relative rarity in a field that now presumes that readers have a certain amount of knowledge. As well as ongoing discussions of authorship, order of composition, and relations of various versions as extant in the manuscripts, Langland studies have tended to produce analyses of a single episode or of a selected thematic or topical concern. Along with Anne Middleton's two essays on the critical tradition ("XVIII"; "Introduction"), "The Poem in Time" essay in the second volume of Schmidt's parallel-text edition (Piers [2011] 269–304) offers a summative overview of leading critical issues including authorship, date, early reception, ordering, revision, and sources for the poems.

Monographs on Langland

Engendered by modern editions and translations, which support teaching Langland at various levels, as well as careful study by scholar-critics, Langland studies has seen strong growth in the last forty years. In broad terms, it may be said that older questions of authorship of the multiple versions, addressed in Donaldson's study of the C text, and of potential historical allusion, which occupied Langland studies in the century including and following Skeat's work, yielded to more literary appreciations of the poems and then to concerns with historical currents of theology, particularly that of the *moderni*, those fourteenth-century theologians such as Duns Scotus, William of Ockham, and Robert Holcot. Following such interests, issues of potential heresy, including Lollard and Wycliffite associations, and revolt, including purported references in letters associated with the Rising of 1381, have given way to interests in Franciscanism and Joachinism, literacy and heresy, Reformation and post-Reformation reception, and thence to renewed close study of manuscripts, leading toward a more complex sense of Langland as "author" of a poem—and of poems—that we call *Piers Plowman*. With few exceptions to date (W. E. Rogers; Zeeman, Piers; Zeeman, "*Piers Plowman* in Theory"), Langland's readers have been given more to formalist and historicist analyses than to those shaped by hermeneutics, postmodern theory, and cultural studies.

The following selective list suggests some of the topics that have occupied scholars of the poem and its poet over the past fifty years: Kane, Piers Plowman*: The Evidence for Authorship* (1965); Elizabeth D. Kirk, *The Dream Thought of* Piers Plowman (1972); Mary Carruthers, *The Search for St. Truth: A Study of Meaning in* Piers Plowman (1973); John M. Bowers, *The Crisis of Will in* Piers Plowman (1986); Schmidt, *The Clerkly Maker: Langland's Poetic Art* (1987); Mary Clemente Davlin, *A Game of Heuene: Word Play and the Meaning of* Piers Plowman *B* (1989); Wendy Scase, Piers Plowman *and the New Anticlericalism* (1989; 2007); Malcolm Godden, *The Making of* Piers Plowman (1990); Kathryn Kerby-Fulton, *Reformist Apocalypticism and* Piers Plowman (1990; 2007); John Alford, Piers Plowman*: A Guide to the Quotations* (1992); John A. Burrow, *Langland's Fictions* (1993); Britton J. Harwood, Piers Plowman *and the Problem of Belief* (1995); Lawrence M. Clopper, *"Songes of Rechelesnesse": Langland and the Franciscans* (1997); C. David Benson, *Public* Piers Plowman*: Modern Scholarship and Late Medieval English Culture* (2005); David Aers, *Salvation and Sin: Augustine, Langland, and Fourteenth-Century Theology* (2009); and Nicolette Zeeman, Piers Plowman *and the Medieval Discourse of Desire* (2009). Aers's *Beyond Reformation? An Essay on William Langland's* Piers Plowman *and the End of Constantinian Christianity* (2015) departs from the bulk of writing on Langland in its closely argued reading of the C text.

Given Chaucer's central place in Middle English studies, three books that examine Chaucer alongside Langland deserve mention: Aers, *Chaucer, Langland, and the Creative Imagination* (1980); Kane, *Chaucer and Langland: Historical and Textual Approaches* (1989); and John M. Bowers, *Chaucer and Langland: The Antagonistic Tradition* (2007). The essays in this volume by Lawrence Clopper and by Ian Cornelius also offer comparative examinations of Langland and

Chaucer; those by Mary Clemente Davlin, Andrew Galloway, Ralph Hanna, David Lawton, Elizabeth Robertson, Emily Steiner, and Stephanie Trigg invoke Chaucer in passing.

Essays and Essay Collections Relevant to Langland

The following essays may be recommended particularly to students as starting points in the critical literature, as they have been cited frequently since their original publication: John Lawlor, "The Imaginative Unity of *Piers Plowman*" (1957); Pamela Gradon, "Langland and the Ideology of Dissent" (1980); James Simpson, "From Reason to Affective Knowledge: Modes of Thought and Poetic Form in *Piers Plowman*" (1986); David Lawton, "The Subject of *Piers Plowman*" (1987); Helen Cooper, "Langland's and Chaucer's Prologues" (1987); John Alford, "The Idea of Reason in *Piers Plowman*" (1988); Elizabeth Kirk, "Langland's Plowman and the Re-Creation of Fourteenth-Century Religious Metaphor" (1988); Steven Justice, "The Genres of *Piers Plowman*" (1988); and Anne Middleton, "William Langland's 'Kynde Name': Authorial Signature and Social Identity in Late Fourteenth-Century England" (1990).

Kathleen M. Hewett-Smith's *William Langland's* Piers Plowman: *A Book of Essays* (2001) includes ten essays that are subdivided into four sections addressing legal and literary historical contexts, Langland's alliterative line compared with Chaucer's verse, literary theory with regard to authorial naming and to gender studies, and allegory and personification in Langland.

Steven Justice and Kathryn Kerby-Fulton's *Written Work: Langland, Labor, and Authorship* (1997) offers an introduction and five extended essays speaking to the passage of just over one hundred lines in passus 5 of the C text often referred to as autobiographical, wherein the poet appears in his own voice to wrestle with the ethics of his employment status, including his work as a poet. Justice's "Introduction: Authorial Work and Literary Ideology" is followed by Derek Pearsall's edition and translation of the passage, "Will's 'Apologia pro vita sua.'" The essays that follow offer historicist readings that sustain dialogues with the circumstances—legal, cultural, religious discursive, and urban—in which Langland wrote.

Barbara Hanawalt's *Chaucer's England: Literature in Historical Context* (1992) brings together ten essays exploring late medieval English literature through historicist lenses. All the essays take up questions of historiography, disciplinary differences, and evidential viability; four directly address Langland's poetry. Another collection of essays devoted to Langland is Míċeál F. Vaughan's *Suche Werkis to Werche: Essays on* Piers Plowman *in Honor of David C. Fowler* (1993), which examines aspects of style, iconography, and manuscript traditions.

Two essay collections by prominent scholars of Middle English studies, and of *Piers Plowman* in particular, merit special note. These are *Earthly Honest*

Things: Collected Essays on Piers Plowman (2012), which brings together eighteen of Schmidt's essays on the poems; and a volume that collects Middleton's writings, *Chaucer, Langland, and Fourteenth-Century Literary History*, edited by Steven Justice (2013), which offers, among other work, one new and four previously published essays on *Piers Plowman*.

Earlier essay collections reveal the turn from older questions of authorship, texts, and language toward literary appreciation of Langland, including close readings of particular passages. These include S. S. Hussey's Piers Plowman*: Critical Approaches* (1969), and Robert J. Blanch's *Style and Symbolism in* Piers Plowman (1969).

Monographs in Middle English Studies

The following selective list of monographs, including a few earlier titles with continuing influence, can only suggest the depth of recent strong work in Middle English studies: Jill Mann, *Chaucer and Medieval Estates Satire* (1973); Penn R. Szittya, *The Antifraternal Tradition in Middle English Literature* (1986); Anne Hudson, *The Premature Reformation: Wycliffite Texts and Lollard History* (1988); Steven Justice, *Writing and Rebellion: England in 1381* (1994); Richard Firth Green, *A Crisis of Truth: Literature and Law in Ricardian England* (1999); Emily Steiner, *Documentary Culture and the Making of Medieval English Literature* (2003); Eamon Duffy, *The Stripping of the Altars* (1992; 2005); Ralph Hanna, *London Literature, 1300–1380* (2005); Andrew Cole, *Literature and Heresy in the Age of Chaucer* (2008); Brian Cummings and James Simpson, *Cultural Reformations: Medieval and Renaissance in Literary History* (2010); Kathryn Kerby-Fulton, *Books under Suspicion: Censorship and Tolerance of Revelatory Writing in Late Medieval England* (2011).

Collections of Primary Sources Relevant to **Piers Plowman** *and the Middle Ages*

Historical and literary-historical approaches to Langland have often predominated in pedagogy and in critical response, drawing on other poems and on documentary sources, especially from late-fourteenth-century England. Many such sources suitable for nearly any course on the later Middle Ages are available in anthologies, indicating the support of teaching scholars and of publishers for study of the period.

An important approach to teaching the influence of Langland and of the plowman figure is offered by Helen Barr's *The* Piers Plowman *Tradition: A Critical Edition of* Pierce the Ploughman's Crede, Richard the Redeless, Mum and the Sothsegger, *and* The Crowned King (1993). An introduction, bibliography, and a chronology of historical events precede a glossed text of the four poems, followed by notes and commentary (but no glossary). Also pertinent is the section "Plowman Writings" (243–65) collected in James M. Dean's *Medieval English Political Writings* (1996).

The World of Piers Plowman (1975), edited by Jeanne Krochalis and Edward Peters, was the first book offering support for students and instructors of the poems by means of a substantial selection of literary and documentary sources. Sources in Latin and French appear in translation, while sources in Middle English prose and verse are given in the original. It remains available in print and electronic formats.

Goldie's *Middle English Literature: A Historical Sourcebook* (2003) presents an excellent anthology of primary sources for Langland's poetry. In seven sections, the editor sets out selections mostly from fourteenth- and fifteenth-century sources covering medieval institutions, economy, sexuality, and textualities. Documentary sources range from the Benedictine Rule to the *Anonimalle Chronicle* and the fifteenth-century Paston family letters. There is a succinct table of dates, 1325–1500; a glossary; suggestions for further reading following each introductory essay; and a generous bibliography. It is available in both print and electronic formats.

Laurel Amtower and Jacqueline Vanhoutte's *Companion to Chaucer and His Contemporaries: Texts and Contexts* (2009) offers 120 documents arranged in eight chapters, each with an introduction, covering political ideology, social structure, religious practice, knighthood, war, literacy, education, and medicine. The first half of the book focuses on aspects of English life; the second draws on sources from, and addresses (or imagines) a wider Western European world, and beyond.

Carolyn P. Collette and Harold Garrett-Goodyear's substantial volume, *The Later Middle Ages: A Sourcebook* (2010), is directed toward student readers. Following an introduction to the period, more than one hundred documentary excerpts, arranged in eight topical areas, address spirituality, chivalry and violence, manorial life, mercantilism, and book production. Introductory and supporting commentary helps readers understand the context and ethos of the sources. The editors also provide a comprehensive bibliography of print and online sources for further study.

William R. Cook and Ronald B. Herzman's *The Medieval World View: An Introduction* (2011) frames selections from primary texts along with images to construct a narrative account from late antiquity through the rise of the mendicant orders, though the epilogue, "From Medieval to Renaissance," addresses the fourteenth century. The historiography of the book subdivides the long reach of this account conventionally into four major parts: late antiquity and early Christianity; the Mediterranean world (including Byzantium and Islam); the early Middle Ages and the foundations of monasticism; and what have been termed traditionally the High and late Middle Ages, including the emergence of the mendicant orders.

Histories of and Guides to Medieval English Studies

Literary Histories

David Wallace's *The Cambridge History of Medieval English Literature* (2002) includes Hanna's "Alliterative Poetry" and Kerby-Fulton's "*Piers Plowman*." Published to some controversy due in part to its starting date of 1066, thus excluding Old English and earlier Latin literature in Britain, the book is deliberately inclusive of Latin, Irish, Welsh, and Scots literature and expansive in its topical treatment of the field. The earlier period has since been addressed in Clare A. Lees's *The Cambridge History of Early Medieval English Literature* (2012). And for an intricate look at networks and exchanges among peoples, cultures, literatures, and places that is geographically wide-ranging, see Wallace's *Europe: A Literary History, 1348–1418* (2016).

Christopher Cannon's *Middle English Literature* (2008) makes a strong case for the medieval period as a source for the very category of literature. A literary history encompassing much more than the literary or the textual, the book contains chapters on technology, insurgency, statecraft, place, and jurisdiction, among other topics, offering a critically attuned account of how English was made into a medium for serious literary expression as well as a documentary register.

Companions and Handbooks

Larry Scanlon's *Cambridge Companion to Medieval English Literature, 1100–1500* (2009) offers a full yet compact compendium of eighteen essays in two parts. Especially relevant is Steven Kruger's essay, "Dialogue, Debate, and Dream Vision," for its address of *Piers Plowman* as participating in these discursive modes, implicitly offering important pedagogical possibilities not explored in this volume. Useful alongside this volume is *The Cambridge Companion to Medieval English Culture*, edited by Andrew Galloway (2011). Its extraliterary range is patent in chapters on archaeology, visual texts, and literacy and education.

Middle English, edited by Paul Strohm (2007), presents in thirty essays a provocative intellectual geography that foregrounds areas of critical debate while offering topical perspectives distinct from those conventionally centered on genres and authors, intending interventions less authoritative than conventional guides and handbooks generally suggest. Elaine Treharne and Greg Walker's *Oxford Handbook of Medieval Literature in English* (2010) is a comprehensive volume, available in print and electronic formats, of thirty-five chapters and an epilogue. Peter Brown's *Companion to Medieval English Literature and Culture, c. 1350–c. 1500* (2007) presents a formidable resource for study, dealing with topics such as textual production and reception, encounters with other cultures, and literature and law. *The Medieval British Literature Handbook*, edited by Daniel T. Kline (2009), presents an excellent introduction to the field, especially in terms of critical approaches. The book describes a broad range of primary literary and documentary sources, a host of persons and events relevant to reading the later Middle Ages in Britain, and an array of critical concepts and currents and their respective relevance to the field. It is accompanied by an online appendix on teaching medieval British literature in the twenty-first century.

Marion Turner's *Handbook of Middle English Studies* (2013), available in print and as an e-book, comprises twenty-six essays that bring medieval conceptual and material topics into dialogue with contemporary theory. *A Concise Companion to Middle English Literature*, edited by Marilyn Corrie (2009) and available in print and as an e-book, offers twelve essays in four sections: key contexts, the production of medieval literature, writing in Middle English, and Middle English literature in the postmedieval world. Thorlac Turville-Petre's *Reading Middle English Literature: An Introduction* (2006) offers six thematic chapters that address the use of English, texts and manuscripts, literature and society, history and romance, piety, and love and marriage. The subtopics in each chapter are brief, suggesting the book's introductory nature; "Ploughing Piers' Half Acre" (68–78) is of special interest to students of Langland. *A Companion to Medieval Poetry*, edited by Corinne Saunders (2007), offers a comprehensive discursive introduction to the sweep of literary production in Britain from the Anglo-Saxon period to the fifteenth century. Especially relevant are two essays by John Scattergood on alliterative poetry (329–48, 349–66) and one on Langland by Lawrence J. Warner (401–13).

Historical Studies of Late Medieval England

Print Sources

May McKisack's *The Fourteenth Century, 1307–1399* (1959) has long been the standard account of the period. Sylvia L. Thrupp's *The Merchant Class of Medieval London* (1948) has remained an essential source about a social group important to many changes in the period, including the spread of literacy. Rodney Hilton's *Bond Men Made Free: Medieval Peasant Movements and the English Rising of 1381* (1973; 2003) offers a widely referenced account of the Rising of 1381.

Web Sources

E-Medieval: Teaching, Research, and the Net is a special issue of *Literature Compass*, edited by Elaine Treharne with Orietta Da Rold, directed at digital humanities and pedagogies for medieval studies.

The Web site *Luminarium: Anthology of English Literature* is one of the oldest online resources for study of the Middle Ages, along with *The ORB: Online Reference Book for Medieval Studies*, which includes the *Internet Medieval Sourcebook*, sponsored by the Fordham University Center for Medieval Studies. *The Labyrinth: Resources for Medieval Studies*, sponsored by Georgetown University, offers an impressive network of sources organized in forty-two searchable categories, including "English, Middle."

The *Middle English Texts Series*, published by the Teaching Association for Medieval Studies (TEAMS), publishes Middle English texts in print and, more recently, in digital format; most of the content of the print volumes is also freely available online ("Middle English Text Series").

NOTES

[1]For a fuller discussion of student editions, the long fallow period in modern editions of Langland's poems, and its probable impact on pedagogical and scholarly attention, see Goodmann.

[2]The *W. W. Norton* Web site offers free resources that support the anthology for instructors and students with registered access, including summaries of introductory material from the print volume and maps.

Part Two

APPROACHES

Introduction

Thomas A. Goodmann

The contributions to this volume offer many paths for engaging readers of *Piers Plowman*, from those outside the conventional classroom to those in graduate seminars, and those reading Langland in translation and in Middle English and in manuscript. What makes Langland so interesting to teach is also what makes his writing most challenging: the multiplicity of modes and registers in the poems as well as a long and lively critical conversation regarding the poet's identity, purposes, and affiliations. That said, neither instructors nor students need a sense of mastery to read the poem; the point of this volume is to encourage readers simply to do so.

Over the past century and until recently, the B text of the poem has received the most attention from critical respondents and translators, and it is the version taught and cited most frequently, in A. V. C. Schmidt's Everyman edition (Vision), by the contributors to this volume. Against the weight of interest in the B text, two essays argue the particular benefits of teaching the other versions: Míċeál F. Vaughan for the A text and Kathryn Kerby-Fulton for the C. A, B, and C versions aside, readers will note that there is not a text or edition uniformly cited by contributors, for instructors of Langland have recourse both to Middle English editions for all three texts and to several translations of B and one of C currently in print. (There is no student edition of the unique Z text, and it is unlikely to gain such support). Nor among scholar-critics is there a single text of reference, as neither the three-volume Athlone Press edition (Kane, Piers [1988]; Kane and Donaldson; Russell and Kane) nor Schmidt's three-volume parallel-text edition (Piers [1995]; Piers [2008]; Piers [2011]) predominates (whereas for Chaucer, the Riverside edition, under the general editorship of Larry D. Benson, has been predominant since its publication in 1987). Moreover, most writing on Langland today attends to the multiple versions and the complex manuscript tradition. The essays in this volume, however, do not address themselves to specialists but to all manner of instructors, encouraging them to begin reading and teaching Langland—and to enter the waters almost anywhere in the current high tide of texts, translations, and supporting sources.

After choosing an edition, a translation, or selected excerpts (or a combination of these), instructors will want to select from supporting works by Anna Baldwin, Michael Calabrese, Andrew Cole and Andrew Galloway, James Simpson (Piers), and Emily Steiner (*Reading*), supplemented by documentary sources drawn from one of the source anthologies and by critical studies (see part 1, "Materials"). Annotated and glossed editions such as Schmidt's B text (Vision) and Derek Pearsall's C text (Piers), the complementary-text edition of Elizabeth

Robertson and Stephen H. A. Shepherd, selections in anthologies, and stand-alone translations will support a variety of instructor preferences and types of courses.

David Lawton's reflective essay, "Unliterary Langland?," serves as a prologue to the volume, offering a critical history of some of the key lines of inquiry academic readers have entertained. Coursing a panoply of topics for engaging *Piers Plowman*—including the value of poetry in the poem, the production of vernacular literature among professional scribes, alliterative verse from *Beowulf* forward, the good of earthly treasure, and reading Langland alongside Chaucer—the essay frames many of the approaches that follow in charting the vale between the tower of the literary and the dungeon of the unliterary.

No single critical method predominates in the essays that follow. The capacious terms of critical reception mapped by Lawton are in some degree echoed in essays taking up issues of interpretation intrinsic to the mode of *Piers Plowman* (William E. Rogers, Thomas A. Prendergast, Nicholas Watson). Two essays model a Socratic dialogue with students to examine modes of discourse (Ralph Hanna) and unrhymed alliterative versus end-rhymed verse (Ian Cornelius). Others engage historical issues of hunger (Madonna J. Hettinger), poverty (Kate Crassons), and extratextual invocations of literary characters (Gina Brandolino) to suggest how students might extend such issues in contemporary terms of research or in community service. Still others examine the literary and historical resonances of community (Steiner), the gendered dimensions of topical and allegorical representation (Robertson), and Langland's self-conscious anxieties about poetry and popular culture (Stephanie Trigg). The plowman as a figure with a long afterlife—along with the early modern and Reformation reception of *Piers Plowman*—is the subject of Sarah A. Kelen's essay. Translation as a medium (Thomas A. Goodmann) or as a mode of dramatizing excerpts for classroom performance (Galloway) offers ways to facilitate active learning with students. Allegory as a mode of literary representation with a long history is the subject of Judith H. Anderson's essay, which shares some concerns with Robertson's discussion of gender.

Several contributors invite comparative readings with Dante (Lawrence Warner) and, predictably, with Chaucer, especially the General Prologue (Lawton, Hanna, Lawrence M. Clopper, Cornelius) and other parts of *The Canterbury Tales* (Mary Clemente Davlin, Galloway, Robertson, Steiner, and Trigg). The possibilities for reading selections from Langland and Chaucer together are too many to discuss here. Just a few of these pairings include Lady Meed and the Wife of Bath; the treatment of money in *Piers*, B text, passus 2–4, and in the Shipman's Tale; the pardon in the B text, passus 7 (and C.9), and the Pardoner's Prologue and Tale; knighthood in *Piers* (B.1, 17–18) and in the Knight's Tale; and the value of learning as explored in the central passus (B.9–15; C.10–16) and in the Nun's Priest's Tale.

Many essays offer brief, demonstrative close readings (Davlin, Hanna, Clopper, Goodmann, Robertson, Steiner, Trigg). Course contexts for teaching Langland are also addressed, from the widely taught survey of British literature to 1600 or 1800 (Anderson, Clopper); to a survey of Middle English (Hanna); medieval history (Hettinger); interdisciplinary courses in topics such as medieval English literature and history (Galloway) and in apocalypticism, medieval London, and monasticism (Richard K. Emmerson); an advanced undergraduate seminar on poverty (Crassons); and (nearly) all of the above, including students of spirituality outside the classroom (Davlin).

The first group of essays, "Practices of Reading in *Piers Plowman*," offers formalist and theoretically informed approaches to Langland's poetry, each of them assuming little prior familiarity with Middle English literature beyond perhaps some reading of Chaucer. Hanna's essay describes how he opens the B text prologue with students, modeling a Socratic inquiry that attends especially to Langland's blend of discursive cues and strategies. The approach is not specific to Langland, but proceeds from questions fundamental to understanding any literary work: for example, What would constitute an adequate explanation of a literary work? C. David Benson addresses the perceived difficulty of Langland, which may hinder many instructors from opening *Piers Plowman* with students. Benson advises using this perception of difficulty as a drawbridge to understanding rather than as a moat of nonengagement. His sanguine view is that the poem is its own sufficient guide for reading, especially for limning some of the abiding concerns of the author: ethics and practices of work, play, and desire; issues of equity and merit, especially in light of salvation; the role of the intellect in the realm of the spiritual; and the intractable fallibility of human institutions.

Cornelius's essay describes a formalist method for teaching Langland's alliterative verse in two curricular settings, a survey of Middle English literature and a course on Late Middle English alliterative verse. In both instances one objective is to find fitting language to account for the metrical workings of Langland's verse in service to a yet larger question: "why—other than because it is printed in lines—we call *Piers Plowman* a poem." Cornelius makes use of Chaucer's General Prologue for comparative purposes and provides a model of interrogative analysis that instructors may apply to any passage in the poetry of both poets (and, with adjustments, to other poems in the late Middle English alliterative corpus). Rogers draws on the semiotics of Charles Sanders Peirce to explore sign-making and sign-meaning in *Piers Plowman* with students, connecting such exploration to the enterprise of liberal education—"to think about how people think"—the value of which has been under continuous scrutiny of late. Rogers offers that his practice "to read dramatically means to see *Piers Plowman* as the site of contending texts that themselves function as dramatis personae. . . ." To read Langland, argues Rogers, is to engage a text that enacts the difficulties of interpretation with which all readers struggle.

The four essays gathered under the rubric "History and Historicism: Contexts for *Piers Plowman* Then and Now" take up settings and inquiries contemporary with the poems and with our own time. Prendergast explores the teacher's obligations to students regarding freedom of belief and of interpretation in a post-secular world. He models interrogatively the metatextual nature of the pardon scene in version B, passus 7, for the ways in which "the analogy between the readers in the poem and the readers of the poem is part of the essential message that the poem is trying to communicate" about interpretive complexity. Invoking Habermas, he proposes an ethical imperative about freedom of interpretation in the classroom, acknowledging the inevitability of interpretation in choice and of choice in interpretation.

Nicholas Watson reads the poem with students "as a secular kind of theology," a poem deeply, if critically, committed to one particular religious system. Watson's map for teaching the poem as theology leads to sustained engagements with the problematical, even paradoxical, and dynamic representations by which Langland shapes his poem; the approach makes good use of contemporary medieval debates over poverty, social assistance, equity, and just deserts. Yet in acknowledging the difficulties of the poem, Watson shapes a case for the estrangement of Langland—his lack of canonicity compared with *The Canterbury Tales*—as a powerful vehicle for studying pastness, ever a ghostly presence in the forward-looking ethos of modernity. And, finally, his essay suggests how "the poem's intense commitment to its own present moment" may instruct readers in how to know things as Will seeks to know them: *kyndely*; that is, in a vitally and disturbingly lived present.

The concerns of Prendergast's essay overlap with those of Watson's with respect to the ethical problematic of historicist and presentist readings of Langland. While Watson reads the poem as an enactment of theology and as an instantiation of pastness, Prendergast unpacks the ways that the pardon scene looks to the past as well as to the future. Like Rogers, Prendergast examines the scene for the ethical possibilities of reading, for the urgencies of interpretation it represents for readers in the text and of the text, readers resistant to objective closure and open to individual choice.

Hettinger's one-semester survey of medieval history draws on the Goodridge translation of Langland, especially the figure of Hunger in version B, passus 6, to explore issues of agricultural labor, economy, ethics, and food in the Middle Ages and in the present moment. She invokes statistics about food and diet in the United States to engage students with the ethics of excess and of privation. "If we can read only one passage to help us understand the marginal economy that guaranteed the social structure of the three orders," Hettinger observes, "Hunger's appearance when Piers sets out to plow his half acre is a good choice."

Brandolino focuses on the enigmatic figure of Piers himself and his invocation in the letters associated with the Rising of 1381, so that Piers becomes a figure alive in the culture at large, an extraliterary persona. Her essay narrates the ways in which her historical investigations of the fourteenth century with students have been enlivened by a modern analogue, comic book superheroes. Similarly summoned, like the plowman figure, into "historical" action, superheroes during World War II were made to engage the Nazis long before the United States actually entered the war. She acknowledges a deep history in the *golem*, a figure both analogous to and distinct from Piers and one pertinent to the many Jewish artists in the history of comic book narrative and art.

The next section, "*Piers Plowman* in Literary Dialogue," contains essays framing how instructors may pair Langland's poetry with that of other medieval writers, including Dante and Chaucer, and explore Langland's poetry across the early modern period, from the sixteenth through the eighteenth centuries. Warner's essay takes up what is perhaps the most famous literary pilgrimage of the Middle Ages, rivaling that of Chaucer, in his discussion of teaching Dante alongside Langland. Warner encourages students to join the critical conversation and instructors, as Gerald Graff says, to teach the conflicts. Drawing on two points of parallel—the age of each narrator in midlife, and each poem's invocation of the virtuous pagan, Trajan—Warner outlines how students might address large questions of historical reference and allegorical method. He also suggests what students may learn from the dramatic and contrastive uses of Latin by each poet, raising arresting possibilities for authorial intent versus scribal practice that go to the heart of literary interpretation and investigation. The topic of pilgrimage is not explicitly addressed among these essays, but will no doubt occur to many readers; a good starting point is Dee Dyas's *Pilgrimage in Medieval English Literature, 700–1500.*

The essay by the late Lawrence M. Clopper discusses how to teach the General Prologue to *The Canterbury Tales*—the medieval text most likely to be familiar to some students and nearly all instructors—in comparison with Langland's B prologue, reading both texts in Middle English. His historically focused analysis draws on the trifunctional social model of knighthood, clergy, and commons evident in both prologues and interrogates the model's ideological interests and descriptive limitations. This essay follows neatly from Ralph Hanna's model of close inquiry of discourses invoked in the opening lines of the B prologue.

The final pair of essays in this section concern reading Langland after his own moment, from the so-called *Piers Plowman* poems to the 1550 editions of Robert Crowley. Kelen's essay addresses some of the pedagogical possibilities for historically situated postmedieval readings of Langland in a British literature survey course and as a component of medievalism in an early modern literature course, suggesting some implications of early modern medievalism. Anderson's pedagogy of the poem engages a specific case of such medievalism in Spenser's *Faerie Queene*, drawing on allegory in particular as a system of signification, a topic useful to nearly all instructors. She addresses primarily the

British literature survey course—one of the most common contexts for including Langland—and her essay references, as well as Spenser, *Pearl*, *Everyman*, and elements of *King Lear*. Possibilities for exploring Langland within a long allegorical tradition include the *Commedia*, as Warner shows, as well as the *Roman de la Rose*, the *Pèlerinage de la vie humaine*, and *The Pilgrim's Progress*; Anderson cites useful resources for grounding any such study of allegory.

Anderson's essay on allegory makes a bridge to the next section of essays, "Topics and Tropes." These engage a range of themes including poetry writing, community, gender, and translation. Trigg suggests how instructors might explore the aesthetic and ethical issues involved in writing poetry as a form of justifiable work—not making idle songs—a key concern in Langland's writing. Trigg draws attention to the range of words Langland uses for the making and makers of poetry and song, whose distinctions are often not clear or stable. Among potential contemporary comparisons, she suggests that students consider the self-presentations of Chaucer and of Hoccleve as writers. Equally compelling is her outlining of the tension between the morally critical, ethical view of the world at large at the close of the B prologue and the aesthetic energy of the writing. Next, Steiner's essay on the theme of community in the poem offers several possibilities for students to wrestle with Langland's "experimental poetics" in its deep ethical commitments to social reform. Chief among the paths she suggests we trace with students is the aristocratic language of "blood brothers" invoked in the poem and its limited legibility among nonaristocrats. Social difference, which Langland elsewhere affirms, reifies linguistic limitations that inhibit the very reforms for which the poem calls. Likewise, tracing tensions between exclusion and inclusion, between differences and affinities, which underwrite Langland's interests in community, can open the poem for students.

Robertson addresses gender and the role of the feminine in Langland. While acknowledging that such issues are less obvious or insistent than in *The Canterbury Tales*, she demonstrates how Langland's representations of women are distinctively broad and various, if intermittent, suggesting a good deal of material for instructors regarding women's roles in work and marriage. And she offers trenchant readings of Animus/Anima and of Will himself that suggest a blurring of conventional gender categories. Goodmann explores translation in its conventional sense, providing an account of available renditions of the B and C texts, while encouraging instructors to use translations to engage students with the Middle English in selected passages or at greater length. The essay offers a close reading of the opening lines to show how students may become critical readers by comparing translators' choices with one another and with the source. Treating translation more expansively, Goodmann suggests that students might turn Langland's verse into prose, as some translators have chosen, or cast and perform dramatic episodes with contemporary figures, an approach realized in more dimension in Galloway's essay.

In the section "Curricular Contexts," Davlin outlines her eclectic approach to teaching the poems, focused on the B text, both in classroom and extracurricular settings, which takes *Piers Plowman* public in a spirit closer to the intentions of its author than most academic settings offer. She presents an array of potential selections and approaches, including the figure of Will, select themes of the poem, key words and their polyvalency, and the errancy of some confident-sounding figures. In citing the visual and dramatic elements in Langland that invite illustration and dramatization, she too anticipates the approach described by Galloway. Emmerson describes two courses, The Apocalyptic Imagination in the Middle Ages, a course for advanced undergraduates and graduate students on medieval London that makes use of visual as well as verbal sources; and Monasticism and the Arts, which likewise draws upon visual and material sources. These courses are addressed primarily to students in fields other than English or literary studies and read the poem in translation. Galloway's essay describes his inventive collaboration with the historian Paul Hyams to dramatize passus 18 of the B text, the Crucifixion scene, with their students. Exploring the poem's literary qualities as well as its social and historical dimensions, Galloway and Hyams sought to test a general theory that *Piers Plowman*, in spite of its complicated ideas and speeches, has a strong dramatic conception and potential. Staging passus 18 perforce involved many decisions that raised further interpretive questions regarding author, narrator, and spectators in the narrative scene as dramatized. As Davlin suggests in her essay, this is a teaching technique that may be used to open up this and other expressly dramatic episodes in the poem. Equally, Galloway and Hyam's course suggests one productive path for collaboration across disciplines, such as English and history, that could easily extend to art history, architecture, archaeology, religious studies, and philosophy.

Crassons discusses how she uses the C text in a service learning course that examines poverty through literature, for which students give at least twenty hours during the semester to local community-serving organizations. Like Hettinger's essay on hunger, Crassons's approach asks students to engage the world around us, using economic investigation to advance ethical inquiry and service activity.

The section "Beyond the B Text" offers two alternatives to the version of the poem that has predominated in teaching and criticism for decades (although critical currents are now more complex). Vaughan makes the case for teaching the relatively short and structurally comprehensible A text, which he has recently edited, while Kerby-Fulton seeks to raise the relatively "oppressed" status of the C text. The C text is supported by George Economou's translation, and the so-called autobiographical passage in passus 5 of the C text is one of the most widely excerpted and commented upon extracts.

To follow Kerby-Fulton's essay, Axton Crolley offers an appendix that outlines Langland's language in the C text (though it is plainly relevant to A and B as well). The late Lawrence M. Clopper closes the collection with an appendix for instructors on the clerical orders that aims to help students understand the complex structure of the medieval Catholic Church.

The approaches offered in these twenty-three essays do not begin to exhaust the possibilities for reading Langland's poetry. It is hoped nonetheless that these essays may encourage more instructors who teach literature, history, religious studies, iconography, ethics, and other subjects to take up Langland's remarkable poems and that this volume may inspire yet more ways to do so.

Unliterary Langland?

David Lawton

What follows is not an argument that Langland is unliterary—my title has a question mark. The point is to ask, What happens if we think of him as unliterary? What happens, not least, to our conception of what literature is now and was then?

When, in the 1960s, I first started reading *Piers Plowman*, I was surprised by how much of the criticism I read failed to engage with the work as a poem at all. The great early exception before the 1960s was E. T. Donaldson, who had the temerity to include the word *poet* in the title of his 1949 book, Piers Plowman*: The C-Text and Its Poet*.[1] I did my first graduate work on Langland's poetics, not so much his meter—which looks quite different now from the "splendidly simple subject" W. W. Skeat thought it in 1868 ("Essay" xi)—as his semantics: the key alliterative words he collocates throughout the poem, making a network of meanings separate from, and just as important as, those of narrative and syntax (Lawton, "Style"). Quite recently, I have written on Langland as a poet-humanist, comparing him to Petrarch in the *Secretum*: Petrarch represents himself arguing with a fictionalized Augustine and politely refuses to give way when his Augustine strongly urges him to renounce the vain pursuit of poetry (Lawton, *Voice* 120–24; Petrarch). This seems to me exactly what the writer of *Piers Plowman* does at several moments in the text, when his proxy is examined by Reason and Conscience in passus 5 of the C text and when he is chastised by Dame Study in passus 10 of B. Like Petrarch, Langland is really interested in finding what might be called the space of literature, which can license him to push back against authority. The form stems from Boethian debate, which was extraordinarily influential in the development of vernacular poetry in the late fourteenth century (E. Johnson; Miller). But Langland is more Boethian than Boethius, if most modern readers of the *Consolation of Philosophy* are right when they judge that the prisoner Boethius finally capitulates before Lady Philosophy's intellectual correction.[2]

So my intellectual and critical sympathies are instinctively with those readers who appreciate Langland's poetic artistry in major episodes (the fair field, the confession of the folk, the Crucifixion, and the harrowing of hell) and are aware of Langland's knowledge of a wide range of poetry in three languages. Such readers historically have noted his feeling, albeit experimental, for literary genres, above all dream vision, and they have attempted to validate it by looking for a literary structure overall in the poem's quests—for Truth, "kynde" knowing, Dowel, Piers Plowman, and so on. Yet in my reading, and certainly in my teaching, I find that I cannot disregard the testimony of readers for whom a range of extraliterary discourses in the poem—and the historical contexts of those discourses—so problematize their reading as to leave them distrustful of their own, and, by inference, Langland's, literary instincts. Such (often advanced) readers may contrast Langland with, in their view, the literary Chaucer; they may even claim that Langland allows them more direct access to the world of late-fourteenth-century England than they find in Chaucer or texts more conventionally literary.

These different reactions model standard scholarly and critical approaches to the poem, some dating back to the fifteenth century, and serve to introduce the complex history of its reading and editing. Derek Pearsall has presented the criticism of the poem in the last half century or more in terms of a sequence from formalism to historicism (*Annotated Critical Bibliography*). The generation influenced by New Criticism, reacting against an often reductive use of the poem for historical illustration, wanted to read it for what John Lawlor called, in a splendid and foundational essay, its "imaginative unity" ("Imaginative Unity"). Such reading stressed process, not product. It bought the reader out of some of the poem's vertiginous intellectuality by emphasizing not only its provisionality but also its dramatic context. It responded to a dreamer and his restless, dissatisfied questing, though at the same time distancing his experience from that of the (wiser) reader. Like most New Criticism, it played well enough with structuralism, responding to narratology such as Tzvetan Todorov's on the quest, and managed to accommodate itself to early, allegorical deconstruction such as Paul de Man's. It came decisively unstuck, however, when it encountered Michel Foucault, and the consequent drawing of literature into what some saw as the black hole of discourse. This was the historicist move noted by Pearsall, strongly inflected by late Marxism or Catholicism or both, and to some extent it returned to prior insights, against which the formalists had reacted, and to the work's address to the academic, theological, legal, parliamentary, and social. If formalism had strayed too far in the direction of well-wrought urns, this criticism sometimes declined to gesture toward the poetic at all. The most extreme modern statement was Judson Allen's at a 1982 conference: "*Piers Plowman* is not a poem but a *distinctio*" (J. B. Allen, Conference paper).[3]

In a long historical view this kind of historicism is another moment in the recruitment of Langland in terms of what we now call vernacular theology, which began with Wycliffites and continued through the Reformation. In its modern academic form, however, the argument derives from a North American quarrel. On the one side, D. W. Robertson, Jr., and his medievalist colleagues at Princeton University were early advocates of the alterity of medieval literature and argued that the reading of Langland, or indeed Chaucer, was impossible without intense study of the Latin textual culture and iconography from which they sprang (D. W. Robertson; Robertson and Huppé). In many respects, this position was an important precursor of modern historicist study of medieval literature;

however, Robertson's exposition of medieval culture, while intensely learned, lacked diversity, tending to be Catholic, orthodox, and overall dogmatic. On the other side was the redoubtable Donaldson at Yale University, who insisted on the intelligibility of late medieval vernacular literature for modern readers and on the difference between the normative cultural reading of the Robertsonians and the literary purposes of late-fourteenth-century poets. While Robertson and his school can fairly be described as historicist, it would be a travesty to call Donaldson, by contrast, merely formalist; his work, above all on *Piers*, is informed as much by historical scholarship as by his excellent critical skills. Equally, Robertson was a subtle reader who paid attention to form.

It follows that the dichotomy between historicist and formalist is no more than a useful simplification. The true contrast is between those who claim for literature a degree of autonomy and those who maintain that it can be read only in terms of a broader social and intellectual network. The underlying issue is the one I have posed here: literary or unliterary Langland? In the current generation of scholarship, the still open question is to what degree Langland can be simultaneously literary and unliterary. Ingrained approaches may mistakenly fall along a post-Reformation fault line between religious and secular, with Langland parked on one side and Chaucer on the other. Much recent work helps us rethink this in ways that are equally literary and historicist. The structuralist term *literariness* remains useful here, to signify an unfolding concern with what literature may be as, or if—as if—distinct from other discourses. Scholarship of the last twenty or so years has contributed many tools for historical understanding of Middle English literariness: on voice (Zumthor, *Introduction*, *Oral Poetry*, and "Pour une poétique")[4]; on interpretive communities (Stock); on medieval rhetorical poetics (Copeland, "Pathos" and *Rhetoric*; Camargo); on vernacular composition and the difference between a Latin *auctor* and a vernacular *compilator* (Minnis); on multilingualism and translation more generally, viewed as a cultural project; and, not least, on medieval memory systems (Carruthers, for *Piers* especially) and on vernacular theology (Gillespie, "[S]he"; "Vernacular Theology"). The most exciting opportunity of the present moment, and one immediately attractive to most students, lies in the advances the new codicology has made in charting the relation between literature and other forms of textual activity and public service. It really matters to know the identity of Adam Pynkhurst and to know that he, like Thomas Hoccleve, worked (among much else) on manuscripts of both Langland and Chaucer (Mooney; Horobin).[5] A. I. Doyle and Malcolm Parkes proposed more than thirty years ago that the emergence of English literary manuscripts beginning in the late fourteenth century is a story that concerns government scribes moonlighting in English classics as a form of private enterprise. Subsequent investigations have found a mass of corroborative evidence that links scribes and vernacular authors, translators and compilers, sometimes all in one person (such as Hoccleve). Cultural construction did not just happen;

it was made. For all that its reception makes it appear securely foundational, the writing itself is edgy, unstable, and experimental. Codicology allows us to see the processes of revision and indecision through many stages, not all distinct. Both *Piers Plowman* and *The Canterbury Tales* can be seen as playing with the (hitherto dominant) production model of the miscellany, while at the same time they break with it in favor of a more exclusively literary model. Both are involved textually in the production of literature as an institution at the hands of scribes employed by government. So far, so literary.

Yet there are obvious and major differences in which *Piers Plowman* contrasts with the work of Chaucer and of John Gower, and indeed with that of John Lydgate and of Hoccleve. There is little of Chaucer's work to suggest he would have been antipathetic to literary formation; Langland, however, is at best impervious, and more often than not hostile. Nor does he seem interested in fashioning a new model of vernacular eloquence: his alliterative style is as far removed as possible from the ornate high style of works such as *Sir Gawain and the Green Knight*; his conception of writing in the vernacular seems grounded less in speech acts than in material deeds and doing well. Nor do any of the newly canonical writers of the fifteenth century claim him as a literary precursor in the tradition of classical or Chaucerian fame. While Hoccleve's work is steeped in Langlandian ideas and phraseology, he pays no such tribute to the poet of *Piers Plowman* as he does to Chaucer, or even to Gower (Lawton, *Voice* 183–94; Burrow, "Autobiographical Poetry"). There is no conceptualizing of poetry in *Piers*, unless of the wrong kind of poetry. While Chaucer in *Troilus and Criseyde* is anxious in the end to place his work in a tradition of "poesye," Langland uses the word "poete" only once (B.12.148), and it refers to the biblical Magi.[6] Indeed, there is good reason for placing Langland in a line of vernacular Bible Englishing that produced the contemporary Middle English ("Wycliffite") Bible; its translators would not have been thrilled for their work to be regarded as literary.

Moreover, Langland's poetry differs in that it is not essentially translation. Reliance on the term *compilation* has blurred this difference. The other poets can appear inventive by deviating from their sources, by establishing difference: Langland's poetry is based not on translation but on citation, and much of the content of his citation is hidden in most of his manuscripts. His is not like the business of honest importation, which is translation; it is like that of smuggling goods that are often, as it were, impounded. He therefore has no model. The translator-poet has a textual ground for the difference he makes; Langland, by contrast, must invent his own form from allusions often left uncontextualized, literally disoriented. His poetry is discontinuous in a way different from Chaucer's: whereas Chaucer's ruptures stem from the pressure and exuberance of narrative, and the effort of framing it, Langland's arise from a distrust of narrative, a desire to awaken from the nightmare of history. By refusing to have a single source, Langland's poetry must continually confront a world of texts outside itself, especially works of learning, by which it is constantly under examination. Or, to put it more positively, Langland's work is by design always and unboundedly open to discourse. Using strategies from literary and extraliterary genres, it deliberately lays itself open to invasion from the world outside it—like a newspaper, or, better, like a sophisticated, anxious, irascible, and necessarily anonymous blog. Such work, unlike Chaucer's, is not a multiplicity, one work in a series of works, but a rhizome: a multiply focused single work that can admit or be no other. By not withdrawing into a form other than its own, it remains in the fair field, which is our world of discourse. In writing about the multiplicity of Chaucer's work, therefore, I think more about voice, which is literary, but with Langland I think more about subjects, which are discursive.[7]

For Langland, therefore, there is no separate space for the literary—certainly not according to the interlocutor represented in his work, for whom poems exist not as speech acts but as material deeds, like prayers sold for money, albeit deeds too vain and unloving for one who would do well. Hence the paradoxical representation of the narrator's profession as idleness and his concern for all "the moneye of this molde" (B.1.44), when Holy Church would prefer to direct him to treasure, which for her, in denial of all worldly riches, is the treasure inherent in the human heart. In its discursive trajectory, the poem keeps returning to Holy Church's absolutism and the effort to internalize it: the only true treasure is truth. Learning itself is a form of material enrichment and must ultimately fall away in spiritual transformation. In its most poetic sequences, the poem returns again and again to this run of discourse, to the poetic praise of patient poverty, and to the advice that one must not only commend poverty but be poor oneself as Christ was poor. Yet the call to absolute poverty as a spiritual imperative is at odds with the literary impulse of the poem, otherwise the poem as a material object must consent to its own annihilation; and no sentient being, other than one in a poetic flight, can recommend poverty for all, since this condemns to poverty the selfsame poor for whom one cares. Langland all but ends his poem with the wish that friars, who are both the spiritual poor and worldly beggars, might have a "fyndyng" (B.20.383), an income. Poverty in their case—voluntary poverty—can function only as evasive transcendence, when in this world the demand is to do as well as to be, and making is a form of doing. No one discourse fits any better than a single form. The poem looks for a way of justifying its own work, but in the end all it can do is persist, at a perpetual crossroads, as a site "like social situations, where multiple forms cross and collide" (Levine 122). Much less than Chaucer can Langland find a separate space for literature. If it exists at all, it exists not conceptually but as endurance (suffering, patience), as no more than the refusal to accept authoritative advice voiced in the text itself to stop messing around (meddling with makings). This falls within the ambit of Petrarchan clerkship, not that of spiritual renunciation, so it does not make for a literature of poverty. But in comparison with the pretensions not only of Chaucer but also of Gower, Lydgate, and Hoccleve, it could nevertheless pass for a poor literature.

This makes what happens at the end of the poem all the more radical, unnerving, and anguished. The collapse of Unity is a far cry from Chaucer's retractions to the Parson's Tale or his palinode to *Troilus*, both of which combine a moment of renunciation with the main business of exculpation and self-congratulation. I offer my students the closest analogy I know, a modern parallel, drawn from another author whose life's work becomes a single series extending as long as life permits: Proust (Proust; Tadié 731–79). In 1921, as he lies on what will shortly be his deathbed, Proust hesitates over the proofs of his final volume. He has a decision to take that affects his whole book and his sense of his relation to his book and his life. Like Langland, Proust narrates his work in the voice of one who is and is not the biographical author: Will is named only once in *Piers*, Proust's narrator not at all. The whole fabric of Proust's massive work rests on the narrator's childhood, and particularly the parts of it spent in the family's summer residence in Combrai where his grandparents and aunt lived. It is here that many of the moments occur that are to be recovered in the work's process of involuntary memory: the famous madeleine at tea in his aunt's house, the smell of hawthorn, the main street, the Gothic church, the parks and estates through which he wanders. His conception of Combrai is an amalgam of two places, the more dominant of which, Illiers, is where the Proust family spent their summers; Illiers was more or less destroyed toward the end of World War I. So Proust hesitates: he can spare his fictional world, or he can follow the course of events by reducing it to rubble—no more house, street, church, hawthorn, or parks. And then he makes the discreet correction, noting quickly that Combrai is lost and the childhood eradicated, irrecoverable now except in memory. Because the book still holds the memory, one might still see this authorial decision as a triumph of the literary—but it takes place on a scorched earth and plays out on a sickbed. Any idea of the autonomy of literature gives way before mortality and history.

So it is when Conscience leaves Unity at the end of *Piers Plowman*. It is the last in a series of departures and cancellations in Langland's text, such as Conscience's leaving with Patience from the feast in passus 15 of the C version or the tearing of the pardon in passus 7 of B. Yet it is the last, and there can surely be no more: the narrator has dreamed himself grown old, bald, toothless, and impotent, and his waking to Conscience's groans—"And siththe he gradde after grace, til I gan awake" (B.20.386, C.22.386)—sounds uncannily like a death. Conscience's departure all but cancels out the whole poem, like war has annihilated the scene of memory in Proust: outside Unity, there are no sacraments, no libraries, perhaps even no grace. What has seemed like the only solid ground in the whole work subsides: Conscience exits not so much into poverty as into destitution and homelessness. At the point of his departure, the work ends. In many ways, gauging what happens here seems to me the crucial act in interpreting the poem:

as apocalypse, as an enigma of submission and hope, as an invitation to reread the poem (but with what measure of changed understanding?), or as bathos. It can be approached only through the entirety of the work, yet—like Proust's last-minute revision—it happens suddenly, without development. I would resist any impulse to moralize it or even explain it. It is just a line of flight, but one in which the work surrenders its autonomy and steps away from its readers, its author, and itself. In the end, it is unliterary. As Conscience leaves Unity, so Langland evacuates the literary. What remains is the battleground of time and discourse.

NOTES

[1] I was also encouraged by Salter, Piers Plowman*: An Introduction* (1962).

[2] For a more nuanced view, see Lerer, *Boethius*.

[3] Allen developed the point in his book *The Ethical Poetic of the Later Middle Ages*.

[4] See also Lawton, "English Literary Voices."

[5] For a challenge to this view, see Warner, "Scribes."

[6] In this essay quotations from *Piers Plowman* are from Schmidt, Vision.

[7] On Chaucer's voice, see Lawton, *Voice*; on Langland's subjects, see Lawton, "Subject."

PRACTICES OF READING

The Subject of *Piers Plowman* / *Piers Plowman* and the Discursive

Ralph Hanna

My conjoined titles allude to the two topics I use as proper tools to teach *Piers Plowman*. Both halves are derivative, not of my invention; they follow from the particularly generative and provocative writings of David Lawton ("Subject") and David Aers (*Chaucer*). But teaching, at least the way I do it, isn't an involvement in some conversation with a world of cognoscenti out there, but rather immediate, a performance. Unlike the most flamboyant academic assays in the genre, the performative here does not involve professional self-credentialing but a reconstruction of the act of reading itself.

I customarily teach the poem in two rather different undergraduate contexts. Both my usual contexts share some features: they are usually Middle English surveys (often limited to non-Chaucerian materials); the students have a syllabus and a set of suggested additional readings (one page of really basic stuff: for example, John Alford's *Companion*, James Simpson's *Introduction to the B-Text*, Wittig's *Concordance*, and Kane's *Glossary*); and we read from A. V. C. Schmidt's paperback edition of the B version (Piers [1992]), in spite of its problems of underannotation, a real difficulty for a beginning audience.

But the contexts (and what I can assume about the students) vary. With American undergraduates, I cannot assume they know much more than what they have read in my course before they come to *Piers*. Usually, I teach Langland second, after a warm-up text, often Robert Henryson's *Testament of Cresseid*. These students will read a substantial part, but by no means all, of the poem: prologue to passus 7, passus 18–20, the autobiographical passage from C, passus 5. In Oxford undergraduate classes and tutorials (a setting analogous to independent study courses for American undergraduates), I can assume a little more. Students will come to the text after a term of Chaucer, Middle English dream visions, and some Henryson; they will read the entire B version and write at least two tutorial essays (a teaching situation that is what is described in subsequent paragraphs as run amuck); they will have, as a prominent option, the opportunity of commenting a piece of passus 16–20. But generally it doesn't matter, since my teaching *Piers* all starts off the same. This occurs because I have a fairly definite, if performatively flexible, sense of how to site my pedagogy. I work best through a generally unprogrammed, if implicitly stable, framework that proceeds Socratically, by what a blues historian would designate as call-and-response. This enacts a commitment to literary study as "conversation," some variety of community search.

However, in teaching this poem (as all other poems I teach), the most relevant questions are always not about *Piers Plowman*, which just happens to be the daily or weekly exhibit, but are broadly educative. What would constitute an adequate explanation of a literary work? What tools do you have that would help you deal with such a thing? What tools would you need, if you haven't got them? And where and how might you go about acquiring them? How would you imagine different tools as differently prioritizing different aspects of the same verbal object?

I am most strongly committed to giving a whole series of kinds of explanation. This, whether provocatively or confusingly, regularly includes multiples of the same thing: "You could argue. . . . But, then again, you might argue. . . . How do you think these different views would differently dispose pieces of the text?" Nor will I ever shut down anything that comes back to me, no matter how misbegotten it appears. If it's truly off-the-wall, discussing it will show difficulties; if it's not, then the group ought to see where it would get us as an approach.

The process is always guided by A. E. Housman's comment that "[i]t is not important that I explain Juvenal; it is important that Juvenal be explained" (qtd. in Kane, Piers Plowman*: The A Version* 54n). So my role is mostly facilitative and not about my interpretation (although I always hope I'm earning my keep and that it's, in some terms, better than my audience's). Rather, I'm always trying to communicate something about the parameters in which interpretation might proceed. Thus, the only given is enforcing thought and a passionate attentiveness.

This also means that the great bugbear of the study is the facile and the conventional. I'm particularly interested in ensuring that the group gets rid of fixed and conventional expectations. In the context of *Piers Plowman*, this is most pressingly represented by a comment that came from a committed Catholic student of the late 1960s. He told me, "I don't like this poem, 'cause it's just like catechism class." (Given the way I operate, the class will eventually see how some version of that response might be descriptive as well as the limits of its descriptiveness.)

So what I have to offer here isn't an overarching lecture (or set of them) on the poem. Rather, I can give you an idealized version of a pretty usual script. This is how the first couple of hours, devoted to the prologue, might go. As a pedagogical exercise, it turns out to be slightly perverse (but a perversity programmed by Langland himself): teaching the prologue is one of those situations in which the less experienced students are ultimately going to end up looking like stars, all their confusions ratified.

In my form of teaching, the first and most important step is to try to find out where the median to start from is. (You do need to know where you should start pitching things.) So I ask the class what they have noticed in the reading that they think is of interest and want to talk about. Astute students are going to home straight in on the fact that they think this is all already déjà lu—that it's Chaucer all over again—and they will promptly want to start making some comparative gestures.

That's intriguing enough, but I fob them off for a while, and eventually someone either asks me about the Latin or professes confusion about where the rats came from at line 146. Now we are in business, because it allows me to ask what either of those things have to do with what the other students are up to (doing Chaucer comparisons) and to force them to confront the fact that the appropriate answer to the question is "ostensibly very little." This answer opens out the basic problem about *Piers Plowman*, that the poem engages in modes of operation that juxtapose things one wouldn't expect and thus that its mode of making meaning isn't going to be quite manageable within the terms the class may think they have got at hand.

We can then branch out a bit. So I ask whether they think there are other parts of the prologue that involve similar kinds of disjunction, things they would have difficulty accommodating to a view that this is like Chaucer somehow. Usually, we come up with a fairly extensive list of exhibits. These I tend to list for them on the blackboard, visual demonstration—the more extensive the list gets, the more evidently pressing the problem is. All of this further exemplifies the poem's centrifugal operations, rather than its developing toward coherence.

At this point, we may do a little close text work. For example, I might invite the class into the first twenty lines of the poem and ask them about the dreamer's falling asleep and his initial moment of vision, towers, and field. On the one hand, this should evoke a recognition of romance, or magnatial, culture. For example, there's the *locus amoenus* of lines 8–10, with the "somer seson" and "May morwenynge" of lines 1 and 4. Alternatively, they may pick up on the world of marvels, diction like "a ferly of fairye" (some may know Chaucer's Tale of Sir Thopas or Wife of Bath's Tale; someone might even know Thomas Chestre's *Sir Launfal*). Or there's "wondres to here" (which would provoke a little subsidiary question: do you normally hear wonders? what do you think of a poem marked as visual and yet heard? does that remind you of other prologue moments?), and the "merveillous swevene" of line 11.

Of course, whatever the problems with digesting this material, it's juxtaposed with something very different. When he falls asleep, the apparently romance dreamer comes squarely up against universalizing two-way religious allegory (lines 13–19). The group might have some past-reading referents for this material as well: "the sonne" of line 13 may recall for them Dante, or notes may have told them they should associate what is here "seen" with a morality play and its staging.

Thus, students have become aware of some range of texts lurking behind Langland's. But these are diverse, not customarily thought of in the same universe, and behind them all is that strange disjunction of seeing and hearing. This collision, about which I again remind students as a problem that has implicitly occurred earlier in the discussion, raises the specter of genre, wide-mouthed wonder (about mouthiness) versus moral directness. So we'll try to talk a little about what genre (literary "kynde") means, how people go about distinguishing genres, and so forth. The hope is that students come to see that genre is constituted out of specific literary topics and rhetorical features, supposed to be distinctly separate (I can remind them of the compositional rule of generic diversity in *The Canterbury Tales*). At this point, I can spring my trap (the same one I use on everything, Chaucer, Shakespeare, Milton, what have you), the idea of specific realms of discourse. And that what may have been troubling them is that the poem has got more of these than they are used to, exhibited in brief compass without particularly overt markers to designate the switch points.

At this point, we can step back a little. So I ask, assuming that their ways of doing literature rely on coherence theories of meaning, whether they can see ways to reduce the amount of apparent multiplicity in Langland's poem. I do this with a kind of indirection that's momentarily calculated vertiginousness, by asking them whether they recall any references to romance, the romantic, or people who might be romance hearers after the dream setup. With a little prodding, they usually get to "Thanne kam ther a king, knyghthod him ladde" (112). (They probably need a momentary gloss on this line, especially given Schmidt's capitalized "Knyghthod," a warning to take with them through further reading. It's often unclear in the poem whether one treats abstract nouns or personifications or "characters.") So then, I say, are this king and the scene he's in quite what you think of when you consider "romance"?

Well, no it's political, not the romance of dragons, ladies, and knight errantry. Rather, it describes what knights do most of the time after they are grown up, function as the king's local supportive administrators. Pause. So does this strike you as literary? or as something else? What does that say about Langland and the value of romance? About the relation of a poem that is literary and some "real" that it is trying to present verbally (heard or read, not seen, I remind them)?

It gets worse from there. For example, I'm now ready to remind the group of the worry over Latin that some students raised. They need to see that that language isn't monolithic or just some kind of code-switching (the poem relies on people in possession of a single, trilingual code that can be disposed ad lib, a view that might lead to a momentary digression to look at 15.371–75). "Ve terre" at line 196 is clearly marked as prophetic Bible, but "Dum rex a regere" (141) isn't. It's a certain kind of academic wit, here a kind of pop political science that ultimately goes back to something like Isidore's *Etymologies*; from that source, it conveys a view that the form of language itself indicates a proper real. So the Latin involves different codes, different discourses as well. But there's more to say about "Dum rex." I momentarily ask them to reconsider that proposition: In terms of that precept and its implications, does the poem seem to be "proper"? How might you think about addressing that issue? Does it remind you of other "improprieties," perhaps related to the poetic speaker? (A little jab that may lead off into lines 1–4 and some warnings about handling clearly narrative statement.) What if it reminded you of other "improper" speeches?

Then I'd add just one further complication. Who says "Dum rex a regere," and where does that person come from? Do you recall any other odd conversations (things heard, not seen) here? So we see that Langland presents in lines 123–42 the surreal just-popping-up-from-nowhere of three characters. (I'll remind students in passing of the rat parliament question at the start of the discussion.) Who are these speakers—angel, *goliardeys*, lunatic? Have they anything in common? Do they seem to "have credentials" that might underwrite this conversation? All of them? All of them equally? (In passing, I might point out that Chaucer calls the Miller a *goliardeys*, in ways that might associate the term with low stories or jesting, and that the lunatic has got play as the poet's self-identification in parts of the poem students don't read—but they could recall his queer self-introduction at lines 1–4, or perhaps we'd make a quick run to look at the lines following 13.440 and 15.3–10.) I then point out that all this detail, down to "histriones," refers to a real historical situation, the coronation of Richard II, known to us from the St. Albans historian Thomas Walsingham.

So at this point, we need to summarize and develop a little bit. Unlike everything else they know, Langland's poem seems to depend on an absolute historical siting, a very specific sense of place-time-event. Langland responds to the contemporary: on one hand, this raises a broad literary question about whether there might be a meaningful distinction between art and journalism. More to the point, we can have a little disquisition on Edward III's dotage (for now, death of the Black Prince, why there's a kitten, the Good Parliament, why they will get to read about Lady Meed next class), allowing us to see how the rat parliament might be related to the discussion. But equally, we see it as discursively nonrelated: if the description is some fictionalized history, when we get to the rats, we slip into a different literary kind. So we talk a bit about Aesopianism, and the satiric use of beast fables (I remind them of at least Chaucer's Nun's Priest's Tale). But we also talk about Aesop as a text for somebody: who originally? who in the Middle Ages? The poet, whether or not he's the opposed lunatic, seems to share the *goliardeys*'s grammar school background. This probably leads into a little disquisition on Clergy and the need to manage the world's discourse, perhaps not just learned discourse.

We can now circle back into the depiction of Richard's coronation. As the angel, goliard, and lunatic show, contemporary emergency provokes wildly diverse responses. Langland's poem thus might be legitimately critical or, maybe better, analytical, a display or development of the world's discourses (note again that they are verbal and heard, not seen). But confusingly, the responses evoked by a single event aren't carefully marked to direct our consumption of the views expressed (whose version are we supposed to believe here?). "Any suggestions for reading strategies?" I ask. We agree that we have to puzzle these out, consider the implications of what each speaker says and what kinds of scenarios each would generate, how we might feel about each of these outcomes. Is this a guide for reading the poem? That it is resistant, and that you as reader have to assess?

Further, thinking about romance opening and "knyghthod hym ladde" indicates the poem's desire to outline and discover the social use for knights. This perception provides an entrée into what we will now be able to see as another discourse, the one shared with Chaucer, that of estates satire. Finally (and so students will certainly think), I let them do the comparison they were chafing for, most especially to see the rather different emphases of Langland's version and Chaucer's. Whatever Chaucer is describing, Langland's estate satire emphasizes working, staying home, and proper provision of religious instruction. We might notice here that Chaucer knows Langland (the Plowman most obviously) but not the reverse, that this poem is earlier and may have very different presuppositions. (A possible digression at this point to remind them of reception theory, anxieties of influence, and so on.)

I'll then encourage them to consider estates satire insofar as it affects clerics (a lot more of them in *Piers* than in *The Canterbury Tales*). Things will focus around the line, "parisshes weren povere sith the pestilence tyme" (84). First a little conversation about demographic disaster (is it an analogy to the disaster of late Edward III?) and another discourse, this one again associated with current events, that of the possibly suspicious nature of poverty and of the sturdy beggar wandering loose (recall lines 40–45).

But the poem's clerics are precisely not beggars. Indeed, Langland seems to present profitability as the top priority of priestly training. Thus, the cure of souls gets automatically, it appears, swapped for bureaucracy. Is this a move one might see as analogous to idealized romance knights as administrators? Is one to think it equivalent? or better? or worse? Here we might turn back to the text and examine Langland's abusive language more carefully, for example the venomous portrayal of friars (58–67). I'll encourage the group to unpack language like "charite [the] chapman" (64) to see the intersection of what may be an attractively inappropriate discourse set with religious language. What obvious word has "chapman" replaced? (Intruded general moral: try to listen [wondres to here], to hear what's not there and might be?) But more germane will be questions like the following: How do commerce and associated languages figure in the portrait? What is it shoving out (why "glosed" [60] and "construwed" [61])? What gets lost when public teachers become enamored of getting and spending? What does that answer imply about "profit"? Does that answer imply what Langland wants to retrieve for us but that his available discourses, the only ones he can write intelligibly in and be socially comprehensible, shroud?

We could again return to the comparison with which we came upon the discourse of estates satire. Is Langland's representation pointed differently from Chaucer's? Does the younger poet's delight in showy individual impulse leave out something that's more interesting to Langland? Does Chaucer ever stop to consider social effects? Or does he rely on some implicit notion of victimless crime? What do students think of that? Or of this poem as "public" or "communal" (remind them of uses of the words at, for example, lines 113, 115, 117)? Is Langland more "committed" than Chaucer, more prone to see social disaster, not just glamorous cheekiness? But is there then a conundrum about the discovery with friars that worldly language might have been co-opted into unhelpful forms?

That last perception will give us one way of framing the sort of controlled chaos we're discussing. It is a way of representing an undesirable state of social crisis. Then, the collision of discursive frameworks we're accustomed to keeping separate or that we think of as extraliterary—and are thus shocked to find in this (or maybe any?) poem is one way of expressing that issue. But correspondingly, implicit in all this is a view that these discourses are sensible and that they should be orderly. The problem in Langland's poem, which never gets resolved, is how to put them together—again. The most particularly pressing issue might appear to be clerical instruction itself, since that (recall the allusions to grammar, "dum rex" or "glosed") is the way medieval society articulates how one ought to police discourse.

That would be one kind of (pretty structured) conclusion. But along the way, I'm nagging at students, inviting them to offer examples of things that are getting left out, things they feel are not adequately explained yet, things that require inclusion or integration. (Essentially, I'm trying to enact a model of completeness, not just coherence of explanation, within the precept that no one can ever drain the text or fully empty it out.) Thus, this remains a pretty idealized description, since the class might equally end as summary of what we have discovered, what stands as unfinished business, with an invitation to consider whether what's been found actually will stand up to a scrutiny predicated upon the superflux, what can't (or hasn't yet come to) be integrated.

And I'll remind them that this discussion has been predicated upon an "opening." Our exfoliation of textual problems mirrors the poet's. He's set a whole complex of issues in train, opened and revealed them for scrutiny and discussion. So one thing to look for as they read is how the text responds to the opening it has created, how it develops (or does it develop at all?) the issues it has raised. The friars at the end of the class are a perfect setup: after all, the rest of the first vision (reminder that that's reading for next time) is going to play off that same collision of doctrine and dollars, Lady Holy Church and Lady Meed.

So that would be a first class or two about the poem. The remainder of this teaching stint would go on developing analogously the poem's variety of discursive issues. And, raising the issue of poetic narrative, it would necessarily inflect these issues against ideas like time and order of argument: Why address this issue now? What might this apparent resolution gain? What does it leave out, or what issues remain outstanding, potential matter for the poem's continuing discussions?

"Lewed" Langland and the Delights of Difficulty

C. David Benson

William Langland is often regarded as fourteenth-century English poetry's compulsive intellectual, even its nutty professor—and this by his supporters. Not without some reason, his work is said to be stuffed with academic arguments and obscure allusions accessible only to those thoroughly grounded in such disciplines as medieval theology, history, biblical exegesis, and political thought. The title of one essay echoes a cry uttered by many students (and their teachers): "What Makes *Piers Plowman* So Hard to Read?" (Chamberlin). As a leading scholar of the poem has observed, "With every new book on Langland, it seems, the poem gets more and more difficult. Soon it may be inaccessible except to a handful of specialists—literary high priests who have prepared themselves for its mysteries by a lifetime of reading in Thomas Aquinas, Duns Scotus . . . and so forth" (Alford, "Langland's Learning" 2).

I reject such a cult-like treatment of *Piers Plowman*, which would deny this rich and often funny work from all except a small band of initiates who know the secret (Latin) password. Instead, I want to argue for the accessibility of *Piers* and suggest that the poem itself is the best guide to how it should be read. As indicated by my title (it is not absolutely required that essays on *Piers* themselves alliterate, but an amazing number of them do), I have two major points: first, while knowledge is always a good thing, *Piers* is less exotically learned than it may initially appear and is approachable by an alert reader with little prior training; and second, difficulty is not only a problem in *Piers* but also the source of much of its pleasure and delight.

"Lewed "Langland

By calling Langland *lewed*, the Middle English word for someone who is ignorant or uneducated, I am not suggesting that Langland was an unlettered oaf. *Piers Plowman* is, among other things, a poem by an intellectual for intellectuals, and the poet wrestles with a variety of ideas and other texts (especially the Bible). But I am convinced that most of the knowledge needed to enjoy *Piers* is supplied by the poem itself. We need not recognize the full range of sources behind Langland's portrait of the Seven Deadly Sins in passus 5, for example, to respond to the desperate (and often comic) plight of these all-too-human personifications, who are unable to treat others except as the objects of their lust, envy, and covetousness. *Piers Plowman* is firmly set in the realities of the everyday world. The poem demonstrates that abstract academic thought is of limited help in reaching metaphysical truth and that the reader can best glimpse this truth through the images and enigmas of vernacular poetry. Learned interpretations of *Piers* are often impressive and enlightening, especially for advanced readers, but they are no substitute for reading and appreciating the poem itself.

For example, the fable of the attempted belling of the cat by mice and rats at the end of the B prologue (146–210) has led scholars to try to connect the participants with real historical figures: the cat has been identified as John of Gaunt and the "rat of renown" as the speaker of the House of Commons Peter de la Mare. Undoubtedly these identifications provide a possible political context, even if not all scholars agree on them, but such knowledge is not required for readers to enjoy the vivacity of Langland's rodents or to interpret the meaning of the fable, as its last lines encourage us to do (209–10). Many assume that the mouse who insists on the futility of attempting to bell the cat is expressing Langland's own opinion that resistance to state power is pointless. Yet, prompted by the fable's closing invitation to speculate, we might wonder whether the mouse's advice is indeed prudent or merely the response of a timorous beast and therefore not to be imitated by human beings.

Although Langland assumes a basic knowledge of Christianity not everyone possesses today and some of his concerns are undoubtedly less immediate to us than they were to his readers six hundred years ago, the learning of *Piers Plowman* is not really as esoteric as sometimes claimed, for the poem shares much with the wide general culture of late medieval England, as I have recently argued in my book *Public* Piers Plowman*: Modern Scholarship and Late Medieval English Culture*. That *Piers* can be read without extensive outside commentary is shown by a major allegorical personification, Imaginatif, near the end of his speech in B passus 12 in which he wonders whether pagans will be rewarded by God for faithfulness to their own creeds:

> Ac trewth that trespassed nevere ne transversed ayeins his lawe,
> But lyveth as his lawe techeth, and leveth there be no bettere,
> And if there were he wolde amende, and in suche wille deyeth—
> Ne wolde nevere trewe God but [trewe] treuth were allowed.
> And where it worth [of treuth] or nought, the [worth of] bileve is gret,
> And an hope hangyng thereinne to have a mede for his treuthe. (12.287–92)
>
> But truth that never trespassed nor transgressed against his law,
> But lives as his law teaches, and believes there is no better,
> And if there were he would adopt it, and in such a will dies—
> Would never true God wish but true truth were allowed.
> And whether it's witness of truth or not, the worth of belief is great,
> And a hope is hanging in it to have reward for his truth. (12.287–92)[1]

Searching for the source of this apparent challenge to the medieval doctrine that salvation was possible only within the Church, scholars have pointed to the arguments against this by the extreme (and censured) Uthred of Boldon or the advanced theologians known as the *moderni*.

But these arcane analogues are not necessary, for Imaginatif's words are not a formal statement of an intellectual position but a playful poetic exploration of the question, which is full of ambiguities and hesitations that resist epitome or resolution. The energy of Langland's lines is not revealed by learned scholarly annotation but by careful reading. First of all, the author is not necessarily giving his own opinion but speaking in the voice of a dramatic character, Imaginatif, whose words are highly literary, especially in his ringing changes on different forms of the word *truth*. The case for the salvation of the heathen is made not through argument but through word play: they are true and so is God and therefore to be true to himself he must allow their truth. If we are persuaded, it is not by the logic of argument but by the suggestiveness of poetic language. The resistance to simple paraphrase in these lines (as throughout *Piers*), which requires them to be read closely, continues in the final line of the passage: the salvation of righteous pagans is not directly asserted by Imaginatif; rather, it is his "hope" that such non-Christians will "have a mede for his treuthe." With characteristic subtlety, this hope is expressed by using (and redeeming?) one of the most negative words in the first part of *Piers*, *mede*. The lady called Meed in B, passus 2–4, epitomizes earthly corruption and bribery, but here the word is transformed to mean the divine reward of those who do well.

The Delights of Difficulty

My brief discussion of a few of Imaginatif's many words shows that Langland's poetry requires alert, careful attention—skimming just doesn't work—and this is one of the reasons *Piers Plowman* may be the least read masterpiece in our language. But, far from being an impediment, this difficulty, if understood rightly, is the key to the poem's special delights. My experience in reading, teaching, and talking about *Piers* has persuaded me that readers from beginning undergraduates to professional medievalists can find immense pleasure in Langland's poetry once they accept and engage with its difficulties, like travelers in a foreign land exploring and savoring rather than resisting the new customs, foods, people, and sights they encounter. The profit and pleasures of difficulty in both scripture and secular poetry were emphasized by medieval theorists from Augustine to Boccaccio, and we, too, should embrace such difficulty rather than trying to shield our students from it.

A primary difficulty with *Piers*, which some critics attempt to ignore, is its lack of clear and consistent structure and narrative. Derek Pearsall has observed that what many think of as "the major school of modern Langland criticism" is composed of those "who believe that the poem has a completed coherence of design, and that careful enquiry into its background in intellectual, scriptural and patristic tradition will gradually reveal and elucidate that design" (*Piers* 5). I would argue against design, or at least against a completed coherence of design, and emphasize instead the tensions, contradictions, and irresolution in the poem. These are not failures of the poet but his deliberate attempts to represent the complexity of his themes.

Nevill Coghill memorably observed that the organization of *Piers Plowman* was less a coherent, developing structure than a series of "foretastes and echoes" (147), though this is often forgotten in an understandable desire to create order from an unruly poem. Coghill's suggestion is supported by the fact that the poem's first-person narrator is not obviously wiser after his long journey: in the closing lines of the work we find him setting out, once again, in pursuit of Piers the Plowman. Nor are we ever given answers to some of the key questions in the poem: Who is Piers Plowman? What is Truth's pardon? What is the relation between justice and mercy? How do I save my soul? Instead of an absence of structures or answers, *Piers* contains too many. Everything is kept in motion, as if by a literary juggler. Important themes, like the idea of a blood brotherhood that unites human beings (including Christ), are introduced casually, while others are discussed at length but never finally abandoned. The poem is more an endless debate than an argument with a clear conclusion. Thus, the value of learning, which is questioned by the narrative "I" at the end of passus 10, is affirmed by Imaginatif in 12, only to be shown at its worst in the Doctor of Divinity in 13, whose learning, however, is perhaps not as corrosive to the soul as the life of action led by Haukyn. It has been suggested that *ac* (a form of *but*) is the most important word in the poem. Again and again positions that seem most central to the poem, such as the condemnation of the behavior of the rich, are qualified, then reaffirmed, then qualified in a new way by a series of "buts" (e.g., 14.140–70).

Everyone knows, but not everyone always remembers, that *Piers Plowman* is poetry, not theology. It challenges, provokes, delights, and even frustrates, but it doesn't indoctrinate. The more carefully we read the poem, accepting its intricacies, ambiguities, contradictions, and lack of final conclusions, the more exciting it will become for us and especially for our students. Previous critics have identified puzzling scenes and characters in *Piers*, such as Lady Meed and Truth's pardon, the latter being what Elizabeth Kirk correctly calls an "aenigma" that ought not be explained away (*Dream Thought* 82–83). I agree and urge that we extend this attitude to the rest of the poem. For example, Patience is clearly an ideal figure in the poem and his concluding praise of poverty important, but what exactly do we make of some of his doubtful statements to Haukyn, such as that the poor are never guilty of the sin of anger because when they must ask others for food or money they look "lowly" and are "loveliche" ("pleasant") in their speech (14.228–29)? Anyone who has ever had to beg for a favor knows that one's outwardly pleasing appearance in such situations is often only superficial and does not necessarily reflect one's deepest feelings.

When a student says something like, "I'm confused; just who is Piers Plowman?," perhaps we ought to respond, "Yes, that's the way to read the poem." This question and others like them are not to be answered so much as explored. We should relish the poem's puzzles without feeling that we must resolve them. *Piers Plowman* proceeds by means of puns, debates, prophecies, and parables. It is, as the Doctor of Divinity scornfully says of Patience's words, "a dido . . . a dysoures tale" (13.172)—a poetic fable like that of Dido or a minstrel's tale.

A famous passage early in the poem, spoken by the first personification the "I" meets, Holy Church, demonstrates well the poetic difficulties and delights of *Piers Plowman*, whose art is far from serene and settled but instead dynamically fractured and dissonant (1.138–62). Although Holy Church is sometimes treated as a didactic and remote figure of authority, in these few lines she is anything but. Holy Church begins with a sharp, salty dismissal of the narrator's request to explain herself more clearly: "'Thow doted daffe!' quod she, 'dulle arne thi wittes'" ("'You doting dolt,' said she, 'dull are your wits'"; 140). But a mere dozen lines later, she speaks some of the most sublime words in Middle English poetry: the dazzling, paradoxical, metaphysical lines about divine incarnation that describe Christ as, among others things, a "plant of peace," which heaven cannot hold because of its heaviness—though, after eating its fill of the earth, it becomes as light as a tree leaf and as piercing as the point of a needle (152–58). The deepest literary pleasure in these lines, which I do not have space to adequately discuss here, will come not from tracking down possible sources, though many have been proposed, nor from uncovering a consistent argument, but from responding to the tangled suggestions and sharp shocks as the passage unfolds. Langland is responding poetically to the incarnation rather than presenting doctrine—his profusion of comparisons never coheres into a single, stable image. As throughout *Piers*, thought does not so much develop as oscillate back and forth, an occillation reflected in both style and content. We not only see concrete examples of contrary things (such as heavy and light), we also hear changes in sound and rhythm, from salty insult to holy rapture. The passage concludes, perhaps even more daringly, by comparing Love as Christ to a mayor who mediates between king and commons. After the pyrotechnics of the "plant of peace," this association may seem prosaically anticlimactic, but this new jolt—daring to compare divine love to a mere city mayor—shows how Langland's poetry keeps challenging its readers. The last line of the excerpt describes the power of mayors to enforce laws and assess fines, but the term used for the latter, "merciment" (162), is a Middle English word that contains its opposite, the word "mercy." Thus, Langland again demonstrates his art, which is able to reconcile justice and mercy in literary language, if not in strict logic, as it invites readers to enjoy the difficult, cunning, early postmodern poetry of *Piers Plowman*.

NOTE

[1]Quotations from *Piers Plowman* are from Robertson and Shepherd, and translations are from Donaldson (*Alliterative Verse Translation*). Donaldson notes that in the passage quoted here "truth" (line 287) means "a true person."

FURTHER READING

A remarkable group of publications in the 1970s and 1980s emphasized the literary achievements of *Piers Plowman*. They include Mary Carruthers's *The Search for St. Truth: A Study of Meaning in* Piers Plowman, Elizabeth D. Kirk's *The Dream Thought of* Piers Plowman, and Priscilla Martin's Piers Plowman*: The Tower and the Field.* See also A. C. Spearing's essay "Langland's Poetry: Some Notes in Critical Analysis."

This careful attention to Langland's artistry, which did not ignore the poet's social and religious contexts, was continued by others, such as Mary Clemente Davlin, Jill Mann, William Rogers, James Simpson, and Emily Steiner. See, for example, Davlin's *A Game of Heuene: Word Play and the Meaning of* Piers Plowman *B*, Mann's *Langland and Allegory*, Rogers's *Interpretation in* Piers Plowman, Simpson's "From Reason to Affective Knowledge: Modes of Thought and Poetic Form in *Piers Plowman*," Simpson's Piers Plowman*: An Introduction to the B-Text*, and Steiner's *Reading* Piers Plowman.

Versification

Ian Cornelius

I teach *Piers Plowman* in two upper-level undergraduate courses, a survey of Middle English literature and a seminar on Middle English alliterative poetry. In the seminar, versification is an organizing principle of the syllabus and is addressed early in the semester, before we reach *Piers Plowman*. In the survey, the question of versification need not arise at all, but I place it on our agenda to shake up the routines of thematic reading and because some students will want to know why we call *Piers Plowman* a poem. My preferred teaching text is A. V. C. Schmidt's Everyman edition (Vision), from which this essay quotes, and I situate this lesson in the prologue, an especially rich announcement of the poet's project and one that repays repeated examination on the second or third day of engagement with the poem. (Other aspects of Langland's art take priority on day one, for which see Hanna's contribution to this volume).

I can count on students having read a portion of Chaucer's *Canterbury Tales* before they arrive in my classroom. I therefore structure this lesson as a sequence of comparisons between Langland's prologue and the opening lines of Chaucer's prologue. I supply Chaucer's lines on a handout; they allow us to reprise and deepen comparisons previously ventured between the pilgrim portraits and Langland's fair field of folk.

I begin asking questions, aiming to flush out the observations that Chaucer rhymes, Langland doesn't, and a lot of words in Langland's poem begin with the same letter. I will pause to ensure that students perceive the alliteration: it is part of Langland's verse form, just as end rhyme is part of Chaucer's. Yet I am now headed deeper into the form, so I put alliteration on hold. We return to Chaucer, this time reading aloud and listening to the rhythm, until we perceive that Chaucer's verse is structured by a regular alternation of beat and offbeat, with five beats to a line. Calling it iambic pentameter will do. Turning back to *Piers Plowman*, I allow students to flounder a bit, attempting to fit Langland's verse to a similar pattern of alternating stress.

The positive result of this floundering should be a recognition that Langland's lines are generally longer than Chaucer's. Here our inquiry reaches a deadlock, for Langland's line is organized by a surprisingly different system. The meter of alliterative verse distinguishes between two basic types of words: those that establish the surface structure of an utterance (called function words) and those that carry its core meaning (called content words). The words that carry the core meaning usually also supply the metrical stresses. The easiest way to deliver this principle is in a table that I write on a whiteboard or project from my computer:

Usually supply a stress	*Usually don't supply a stress*
nouns, adjectives, derived adverbs, and most verbs	articles, pronouns, prepositions, conjunctions, tiny adverbs, auxiliary verbs, and forms of *to be* and *to have*

Before we operationalize this new knowledge in Langland's poetry, I guide the class back to the behavior of these word classes in Chaucer's verse:

Bi**fil** that **in** that **se**son **on** a **day**
In **South**werk **at** the **Ta**bard **as** I **lay**
Redy to **wen**den **on** my **pil**gry**ma**ge
To **Caun**ter**bụry** with **ful** de**vout** co**ra**ge
At **nyght** was **comẹ** in**to** that **hos**tel**ry**e
Wel **ny**nẹ and **twen**ty **in** a **com**paig**ny**e
Of **son**dry **folk** by **a**ven**tur**e y**fal**le
In **fe**lawẹ**ship**e and **pil**grimẹs **wer**ẹ they **al**le
That **to**ward **Caun**ter**bu**ry **wol**den **ry**de
(L. D. Benson, *Riverside Chaucer*, General Prologue, lines 19–28)

Here I place in bold the syllables that support a metrical beat; dots under vowels indicate that the letter is elided, silent, or slurred, as in *Canterb'ry* at line 22. I want students to see that ordinary word stresses of content words supply the anchoring beats in Chaucer's verse, but only the anchoring beats. To fill out the five-beat template, Chaucer's verse does two things: it promotes function words (e.g., *in*, *on*, *at*, *as*, *ful*) and it assigns a second stress to polysyllabic content words (e.g., *pilgrymage*, *felaweshipe*). When we read aloud the first line above, we will probably not stress the prepositions *in* and *on* as heavily as either *day* or the first syllable of *seson*. Nevertheless, the template, or abstract metrical pattern, directs us to stress *in* and *on* slightly more than the syllables on either side of them. The beats supplied by these words are essential to Chaucer's verse form.

We now return to *Piers Plowman*. The metrical rhythm of this poem is similarly anchored to the ordinary word stresses of content words. Yet, unlike Chaucer, Langland allows all other syllables to fall into strings of unstressed material. Function words do not usually supply a stress, and even long words supply only one stress each:

In a **so**mer **se**son whan **sof**te was the **son**ne
I **shoop** me into **shrou**des as I a **sheep** **we**re
In **ha**bite as an **he**remite un**ho**ly of **wer**kes
Wente **wi**de in this **world** **won**dres to **he**re
Ac on a **May** **mor**wenynge on **Mal**verne **Hil**les
Me bi**fel** a **fer**ly of **Fai**rye me **thogh**te (prol. 1–6)

We consider this array of stressed and unstressed syllables. Alliteration—which students noticed at the beginning of our inquiry—now returns with a deeper relevance. It is used (not invariably) as a cue to the placement of metrical stress. The last stress of the line doesn't usually have alliteration, but sometimes it does (e.g., line 1). There are usually four stresses per line, but perhaps there is a fifth in line 4. (Here we might take a quick look at prologue lines 15–16, which also have an extra stressable word.) Finally, I want students to notice that the word *were* is a form of *to be* and so, according to the table above, should not be stressed. Does line 2 therefore have only three stresses?

This puzzle allows me to reveal a second surprise about Langland's form. The first surprise was the binary division between content words and function words. The second is that Langland's verse, like Chaucer's, has a metrical template—sort of. I write the following on the board:

Chaucer: (x)SxSxSxSxS(x)

Here "S" indicates a stress, or beat, and "x" a single unstressed syllable, or off-beat; "(x)" represents an optional unstressed syllable. Chaucer's template consists of regular alternation of strong and weak positions throughout the line, with some standard variations, such as the initial inversion at the head of line 21: "**Re**dy to **wen**den" (SxxSx). By contrast, Langland's template obtains only at the end of the line and is a good deal more complex. There are two basic patterns, which I call "Langland 1" and "Langland 2":

Langland 1: . . . (x)Sxx(x . . . x)Sx
Langland 2: . . . xx(x . . . x)S(x)Sx

Here "xx(x . . . x)" indicates a string of two or more unstressed syllables. Though relatively complex, this template is invariant at its conclusion: lines end with a stress followed by a single unstressed syllable. We have seen how Chaucer's template frequently elevates function words to supply metrical beats. The same thing happens, though more rarely, in Langland's verse. In line 2 of the prologue, *were*, which is here disyllabic, carries a stress on its first syllable. Metrical promotion occurs most frequently at the end of the line, but it may occur elsewhere: in line 161 of the prologue the preposition *about* supplies the line's penultimate stress: "a**bou**ten hire **nek**kes" (xSxxSx).

Working from the end of a line to its beginning, we come next to the string of unstressed syllables that flank the penultimate stress, and we attempt to classify each of the lines in our sample into one of the two patterns. Does the string of unstressed syllables occur before or after the penultimate stress? Line 2 fits the second pattern: here the unstressed syllables precede the penultimate stress. I next direct students to line 4. It fits the first pattern. But what of the other lines in this passage? They seem to have strings of two or more unstressed syllables on either side of the penultimate stress. This is not what the template patterns led us to expect.

The problem allows me to reveal a third and final surprise. The patterns I have written on the board aren't just line-ending patterns, as I have called them. They map onto a discrete unit of verse. In line 1, the second syllable of *seson* does not count as part of the template because *seson* does not belong to the same verse unit as the *whan* that follows. Thus, the line's penultimate stress (on *softe*) is preceded by only one unstressed syllable in the verse unit.

Here we need to take one or two steps back. Langland's poetry is built up from smaller chunks of language. The line is not the smallest metrically relevant unit of composition, for it is itself composed of two short verses, or half lines.[1] I divide the lines in our sample passage, placing the half lines in separate columns labeled "a-verse" and "b-verse":

a-verse	*b-verse*	*b-verse scansion*
In a **so**mer **se**son	whan **sof**te was the **son**ne	xSxxxSx
I **shoop** me into **shrou**des	as I a **sheep were**	xxxSSx
In **ha**bite as an **he**remite	un**ho**ly of **wer**kes	xSxxSx
Wente **wi**de in this **world**	**won**dres to **he**re	SxxSx
Ac on a **May mor**wenynge	on **Mal**verne **Hil**les	xSxxSx
Me bi**fel** a **fer**ly	of **Fai**rye me **thogh**te	xSxxSx

Line 1 of the prologue corresponds to the first of the two template patterns, with the unstressed syllables between the two stresses. With the exception of line 2, all other lines in the passage also correspond to this pattern. Here we might flag one or two other instances of the rarer pattern with unstressed syllables in the initial position: for example, the b-verse of line 19 of the prologue, "as the **world as**keth" (xxSSx), and the b-verse of line 54, "and hire **wen**ches **af**ter" (xxSxSx) (the pronoun *hire* is monosyllabic).

As illustration that Langland's verse is composed in half lines, I observe that a-verses convey the core sense and narrative action of our sample passage. They even make sense on their own: "In a summer season, I dressed myself in garments, in the habit of a hermit, [and I] went far in the world. But on a May morning I saw something special." The b-verses consist of modifying material, subordinate clauses and adjectival and prepositional phrases that enrich the sense of this passage but become meaningful only in connection with the a-verses. This grammatical observation lends itself to literary-critical interpretation: Langland is expressly traditional in the first lines of his poem, making a performance of traditional alliterative style at the same time that he alludes to the traditional genres of romance and dream vision. Elsewhere in *Piers Plowman*, the stunt of reading only the a-verses will often fail, but the half-line unit remains foundational throughout Langland's poem.

We can now wrap up, having absorbed three principles of Langland's versification: lines are composed of half-line units, metrical stresses are typically supplied by content words (only one stress per word), and the pattern of syllables is governed by a template in the b-verse. These three principles are interdependent; together they establish Langland's form, and each functions only in combination with the other two.

Of course, this presentation is far from complete. What about a-verses? Or any number of apparent and real exceptions? Readers of *Piers Plowman* will not infrequently encounter b-verses that diverge from the accentual templates I have presented. A significant minority of b-verses in the poem have strings of unstressed syllables in both the initial and medial positions; an example from the prologue is the b-verse of line 186, "though we **cro**pen under **ben**ches" (xxSxxxSx). More rarely b-verses will seem to have three stresses. These patterns usually reside in the a-verse; their appearance in the more tightly constructed second half of the line shows that Langland did not distinguish between a-verse and b-verse quite so sharply as some of his contemporaries did. Even more remarkably, Langland occasionally switched out of alliterative meter at mid-line, pairing an a-verse with an unmetered segment consisting of a Latin quotation. An example is passus 5, line 507: "Thanne hente Hope an horn / of *Deus tu conversus vivificabis nos*" (the slash marks the end of the a-verse). These features lie beyond the scope of my introductory lesson; however, the introductory lesson enables us to perceive complexities as such, set off against a background of formal regularity.[2] The formal features of alliterative verse provide readers with a bracing experience in thinking the relation between norms and the practices they animate.

At a more practical level, knowledge of Langland's meter can guide students to probable readings of Langland's verse, in the absence of full command of his language. Identifying the half-line boundary often helps students construe the meaning of a difficult line, while the b-verse templates can guide pronunciation. Chaucer's simpler metrical template has served generations of readers in this way: one can trust oneself to the template, sounding a final *-e* where it separates beats and ignoring written *-e*'s that, if sounded, would result in a second unstressed syllable between beats. Alliterative verse is more variable than Chaucer's form, so readers of Langland need to know more grammar than readers of Chaucer. This is a challenge of teaching Langland's form, but it is also a benefit: it stages an encounter with difficulties at the intersection of language history, literary history, and literary form. Metrical analysis of even the briefest passage of Langland's verse will provoke intriguing questions, all quite different from the standard offerings of literary thematics.

I conclude with some reflections on literary history. Students will want to know where Langland's verse form came from, why it is so unlike Chaucer's, and why it presents so many difficulties for readers. I answer these questions by zooming out to the *longue durée* of English literature. The tradition of versification in which Langland worked had a long prior history but would continue to generate new English poetry for only a little over a century after our poet's death. Although the form's deep past was probably as hidden from Langland as its future, both are important for understanding his art. In the Anglo-Saxon period, alliterative verse was simply the way of making poetry in English. After the Norman conquest, poets developed a second basic way of versifying in English, modeled on French and on medieval Latin but adjusted in various ways to the specificities of English prosody. The English language therefore had two systems of versification in the later Middle Ages. Among the representatives of the alliterative tradition are Lawman's *Brut*, *Sir Gawain and the Green Knight*, and *Piers Plowman*. Chaucer belongs to the other tradition. During the second half of the fourteenth century, when Langland was writing, both verse types were well represented in English literary culture. But the alliterative tradition became defunct at the end of the Middle Ages, while the English iambic verse would reign triumphant from the sixteenth century forward, claiming Chaucer as its founding father. As a result medieval alliterative verse has necessarily appeared to modern readers as something strange and different. It is a deeply historical form that, several centuries ago, slipped into the past, where it remains today. My approach to Langland's versification aims to make its peculiar qualities available and meaningful to students and thereby to supply a fresh perspective on *Piers Plowman* itself and on the broader history of English literature.

NOTES

[1]When the location of the boundary between half lines is in doubt, the best course of action is to consult with the poem's scribes, who consistently recorded this most basic feature of Langland's versification. Record of scribal punctuation is conveniently accessible in the editions published online by the *Piers Plowman Electronic Archive*. The metrical punctuation editorially reconstructed in John A. Burrow and Thorlac Turville-Petre's edition of the *The B-Version Archetype* is especially accurate.

[2]I provide a fuller account in *Reconstructing Alliterative Verse*.

APPENDIX

This appendix extends the introductory lesson by engaging a more complex passage. Lines 123–131a of the prologue reveal features of Langland's versification not evident in the opening lines of the poem:

Thanne **lo**ked up a **lu**na**tik**   a **lee**ne thyng with**al**le
And **kne**lynge to the **Kyng**   **cler**gially he **sei**de
Crist kepe thee sire **Kyng**   and thi **kyngry**che
And **le**ne thee **le**de thi **lond**   so **leau**te thee **lov**ye
And for thi **right**ful **ru**lyng   be **re**warded in **he**vene
And sithen in the **eyr** on **heigh**   an **aun**gel of **he**vene
Lowed to **spe**ke in **La**tyn   for **le**wed men ne **kou**de
Jangle ne **jug**ge   that **jus**tifie hem **shol**de
But **suf**fren and **ser**ven

The long words *clergially* (124) and *justifie* (130) supply only one stress each, as usual, but *kyngryche* (125) is an exception: here both b-verse stresses are loaded onto a single word. Like Chaucer's meter, Langland's is able to recruit a second metrical stress from polysyllabic and compound words. The stresses carried by *koude* (129b) and *sholde* (130b), at the ends of their lines, instance the more usual type of metrical promotion, already observed in line 2 of the prologue (where the word promoted was *were*). This passage also allows us to observe the reverse process, metrical demotion: the noun *thyng* is presumably demoted into a string of unstressed syllables in 123b, and the same happens to *men* in 129b. Promotion and demotion are the outcome of conflicts between two core principles of the meter—accentual template and word class—and result in lines more complex than the ones at the opening of the prologue.

The syntax of this passage is also more complex. Whereas the opening lines had packed core syntactic elements into a-verses, the sentence beginning in line 128 locates its grammatical subject—"an aungel"—in a b-verse. In a second contrast with Langland's usual practice, this passage has strong syntactic continuity between lines 129b and 130a: "for lewed men ne koude / Jangle ne jugge." Lines are usually end-stopped, but not invariably so. The next b-verse, "that justifie hem sholde," is an intrusion that supplies an object-clause for the verbs *jangle* and *jugge*. The main line of thought resumes (and concludes) in line 131a. One may translate lines 128a–131a as, "And then, up high in the air, an angel of heaven descended to speak in Latin so that uneducated people would not be able to dispute or challenge those who must govern them, but instead submit and serve." This intricate sentence ends mid-line. Line 131b is a syntactically independent unit introducing the angel's subsequent Latin speech: "Forthi seide the aungel / Sum Rex, sum princeps, neutrum fortasse deinceps. . . ."

Repeating Our Agonies: An Approach to Teaching Langland

William E. Rogers

A few years ago I wrote a book about *Piers Plowman*. Deeply informed by my adventures in teaching the poem, the book contained scarcely anything that was completely new or original. Its value, if any, consists in its thoroughgoing insistence on an approach: in brief, I argued that *Piers Plowman* is about (among other things) Langland's quest for a viable hermeneutic and that "Langland connects signs as if he were interpreting a text. He reads his world as if it were a book" (W. E. Rogers 13). In this essay I consider some of the pedagogical implications of that approach.

How one teaches Langland depends on where one teaches. I taught *Piers Plowman* to undergraduates at a small liberal arts college, an enterprise that I judge to be quite different, for example, from teaching *Piers Plowman* to graduate students at a research university. But most of what I say applies generally to teaching *Piers Plowman* to undergraduates, whether the poem is taught in part or as a whole, in Middle English or in translation, as part of a survey or as the subject of a seminar.

The vocabulary of connecting signs derives from the philosophy of Charles Sanders Peirce. Peirce envisioned a field of inquiry he called "methodeutic": "Its task is to ascertain the laws by which in every scientific intelligence one sign gives birth to another, and especially one thought brings forth another" (Peirce 2: 229). I would propose "hermeneutic intelligence" in place of "scientific intelligence," because I think Peirce's term *scientific* has baggage for us that it did not have for him. With this substitution, thinking of liberal study as Peircean methodeutic helps to clarify some of the issues that always arise in discussions of the nature, the value, and the ends of liberal education. When I say "Homer," do you think "*Iliad*," or "Simpson," or "Babe Ruth"? What laws of nature or culture determine the processes by means of which such connections get made? In short, to experience liberal education does not mean to receive instruction in operating some particular interpretive system, such as chemistry or literary criticism. It means to think about how people think. Human thought is semiosis. Semiosis is connecting signs.

How one teaches Langland also depends on how one reads Langland. But as George Kane once wrote, in his experience "no two people genuinely familiar with the text of the poem will agree about its larger meaning" (Kane, "Reading" 17–18). Where there is no dogma to hand on, interpretation itself moves to the foreground.

I want to make a virtue of necessity. That is, I want to push the issue of interpretation as far as it will go and to regard the act of interpretation, the practice of textual hermeneutics, as the primary focus for the study of *Piers Plowman*. That means to read the poem as an echo of the interpretive agonies that *Piers Plowman* induces in its readers. The points at which Langland most deeply engages students who are committed to liberal study—to thinking about how people think—are the points at which his poem talks about the same sorts of things that happen to those students when they try to read the poem. Namely, readers are, and Langland is, struggling to interpret a complex text that itself embodies the struggle between contradictory authoritative texts. For the students, that complex text is *Piers Plowman*. For Langland, that text is his world. As Steven Justice says of the *vita*, "the fluidity and digressiveness of the poem signal not exactly a 'decentering,' but a proliferation of competing discourses, each of which tries to promote itself as the authoritative center" (*Writing* 113). I would extend the principle to the *visio* as well.

I believe that there is after all a narrative of the dreamer in *Piers Plowman*—a progression of a certain sort, as opposed to a random walk through various authoritative texts. But, in a way, whether there is a narrative is beside the point here. I am arguing for a pedagogical approach that focuses on the process of interpretation, wherever that process might lead. If a class on *Piers Plowman* begins to look like random motion, that is not always a bad thing, because it signals that the difficulty of interpretation and the explicit construction of methodeutic have come to the fore.

Now I want to consider some pedagogical tactics associated with the general approach I have outlined. I characterize Langland as a medieval intellectual who lives his life in and through texts. To specify further, I characterize Langland's poetic technique as dramatic and recursive. The possibilities for reading Langland as a highly dramatic poet have been somewhat neglected. For obvious reasons, we tend to approach his work as didactic or as a satire emanating from a single center of consciousness. But, as Anne Middleton says, "[T]he episode in *Piers* presents a combat . . . at some point the interaction becomes charged with opposition. The injection of a countervening force, rather than the logical or rhetorical limits of the discursive topic, shapes the further course of the episode and determines its often abrupt end" ("Narration" 96–97). Dramatic reading needs to be close reading in Langland, because dramatic interactions are usually implicit and much is left to inference. But to read dramatically means to see *Piers Plowman* as the site of contending texts that themselves function as dramatis personae and thus to foreground the hermeneutic processes that are (in my reading, anyway) the main concern of the poem.

But Langland's recursiveness has always been evident. He returns again and again to the same terms, but the terms seem to mean different things in different contexts. The great example is the evolving meaning of Dowel. Reading Langland as a recursive poet—taking into account all the contexts in which his crucial terms appear—complements the relentless concentration on local effects that characterizes dramatic reading.

Here is an example of what I mean by reading Langland dramatically. After the first foundation in the prologue, the king receives four pieces of advice. The lean "lunatik" ("lunatic"; prol. 123) says, "Crist kepe thee, sire Kyng, and thi kyngryche, / And lene thee lede thi lond so leaute thee lovye, / And for thi rightful rulyng be rewarded in hevene!" ("Christ keep you, sir King, and the kingdom you rule / And grant you to lead your land so that Lewte loves you, / And for your righteous ruling be rewarded in Heaven"; prol. 125–27).[1] The "aungel of hevene" ("angel of Heaven"; 128) then offers, "*iustus es, esto pius! / Nudum ius a te vestiri vult pietate*" ("as you are just, be godly! / Naked law requires to be clothed by you with a sense of your duty to God"; 134–35. The "goliardeis" ("goliard"; 139) responds to the angel, "*Dum 'rex' a 'regere' dicatur nomen habere, / Nomen habet sine re nisi studet iura tenere*" ("Inasmuch as a king has his name from (the fact of) being a ruler . . . , he possesses the name (alone) without the reality unless he is zealous in maintaining the laws"; 141–42). Finally, "al the commune" ("all the commons"; 143) chime in with "*Precepta Regis sunt nobis vincula legis!*" ("The king's bidding has for us the binding force of law"; 145).

We have, then, four contending texts with at least the force of proverbial wisdom. But the texts are potentially contradictory: the goliard points out that if the king dispenses too much mercy by following the angel's advice, the king will not deserve his name of *rex*. The commons seem to be saying, contrary to the goliard, that the law is the will of the king. And the lunatic's advice, the only text that does not clothe itself in the authority of Latinity, might be accused of being true enough but vacuous: please Christ. Thus, what begins as an exposition of kingship turns into an argument about the correct description of kingship—that is, a hermeneutic struggle and a site of contending texts. In Peircean language: the dreamer is presumably attempting to connect the authoritative texts, as signs of their respective theories of kingship, with the behaviors that are signs of the actual social organization.

But readers face a corresponding hermeneutic struggle. We think our job as readers is to determine "what Langland thinks"—which of these theories of kingship, if any, the poem favors. In Peircean language: we are attempting to connect the authoritative texts, as signs of their respective theories of kingship, with the rhetorical behaviors that are presumably signs of the poet's own preference. Is the lunatic's speech to be favored, because the lunatic seems to be a surrogate for Langland himself (who later becomes at least mentally disturbed, as in 15.3)? Is the angel's text to be favored, just because the angel is an angel? Does the goliard, proud as he is, have a good point about the deep and often occult influences of language on human behavior? Several good books on that theme in Langland attest to its importance (Carruthers, *Search*; Davlin, *Game*; Raabe; Rudd). Or do we want to cast our lot with the cynical practicality with which the commons acknowledge the facts of power and by which the immediately ensuing fable of the rats and mice is most easily explained?

In attempting to answer these questions, we begin to pay attention to the drama of the scene—not just to what is said, but to who says it and how it functions. Thus, the goliard's espousing of his theory of grammar as destiny is perhaps explained by his self-image as the one who masters language, the "gloton of wordes" (139). And the commons perhaps prefer the arbitrary dictates of the king to the tender mercies of his councillors, who will, under the goliard's theory of government, actually be the ones to interpret the law to the king. And because the chaotic council of the rats and mice comes on the heels of the commons' pronouncement, maybe Langland is trying to indicate that nothing is concluded or resolved by this whole debate.

At this point dramatic reading becomes methodeutic. We are paying explicit attention to how we use Langland's poetic strategies of characterization and dramatic juxtaposition to authorize our connections of the authoritative texts with what we reconstruct as Langland's political theory. What Langland does, paradigmatically, is to postpone the final solution—to force us again and again back into the hermeneutic circle, by forcing his dreamer again and again back into quandary. We should ask, for example, not what unalterable lessons Holy Church teaches us about truth, but rather why Holy Church understands truth as she does; we should ask not what Conscience teaches us about money, but rather why Conscience regards money as he does.

In this pedagogy the teacher's role is not to answer questions about Langland's politics but to open them and then to make explicit the various interpretive strategies that readers use in attempting to address the questions. The role of the teacher is to be bothersome—not to let reading rest in the easy answer constituted by explicating the authoritative texts Langland quotes, as if the point of *Piers Plowman* were to assemble some sort of unimaginable commonplace book in which everything recorded is true and counts equally with everything else. Nor should reading rest in the somewhat more difficult answer that Langland offers several alternatives from which he chooses one. In my reading of the poem, he does not choose. Instead, he offers the impossible choices that real people really face.

The pedagogy that considers Langland as a dramatic poet involves much circling and many false starts, and it involves little accumulation of systematic knowledge about medieval ideas of this or that. If there were any systematic knowledge to be gained from such a pedagogy, it would be systematic knowledge of interpretive strategies—Langland's medieval strategies and our postmodern ones.

Here is an example of what I mean by reading Langland as a recursive poet. In passus 19, the passage about the "lewed vicory" ("ignorant vicar"; 413) sometimes puzzles readers. The moral valency of the vicar's speech is in question.

The speech seems doctrinally unexceptionable in its critique of corrupt cardinals and popes, but the vicar is, after all, "lewed," and his speech fills a niche in the dramatic structure of the poem that ought to contain a specious argument. It occurs in the section of the poem where Langland seems to be showing how the four cardinal virtues themselves can be corrupted. Just before the vicar speaks, the brewer undermines the cardinal virtue of justice (400–06), and just after the vicar speaks, the lord and the king undermine the virtues of fortitude and justice (463–80). The speech of Need (passus 20) immediately follows the vicar's departure, and some readers think that Need undermines the virtue of temperance (20.6–22). The vicar does explain how the "peple" ("people") turn prudence, the fourth cardinal virtue, into "gyle" ("guile"; 19.459), but the dramatic structure of the poem might lead one to expect that the vicar himself—like the brewer, the lord, the king, and Need—would also illustrate the corruption of one of the cardinal virtues. The problem, then, is to determine what, if anything, in the vicar's speech makes the vicar an exemplar of corrupted prudence.

A student in one of my survey courses wrote an excellent paper on this passage. The student pointed out that there was perhaps a clue in the poem about the vicar's moral problem in the penultimate line of passus 19: "The viker hadde fer hoom, and faire took his leeve" ("This vicar's home was far away, and he fairly took his leave"; 484). If the student is right, then this line is typical of Langland's drama: the gesture of departure flashes quickly by and yet turns out to be critically important. This student had been exploring the concept of the Church as it develops through *Piers Plowman*. The Church in passus 19 receives the particular name of Unite (331). Reading line 484 with Langland's recursive poetics in mind led the student to hypothesize that the vicar's departure was a sign of his moral failing: namely, of his unwillingness to participate fully in the Christian community being constructed by Conscience in this final foundation of the poem. The vicar leaves before the indefinitely postponed Eucharist to which Conscience has invited all repentant Christians (19.387–94).

It now becomes reasonable to ask of that student, "Why, then, does the vicar's speech concentrate on corrupt cardinals and popes? Why this further satire on corrupt clergy, of which Langland has by now already provided God's plenty and more?" These are questions about the dramatic function of the vicar's speech. One might suggest at this point that what the vicar is doing—as opposed to what he is saying—is sitting in judgment on his ecclesiastical superiors to project the evils attendant upon the particular organization of the Church that he describes. The vicar calls into question the efficacy of the machinery of the Church, and ultimately of the cardinal virtues themselves, for the salvation of the commons (455–62). Perhaps the vicar illustrates here the corruption of prudence that Need describes: "*Spiritus Prudencie* in many a point shal faille / Of that he weneth wolde falle if his wit ne weere" (20.31–32). I translate these lines as follows: "The spirit of prudence will err in many cases in thinking that something or other would happen if his wit did not intervene to prevent it." That is, the vicar implies that Christians are doomed because the clergy are sinful—that evil must ensue if not everyone thinks as he himself thinks. His malpractice of prudence, in other words, is precisely the wedge that he drives between himself and those who, sinful as they are, ought to be his fellows in Unite.

Whether this counts as a solution to the crux of the vicar is a difficult question that I will not undertake to answer. My point is to illustrate how recursive reading of *Piers Plowman* might complement dramatic reading in order to foreground the hermeneutic enterprise. To see the episode of the vicar as constituting a crux means to recognize explicitly the power of dramatic structures to impel readers to connect signs in particular ways. To attempt to solve the crux by recursive reading is to recognize explicitly the hermeneutic strategy of appealing to broader contexts.

I believe, finally, that Langland's poetry is original in the most profound sense. I mean that we cannot paraphrase Langland's meaning by substituting what we take to be the meaning of the texts Langland seems to treat as authoritative. Langland, while we might interpret him as Augustinian, or as semi-Pelagian, or whatever, is not a mouthpiece for Augustinianism, or semi-Pelagianism, or any ism. He does not preach doctrine but instead struggles with it. Just as he is no author's mouthpiece, there are strong arguments that, mutatis mutandis, none of Langland's characters is simply Langland's mouthpiece.

I mention a corollary to that principle: there is, in the economy of the liberal arts college as I conceive it, no meaningful pedagogy of Langland that depends primarily on lecture. This sounds paradoxical. There is so much about Langland, of all authors, that is strange and medieval, so much information that needs to be conveyed, and so much intellectual history that needs to be explained before students can even begin to come to grips with *Piers Plowman*. But lecture is ultimately reading, and with Langland in particular that is always only my reading. The task is rather to expose and explore different readings, to bring the hermeneutic process into the spotlight, and to map our own hermeneutic struggles onto the struggles proposed in Langland's text. When students read Langland, the teacher's imperatives are to decentralize hermeneutic authority and to authorize students to be honest about their own processes of reading. There are various ways to do this, and the effectiveness of these ways depends more on institutional culture and individual personality than on the nature of *Piers Plowman*. And so determining how to make one's students honest is an exercise I leave for the teacher.

NOTE

[1]Unless otherwise indicated, quotations of the poem are from A. V. C. Schmidt's edition (Vision), and translations of the poem are from Donaldson (*Alliterative Verse Translation*).

Postsecular *Piers*

Thomas A. Prendergast

> Credo ut intelligam.
>
> —Anselm of Canterbury

> "Believe in order to understand, understand in order to believe"—such is its maxim; and its maxim is the hermeneutic circle itself of believing and understanding.
>
> —Paul Ricoeur

Whenever I deal with the Bible in my undergraduate courses, I preface my discussion with a disclaimer that might be familiar to medievalists. I say that we'll be approaching the Bible as a literary text as opposed to a faith document. I tell the students that they shouldn't take anything I or others say as a challenge to their religion or beliefs. I tell them that our analysis of biblical narratives in the course should not interfere with their understanding of the Bible as an expression of divinity or religion. I've often felt somewhat disingenuous about such claims, because my approach to the Bible presupposes that the text is figurative, while some faith-based readings rely on the idea that there is only one way to read scripture—literally. Recently, my private misgivings became a public problem when a student stopped my exegetical excursus into the contradictory narratives of Genesis 1.25–27 and 2.21–23 with a question: What did I think Moses was doing in writing two dissimilar accounts of Eve's creation? I knew, of course, of the ancient tradition that Moses had written the Pentateuch, but I didn't expect to encounter it in my twenty-first-century classroom. I fumbled around a bit, said something about how religion and textual analysis were not incompatible and, I'm sure, left everyone thoroughly confused.

This incident and others led me to reconsider what my ethical commitments were in the classroom. Specifically, do we have ethical commitments to those who approach religious texts with faith? Do we insist that, as with other kinds of texts, we must keep open the possibility of multiple interpretations? Some might argue that this is precisely the job of liberal education—to demonstrate that textuality is by its very nature polysemous. But if the basis of liberal education is also the cultivation of freedom, can we insist that a certain kind of text has more than one meaning? In writing about the duties of the postsecular state, Jürgen Habermas makes the case that the liberal state "may not demand anything of its religious citizens which cannot be reconciled with a life that is led authentically 'from faith'" (21). His argument is that because liberalism is fundamentally implicated in guaranteeing freedom, it must guarantee everyone's freedom of conscience and of religious belief. Of course, the classroom is not the state and the students are not its citizens, but I think that most professors would maintain that the classroom should be a locus of free inquiry. How far should that freedom extend? Should students be free not to accept that certain kinds of texts are ambiguous?

There's no easy answer to this question. Medievalists have a debt to past readers who read biblical texts in many different ways, and teachers have an ethical commitment to communicate this to our students. How do we balance these competing imperatives? Perhaps positing one unambiguous answer to a question about ambiguity is the wrong approach. It seems to me that a literary approach that deals with faith, reading, and scripture might be more productive. And we are offered just this kind of approach in the B version of *Piers Plowman*. James Simpson has drawn attention to the metatextual nature of the poem, saying that "we should look to models of reading from within the poem itself" if we are to make connections between the "correction of the will" (or Will) and reading ("Desire" 219). I would extend this insight to claim that at least one episode of reading in the poem reflects something more—what happens when we read with others.

Famously, at the beginning of passus 7 of the B version, Truth sends to Piers "a pardoun *a pena & a culpa*" ("a pardon from punishment and from guilt"; 7.3).[1] This pardon, so the poet tells us, is for Piers, his heirs, and any who would help him "to eyre or to sowe" ("plow or sow"; 7.6). Later in the passus, however, a priest asks to read the pardon:

> And Piers at his preiere þe pardon vnfoldeþ,
> And I bihynde hem boþe biheld al þe bulle.
> In two lynes it lay and noȝt a [lettre] moore,
> And was writen riȝt þus in witnesse of truþe:
> *Et qui bona egerunt ibunt in vitam eternam;*

> *Qui vero mala in ignem eternum.*
> "Peter!" quod þe preest þoo, "I kan no pardon fynde
> But do wel and haue wel, and god shal haue þi soule,
> And do yuel and haue yuel, [and] hope þow noon ooþer
> [That] after þi deeþ day þe deuel shal haue þi soule."
> And Piers for pure tene pulled it [asonder]
> And seide, "*Si ambulauero in medio vmbre mortis*
> *Non timebo mala quoniam tu mecum es.*" (7.109–21)
>
> And Piers unfolds the pardon at the priest's prayer,
> And I behind them both beheld all the bull.
> In two lines it lay, and not a letter more,
> And was worded this way in witness of truth:
> *They that have done good shall go into life everlasting;*
> *And they that have done evil into everlasting fire.*
> "Peter!" said the Priest then, "I can find no pardon here—
> Only 'Do well, and have well,' and God will have your soul,
> And 'Do evil, and have evil,' and hope nothing else
> But that after your death-day the Devil will have your soul."
> And Piers for pure wrath pulled it in two
> And said, *"Though I walk in the midst of the shadow of death*
> *I will fear no evil; for thou art with me."*

This passage, of course, has occasioned a multitude of scholarly interventions and remains central to any sophisticated understanding of the theological meaning of the poem. But for the moment I would like to consider the episode simply as a reflection of the scene of reading and interpretation. It is set up as a kind of tableau—Piers and the priest in front and Will behind. The priest treats Piers as a student, saying that he will "construe ech clause and kenne it þee on englissh" ("explain each paragraph to you and put it in English"; 7.108). When Piers hears the priest's interpretation and learns what the pardon actually says, he is, as students sometimes are, apparently frustrated, and he takes it out on the text. When the priest pokes fun at his exegetical skills, Will transfers his frustration to the interpreter of the text, labeling him a "*derisor*," or scoffer (7.143).

If we take this as an enactment of what can happen in the classroom, it might be seen as a teacher's nightmare rather than a dream. The student physically destroys the text, and the dispute between teacher and student becomes so heated that it wakes Will from his dream. Yet the questions posed by the scene could enable a class to come to terms with the difficult power dynamic that characterizes both Piers's relationship to the priest and, by analogy, the relationship of a student (particularly one who is used to reading literally) to a professor. As this reading of the Pardon scene folds back into how we read the text, it enables students to come to terms with how interpretation of the work before them might be carried out and highlights the extent to which the analogy between the readers in the poem and the readers of the poem is part of the essential message that the poem is trying to communicate.

Bringing students to the understanding of the metatextual nature of *Piers* could be carried out a number of different ways, but I would advocate a series of questions generated from the extensive secondary literature focused on the interpretive subject positions of the text's actors. For instance, one of the first questions that one might ask is, Can we dismiss the Priest as a mere "*derisor*" (as Piers does) or "*detractor*" (J. B. Allen, "Langland's Reading"; Lawler, "Pardon" 137)? And, if so, is his derisiveness a product of his interpretation of the pardon as no pardon at all, or is it his mocking reference to Piers's interpretive skills? Or are the two linked? And what of his interpretation of the pardon itself? His explication of the text is not so far removed from what the Latin actually says. Can we characterize his behavior as a misuse of his superior interpretive skill?

What are we to make of Piers's reaction to the interpretation of the pardon? The text tells us that he reacts out of "pure tene." One might well admire his affective commitment to the meaning of the text, but the actual destruction of the pardon is incommensurate with what the priest says. What of Piers's reaction to the priest's mockery—impugning the priest's knowledge of the Bible? And what of Will's involvement in the scene? Is he, in some sense, meant to stand in for the reading audience? In other words, are we interpellated into the position of Will to witness this scene of reading and interpretation? Or do we occupy a separate, more objective interpretive position? At least initially, Will's role as witness appears to be simply as a *testis*—someone "in the position of a third party" who can provide testimony about a dispute between two parties (Agamben 17). After waking, however, Will casts doubt on the veracity of dreams (as he had earlier in the poem), wondering "if it so be myȝte" ("if it might be so"; 7.150). Are we meant to feel Will's doubt? He also offers as an interpretation of the episode that the "preest inpugned it [the pardon] wiþ two p*ro*pre wordes"; "priest impugned it [the pardon] with two proper words"; 7.153). Once he enters the waking world, he himself becomes an interpreter of what he has seen and suggests that two words—"*Dixit insipiens*" ("the fool hath said")—were what lessened the authority of the pardon (7.141). But, of course, these two words have little to do with the pardon and everything to do with Piers. Is it Piers's possession of the pardon that leads to its dismissal as a pardon, as some have suggested (Middleton, "Narration" 108)? Like the scene itself, questions are designed to return students again and again to the interpretive actors in order to get to the crux of the matter: who (and, by extension, what) do we believe and why do we believe them?

I'm advocating an approach that should lead to what Clifford Geertz characterizes as "epistemological empathy" with the characters—we attempt to come to terms with the text they have before them (357). That is, we choose to inhabit the subject positions of the various characters in the poem in order to figure out, for instance, why Piers acts out of "pure tene," or why the priest impugns the pardon and seemingly insults Piers, or what Will makes of the interaction between Piers and the priest. Of course, empathizing already implicates us in a number of beliefs—the belief that we are meant to inhabit the characters, the belief that this inhabitation is actually possible for a twenty-first-century audience, and the belief that inhabitation will render an understanding of the character (as opposed to a mere narcissistic projection). We're aided in these beliefs by the priest's jeering reference to Piers ("*dixit insipiens*"), which recalls not only Psalm 13 but also punningly refers to "the three days of disputation that culminated [the university student's] proof of himself as a beginner or *incipiens*" (Middleton, "William" 39–40; D. Smith 195). Having his characters occupy roles familiar from university life, Langland means for us to understand this scene in an educational context.

But what of the student who takes the position that these beliefs are unwarranted? It is important to maintain the possiblility of not engaging in this empathetic reading and allowing an approach to the poem—in general and this scene in particular—that resists the text and distrusts the author. From this point of view the entire Pardon narrative might be seen as a kind of elaborate setup. The poet tells us early in passus 7 that Truth "p*ur*chased hym [Piers] a pardou*n*" ("procured him [Piers] a pardon"; 7.3). And the actors in this interpretive drama (at least until line 115) all believe that the document lays claim to the name of pardon.[2] But it's possible to read the idea of the pardon as a confection of the poet. The readers of the poem have been "led down the garden path" (Frank 25) by Langland, who perhaps misleads them about the nature of the pardon, but only in order to lead them to truth (D. Baker 725).

The pardon scene is useful as a kind of hermenutical module because it simultaneously enables belief and skepticism, knowing and not knowing—a kind of interpretive suspension that offers the reader a choice.[3] This choice, I think, results from the text consciously projecting itself into a future that is known but still requires interpretation. The pardon, of course, is all about the future—characterized, as it is at passus 7, line 4, as a promise for all time—"For hym and for hise heires eueremoore after" ("For him and for his heirs for evermore after"). And even the text, from the Athanasian Creed, describes a future in which all of the actors believe. Finally, in "musynge on þis metels" ("musing on my dream"; 7.148) Will turns to the biblical past, but only to foreground the extent to which dreams can be predictive. We have to wonder, Is he thinking about his own dream here? Is he projecting his witnessing of the scene of reading as a scene that will happen in the future? Langland here is not only "making a place for the future" but making a future place for the interpretation of the future (Certeau 85). As we might expect, he leaves open the possibility that the dream means nothing, telling us that "Caton and Canonistres counseillen vs to leue / To sette sadnesse in Songewarie for *sompnia ne cures*" ("Cato and canon-lawyers counsel us to cease / Assigning certainty to dream-lore, for "Pay no attention to dreams"; 7.155). Thus, the scene of interpretation is not predictive. The space is seemingly uncreated. Yet choosing not to pay attention to dreams is itself a belief and an interpretive act.

Focusing on the nature of interpretation and the ways in which the poem encourages us to perform interpretive acts is a start toward encouraging the understanding that all textualities ultimately require interpretation. I realize that I might sound like a Pollyanna here, but to claim that it is a "lost cause" to try to convince some readers that texts, and especially biblical texts, have multiple meanings seems to me the counsel of despair (Simpson, *Burning* 8). One of the lessons of *Piers Plowman* is that we always have a choice, and it is incumbent on us to communicate that choice to our students. We might not have faith in the choices they make, but whether they engage in a hermeneutics of suspicion or a hermeneutics of faith, they may begin to understand that however they approach a text, that itself is a choice that they make freely.

NOTES

[1]Quotations of the poem are from Kane and Donaldson's edition of the B version. Translations are from Donaldson's *Alliterative Verse Translation*.

[2]The priest says to Piers "þi pardon moste I rede" ("your pardon must I read"; 7.107) before he pronounces it no pardon at all. Piers's reaction to what the priest has to say suggests that Piers believed it was a pardon. And even after Will wakes up, he refers to it as a pardon.

[3]Skepticism is not borne out of an allegory that fosters distrust by self-consciously foregrounding the extent to which we can't read allegory literally. I'm thinking here of allegories like *The Faerie Queene*, in which Red Cross's defeat of Error in book 1 doesn't really mean that he's defeated error. Some critics have, of course, argued that Langland meant for the pardon scene to remain open for interpretation: see, for instance, Astell 68.

Piers Plowman as Theology: Pedagogy, Politics, Pastness

Nicholas Watson

I teach *Piers Plowman*—to graduates and undergraduates, in scholarly editions of the B or C texts, in translation, in excerpt—not merely in relation to theology but as a secular kind of theology, by which I mean something that emerges only at the end of this essay. There is much talk among literary scholars about the disappearance in society at large of general knowledge of Christianity as an intellectual and dogmatic structure and about the problems this causes for reading much of the premodern English literary canon, even for students who come from families with Christian backgrounds and those who have been raised as Christian believers. Recent handbooks and other aids address this aspect of the crisis of literary studies. I have contributed a prequel to this essay to one such handbook (Watson, "Chaucer"; Hass et al.). But if *Piers Plowman* is clear about anything, it is that catechesis is of limited value, even for a pedagogy more organized around memorization than our own. To be usable, knowledge must be "kynde": perceived as natural, innate, or integral to awareness, tasted like apples on a Tree of Charity, not reduced to a list of the way stations on a pilgrimage to Truth (*Piers Plowman* 16.1–23, 5.561–629).[1] Thus, in teaching *Piers Plowman* as theology I am only secondarily interested in promoting a better understanding of the particular, medieval, Christian religious system that subtends the poem or, indeed, a better understanding of how religious systems generally work and can be imaginatively realized by poets. Such approaches result in students arriving at "kynde knowing" neither of the poem nor of the particular religious sensibility to which it gives access.

Of course, given the geopolitical significance of contemporary religions, it is vital that students know about the role such systems play in the construction of human societies, thought, and art. Since Western society is bound by a set of secular dogmas clustered around the numinous term *modernity*, it is equally vital that students understand how religious ideologies differ from secular ones. For example, religious ideologies have an unmatched ability, for better or for worse, to synthesize models of human selfhood within a single understanding of the enfolding familial, communal, institutional, civic, national, environmental, and cosmological habitats in which people live, giving a total account of the entire shape of human life and death. Students need to understand that religious societies are by no means inferior to secular ones in producing the conditions necessary for human self-fulfillment. By this understanding students learn to reflect critically on the status of the secular West in its narrative of progress.

Self-knowledge that comes from the experience of alterity is thematized in *Piers Plowman*, where knowledge is represented as sciential before it is sapiential and involves constant, confusing recognitions of the self in and against the world. In the third vision, Will's search for the ethical life begins with his encounter with himself as Thought but moves away into talk with more abstract figures until he childishly refuses further schooling (passus 8–11). Once he has slowly learned patience—through scrutinizing not himself but the world (12–14)—a second self-encounter, with Anima, teaches him nothing about himself except what he gleans from Anima's discursive tour of time and space (15). Before Will can take the apple of knowledge, he must know the world as different from himself.

Of course, *Piers Plowman* is also a remarkable resource for the deep study of one representative religious system, late medieval Catholic Christianity, observed in what is widely understood as the early stages of its last, most destructive crisis. The poem brilliantly represents this system as an intensely moving narrative of salvation history, from creation to fall to incarnation to passion to doomsday; as a coherent set of dogmas and practices, developed out of the authoritative texts that the poem quotes as sententiae and uses in the most varied ways, and summated in the creeds, prayers, and syllabuses that underlie much of its formal structure; and as a highly problematic intellectual and political institution, in principle still committed to instantiating Christian belief and ethics in individuals and in society but viewed by many—even among its own members—as increasingly compromised by its economic integration with that society and a growing disparity between idea and fact, word and work.

Although the poem subjects this system to a sustained, corrosive, yet heavily self-critical analysis, it remains a work of belief, enmeshed in the system it criticizes (at least in its ideal form) and unable to imagine any alternative to it. Because the poem takes the form of a great imaginative work and its critique remains internal to medieval Catholic Christianity, *Piers Plowman* thus also testifies to the reformist possibilities within vibrant religious systems, confuting the common modernist association of religion with reactionary fundamentalism. It also speaks to the urgency of such systems for those who live in them, to the multiplicity and inner contradictions of those systems, and to the ability of those systems to move those who inhabit them in emotional, artistic, and intellectual ways so that they may engage the whole of human experience.

Of course, my classroom approach to *Piers Plowman* deals with the poem's intricacies by relating them to general issues such as those mentioned above. In describing the integrative aspirations of religious systems, I focus, for example, on the play of the personal and the communal throughout the first two visions; the complex movement between individual and social critique in the episode of the confession of the sins episode and the pardon episode in particular (passus 5.62–506, 7.1–110); and how both episodes argue, with equal force, exactly opposite positions: that individual reform can be sustained only in a reformed society and that such a society can come into being only through reformation of the individuals in it. Working an analogy with modern secular society, I relate the tension between these positions that emerges in the episode of the plowing of the half acre (passus 6) to that between opposing modern social policies on indigence: Piers's words and behavior in this passus reflect both the socially oriented position that it is the state's responsibility to care for those in need and the individually oriented position that the provision of such care actively promotes indigence. But I then complicate this analogy to contrast how religious and secular societies think about the same issues and to show the real-world consequences of specific religious doctrines, which can give the appearance of abstraction and foreignness.

First, I note that the intellectual substructure of the half-acre episode includes the doctrine of the Fall—"Tho Adam and Eve eten apples unrosted" ("when Adam and Eve ate unroasted apples"; 5.603), as Piers describes it—which holds that there is a gap between the world as it is and the perfect world God created. The idea that perfection belongs to a lost past, not a latent future, differs from the ideas of modern secular progressivism. Leftists accuse this doctrine of fatalism and thus of failure to promote radical social progress, and the episode gives credence to this accusation: Piers assumes that we always have the poor with us (Matt. 26.11), and never mentions the desirability of eliminating Hunger. Yet the episode shows two understandings of the Fall in dynamic tension: Piers's realistic view that many beggars, corrupted by idleness, refuse to work even if they can is complicated by his idealistic view of even the laziest of them as his "blody bretheren" ("brothers by blood"), made in God's image as they are, and "bought," like him, by the death of Christ (6.207). Such a view puts pressure on him to care for beggars, even at the risk of worsening Hunger's grip on society.

Piers's realism is based on an understanding of the Fall as a fundamental disordering of the cosmos, an understanding that voids the purpose of programs aimed at bettering society and radically divides society between those who avail themselves of grace, the sole solution to sin, and those who do not. His idealism is committed to a less drastic view of the Fall, which holds out hope of amendment for all and even insists that, because it brought Christ to earth, the Fall was a "*felix culpa*," a fortunate or happy fault (5.484).

Medieval Catholic orthodoxy holds both understandings of the Fall true; it is characteristic of religious systems to embrace opposed interpretations of their own dogma. *Piers Plowman* also holds both true, but invests huge energies in the view that society can be bettered. Reform movements ripple through the poem: the half-acre episode is part of one such movement. Throughout the poem, Piers seems to embody the belief in the innate goodness of human beings, despite the Fall, and in humanity's ability to aid its own regeneration, not leave all to God. In class, we flash forward to Piers chasing the devil, brandishing a stick representing God the Son (16.86–87). Reform always fails, never more drastically than at the poem's close, but Langland remains committed to reform as a social and ethical ideal—as something that takes place in this world rather than directing attention to the next.

Second, I return to the issue of poverty and the difference between the poem's conception of social justice and that of the modern secular left. The poem evokes utopian dreams of social leveling, in which, once Meed has been banished and rational rule established, "lawe" will be "a laborer" and "lede afeld donge" ("lawyers" will become "laborers" and "manure the fields"; 4.147). In the second vision, society reorganizes itself around the peasant's role in the production of "liflade" ("daily necessities"); the figure of the peasant was understood in radical terms by the rebels of 1381. A thin line joins the medieval plowman figure with the radical movements of the seventeenth century and their American (Puritan) and later European (proletarian) descendants. Yet in most ways the poem is socially conservative: Piers is happy to work for the knight and encourages social distinctions, for example, when it comes to the manufacture of different kinds of cloth by women of different classes (6.1–25).

This conservatism bodes ill for the social ideals of destratifying society and distributing capital equitably. But there is compensation on the discursive level because of the ways in which poverty signifies spiritually in medieval Christianity. The pardon confirms an implication of the half-acre episode, that the patient poor are exempt from social responsibility (7.98–104). In class we tiptoe gingerly into the difficult third and fourth visions to see how poverty becomes an increasingly important spiritual ideal—associated not only with material lack but also with authenticity, spiritual self-abandonment, and antimaterialism—and a powerful site of opposition to the prestige that inheres in social and educational institutions, and in clerical learning in particular. As Trajan says, "[O]ure joy and oure juele, Jesu Crist of hevene, / In a povere mannes apparaille pursueth us evere" ("our joy and our jewel, Jesus Christ from heaven, constantly pursues us in the garb of a poor man"; 11.184–85). The ideal of poverty generates its own exclusions. No more than any other ideal can it provide final solutions, especially for those who by definition are unable to embrace it, such as the merchant, Haukyn. But the poem's translation of the material fact of poverty into a spiritual ideal both gives status to the poor—refusing their objectification as mere objects of charity—and exemplifies the powerful capacity of Christian religious systems to read social hierarchies upside down and to sustain a discursive gap between social reality and its meaning. Since *Piers Plowman* develops into a poem of protest, especially against the failure of Christian institutions to live up to their ideals, the poem itself comes to be situated within this gap, in the dangerous but powerful space of the prophetic.

Class discussion of one of the more accessible portions of *Piers Plowman* thus aims to show both similarities and differences between secular and religious systems and especially to give a careful account of the real sociopolitical and ethical consequences of the idea of the transcendent in religious systems. For it is through the transcendent—the imposition of a spiritual value system on a material one—that the poem gives positive valency to poverty, both in an obvious way, by offering the poor eternal salvation on easy terms, and in less obvious ones, for example, by identifying Christ with poverty, not power, and by using poverty metaphorically as part of the poem's attack on intellectual pretension. The transcendent, in other words, can be yoked to many ends but is by no means a conservative or socially quietist idea, any more than the doctrine of the Fall is. Nor does the rule of social distinction set in place in the prologue, "ech lif to knowe his owene" ("each person to know his own station in life"; prol. 122)—interestingly, never claimed to have a transcendent source—translate into a hierarchy of discursive power.

By expounding parts of the poem in these ways, I hope to convey something of the particularity of *Piers Plowman*'s theological analysis of late medieval English society while at the same time using the poem in an exemplary fashion, as a powerful instantiation of a religious world view. It is probably clear that my approach also has a genealogical component—that is, it is interested in how late medieval theology might be considered a source of modern, secular conceptions of society and social justice—and that it encourages analogy, placing Langlandian social ideas in dialogue with a (somewhat generically conceived) modern response to essentially the same social issue, the problem of indigence, or the role of welfare.

It may not be clear from the above that I do read *Piers Plowman* as a poem, focusing on the refusal of Langlandian allegory to behave in the stiff ways Coleridge's attack on the mode assumes (Halmi). Indeed, the poem's interest in how ideas and spiritual energies interact with or become incarnate in persons and communities, inhabiting them but seldom permanently fusing with them, has obvious resonances with Langland's theological concern with matters like conversion, reform, and pedagogy. In the prologue Langland's narrator envisions a society ignorant of the outside forces that act on it; its members are existentially positioned between heaven and hell but their lives go, for the most part, "as the world asketh" (prol. 19). Allegory in *Piers Plowman* analyzes society but also energizes its account of society in a literary sense, allowing the field full of folk to develop into narrative (since allegory is narrative argument). Yet whenever the narrative shifts or drops, as personifications or allegorical motifs give way to others, whatever reforms have been gained disappear. If the society depicted in *Piers Plowman* pays lip service to religious categories that the poem itself understands as real, through much of the poem the secularization of this society proceeds apace.

"Yet have I no kynde knowynge . . . ye mote ye kenne me bettre" ("yet I have no inward knowledge . . . you must teach me better") says the narrator to Holy

Church, causing her to respond more in the voice of Dame Grammar with her birch than of *Ecclesia* ("the Church") the *sponsa Christi* ("spouse of Christ"): "Thow doted daffe!" ("You stupid idiot!"; 1.138, 140). The trouble with my own practice as outlined here is that students tend to echo the narrator's words, and rightly so. None of the suggestions I have made about the usefulness of studying *Piers Plowman* argue that it urgently belongs in an undergraduate English student's curriculum, given the small number of specialist courses North American students take and the students' usual preference for the familiar modern over the unfamiliar medieval.

My students see little cultural capital to be accrued by reading *Piers Plowman*, the greatest work written in English without a secure place in the literary canon. A *Google Ngram Viewer* search of books in English published between 1950 and 2000 shows that the name "William Langland" has kept roughly level with "John Lydgate" across this period but has steadily lost ground, since the 1970s, to "Margery Kempe" and "Julian of Norwich." By the 1990s, references to the latter two names outnumbered those to the former two by a factor of roughly six to one, almost equal to references to "Geoffrey Chaucer," which outnumbered references to Langland and Lydgate by seven to one, though still far behind references to "William Shakespeare," which outnumbered references to "Geoffrey Chaucer" by five to one. Across the whole period, for every reference to Langland there are about twelve references to Chaucer, and for every reference to Chaucer there are five to Shakespeare.

Students are interested in religion and can become interested in much else *Piers Plowman* has to offer, including the singularity of its form and its status as a pioneering work in an unfamiliar literary medium and language. But the poem is tough, and much of what they can learn from it—for example, about the nature of religious societies, indeed even of medieval Catholic society—might be learned elsewhere. A different justification is needed for subjecting them to the labor of reading and understanding this work. Above all, its very difficulty offers something unique to students' experience of the literary—something, moreover, they can be taught to know "kyndely," tasted as part of their innermost experience.

Over the last several years, I have therefore slowly and tentatively reframed my classroom approach to complex medieval materials such as *Piers Plowman* as an exercise in the experience of pastness, an exercise that involves asking students to affirm, at least provisionally, two kinds of belief: the belief that the past was once the present, with all the sense of possibility this implies, and the more difficult belief that the past still lies latent in the present. I base my initial claim for *Piers Plowman* as an object of study squarely on the double facts of its greatness and its obscurity. The text's lack of canonical purchase and its difficulty make it ideal for the exploration of pastness. When undertaken in the company of a prophetic pedagogue like Langland, this exploration, I claim, can reinvigorate our entire understanding of the past and, crucially, deepen our experience of the present and, by extension, of ourselves. This is the "kynde knowing" that I have come to believe the poem can offer modern students.

Such an approach presupposes a polemical understanding of our own cultural moment as future-directed—urgently concerned with the possible outcomes of a present that is experienced as a moving threshold of individual and aggregate decisions pointed toward futurity. Our dominant narrative forms (the movie, the newspaper, the novel, the stock market) offer images of this present as ideally unencumbered by a past whose metaphoric hallmark is its inert, constricting deadness. When the past does show up in a positive way under the aegis of modern thought, ethics, and art, it does so as the tasteless gruel of heritage or, worse, as the inedible lessons of history: didactic forms as nearly useless to us as Holy Church's generalities are to the narrator of *Piers Plowman*. As moderns, we therefore neglect pastness as such whenever we can, alternately monumentalizing and resenting those aspects of the past that appear to bear on us directly and treating the past as a utilitarian resource but hardly ever as formerly present, pregnant with its own futures, mostly very different from the one we happen to occupy. In suppressing the past's erstwhile presence we also suppress our awareness of its latent presence, by which I mean its mode of survival, not as monuments but as ghosts in contemporary culture: unexplained breaks in the fabric of modernity through which forgotten energies can suddenly erupt, as they have so unexpectedly (yet so predictably) in recent years—as, for example, in the case of the new "fundamentalist" versions of Christian and other religious systems, which feature a strange mix of elements drawn from the distant past and elements particular to our modernist moment. Whether ghosts or monuments are in question, by allowing the past to be only about us, by understanding time teleologically, we render the past doubly dead because we effectively deny it ever had life.

Given this admittedly lopsided account of modernity, the study of *Piers Plowman* can be presented as urgent on three linked grounds. First, to an extent never true of a canonical work such as *The Canterbury Tales*, which employs (and reinterprets for the future) a set of preexisting and still-surviving high-art literary forms and hermeneutic habits, *Piers Plowman* requires us to exhume the past, demanding that we reconstruct it as we read it and slowly come to understand it on its own terms (as open-ended, incomplete). We have to learn this art of exhumation, I argue, because we need to reconnect with the past by attempting to realize something of its former presence (its logic, tensions, vibrancy), and so experience it as other than monument or phantasmal cultural presence.

The difficulty of this project is a given, since the past had its own coherence, many of whose elements have long since metamorphosed and become unrecognizable or recognizable only factitiously: they are like the so-called false friends that may trap the unwary translator or like our initial encounter with, say, Langland's economic thought in the long Lady Meed episode, where what seems a straightforwardly moralistic account of late medieval England's culture of bribery slowly opens out to reveal a tangled complex of associations around the practice of gift-giving, in which the possibility of divine mercy itself can suddenly be at stake (passus 2–4). But difficulty, including the always revealing species of difficulty we name boredom (*acedia*), is also part of the point of exhumation, since difficulty is a kind of journey—or quest, to invoke one of the medieval past's uncomplicated gifts to the present. (This argument for the value of exhumation, of course, follows the logic of psychoanalysis and the ghost story, modern cultural forms that are of interest to many students and that can be seen in this context as implied commentaries on modernity's forgetting of the past.)

Second, we can learn to enter into dialogue with *Piers Plowman*, for example, along the lines of the formal, sociological, and theological discussion of the half-acre episode sketched above. This dialogue reveals parallels and direct connections—as well as disconnection—between Langland's thought world and ours, reviving the past by allowing it to say all it has to say, not forcing it to conform to the uses we want to make of it and suppressing the rest. Because the past is still inherent in the present, what at first seems a disconnection may turn out to be a connection. While Christian salvation history, defined by the primal event of the Fall, and the modern West's understanding of time, defined by its hope in progress, seem naturally in opposition, *Piers Plowman* helps in mapping one onto the other. Because the past is now gone, displaced by the present, the opposite may also be true; the easy commerce between microcosm and macrocosm (individual, community, cosmos) and between material and abstract (material indigence and spiritual power) in Langland's thought—as well as the disruption of the metaphysical structure that makes this commerce possible in modernity—generate many false friends. Disconnections are as interesting as connections because they help us displace the heritage model and the lessons-of-history model of the past. It is vital to know about medieval Christianity or the political implications of the doctrine of the Fall because our connection to both is now so uncertain and because we can never be sure what the past may do to us next.

Third, and most important, our dialogue with *Piers Plowman* can be shaped to show that the poem is, on one level, an analysis of a particular, late medieval experience of living in the present and a study of how to learn to do so "kyndely." The poem's intense commitment to its own present moment accounts for much of its difficulty, for example, its indifference to formal and generic norms and infuriating habits of self-cancellation and perpetual discursive revolution, features of the poem that may have been as troublesome to early readers, indeed to Langland, as they are to us. The quest that gradually shapes itself around the narrator and his avatar, Will, can be understood as a quest to learn to live in the present with urgency, that is, to understand the claims made by the present moment.

Throughout the poem, Will dreams possible presents—models of how things are, or should be, or would be if certain conditions were met—many of them aimed at renewed futures or designed to expose the present's failures to work toward such futures. All these models fail, in that they remain only models imagined in a dream, but they do slowly generate the urgency toward the present that is one of the poem's ethical absolutes. By the last passus, this urgency has recast the aimlessness of the prologue in eschatological terms. Now Will's present—secular in the sense that it is still mainly motivated by worldly human desires—is like a dystopic version of our own, pointing toward a desperate future while still (barely) holding out the hope of renewal. Will, initially a partisan observer of the field of the world, has recognized his place in its great drama, even his responsibility to it. How has he come to this recognition? Specifically by acknowledging the present's relation not only to the future but also to the past: the redemptive past that he experiences "kyndely," tastes as an apple of knowledge in re-creative and dialogic meditation from the episode of the tree of charity onward (passus 16–19), and that radically resituates his relation to his cultural moment. Will's journey, in other words, is a journey through time toward an understanding of what it is to live in time. This is the journey I argue the poem challenges our students to appropriate.

NOTE

[1]Quotations from *Piers Plowman* are from Schmidt (Vision). Translations are my own.

Hunger Bites: Medieval Malnutrition and a Pedagogy for the Overfed

Madonna J. Hettinger

Bringing Hunger to the Table

It is usually safe to assume that most students who have signed up for an undergraduate course on medieval history arrive with either a romantic or a violent view of medieval Europe. Both types of imaginings will tend toward sensationalism, and it often takes a semester's worth of readings on the social structure and material culture of the Middle Ages to loosen the grip of Hollywood knights. Slowly, the tournaments and feasts of students' imaginations give way to the fields full of folk and the peasants who put the food on the table. It is also safe to assume that on any given day many students will have skipped breakfast. At the liberal arts college where I teach, most of them can afford to. Abundance awaits them in the cafeteria for lunch, included in the price of the comprehensive fee. In other academic settings, however, such as the public elementary school just a few blocks from our campus, skipping breakfast was probably not a choice but the default situation for a good number of students. Though my students may romanticize the past, most of them are keenly aware of the class differentials in their own world and their position of relative privilege; the majority of them, some eighty-five percent, regularly volunteer in the local community. But hunger—medieval and modern—still surprises them, much as it does the idle workers in Langland's poem.

Piers *Sets the History Classroom to Work*

A one-semester survey course that attempts to cover roughly the thousand years between the fall of Rome and the Renaissance necessitates that every reading is substantial—not in pages but in entry points to the political realities and cultural codes of the Middle Ages, which seem foreign, illogical, or quaint to many students. In this respect, Langland never fails. Because my course is an intermediate undergraduate history course without prerequisites, I usually assign a translation edition (Goodridge). *Piers Plowman* is well suited to a pedagogical approach that relies on discussion rather than lecture. Admittedly, discussions in my classroom often impede the brisk march through a thousand years of history, but I prefer that students grapple with a few good puzzles and leave the classroom with more of their own questions than with facts and answers. Toward that end, Langland is the perfect host.

I assign the whole poem near the end of the semester to discuss the sweeping social changes of the fourteenth century, but I often use brief readings from

Langland earlier in the course to introduce elements of the medieval *mentalité* that are particularly difficult for students to grasp. My approach is informed by Robert Darnton's suggestion, in his introduction to *The Great Cat Massacre*, to explore a culture by starting with a joke we don't get (4). For our purposes, a paradox works as well as a joke. For example, my students find paradoxical the coexistence of a worldly, politicized Catholic Church and a deeply felt, popular attachment to religion: How did belief endure through centuries of poor spiritual leadership? Why did people buy into the idea that some few were born to pray, some few were born to fight, and the great many were born to work? Why did people for centuries accept their assignment to work and, moreover, to work in conditions that reinforced their lack of personal freedom? These are really good questions. Langland's dreamer articulates many of the things students don't understand, even as he stumbles between the particular realities of postplague English society and the more universal ambitions of a medieval spiritual quest. If we can read only one passage to help us understand the marginal economy that guaranteed the social structure of the three orders, Hunger's appearance when Piers sets out to plow his half acre is a good choice (B.6.112–90).

Hunger is best discussed before lunch. Approaching Hunger in *Piers Plowman* at eleven o'clock in the morning accomplishes many of my course goals. First, against the subtle accompaniment of stomachs growling, Piers's enraged call for Hunger to set the world to work and Hunger's bone-thrashing, gut-wringing answer alert students to the persistent realities of malnutrition, inequality, and social obligation in the Middle Ages. Neither romantic nor sensational—but sometimes violent—hunger pangs go a long way toward understanding why medieval peasants put up with a status quo that restricted them to a life of labor with limited rewards. In *Piers Plowman*, Hunger still has power, even in Langland's time of relative plenty, because the memory of hunger was strong.

Second, Langland's text invites students to grapple with the complex moral and intellectual challenges of a late medieval worldview. The deep roots of that worldview include the concept of a trifunctional society (see Lawrence Clopper's essay in this volume, on Chaucer's and Langland's prologues) and the collective memory of dearth. In Langland's time, after the depopulation caused by the black death, both the economic underpinnings of the trifunctional society and the daily transactions of the marketplace confronted the possibilities of surplus. Workers with full bellies could afford to negotiate the value of their own labor and, through those negotiations, shape their working lives differently. They could now work more or less on their own terms, when and where they wanted to, as Piers knows all too well.

Third, Hunger's power opens a conversation on the comparative malnutritions of Piers's world and our own. Students are of course shocked by the poverty, both quantitative and qualitative, of the medieval diet and by the susceptibility to disease and high rates of infant mortality that came with it. I push the conversation a step further and provide students with recent statistics on hunger, infant mortality, eating disorders, and the confounding evidence of several types of malnutrition that currently coexist—the problem of the underfed, the problem of the improperly fed, and the problem of the overfed. The intent is not to produce guilt or to thin out the line in the cafeteria but to demonstrate the far-ranging impact of food, or the lack thereof, on human behavior and thus to show the fullness of the political and social power of hunger.

Hunger, as Langland breathes life into it, also gives history students access to a basic understanding of allegory. Less abstract than some of the other figures in the poem, Hunger's physicality can be played with, albeit sometimes uncomfortably, in a classroom of diet-conscious students.

To give Hunger its full head of steam, I usually wait until the last minute to walk into the classroom and, with no introduction whatsoever, start reading at passus 6, line 112, with appropriate roaring by Hunger and appropriate pleading by the idle worker. I close the reading, usually at line 190, with the shortest commentary I can offer: "These were the good times." In fact, they were extraordinary times, and yet here is Hunger, the stalker, lying in wait for those with too much food in their bellies and too few tools in their hands. If time permits, I sometimes let Hunger gain strength more slowly. Again with no introduction, I ask one student to read selected lines on Hunger's confrontation with Waster (B.6.171–90). With no comment, I ask a second student to read the same lines, and then a third. With a little encouragement, by the third reading Hunger is bellowing, no longer an "it" but a "he" who gives lazy mortals a drubbing. Through acting out Hunger, students readily grasp that the allegorical figure is an actor, not a mere abstraction. Now we are ready to talk about Hunger's agency.

After the class has heard Hunger wring the guts of Waster, I provide a quick review of how the relative good times of the late medieval agricultural economy in most of Western Europe came about only through the demographic disaster of the mid-fourteenth century. The black death of 1348–50 reversed the relative values of land and labor: there was simply more land, and therefore more food, to go around. That relatively abrupt reversal, however, followed a far longer period during which the population increased and the availability of resources decreased.[1] The gradual growth and eventual overexpansion of the population in the eleventh and twelfth centuries, the land contractions of the thirteenth century, and the famines of the early fourteenth century (1315–17, and again in the 1320s) all combined to reinforce in the peasant community a collective memory of hunger, which had the power to make men and women work. The inequalities of the tripartite system had set workers against the ruling classes and the government at various times, and local tensions became particularly rife when the land-holding classes used such laws as the Statute of Laborers to enforce retrogressive wage restrictions in the postplague economy (Dobson 63–68). The retrenchment of the ruling classes aside, hunger does the best job of keeping peasants in their place.

We then take a look at Piers's attempt to wave off Hunger once order is restored and Hunger's refusal to leave until he has eaten everything Piers and the peasants have to offer (B.6.277–330). The warning at the end of the passus is ominous. Why does Hunger sleep so lightly, even after he has feasted on new grain and good ale?

Who Are We If We Are What We Eat?

After Piers has used Hunger to set the world to work, I set the students to work thinking about hunger as an agent in history. A survey course is no place for a lengthy discussion of philosophies of history, but I like to pose two not-so-rhetorical questions that a person who suddenly wakes up in a historical culture not his or her own should ask: Who are we?, and What's for lunch? If indeed we are what we eat, then food, or the lack thereof, must have been a major factor in the shaping of medieval identity.

Famine was an all-too-frequent visitor in the marginal economy of medieval Europe. Between episodes of starvation, however, the more persistent hunger of malnutrition shaped not only the activities of daily life but also the life cycles of peasants. Mentioning the bread and beer diet, high in calories from carbohydrates, low in proteins, fats, and the micronutrients that contribute to healthy growth, typically gets a laugh in a college classroom—what's not to like about 3,500 calories of bread and beer? We unpack the joke by unpacking the medieval grocery bag and the modern lunch. Only the long-distance runners in the class will admit to consuming 3,500 calories a day, and most of the students will claim that they have not eaten fast food since they were in high school. So I use the memory of fast food to underscore the difference between the medieval peasant diet and the modern American diet. The United States Department of Agriculture sets a general range of 2,000 to 2,500 calories a day, depending on age and gender, as a nutritional target to maintain good health.[2] For what Americans really eat, any fast-food chain serves as an example, and most of them provide nutritional information on their corporate Web sites. At McDonald's, for example, a Big Mac is 540 calories, small fries 230, and a small, chocolate, shake-like substance 530, for a total of 1,300 calories.[3] That's just for lunch, and we haven't super-sized anything yet. To better compare the composition of medieval and modern calories, we might look at the Big Mac's nutritional values: 25 grams of protein (approximately half of the United States Food and Drug Administration's recommended daily value); 28 grams of fat (43 percent of the recommended daily value), most of it saturated or monounsaturated; 80 milligrams of cholesterol (26 percent of the recommended daily value); a tiny smattering of vitamins A and C; and a few minerals that, as paltry as they are compared to the fats, range between twenty to thirty percent of the government's recommended daily values.[4] So, as problematic as the meal may be, it has a lot of protein and a fair amount of iron and calcium. The proteins and fats would go a long way if we were to plow anybody's half acre but are really not well suited to our long hours in front of computer screens.

But we are plowing Piers's half acre, after all, so let's see what's left of our lunch after a medieval harvest. The meat is gone; grazing cattle for beef would simply take up too much of the arable land, all of which is needed for the production of wheat, rye, barley, and oats, the staple crops necessary to maintain the marginal existence that pertained before the black death. Losing the meat takes away about 170 calories and many of the fats. The processed cheese is also gone; milk-fat products have to be used for the production of cheese and butter, market products that could bring in the necessary cash for the repair of essential agricultural tools. Our lunch has lost another fifty calories. The sauce of the Big Mac is worth about ninety calories; among its mysterious ingredients are also soybean oils and processed sugars, inaccessible to our medieval diet, as well as egg yolks, another product more often taken to market for cash than consumed by peasants. Pickles, onions, and ketchup add a few calories and a lot of flavor, but, except for the onions, they would not be found on a medieval table. In the end we are left with just the bun, which provides about 220 calories. We would have to eat about ten buns to meet the Department of Agriculture's recommendations for 2,000 to 2,500 calories a day, and about sixteen buns to reach the 3,500 carbohydrate calories that were necessary for the back-breaking labor required to plow Piers's half acre. Sixteen buns corresponds nicely, in terms of volume and nutritional value, with the measures of bread that were often included in medieval maintenance agreements for pensioners as well as in food allowances for various labor arrangements (Hanawalt, *Ties* 58–59).

Unfortunately, we can't look to the fries or the shake to supplement our meager buns. The fries are the product of a New World crop that would not have a significant impact on the European diet until the early nineteenth century. The shake, as another milk-fat product, goes to the market with the cheese. So, if we are what we eat, are we just protein and fat and unpronounceable by-products today? Were medieval people basically sixteen buns a day with an additional few hundred calories from good ale to relieve the boredom? More important, what do either of these nutritional disasters mean for the life cycles of individuals or the survival of communities?

For the first part of this question the medieval answers may be somewhat simpler, albeit harsher, than the modern answers. Early childhood death rates for the Middle Ages, primarily from malnutrition, range around fifty percent for the first five years of life. Undernourished infants were particularly vulnerable to death from opportunistic infections and simple diarrhea. Malnourished mothers gave birth to malnourished babies, and the rate of maternal deaths and stillbirths was high. Slow growth rates for those who did survive the most vulnerable infant years would have meant a greater susceptibility to childhood accidents. Although a life of work began early, biological maturity arrived late, with puberty usually beginning around age fourteen (Hanawalt, *Ties* 156–68, 189). For those who reached adulthood, middle age was possible and old age was not unknown. Nonetheless, accounting for infant mortality rates, the average life expectancy at birth was about twenty-five to thirty. This was hunger's power in years of average harvests. In years of poor harvests—or in the worst-case scenario, famine—hunger preyed even more heavily on the youngest and oldest individuals.

The modern nutritional disaster is in many ways more complex and contradictory, particularly in the United States. The conundrum is that there is an abundance of nutritional resources but serious problems of poor nutritional health. As a historian, I never overwhelm my students with dates, but I occasionally overwhelm them with statistics. With statistics, we have to look at how questions were asked and remember that numbers, like words, are subject to interpretation. Yet, even if taken with a grain of salt, the answers to questions on the distribution of food resources in the United States are unpalatable. Until the increases in food prices that began during the recession of 2007–09, the government regularly bought food surpluses in order to keep agricultural prices from falling to an unsustainable low. While some of those surpluses made it to food distribution programs such as Women, Infants, Children (WIC), the Supplemental Nutrition Assistance Program (popularly called food stamps), and school-lunch programs, other surpluses, including wheat, milk, and cheese, ended up in warehouses and often went unused. In the recent period of recovery from the recession, the government has resumed many of the programs to support agricultural prices and further stepped in to buy and redistribute oversupplies of meat, fruit, and vegetable products (Kirchhoff).

Our times are characterized by an embarrassment of abundance, yet food has become difficult to obtain for a significant number of Americans. The Department of Agriculture's most recent survey of food consumption found 41.2 million people in the United States living in "food insecure" households at some point in 2016.[5] Of those, 28.3 million were adults and about 12.9 million were children. About 16.5 percent of households with children experienced food insecurity in 2016, although about half of these reported that only the adults in the households went without food. The term *food insecurity* sounds softer than *hunger*. Yet food insecurity is comparable to the chronic malnourishment that pertained for most of the Middle Ages in that it accounts for the accessibility, quality, and variety of food intake, not merely the caloric value. Food-secure households can afford to spend about twenty-nine percent more on food than food-insecure households of the same size. Among the effects of food insecurity are developmental delays in children, learning difficulties, low productivity, damage to physical and psychological health, and family stress. According to the same government survey, 4.9 percent of households in the United States experienced a level of food insecurity low enough to be labeled hunger in 2016.

Recent government figures report that Americans as a whole spent about fifty percent of their food dollars on meals eaten outside the home, but a 2007 study complicates the picture. At that time, 18.28 percent of the average food budget for all households was spent on fast food, while 18.4 percent of American households spent, on average, half of their food dollars on fast food (Fan et al.). There is little to suggest that Americans have changed their fast-food habits in recent years.

The Centers for Disease Control uses a body mass index to define obesity. Its figures for 2013–14 found 37.7 percent of American adults over the age of twenty to be obese, while about seventy percent of the adult population falls into the categories of overweight or obese. The same data identify seventeen percent of children ages two through twenty as obese, while another 16.2 percent of American children are overweight, putting one-third of children in the categories of overweight or obese.[6] Here is where medieval people would have trouble getting the modern joke. Abundance is apparently contributing to health risks, including cardiovascular disease, diabetes, and certain types of cancer. Stranger still, it is not that plentiful harvests are making those with greater resources fatter and more vulnerable to disease. The tragic irony is that—among women and children—those with the most limited resources, the food insecure, and those who do not share in the abundance are most vulnerable to obesity and its health risks. Fast food is relatively cheap food, and its high fat content is reversing some of the life-cycle effects that accompanied poor nutrition in the Middle Ages. Most notably, puberty is occurring earlier, in children who are emotionally unprepared for its physical changes.[7] A host of other health issues lie in wait as malnourished, overweight children reach adulthood. Malnourished and thin in the Middle Ages or malnourished and overweight in modern America, children were and are disproportionately impacted by food insecurity.

Taking Hunger to Task

How do we even begin to approach the question of what these nutritional disasters mean for the survival of communities, medieval or modern? We read the rest of *Piers Plowman*, we read the newspapers, and we look around our own half acre. Not all modern nutritional problems are related to eating the wrong things. Hunger, in its more stark form of undernourishment, is still a powerful force that shapes human experience. Data provided by the United Nations Development Program remind us that infant mortality due to lack of nutrition is still shockingly high in many parts of the world.[8] War and famine still disrupt agricultural production and food distribution. And college students certainly recognize that even the most food-secure individuals can starve from eating disorders.

After this discussion, it is easier to see how Hunger set the world to work, easier even to understand Piers's rage at those who could but would not work. We get it. We may even resent it a bit. We are ready to investigate Gluttony and re-examine Waster and run back to the field full of folk to see what the rats and mice have to say about all this. But first we go to lunch with something to talk about.

NOTES

[1] For a good explanation of the condition of English peasant households in the first half of the fourteenth century, see Bailey, "Peasant Welfare." Jordan demonstrates how deeply the famines of the early fourteenth century cut into the fabric of medieval society.

[2] The government statistics used in this essay are updated frequently. See the *Office of Disease Prevention and Health Promotion* (health.gov/dietaryguidelines/2015/guidelines/).

[3] Nutritional values of various McDonald's products are available at www.mcdonalds.com/us/en/food.html.

[4] See "Changes to the Nutrition Facts Label" at the United States Food and Drug Administration Web site (www.fda.gov/Food/GuidanceRegulation/GuidanceDocumentsRegulatoryInformation/LabelingNutrition/ucm385663.htm).

[5] The Economic Research Service of the United States Department of Agriculture provides a wealth of data relating to the distribution of food resources. For the 2016 report on food security, see Coleman-Jensen et al.

[6] See the *Centers for Disease Control and Prevention*, www.cdc.gov/nchs/data/hestat/obesity_adult_13_14/obesity_adult_13_14.htm;andwww.cdc.gov/nchs/data/hestat/obesity_child_13_14/obesity_child_13_14.htm.

[7] For two *Los Angeles Times* articles on the debate about the normal age for the onset of puberty in girls, see Brink; Roan.

[8] For infant mortality rates, see the *United Nations Development Program, Human Development Reports*, hdr.undp.org/en/content/under-five-mortality-rate-1000-live-births.

Super(Plow)man

Gina Brandolino

This essay provides an overview of a lesson plan that I have used in a number of upper-level undergraduate courses in which I teach *Piers Plowman*. My lesson plan grew out of a specific problem I encounter when I teach this text: my students are too content to see Piers exclusively as a religious figure—usually Jesus, sometimes Saint Peter, sometimes a more generic religious figure. They are drawn to this conclusion, I suspect, in part because of the sections of the poem I teach most regularly: passus 1–7 and 18, the tree of charity scene in passus 16, and the resurrection scene in passus 19 (all from the B text).[1] Given the content of these sections, their conclusion is true; Piers is of course a religious figure, and significantly so, but he is also much more. I sought a way to help my students think about Piers as a social and cultural figure as well as a religious one.

It occurred to me that one approach that might help make these other facets of Piers apparent to my students would be to thoroughly contextualize the character Piers as he exists in Langland's text and beyond it—in short, to historicize, historicize, historicize. But undergraduate courses rarely provide the time necessary for deep historical context; nor does historical context necessarily make for the most captivating lesson plan for the undergraduate classroom. So I settled on a compromise by designing a lesson plan that historically contextualizes Piers through his appearances outside Langland's text, in the letters written by participants of the Great Rising of 1381. Then I helped this historical context along with an unexpected modern analogy: World War II–era comic book covers featuring Superman's fight against the Axis powers.

Piers's presence in the rebel letters and Superman's war efforts on comic book covers are both instances of iconic fictional characters crossing over into historical events. While they are not strict analogs, their similarities are provocative. Studying them together has helped my students see beyond the religious significance of Piers and consider in what wider contexts his character wielded power. In what follows I provide background and context for the components of this lesson plan, describe how the lesson unfolds and what kinds of class discussion it fosters, and explain what rich fruit this unconventional lesson plan bears for students.

Six letters written by participants in the Great Rising of 1381 are preserved in two contemporary chronicle accounts of the Rising: the *Chronicon Henrici Knighton*, by Henry Knighton, and Thomas Walsingham's *Historia Anglicana*.[2] The chronicles are hostile to the rebels and likely do not provide reliable information about them, but they are the only surviving record of the rebel letters. The letters themselves are obscure in meaning, almost code-like, and were written by participants in the Rising for purposes that are unclear and remain a source of scholarly debate (see Green, "John Ball's Letters"; Justice, *Writing*; Hudson, "*Piers*"; Warner, "Plowman Traditions"). Only two letters explicitly mention Piers Plowman the character, though references to *Piers Plowman* the poem are arguably present in all the letters. When my students and I have finished studying Langland's poem, I give a short lecture about the Rising that explains the rebels and their aims. Then I share the complete text of the two letters that make explicit mention of Piers. First, from Walsingham's chronicle, a letter attributed to rebel and priest John Ball:

> Johon Schep, som tyme Seynte Marie prest of York, and now of Colchestre, greteth wel Johan Nameles, and Johan the Mullere, and Johon Cartere, and biddeth hem that thei bee war of gyle in borugh, and stondeth togidre in Godes name, and biddeth Peres Ploughman go to his werk, and chastise wel Hobbe the Robbere, and taketh with yow Johan Trewman and alle hiis felawes, and no mo, and loke schappe you to on heved, and no mo.
>
> Johan the Mullere hath ygrounde smal, smal, smal;
> The Kynges sone of hevene schal paye for al.
> Be war or ye be wo;
> Knoweth your freend fro your foo.
> Haveth ynow, and seith "Hoo!"
> And do wel and bettre, and fleth synne,
> And seketh pees, and hold you therinne.
> And so biddeth Johan Trewman and alle his felawes.
>
> (Dean, *Medieval English Political Writings* 135)

> John Shepherd, formerly a priest of St. Mary at York, now of Colchester, heartily greets John Nameless, John the Miller, and John Carter and urges them to beware of guile about town, and to stand together in God's name and tell Piers Plowman to go to work and chastise Hobbe the Robber. And take John Truman and all his friends with you, but no others, and follow only one leader.
>
> John the Miller has ground finely, finely, finely;
> The son of Heaven's King will redeem us all.
> Beware or be woeful;
> Know your friend from your foe.
> Know when you've had enough, and say so.
> And do well and better, and flee sin,
> And seek peace, and keep yourself therein.
> Thus bids John Truman and all his friends. (my trans.)

The second letter is from Knighton's chronicle and is attributed to one Jack Carter, likely a pseudonym:

> Jakke Carter prayes yowe alle that ye make a gode ende of that ye have begunnen, and doth wele and ay bettur and bettur, for at the evyn men heryth the day. For if the ende be wele, than is alle wele. Lat Peres the Plowman my brother duelle at home and dyght us corne, and I will go with yowe and helpe that I may to dyghte youre mete and youre drynke, that ye none fayle. Lokke that Hobbe Robbyoure be wele chastysed for lesyng of youre grace; for ye have gret nede to take God with yowe in alle youre dedes. For nowe is tyme to be ware.
>
> (137–38)
>
> Jack Carter asks you all to finish well what you started, and do well—in fact, always do better and better, because it is in the evening that men praise the day. For if it ends well, then all is well. Let my brother Piers Plowman stay home and harvest wheat for us, and I will go with you and help as I am able by supplying your food and drink, so that none of you falters. Make sure Hobbe the Robber is chastised for your fall from grace, since you really need God's presence in your deeds. For now is the time to beware.

These letters are admittedly enigmatic; it is uncertain what messages they hope to convey and even to whom they are addressed. And Piers's presence in them is remarkable. Anne Hudson has elegantly commented on the exceptional reuse of Langland's text, noting that "quotation of, or even reference to, a Middle English literary text *within a context entirely different from that for which it was originally written* is very rare" ("*Piers*" 86). Other scholars have doubted that the rebels mined Piers from Langland's text for use in the letters. Lawrence Warner, for example, argues that Piers existed as a folk figure long before Langland's text and that both the poem and the rebel letters therefore hark back to an earlier tradition ("Plowman Traditions" 199–200). Similarly, while Richard Firth Green does not explicitly address the use of Piers in the letters, he considers it likely that they draw on a number of popular and widely available sources, including texts in the tradition of social complaint, sermon collections, and mendicant teaching manuals ("John Ball's Letters" 189–91).[3] Green argues that this takes nothing away from the power of the letters, citing the possibility that, while they may be "entirely conventional" in content, "for some reason their very conventions, however pacific in origin, had become inflammatory by 1381" (189). Green's conclusion provides a useful framework for thinking about Piers specifically: it is indeed possible that the rebel letters and Langland drew on the same traditional folk material in their use of Piers. However, if the character of Piers was "entirely conventional," Langland gave that conventional character shape and definition, so that when the rebels made use of Piers, the character had the potential to mean something more specific. In short, if the figure of Piers "had become inflammatory by 1381," it was in large part due to Langland.[4]

I do not include the details of this debate about Piers's origins in my lesson.[5] Instead I begin with the assumption (made by many scholars) that the Piers visible in the rebel letters is Langland's Piers. I ask my students, What other characters leave the bounds of their narratives and become involved in current events? It is a surprisingly difficult question, because the situation does not arise often. My students' examples are typically from film or television and involve celebrities doing cameo appearances as themselves in fictional settings. Students recognize the shortcomings of their examples—the characters are not fictional but real individuals, and the settings in which they appear are not current events but fiction.

Here is where Superman's involvement in World War II enters the discussion. On comic book covers from the early 1940s, Superman is depicted playing a decisive role in World War II. In figure 1, a cover from December 1941, Superman startles a Nazi paratrooper in mid-air and appears ready to handily disarm him. In figure 2, on a cover from August 1943, Superman thwarts the mission of a Kamikaze pilot visibly reeling from the superhero's blows. A 1942 cover illustration featured Superman collaring Hitler and Hirohito singlehandedly; others depict him straddling torpedoes speeding toward enemy lines, engaging Axis soldiers on the battlefield, and even selling war bonds. And it was not just Superman who was pressed into service to fight the Axis; Batman, Robin, and Captain America did their part as well. In fact, the war was fought on American comic book covers before it was fought by American soldiers: a March 1941 cover

Figure 1. Cover of *Action Comics*, no. 43, Dec. 1941.

Figure 2. Cover of *Action Comics*, no. 63, Aug. 1943.

portrays Captain America punching out Hitler, while the United States did not enter the war until December 1941.

The stories in these comic books show superheroes engaging the Axis powers (or thinly veiled proxies for them) in settings at home and abroad. But I have not found it necessary to use the stories for this lesson; the comic book covers are enough to make the point. Like the mentions of Piers in the rebel letters, the comic book covers manage to insert their characters into real-world events with exceptional agility and in ways that make the characters' presence striking and memorable. Students easily see the parallel and recognize that it is approximate rather than exact; indeed, the approximation of the comparison is what makes it a fruitful pedagogical tool. The use of Piers in the rebel letters and of Superman on the comic book covers are similar enough to kindle discussion and inspire students to discover and explore distinctions between the two that enrich their understanding of both, but of Piers especially.

For example, students comment right away that Superman has the real-world event brought to him, represented in his text, while Piers is appropriated from Langland's text, extracted for use in the letters. Once they recognize this, students almost always ask if Langland approved of the rebels' use of Piers; I explain that, though we cannot know for sure, no evidence indicates that Langland had a hand in Piers's appearances in the rebel letters—and some evidence, most notably Langland's revisions of the poem, suggests that he was disturbed by (or at least unhappy about) the rebels' use of Piers.[6] Inevitably, students want to know what parts of the poem Langland revised. I find it most effective to turn the question back on them: if you were Langland, I ask, and someone hijacked Piers to support the Rising, what parts of the poem would you revise? Without exception, students identify the passages in passus 6 in which Piers organizes labor on the half acre. To a group of women asking how they can help, he gives these directions:

> Somme shal sowe sakke for shedyng of the whete.
> And ye lovely ladyes, with youre longe fyngres,
> That ye han silke and sendal to sowe whan tyme is
> Chesibles for chapelleynes cherches to honoure.
> Wyves and wydwes, wolle and flex spynneth;
> Maketh cloth, I conseille yow, and kenneth so yowre doughtres. (lines 9–14)
>
> Some shall sew sacks to stop the wheat from spilling.
> And you lovely ladies, with your long fingers,
> See that you have silk and sendal to sew when you've time
> Chasubles for chaplains for the Church's honor.
> Wives and widows, spin wool and flax;
> Make cloth, I counsel you, and teach the craft to your daughters.

And he commands a knight to

> . . . kepe Holi Kirke and myselve
> Fro wastoures and fro wykked men that [wolde me destruye].
> And go hunte hardiliche to hares and to foxes,
> To bores and to [buckes] that breketh adown myne hegges,
> And go affaite faucones wilde foules to kille
> For suche cometh to my croft and croppeth my whete. (27–32)

> . . . [champion] Holy Church and me
> Against wasters and wicked men who would destroy me.
> And go hunt hardily hares and foxes,
> Boars and bucks that break down my hedges,
> And have falcons at hand to hunt down the birds
> That come to my croft and crop my wheat.

Students point especially to the imperative verbs in these passages, aware of how these instructions—indeed, commands—draw attention to the dominant, governing role Piers takes in this scene.

Students also often point to Piers's harsh words to the priest in passus 7, specifically when Piers derides him as a "Lewed lorel" ("unlearned lout"; line 142). Interestingly, it is rare that students identify the passage perhaps closest in spirit to the events of the Great Rising: in passus 7, faced with the fact that his pardon is no pardon at all, "Piers for pure tene pulled it atweyne" ("Piers for pure wrath pulled it in two"; 119) and vows to "cessen of my sowying and swynk nought to harde, / Ne about my [bileve] so bisi be namore" ("cease my sowing and not work so hard / Nor be henceforth so busy about my livelihood"; 122–23). Piers's dispute in the text is with the false pardon, but when students are encouraged to think about the similarity of Piers's methods of protest to those of the rebels' they are able to see that this scene is even more inflammatory than the others they identified; like Piers in this passage, the rebels destroyed documents and refused to work. If time permits, it is useful to have students study the parallel passages in the C text (or the lack of parallels, where Langland excised passages altogether) to discuss how the poet revised passages that students identified as potentially attractive to the rebels.

Among the parts of the poem I assign, these passages are the ones in which Piers is most obviously out of order, conducting himself in interactions with others in surprising ways, given his rank as a lowly plowman. Students readily understand that his behavior advances the narrative of the poem, but, looking at Piers in these instances through the lens of the Superman comic book covers, they come to see him as the emblematic rallying figure—indeed, the superhero—that he seems to have been for the participants of the Rising. In class discussion, my student Jon N. commented that Piers is a "powerful ally" for the rebels precisely because he is a fictional character; as such, he is a well-defined symbolic figure. Similarly, my student Courtney G. suggested that by writing Piers into their letters the rebels make him "one of them" and employ him "to legitimize their cause," because "if there is a character who seems to espouse their ideals, then this is a real battle they're fighting, and it's worth fighting for."

What I have described above is just one thread of class discussion produced by this lesson plan; dialogue develops along different trajectories and bears different fruit depending on students' comments. The example I have provided here demonstrates that this lesson plan does its main job very well—after it, students don't see Piers simply as a religious figure, though they recognize that the religious valences of his character certainly enhanced his social capital in fourteenth-century England. But this lesson plan has often surprised me by accomplishing more than expected: it helps my students recognize Piers as a more fully defined figure in Langland's text and outside it. Put another way, my students are interested in what the rebels gain by using Piers in their letters but also in what Piers gains from appearing in them. My student Melissa G. made the point that Piers's appearance in the rebel letters "adds a narrative to his story," suggesting that his character has more dimensions than those presented in Langland's text. Scott D. agreed, adding that thanks to Piers's inclusion in the letters, he is not "locked in the literary" but is a character with "goals, for whom there are things yet to be done." Piers proves these students right. We went on to study the anonymous poem "Piers the Plowman's Crede" (Dean, *Six Ecclesiastical Satires* 1–50), in which Piers offers social and religious commentary to a hapless narrator, and also a section of the late-sixteenth-century poem *The Steele Glas*, by George Gascoigne, in which Piers is acclaimed as an ideal figure. I suspect that some students from that semester's class continue to peer into the texts they study for other courses or read for leisure, asking, like the dreamer in passus 18, "Is Piers in this place?" (line 21).

The comic book covers of Superman fighting Axis powers help my students understand what it meant for Piers, in *Piers Plowman* and beyond, that the rebels commandeered him from the pages of Langland's poem and deployed him in their letters. But the Piers-Superman analogy is not the point of the lesson—a more sophisticated understanding of Piers is. That the analogy is inexact not only fosters discussion but also helps the ancillary part of the comparison fall away more easily once it has served its purpose, leaving students to consider Piers in a new light.

NOTES

An earlier version of this paper was presented in May 2014 at the Forty-Ninth International Congress on Medieval Studies in the session Teaching *Piers Plowman*, which was sponsored by the International *Piers Plowman* Society. I am grateful to members of that session for our rich discussion and for their encouragement and useful feedback on this piece. Thanks also to Christopher Dreyer, who provided invaluable help with research; to Ellen Muehlberger for thinking with me about this lesson plan and about the composition as well as revision of this essay; to Ali Shapiro and Shannon Gayk for help with translations; and to my students, who play a vital role in every good lesson plan, among them especially Jamison Raymond, who introduced me to the Superman comics of World War II.

[1]I teach the B text of *Piers Plowman*, using the Norton Critical Edition (Robertson and Shepherd), from which this essay quotes.

[2]The letters are available in Dean, *Medieval English Political Writings* 135–39; Justice, *Writing* 13–15; and Green, "John Ball's Letters" 193–95. In *Medieval English Political Writings* Dean includes one additional letter from John Stow's late sixteenth-century *Annales*; for an account of the problems that have led other scholars to exclude this letter, see Green, "John Ball's Letters" 180–81.

[3]For a similar argument, see Kane, "Some Fourteenth-Century 'Political' Poems."

[4]Kirk, "Langland's Plowman," makes a similar point.

[5]I see the value of discussing Piers's origins with students and may choose to do so in the future. One promising way to work the scholarly discussion of Piers's potential folk origins into this lesson would be to compare it to the origins of comic book superheroes in the Jewish mystical figure of the golem, a point acknowledged by scholars who study comics but also by the creators of these characters. See, for instance, Weinstein; Hadju.

[6]For the sake of simplicity, I usually adhere to the theory that the chronological order of composition of the texts is A, B, C. In courses in which time allows, I explore with my students the scholarly debate about the order of composition, using several articles to give the lay of the land: Mann, "Power"; Hudson, "*Piers*"; Crane.

PIERS PLOWMAN IN LITERARY DIALOGUE

Teaching Langland and Dante

Lawrence Warner

The juxtaposition of Langland and Dante in the classroom, perhaps even more so than of Langland and Chaucer, sharpens our understanding of some central characteristics of *Piers Plowman*. This essay surveys the most pertinent instances: *Piers Plowman*'s and the *Commedia*'s dramatizations of a first-person protagonist who finds himself spiritually lost in his middle age, the innovative and even shocking roles that the pagan emperor Trajan plays in the spiritual economies of these poems, their contrasting approaches to the relation between allegory and history, and their exploitations of the tension between the vernacular and Latin. Such comparisons have a long history in the scholarship, but this essay ultimately parts ways from earlier treatments by focusing on the process by which Langland's verse form, quite in contrast to Dante's, invites correction and supplementation, whether by the poet himself (hence the existence of numerous versions of *Piers Plowman*) or by the later scribes and readers who produced the poetry and made it their own. In fact, to look at Langland's poetics in the light of Dante's is to recognize that many of the features that we take to be characteristically Langlandian—especially the seemingly open-ended and apocalyptic nature of the poem—might well be absent from the authorial version of what we have come to call the B version of *Piers Plowman*, being instead the products of these later supplements to the poem. This phenomenon is altogether impossible with the *Commedia*, but it raises the possibility that in many ways these two poets' views on the topics listed above were much closer to each other than they might appear if we assume that the surviving manuscripts of *Piers Plowman* B accurately reflect Langland's own vision.

Authorial Protagonists

The most immediate parallel between the two great poems is encapsulated in the title of John Burrow's essay "Langland *nel Mezzo del Cammin*," which alludes to the opening lines of the *Inferno* (1.1–3). The parallel with *Piers Plowman* is not in its prologue, but in the middle of the poem, where the personification Imaginatif tells the dreamer, "I have folwed thee, in feith, thise fyve and fourty wynter" ("I've followed you, in faith, these forty-five winters"; 12.3).[1] "Dante, at thirty-five, is exactly at the middle; Will, at forty-five, is at the end of the middle," observes Burrow. "Morally and spiritually, both have lost their way" (32). And both thus need guidance. Dante encounters three beasts—a leopard, lion, and she-wolf—which impede his progress (*Inf.* 1.31–54) and which early commentators identified as symbols of the three ages of man. Virgil comes to guide him out of the wood and through hell.

Likewise, in *Piers Plowman* Imaginatif claims to have followed the dreamer for many years, having moved him to "amende" his youthful wantonness "in thi myddel age" ("amend it in your middle age"; 12.4–9). Both protagonists, continues Burrow, "from the dubious vantage-point of middle age, see all three ages of human life pass before their eyes. Recapitulating and anticipating their own experience, this vision is, or should be, profoundly shocking and chastening" (32–33). What is striking, though, is not this catalog of similarities, but the remarkable divergence in the consequences of these situations: "Comparing Dante and Langland in this way, one is struck by a certain pointlessness in the English poet's portrait of his narrator in middle age—pointlessness, that is, within the overall plan of the work" (36). Dante's prologue issues in the entire *Commedia*; Langland's equivalent episode is in the middle of the poem and leads only to more confusion. Burrow's reading of this pointlessness—that "Langland was talking about himself" (39)—provides a helpful entry point to classroom discussions about the relation between literary conventions and historical referents, about medieval versus modern conceptions of authorship, and about the very idea that we might have access either to an "overall plan" or to "the work" as Langland conceived it—a topic to which this essay returns.

Trajan

More than for the (potential) self-portrait of the poet, passus 11 and 12 are notable for the memorable appearances of the Roman emperor Trajan. The story of Pope Gregory's tears for the virtuous Trajan, and the latter's subsequent salvation, had been a mainstay of hagiographical literature since the eighth century, a tradition that both Dante and Langland invoke to innovative ends. In *Piers Plowman* the dreamer has convinced himself that baptism is sufficient for salvation and that good works are therefore little needed. Then comes one of the most dramatic entries into this (or any other) poem: "'Ye, baw for bokes!' quod oon was broken out of helle" ("'Yeah? Bah for books,' said one who'd broken out of hell"; 11.140). It is Trajan, who will brook none of the dreamer's smug reliance on the sacraments and dismissal of good works. He points out that he "was ded and dampned to dwellen in pyne / For an uncristene creature" ("was dead and damned to dwell in torment / As an un-Christian creature"; 142–43) yet was eventually "saved, as ye may see, withouten syngynge of masses, / By love and by lernyng of my lyvynge in truthe" ("saved, as you may see, without singing of Masses, / By love and by his learning of my living in truth"; 150–51). In the following passus, Imaginatif elaborates: Trajan, though he "took nevere Cristendom," is nevertheless "saaf, so seith the book, and his soule in hevene" ("never took Christendom, / And he is safe, the book says, and his soul in Heaven"; 12.280–81).

The other major treatment of the Trajan legend in fourteenth-century vernacular literature is that in the *Commedia* (Vickers). In *Purgatorio*, canto 10, the pilgrim sees the "visibile parlare," the "speech made visible" of a sculpted frieze (line 95), in which episodes from the lives of King David, Trajan, and the Virgin Mary portray the figures' humility and devotion to duty (Dante). The emperor, en route to war, encounters a widow who seeks redress for her son's murder and refuses to wait till he returns from battle. Trajan submits to her wishes—and his duty. This is likewise the episode mentioned in *Paradiso* (20.43–48), where Trajan is the fifth part of the eyebrow of the eagle of justice; later the poem explains that Trajan had been condemned to hell for his unbelief (100–18), but, "tornata ne la carne, in che fu poco, / credette in lui che potëa aiutarla" ("back in his flesh for but a while, / believed in Him who had the power to help"; 113–14) and thus was saved. Langland, by contrast, makes no mention of the widow, nor of any "second life": Trajan was saved "Nought thorugh preiere of a pope but for his pure truthe" ("Not through prayer of a pope, but purely for his truth"; 11.155).

The pedagogical possibilities of various modes of comparison here—*Purgatorio* 10 with *Piers Plowman* 12, *Paradiso* 20 with *Piers Plowman* 11, both authors with their predecessors, and so on—are almost endless. In the context of the history of this legend, Gordon Whatley observes, what is innovative is that both poets "relocate the legend of emperor and pope against the backcloth of the 'just pagan' question and treat it (though with varying degrees of intensity) in a spirit of hostility toward the traditional ecclesiastical order" (42–43). But it is perhaps more useful, especially in a classroom setting, to examine how these figures work in the poems themselves. How does Trajan work in the economy of Dante's treatment of his classical poetic models such as Statius and especially Virgil? Why does Langland's Trajan break in so suddenly and dramatically? Such approaches are pertinent not only because of the vast amount of historical knowledge needed to assess Whatley's judgment regarding these poets' uses of their sources but also because Whatley's approach relies on the creation of categories of "orthodoxy" and "heterodoxy" that the poems themselves are interrogating and redefining (Grady, "*Piers*" 67n7).

Rather than get caught up in such theological questions, students might profitably compare each poem's treatment of Trajan as a historical figure. Frank Grady argues that in *Piers Plowman* "[t]he value and affection assigned to classical models like Trajan precedes and enables attempts to rectify doctrinal incongruities, and it is in a sense of historical intelligibility and not theological coherence that an understanding of the saved pagan emperor is grounded" ("*Piers*" 77). The most fruitful classroom discussions on the topics suggested above—how Dante's and Langland's figures of Trajan work in their poems—provide excellent means out of the traps laid by any approach that accepts the terms in which Will and Dante question who deserves to be saved. To invoke theological norms that the poems supposedly violate (e.g., that pre-Christian souls cannot be saved) is to do injustice to the aims of these poems and to risk alienating most modern students, for whom such norms render medieval literature unpalatable, if not unintelligible.

When one broadens the comparison between the *Commedia* and *Piers Plowman* beyond the local figure of Trajan, capacious though he is, important differences between the poems' allegorical and historical visions come into sharp focus. As Grady observes about the Middle English poem, "it is curious and compelling that in a poem populated by ahistorical personifications (like Conscience and Mede) and transhistorical figures (like Christ), Trajan is the only character with a historical reality" (76). The *Commedia*, by contrast, is bursting with historical figures, a contrast that helps us appreciate Langland's approach. "Where Dante surrounds his historical beings with other historical beings, giving them their symbolic force through the allegorical setting in which they are found," argues Howard Schless, "Langland surrounds his personifications with fictionalized human beings or allegorical types, achieving an immediacy by placing them in a background drawn from the daily life of the England of his day" (131).

A student might consider any given personification or figure who appears more than once in *Piers Plowman* and the context in which he or she appears—a good example is Piers himself, who appears, among other roles, as a humble worker (passus 6), a figure for Saint Peter or even for Christ (15.212), the humanity of Christ (18.21–59), and ultimately the object of Conscience's final pilgrimage (20.386)—in comparison with Dante's vision of history. For, as Schless continues, "as opposed to Dante, who wants to show the historical representative of a quality in an eternal condition, Langland wants to show the eternal quality realistically in this historical, representative world" (133). Trajan, that is, represents, in heaven, a virtue (humility) to which the pilgrim and reader should aspire; the figures on the fair field of folk in Langland's prologue or those who want to go to the pub rather than plow the half acre in passus 6 could well be our neighbors in the here and now. Langland's vision is partial and cumulative; Dante's is eternal and, to a large degree, synecdochic, as any given figure embodies a grander truth that participates in the Godhead.

Latin and the Vernacular

A similar contrast comes into focus when we attend to another remarkable feature: each poet's use of Latin in his vernacular poem. In *Purgatorio* and *Paradiso*, Latin mostly occurs in single lines of the poem that rhyme with the surrounding Italian lines (E. P. Nolan 54), such as at *Purgatorio*, canto 29, lines 1–3:

> Cantando come donna innamorata,
> continüò col fin di sue parole:
> "Beati quorum tecta sunt peccata!"
>
> After she had finished speaking
> like a lady touched by love she sang:
> "Beati quorum tecta sunt peccata!"

The Latin, "blessed are those whose sins are covered," a shortened version of (Vulgate) Psalm 31.1, represents an "iconic presence of the timeless in the schemes of time" that "is a working figure of the figural relation itself as well as a demonstration of its validity and power. Embedded Latin functions here as a radical apex of discourse, a figure of *Logos* itself" (E. P. Nolan 54).

Latin is much more pervasive in *Piers Plowman* than in the *Commedia* and as a result serves many more functions. There are certainly moments where Langland's Latin, like Dante's, brings the eternal into the here and now. The peaceful end of the debate of the Four Daughters of God, after which Will awakens and urges his wife and daughter to reverence the cross at church on Easter morning, cites the Psalms as well as a liturgical hymn:

> "Thow seist sooth," seide Rightwisnesse, and reverentliche hire kiste,
> Pees, and Pees hire, *per secula seculorum.*
> *Misericordia et Veritas obviaverunt sibi; Iusticia et Pax osculate sunt.*
> Truthe trumpede tho and song *Te Deum laudamus*;
> And thanne lutede Love in a loud note,
> "*Ecce quam bonum et quam iocundum . . .*" (18.422–25*a*)
>
> "You speak the truth," said Righteousness, and reverently kissed her,
> Peace, and Pease her, *per saecula saeculorum*
> *Mercy and Truth have met together; Righteousness and Peace have kissed each other.*
> Truth sounded a trumpet then and sang *Te Deum Laudamus*;
> And then Love strummed a lute with a loud note:
> *Behold how good and how pleasant, etc.*

In this passage, as in many others, the scriptural quotations "do not merely bolster [Langland's] line of thought, but help to produce it," comments Fiona Somerset, in the most comprehensive survey of Langland's Latin ("Al þe comonys" 111). Righteousness's verse from Psalm 84:11, "Mercy and Truth have met together; Righteousness and Peace have kissed each other," that is, has generated the drama in which the abstractions of that verse, incarnated as the Four Daughters of God, embrace.

E. Peter Nolan focuses on such "reciprocal glossing" in his discussion of *Piers Plowman* (54). Yet, as Somerset has shown, Latin is not merely a monolithic discourse that serves to authorize the poet's theology. "Even when we are reading Middle English, and especially when we are reading Middle English as perfused with Latin as that of *Piers Plowman*," Somerset observes, "variations within Latinity provide a whole realm of reference, shared between writers and to a more limited extent their readers, in which style, genre, and register can become figures for institutionally specific kinds of knowledge, authority, and power" (115–16). A comparison of the iconic, apodictic mode of Latin in the *Purgatorio*, as cited above, with, for instance, the exchange among the lunatic, the angel of heaven who speaks in Latin, and the commoners who cry out in a verse of Latin (prol. 123–43),[2] or with Anima's explanation of his various names (15.23–39*a*)—*Anima*, *Animus*, *Mens*, *Memoria*—would be especially fruitful to heighten students' awareness of the dramatic possibilities inherent in languages that might otherwise seem entirely foreign to them.

Finally, and crucially, let us consider verse form and the question of readerly participation. Whereas, as Nolan points out, the Latin of *Purgatorio* and *Paradiso* "comes . . . in single lines which rhyme (more than phonetically) with the Italian in which they are embedded" (54), most Latin lines in *Piers Plowman*, as Somerset says, "are generally in prose rather than in verse: single words and even sometimes short phrases"—such as "*per secula seculorum*" and "*Te Deum laudamus*" above—"are incorporated into Langland's vernacular alliterative meter just as if they were English words; but half-lines, full lines, or quotations too long to occupy a single line typically stand apart from the alliterative meter in the prose of their source" (135). One register of this difference is the editorial practice of citing stand-alone Latin lines in *Piers Plowman* as separate from the lineage of the English. "*Ecce quam bonum et quam iocundum*" is line 18.425*a*, in recognition that it is not part of the surrounding English verses' alliterative meter or syntax. In the *Commedia*, by contrast, Italian and Latin are integral: the verse form of terza rima (ABA, BCB, CDC, DED, etc.) does not allow for additions or alterations (Freccero).

The same applies to Langland's English verse form: since alliterative long-line poetry does not employ terminal rhyme, one could in theory supplement any given passage. Many readers did just that, most famously John But, who added an indeterminate number of lines—perhaps the entire surviving passus 12—to his copy of *Piers Plowman* A. Scribes could easily copy whole passages in the wrong place or overlook them entirely: the group of thirty-odd lines at passus 15, lines 532–68, for instance, is absent from one B version manuscript group, and put in the wrong place in the other group.[3] Scribes also combined passages from what we now call the various versions of *Piers Plowman*, the most notable instance of which is Huntington Library MS HM 114 (sigil Ht), a fifteenth-century copy that conflates passages from A, B, and C.

I want to make two points about this characteristic of *Piers Plowman*. One is simply its absence from the reception history of the *Commedia*, in large part because of the *terza rima* verse form. The tradition of commentary on Dante's poem—which arose almost instantly—treats the poem like a sacred text (Wallace, "Assessing"). The second point, though, strikes at the heart of a question that should arise for all students and teachers of literature, especially something as evasive as *Piers Plowman*: that of ontology. The B text, to which most critics quoted above refer, "ends in disorder and final sorrow" (E. P. Nolan 53), is a text in which "the job of understanding can never be over" (Schless 139), and is a text whose Latin registers "the dissonance and discontinuity that perhaps more frequently characterizes Langland's poem" than do the integrative possibilities celebrated at fleeting moments in the poem (Somerset, "Al þe comonys" 111).

That is, it is a poem that ends with Conscience departing the collapsing Holy Church Unity and seeking out Piers the Plowman (20.381–87). And yet it seems possible—in my mind, almost certain—that the final two passus, which appear nearly identical in the B and C traditions, entered the latter from the former because of the scribal impulse for complete copies of the poem, instead of remaining unrevised for whatever reason between B and C (Warner, *Lost History* 49–61). If this is so, then Langland's copy of B, and any now lost manuscript tradition that it might have generated, ended after the resolution of the debate among the Four Daughters of God, with Will awake on Easter morning, in a positive, ordered, joyful manner—one in which the relevant adjectives begin with *con-* (conclusive, consonant, continuous) rather than the *dis-* mode to which we have become so accustomed. It was, that is, a much different poem from the one we have been studying for centuries: one much closer to Dante's vision, which might have ended as well on Easter morning 1300 (if he departed on Friday, 8 April, rather than two weeks earlier).[4]

Whether or not my proposal is correct, considering it as a possibility might encourage students to leave behind the notion that the poem they are studying is equivalent to the words printed in whatever edition they have at hand. More particularly, it will raise their awareness to the ways in which poetry's form in many ways constitutes its meaning. In *Piers Plowman* B, whether it ended with Will celebrating Easter or Conscience seeking Piers, this meaning includes the reader and thus takes to its very limit Dante's opening promise that his poem concerns "nostra vita" ("our life"; *Inf.* 1.1).

NOTES

[1] Quotations of *Piers Plowman* are from Schmidt's edition of the B text (Schmidt, Vision) and translations are from Donaldson's *Alliterative Verse Translation*.

[2] This passage is discussed by William Rogers in this volume. See also Somerset, "Al þe comonys" 117–26; E. Peter Nolan 53–54.

[3] See Schmidt, Vision 397 (note to lines 503–09, 528–31). For a different perspective, see Warner, *Lost History* 32–44.

[4] See Hollander's commentary to *Inf.* 1.1, available at the *Princeton Dante Project* (Dante).

Teaching Langland's and Chaucer's Prologues

Lawrence M. Clopper

I teach Langland's *Piers Plowman* in a variety of course formats at the undergraduate and graduate levels. Undergraduate courses include the survey of English literature to 1600 as well as an advanced-level Middle English literature course. At the graduate level, *Piers* may be taught in our lower-level colloquia, which aim at some kind of historical coverage, as well as in seminars organized around a variety of themes. No matter the format, I generally teach Langland's prologue after or in conjunction with Chaucer's because Chaucer's is the simpler of the two and can be used to introduce the trifunctional model on which both are based.

As Georges Duby has shown, the late Middle Ages asserted a trifunctional social structure—there are those who pray, those who fight, and those who labor—despite the fact that this construct did not adequately describe the situation either when it was first formulated or at any subsequent time. Many medieval people were aware of the inadequacy of the categories: where do merchants fit? and women? Chaucer has his persona tell us that he described the pilgrims as best he could in the order of their degree, but the statement itself attests to the inadequacy of the model he was using and accounts, I think, for the contentious atmosphere in which the storytelling is carried out.

One reason that the model was inadequate is that its initial formulator, Bishop Adalbero of Laon, and the person for whom he devised it, King Robert the Pious, were not particularly interested in members of the third estate, the laborers. Adalbero's formulation came about because Robert (purportedly) asked him to describe the relation of powers between the ruler and his bishops, who were to be his advisers. Adalbero, naturally, put bishops, those who pray, first. The ruler was under the tutelage of his bishops. This ordering—those who pray, those who fight, those who labor—is the most common in the late medieval period if for no other reason than that the clergy are the most likely to wield the formula.

I emphasize to my students that this theoretical construct was invented primarily to elaborate the relations between the two ruling estates. At some point, usually after we have read Chaucer's General Prologue, I sketch out the implications of the placement of the three orders, emphasizing the strong binary of laity and clergy. The demarcation insists on the learning and the purity (celibacy) of the clergy, which distinguishes it from the laity, whose members lack learning and are stained by sexual engagement—they are *lewed men*, from which the term *laymen* derives. After pointing out that the clergy are anointed (set aside through a ritual), I assert that the aristocracy's ritual of knighting constitutes a competition for power with the clergy. But the third estate, which I call the commons (that is, the most numerous), is distinguished from both clergy and aristocracy by its lack of anointing rituals and by being stained by sexuality and by labor. By the time we have gone through the portraits from the Knight to the Parson to the Plowman, we have a sketch like this:

LAYPEOPLE	CLERGY
Aristocracy	
Knight	Prioress
Squire	Monk
(Yeoman/servant)	Friar
Commons	
Merchant	Clerk
Sergeant of the Law	
Franklin	
Five Guildsmen	
Their Cook	
Shipman	
Doctor of Physic	
Wife of Bath	
Plowman	Parson
THE TAIL	
Miller	Summoner
Manciple	Pardoner
Reeve	

First, it is important to note that Chaucer does not begin with those who pray; he gives priority to those who fight. This is not particularly surprising. Chaucer is a layman closely associated with the aristocracy. Consequently, he is aware of who has power in his world.

Next, I emphasize that the Plowman and Parson are at the bottom of their respective hierarchies and that, as a result, Chaucer's audience probably assumed that his anatomy of medieval society was completed when he reached these two figures. But then we have the group of rascals ("the tail" in the sketch), which is marked by the binary between the laity and clergy.

I also treat the sequence Wife of Bath, Parson, and Plowman. It is a puzzle that the Wife of Bath should appear so late in the prologue. Her status, the wealth she has accumulated, the prosperous town she comes from, and her position in the parish as indicated by her assumption that she should be first in church to make her offering all suggest that her placement in the hierarchy should be around the level of the merchant. Does she appear where she does because she is a woman, and the trifunctional model is inadequate? I think not. The first thing we are told about the Wife of Bath is that she is a great cloth-maker. Of the ideal Plowman we are told that he performs honest labor; he is a "trewe swinkere" who "dyke[s] and delve[s]" ("an honest laborer" who "makes ditches and digs"; L. D. Benson, *Riverside Chaucer*, 1.531, 536). These terms tip us off to the significance of these portraits. In contemporary representations of the Fall narrative in plays and retellings, we are told that Adam's punishment is that he is to "swinke and swete" ("work and sweat"), to "dike and delve." Eve, on the other hand, is represented pictorially and verbally as weaving clothing to cover her and Adam's nakedness.[1] The Parson, whose portrait comes between these representations of Eve and Adam, is an idealized figure based on Christ's parable of the good shepherd and certain reformist ideas from the late fourteenth century. Visually, the Parson stands between Eve (Wife of Bath) and Adam (Plowman). The Parson is the intermediary but also the mediator; he is the one who can help redeem fallen humankind. But the other implication of the Eve-Adam figures at the bottom of the hierarchy is that the hierarchy—those who pray, those who fight, and those who labor—is a consequence of the Fall. The entire social structure came about because of sin.

In Langland's prologue (lines 13–122) we encounter an entirely different world: "A fair feeld ful of folk fond I þer bitwene / Of alle man*er*e of men, þe meene and þe riche, / Werchynge and wandrynge as þe world askeþ" ("A fair field full of folk I found between them, / Of human beings of all sorts, the high and the low, / Working and wandering as the world requires"; prol. 17–19).[2] Langland begins with neither those who pray nor those who fight but those who labor. And those who wander, a category that does not immediately come to mind as the opposite of those who work. I first ask my students to think about what the categories of working and wandering designate. I have them sort the people mentioned in the first part of the prologue into workers and wanderers. But I also try to make them think about what these terms mean literally and figuratively. For example, does working mean that one performs manual labor? The lines immediately following the initial distinction suggests not:

> Some putten hem to plouȝ, pleiden ful selde,
> In settynge and sowynge swonken ful harde;
> Wonnen þat [þise] wastours w*ith* glotonye destruyeþ.
> And so*m*me putten hem to pride, apparailed hem þ*er*after,
> In contenaunce of cloþynge comen d[is]gised.
> In preires and penaunc[e] putten hem manye,
> Al for loue of oure lord lyueden [wel] streyte
> In hope [for] to haue heueneriche blisse.
> As Ancres and heremites þ*a*t holden hem in hire selles,
> Coueiten noȝt in contree to [cairen] aboute
> For no likerous liflode hire likame to plese. (lines 20–30)

Some applied themselves to plowing, played very rarely,
Sowing seeds and setting plants worked very hard;
Won what wasters gluttonously consume.
And some pursued pride, put on proud clothing.
Came all got up in garments garish to see.
To prayers and penance many put themselves.
All for love of our Lord lived hard lives,
Hoping thereafter to have Heaven's bliss—
Such as hermits and anchorites that hold to their cells,
Don't care to go cavorting about the countryside,
With some lush livelihood delighting their bodies.

These lines provide some keys to Langland's analysis. Workers are those who perform manual labor; wanderers are gluttons who destroy what laborers produce. But wanderers are also defined as exemplars of the sin of pride. Then Langland redefines workers as anchorites and hermits who are good because they do not wander. They do not covet, they do not "cairen aboute" ("go cavorting about," with a pun on *care* and *caro* ["flesh"]), which leads to the next line, they do not engage in a "likerous liflode" ("lush livelihood") to please their bodies.

By this point, we know that workers are manual laborers but also those, like the anchorites and hermits, who simply fulfill whatever function they have chosen. Merchants apparently can fall into the category of worker, though in the pardon sent to Piers later we find out that there are certain conditions merchants must meet. Wanderers might be people who travel about—like the great "lobies" ("lubbers"; "layabouts"; line 55) who are contrasted with the hermits who remain in their cells (53–57)—but wanderers are also any people who sin (the proud, the covetous, and the like). In other words, you do not have to move your feet to be a wanderer.

Having arrived at the top of the secular side of workers who represent the commons (plowman to merchant), Langland throws in another polysemous occupation, the minstrel:

And so*m*me murþes to make as Mynstralles konne,
And getten gold w*ith* her glee [gilt]lees, I leeue.
Ac Iaperes and Iangeleres, Iudas children,
[Fonden] hem fantasies and fooles hem makeþ,
And han wit at wille to werken if [hem liste]. (lines 33–37)

And some make mirth as minstrels can
And get gold for their music, guiltless, I think,
But jokers and word jugglers, Judas' children,

Invent fantasies to tell about and make fools of themselves,
And have whatever wits they need to work if they wanted.

Langland makes a distinction between minstrels who honestly earn their welfare—thus they are workers—as opposed to those who do not. The distinction between good and bad minstrels is not fully revealed here, though it becomes a major issue as the poem develops. Nevertheless, we can deduce that bad minstrels are wanderers who tell japes, janglers, and Judas's children. They pretend; they make themselves appear to be fools to avoid labor. Of course, all sorts of minstrels took to the road, so Langland's point seems not to be that minstrels move about but that the kind of labor they perform defines them as workers or as wanderers. Later we find out that "goddes minstrales" ("God's minstrels"; 13.439) are, among other things, those who can read the Gospels to others and those who are themselves poor, ill, and need to be provided for (13.436–48).

In the prologue Langland then turns to describe groups in the wandering category: bidders and beggars, pilgrims and palmers, unholy hermits, bad friars and "faitours" ("tricksters"; 2.183) and pardoners. These are all people who could labor for their needs but, in various ways, go wandering about—sometimes quite literally. The prologue has been turning toward the clerical orders but Langland does this decisively at line 83, when he begins at the bottom of the clerical hierarchy—"[p]*er*sons and parisshe preestes" ("[p]arsons and parish priests")—and continues to bishops, clerics holding secular office, servants of lords, cardinals, and finally the pope (83–111).

At this crucial point Langland invokes the trifunctional image:

Thanne kam þ*er* a kyng; kynȝthod hym ladde;
Might of þe co*m*munes made hym to regne.
And þanne cam kynde wit and clerkes he made
For to counseillen þe kyng and þe co*m*mune saue.
The kyng and knyȝthod and clergie boþe
Casten þ*a*t þe co*m*mune sholde [hire communes] fynde.
The co*m*mune contreued of kynde wit craftes,
And for p*ro*fit of al þe peple Plowmen ordeyned.
To tilie and to t*ra*uaille as trewe lif askeþ.
The kyng and þe co*m*mune and kynde wit þe þridde
Shopen lawe and leaute, ech [lif] to knowe his owene. (lines 112–22)

Then there came a king, knighthood accompanied him,
Might of the community made him a ruler.
And then came Kind Wit, and he created clerks
To counsel the king and keep commons safe.
The king in concert with knighthood and the clergy as well

Contrived that the commons should provide their commons for them.
The commons with Kind Wit contrived various crafts,
And for profit of all the people appointed plowmen
To till and to toil as true life requires.
The king and the commons and Kind Wit the third
Defined law and lewte—for every kind of life, known limits.

The first things we notice about this passage are the order—those who fight come first—and the mixture of the names of the estates—king and knighthood, clergy, and commons—with a faculty personification—Kynde Wit. In general the statement is traditional: there are three estates, and each has its function in society. The second line throws in an interesting complication: the king rules by might of the commons. This might sound rather startling to the modern ear, but in fact this is a legal maxim expressed in the coronation ritual: the commons must acclaim the new monarch. But I think Langland wants to emphasize that legitimate kingship is founded on the goodwill of the commons (the point is reasserted at 4.182). The second complication is the introduction of the personification Kynde Wit. At a literal level, Kynde Wit seems to be a name for a bishop, because only a bishop can "make clerks" and it is the traditional role of the bishop to advise the king and to save the commons. But the usage also implies some innate understanding that bishops are needed in society to carry out these activities.

The formulation continues in the traditional way: the two ruling powers determine that the commons, the laborers, should provide the needs of all three estates. This assertion is a reminder that neither clergy nor knights are expected to soil their bodies by labor. But Langland again foregrounds the role of the commons. The line "The co*m*mune contreued of kynde wit craftes" has a double meaning: since we earlier read Kynde Wit as an allegorical name for a bishop, we may read this line to mean that the bishop devised crafts for the commons (perhaps following up from the preceding line). But that does not entirely make sense. The line also has an empowering meaning: the commons, by their own natural abilities, contrived crafts necessary for the functioning of society. It is the next line that delivers the knockout: the commons for the profit of all the people ordained plowmen. I have never encountered a like statement in any text that delineates the three-estates theory. It is purely Langland; he alone could conceive that a member of the third estate could be ordained. The sanctification of the plowman is, of course, crucial to Langland's theological and political effort, but the point here is that the plowman, through ordination, as it were, enters into the competition for power that is normally restricted to the two ruling estates.

The last two lines of the passage reassert the traditional position that there are three estates (but still with the double play on "kynde wit"), that each has its function, and that the well-being of the community depends on their mutual cooperation.

A map of Langland's prologue shows how complicated his analysis is (fig. 1). The statement of the trifunctional image at lines 112–22 would look like this:

LAY	CLERICAL
King, Knights	Kynde Wit, Clergy
Plowmen	

Langland fits the trifunctional image within his distinction between workers and wanderers. Workers, like good minstrels, may be either laypeople or clergy. Wanderers are people who deviate in some way from whatever it was they were called to do. Friars are wanderers when they are "faitours," that is, deceivers, especially with regard to begging. But the implication of Langland's analysis is that friars who are itinerant (that is, wanderers) are workers if they perform their apostolic obligations without deception or hypocrisy. When Langland comes to the hierarchy of the secular clergy—parsons to the pope—he assigns them as workers or wanderers, according to however they fulfill their calling. Cardinals, for example, who "in hir holynesse" ("in their holiness"; 19.421) remain in Rome "as hir rule wole þe relikes to kepe" ("as their rule directs, to watch over relics"; 423), are workers, whereas those sent by the pope and "coome among þe comune peple" ("come among the common people"; 420), the latter of whom must "for hir comunes paieþ / For hir pelure and palfreyes mete and pilours þat hem folweþ" ("pay the cost of their provisions, / Of their furs and their palfreys' food, and the pillagers that follow them"; 414–15), are wanderers in several senses.

Langland preserves the first-level binarism between laity and clergy and also the distinction on the lay side between the ruling estate and the commons, but the important binarism for

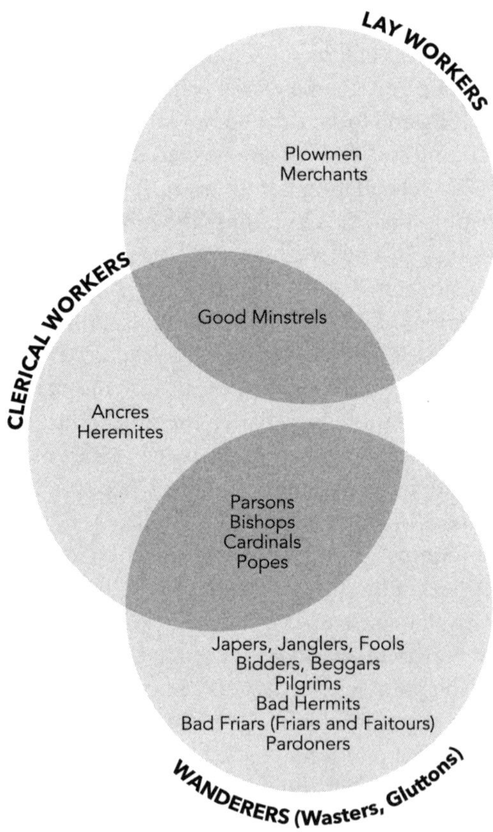

Figure 1

him is that between workers and wanderers in all of the estates. The most significant deviation from the traditional trifunctional image, however, is that he puts plowmen first and centers the hierarchy on the issue of labor—whatever labor that may be. Langland's hierarchy is morally, not socially, based. It values labor over power or status.

Reading Chaucer's and Langland's prologues together—to say nothing of the rest of *The Canterbury Tales* and any version of *Piers Plowman*—offers many such opportunities to explore often subtle and striking distinctions that students may articulate in discussions, schematic and visual presentations, and comparative essays. The social roles imagined by each poem, including ideas of rectitude and apparent rivalries, along with ideas of labor and gender, present further topics, any of which may be concentrated on members of a single group. Other topics reside in the satiric mode of each poem, with Langland's emphasis on the plural and corporate compared with Chaucer's foregrounding of individual pilgrims in their respective invocations of estates satire. The formal differences in dialect and in rhyming versus alliterative verse offer still more possibilities; elucidating what is allegory in Langland, but not in Chaucer, is yet another. Although both prologues clearly make use of a trifunctional social model with a deep medieval tradition (and much deeper cultural roots), each poet invokes the model toward intriguingly complex ends to open his respective, ambitious work.

NOTES

[1]For example, Thomas Walsingham, a monk of St. Albans Abbey, writes in his *Chronica Maiora* that the priest John Ball, a leader of the Great Rising of 1381, preached an incendiary sermon to some 200,000 common people at Blackheath, beginning with the words, "Whan Adam dalf, and Eve span, / Wo was þanne a gentilman?" ("When Adam delved, and Eve span, / Who was then a gentleman?"; Taylor et al. 546–47). In the York Corpus Christi play of the Fall, Dominus (the Lord) says, "Adam and Eve alsoo, yhe / In erthe than shall ye swete and swynke / And travayle for youre foode" ("Adam and Eve also, / in the earth you shall sweat and work / and labor for your food"; Davidson, "Play Five," lines 160–62).

[2]This essay cites Kane and Donaldson's edition of the B version of *Piers Plowman* and Donaldson's translation of the B version.

The Early Modern Plowman in the Classroom

Sarah A. Kelen

> There can be no doubt that some works are felt to have stood the Test of Time better than others. The Test of Time is not simply pass/fail. One of the severest examiners is Time itself. Is it therefore possible to receive a C-minus on the Test of Time? Well, the equivalent.
>
> —William H. Gass, "The Test of Time"

Has *Piers Plowman* stood the test of time? The very existence of this volume suggests that the answer is a qualified yes. In its own day *Piers Plowman* was clearly well known: it gave rise to a genre of protest literature (Barr 1–13; Dean, *Medieval English Political Writings* 243–50) and its language and imagery were appropriated by the laborers of the Great Rising of 1381 (Justice, *Writing* 102–39). Despite its political and literary centrality in the late fourteenth century, however, today *Piers Plowman* is a work read primarily by specialists. Given the poem's lack of contemporary name recognition, it might seem perverse to introduce the early modern reception of *Piers Plowman* into the undergraduate classroom. Who cares what some obscure sixteenth-century scholar thought of a dusty, old fourteenth-century poem, anyway?

By exploring the reception of a medieval work beyond its own period, students can begin to understand the aesthetic and cultural values that guided post-medieval reading, thus understanding better those subsequent literary cultures. Moreover, analyzing the forces that shaped successive judgments on a work's literary value can allow students to see the cultural forces guiding their own value judgments as well as the historically situated context of canon formation (Graff). In particular, the early modern reception and imitations of *Piers Plowman* demonstrate that the literary culture of a period extends beyond works written in that period to include the antecedent works known within a community of writers and readers.

In this essay I outline some ideas for using the early modern history of *Piers Plowman* to expand students' understanding, giving options for a lower-level early British literature survey course and for an upper-level undergraduate course on early modern literature and culture. Undergraduates typically get limited exposure to medieval and early modern literature, so it is hard to resist the temptation to race through as many texts as possible. This essay operates from the premise that students learn more by studying fewer texts from more angles than they do from a necessarily more cursory look at a greater number of texts.

Early Modern Piers Plowman *in a British Literature Survey Course*

Students often first encounter medieval literature in a survey of medieval and early modern British literature. Such courses (and the textbooks that support them) highlight a few greatest hits of each era but rarely address how those works became canonical. *Sir Gawain and the Green Knight*, selections from *The Canterbury Tales*, and excerpts from *Piers Plowman* might all represent the late fourteenth century in a survey course, but those works had different audiences both in their own period and in the centuries between their composition and their appearance in the classroom. Introducing students to the early modern reception of medieval texts alongside early modern literature can foster students' broader understanding of literary history, of the cultural context of aesthetics, and of the literary values that influenced early modern texts.

For *Piers Plowman*, the reception history is both complicated and enriched by the simultaneous presence of texts in the Piers Plowman tradition from the fourteenth through sixteenth centuries—texts that borrowed from, built upon, hid behind, modified, or otherwise responded to the literary archetype of the allegorical plowman (Barr; Kelen, *Langland's Early Modern Identities*; Walker). For early modern readers and editors, the works of the Piers Plowman tradition are often intertwined with the reception of Chaucer (Cummings 844–49; Walker; Warner, "Vision"). By the sixteenth century Chaucer had already been elevated to his position as the "father of English literature" (Lerer, *Chaucer* 3). Yet even when the character of Piers the Plowman was not assimilated into the Chaucer tradition, *Piers Plowman* was far more significant in the early modern period than one might today suspect. Manuscript evidence makes it clear that *Piers Plowman* maintained its readership well into the sixteenth century, independent of Robert Crowley's three 1550 editions and the 1561 reprint by Owen Rogers (Warner, "Vision" 116–17). Wendy Scase has argued that readers of *Piers Plowman* both influenced and responded to sixteenth-century political polemics ("*Dauy Dycars Dreame*" 183, 187).

Many sixteenth-century readers of *Piers Plowman* saw in it a foreshadowing of the Protestant Reformation (King; Kelen, *Langland's Early Modern Identities*). In 1549 the Protestant polemicist, dramatist, and literary historian John Bale notoriously ascribed the poem, which he called "Petrum Agricolam," to the fourteenth-century theologian John Wycliffe, who was understood in the sixteenth century to be a harbinger of the Reformation (Bale, *Illustrium*). In his 1557 revised history of British writers, Bale no longer directly credits Wycliffe with *Piers Plowman* but asserts that the poem's author, whom he calls Robert Langland, was "ex primis Ioannis Uuicleui discipulis unum" ("one of the first disciples of John Wycliffe"; Bale, *Scriptorum* 474; my trans.). Bale's linking of *Piers Plowman* and Wycliffite theology established an interpretive template for the sixteenth-century reception of the medieval work.

If students' exposure to *Piers Plowman* comes from the selections in the standard teaching anthologies, the early modern idea of Langland as Wycliffite, or even as proto-Protestant, would be hard to grasp. The ninth edition of *The Norton Anthology of English Literature* includes half a dozen selections from both the B and C texts of the poem (Greenblatt 373–95). In all the Norton passages, the theology is quite orthodox for the late fourteenth century. In a passage from the B text, passus 5, for example, Piers advocates the veneration of saints in his directions to St. Truth (380–83).

The *Norton Anthology*'s primary competitor, the *Longman Anthology of British Literature* (Damrosch), situates Piers within an oppositional tradition, but in the realm of politics rather than of religion. The *Longman Anthology* emphasizes the poem's political content and context by including a cluster of readings titled "*Piers Plowman* and Its Time" (468–80), which contains selections from contemporary texts about the Rising of 1381, including a selection from the supposed Letter of John Ball preserved in a monastic chronicle. In this English text, putatively a missive sent by the priest John Ball to incite the rebels, Ball "biddeth Pers ploughman/ go to his werk" (475). The *Longman Anthology*'s inclusion of Piers's attempt to order his community in passus 8 (Damrosch 451–56) also situates the text as exemplifying contemporary political philosophy rather than theology.

Because of the allegorical and generic instability of *Piers Plowman*, it's possible for a given set of excerpts to reveal different poems (Justice, "Genres"), but a reader would be hard-pressed to find a Protestant author lurking within the *Norton* or *Longman* selections. Even the tearing of the pardon (included in the *Norton* but not the *Longman*) does not particularly support a Protestantizing interpretation. A Protestant (or Lollard) plowman would indeed reject the efficacy or necessity of a papal pardon, but in this passage Piers's tearing of the pardon is not an outright rejection of pardons but comes from Piers's assessment of it as no pardon (McLeod).

In the process of excerpting *Piers Plowman* for anthologies, twenty-first-century editors choose which poem to present to readers: the theological treatise, the reformist polemic, the allegorical parable, or the social realist satire. There are obviously good reasons for any of these interpretations, but a selection of excerpts that brings forward one of these options unavoidably suppresses others. Showing students selections of *Piers Plowman* unlike those they have already read in their anthology can demonstrate the extent to which editors shape the work by their selections as well as by their headnotes.

If an institution has library access to the Early English Books Online database (EEBO), students can easily access a transcription of the prologue from Crowley's 1550 second edition of the poem, *The vision of pierce Plowman nowe the second time imprinted.* The two pages of the prologue appear as "[leaf motif] The printer to the Reader" and "The Prologe" in the table of contents for the EEBO transcription. Students could compare Crowley's commentary on the poem's style and its highlights to the editorial framing provided by the textbook used in the course.

If reception and the ongoing process of canon formation is a central topic of the course, students could also read the introduction to the "Plowman Writings" section of James M. Dean's *Medieval English Political Writings* to learn about the early-fifteenth-century satirical texts that succeeded *Piers Plowman* (243–50). The authors of these texts interpret Langland's Piers as a voice of political protest and develop the plowman as a literary archetype within fifteenth- and sixteenth-century complaint literature.

The divergent print histories of Chaucer and Langland are another topic to consider in studying the reception of medieval works as a component of early modern literary culture. As discussed in the introduction to William Caxton's *Canterbury Tales* editions on the British Library's Web site, Chaucer's works were among the earliest printed in England ("Canterbury Tales"). *Piers Plowman*, however, was not printed until 1550. As an example of the postmedieval understanding of medieval and early modern poetry, one could assign the students to read chapter 31 of George Puttenham's 1589 *Arte of English Poesie*, "Who in any age have bene the most commended writers in our English Poesie, and the Authors censure given upon them." Puttenham's aesthetics could then be profitably compared to those expressed in Philip Sidney's frequently anthologized *Defense of Poesy*, first published in 1595.

If an instructor wanted to frame a course more extensively in literary metahistory, the course could compare three centuries of historical anthologies of English literature. A college library's shelves might still have back editions of *The Norton Anthology of English Literature* and its predecessors and rivals. Students could be assigned to compare corresponding sections of teaching anthologies produced in different scholarly eras in order to determine the values that may have shaped particular inclusions or exclusions (Shesgreen; Kelen, "Which"). With more time, a class could bridge the centuries between Puttenham's assessment of medieval and early modern literature and those of twentieth-century teaching anthologies by using Laura Mandell and Rita Raley's *Anthologies and Miscellanies* Web site to review the tables of contents of literary anthologies from the eighteenth to the twentieth centuries.

Early Modern Medievalism in an Early Modern Literature Course

Over the last two decades the history of the book has become an increasingly significant focus of early modern English literary studies. With anecdotes like the punitive amputation of the unfortunately named William Stubbs and iconic imagery like the First Folio Shakespeare portrait, this research field translates well to the undergraduate classroom. In teaching the intersection of early modern literary history and print history, there are some obvious monuments—among others, the Tyndale New Testament, the so-called bad quartos of Shakespeare, the King James Bible, Ben Jonson's *Workes*, and the Shakespeare First Folio. One approach to studying the early modern print context of literature focuses on editions of early modern works. However, print culture in the early modern period also included the reproduction of classical and medieval literary works. The importance of Europe's classical inheritance for the early modern period—indicated by the period's traditional name, *Renaissance*—is well known. Recently, the significance of medieval works for the literary inheritance of the early modern period has been emphasized (e.g., Kuskin). A course on early modern literary culture would therefore be greatly enriched by the inclusion of some examples of the early modern afterlives of medieval texts.

Tim William Machan demonstrates the prominence of medieval English works in the early English print canon, arguing that "Early Modern Middle English [is] a genre with its own history, theoretical orientation, and ramifications for the English history of the book" (301). The options outlined above for a survey course apply all the more to a course focused on early modern literature and literary culture. Students in a more specialized course would have more time and scholarly expertise to discuss Robert Crowley's editions of *Piers Plowman* in the context of his larger Reformist project (King) and to consider Puttenham's and Sidney's responses to England's literary inheritance.

The fifteenth- and sixteenth-century reception of medieval literature could be usefully brought to bear on some of the literary and cultural issues that students study in a course on early modern literature and culture. A course that features the Reformation as a central topic would likely draw on some of the recent scholarship that questions the extent to which the Protestant Reformation enacted a decisive break from past ideologies and practices (Bernard; Duffy). As part of that topic, one could draw on the creative co-optation of medieval texts in Crowley's *Piers Plowman* preface as well as the various early modern texts in which a plowman figures as the voice of political and religious protest (Jones).

The generic slipperiness of *Piers Plowman* might also be useful in a discussion of the extent to which genre itself was under construction in the early modern period. The early modern titles of literary works manifest the extent to which genres overlapped and coexisted. In *Hamlet* Polonius's exaggerated praise for the players' generic range nonetheless reflects the complex generic naming practices of the period. The players, he tells Hamlet, are "[t]he best actors in the world, either for tragedy, comedy, history, pastoral, pastoral-comical, historical-pastoral, tragical-historical, tragical-comical-historical-pastoral; scene individible, or poem unlimited" (Greenblatt, *Norton Shakespeare* [1997] 147; 2.2.379–82). For that matter, the early editions of *Hamlet* inhabit three different genres (revenge play, history, and tragedy); the play was entered in the Stationers' Register as *The Revenge of Hamlett Prince (of) Denmarke*, retitled *The Tragicall History of Hamlet, Prince of Denmark* in the two quarto editions; and reduced to *The Tragedie of Hamlet, Prince of Denmarke* in the folio (Berger 164).

The extensive research of R. Carter Hailey on the three 1550 Crowley printings of *Piers Plowman* reveals the many variables of the early modern print shop. On their surface, the different editions seem nearly identical; however, closer inspection shows variation not only among editions but also among copies of the same edition. Although little is known about the readership Crowley intended, Hailey observes that some of the *Piers Plowman* copies were printed on vellum rather than on paper, at a time when vellum printing was exceptionally rare in England. The vellum copies may have appealed to a more well-to-do clientele, or printing on a more durable material may have been Crowley's attempt to help *Piers Plowman* pass the test of time.

Medieval Literature, Early Modern Reception, and the Test of Time

Not only did several medieval literary works stand the test of time, but their early modern readers and editors shaped the reception of those texts in ways that are still felt today (Bowers, *Chaucer* 7–8; Kelen, *Langland's Early Modern Identities* 14–15). The influence that early modern medievalism continues to exert on the field of medieval studies may explain why the early modern perception of the medieval period is more frequently studied by medievalists than by early modernists. Scase remarks with some irony that "[t]he 'early modern' period is one of the most fertile areas in medieval English literary studies today. A vast expanse of unworked, set-aside, or abandoned ground has come into view and medievalists have started cultivating it in earnest" (Scase, "*Dauy Dycars Dreame*" 171; see also Scala).

Piers the Plowman would certainly have something to say to those who leave uncultivated land that could be productive: "But ye arise the rather and rape yow to werche, / Shal no greyn that here groweth glade yow at nede" ("Unless you get up again and begin working now, / No grain that grows here will gladden you at need"; B.6.118–19; Schmidt, Vision; Donaldson, *Alliterative Verse Translation*). Although no one, not even a graduate student, is likely to starve for failing to research early modern medievalism, Piers's threat can nevertheless serve as an incentive for scholars of both periods, medieval and early modern, to attend more closely to the implications of early modern medievalism in the construction of the canon of medieval literature as well as for its role in the literary culture of the early modern period.

Langland and Allegory

Judith H. Anderson

I teach Langland either in an undergraduate survey course or within the context of a more advanced course, in connection with a tradition that extends from *Piers Plowman* into the early modern period, where my primary specialization lies. Although Langland's poem can be taught effectively within a satirical tradition focusing on the figure of the plowman, the approach I have found most fertile, whether in survey, advanced undergraduate, or graduate courses, focuses on allegory as a mode of thought and an organization of experience.[1] Simply put, Langland is a brilliant allegorist, and, questions about his influence on later writers aside, his work offers a basic understanding of the form.[2] This form of trope, in turn, is fundamental to all signification, representation, and interpretation.

Books and essays about allegory exist in stimulating abundance, but the three most useful, foundational discussions I have found for my purposes are those by Cicero and, in modern times, by Stephen A. Barney and by Carolynn Van Dyke — the last two medievalists, by great good fortune for the present essay (Cicero; Barney, *Allegories* 13–42; Van Dyke 15–46).[3] Cicero's *De oratore* considers allegory an extension of metaphor, which is typically located in a single word, and explains that allegory occurs in "ex pluribus [verbis] continuatis connectitur" (a "chain of words linked together"; 2: 130 [3.41.166]). In modern terms, this is the contiguous relation that characterizes narrative. Barney and Van Dyke similarly recognize, whereas a number of otherwise illuminating modern discussions do not, that, properly speaking, allegory is a narrative or dramatic mode.[4] This vital point granted, I value Barney's discussion especially for its compact treatment and tentative summation of characteristics of allegories, namely, their being "allusive, distracting, discontinuous, realistic, and critical," and above all for its brief but cogent discussion of boundary cases, such as emblems or triumphs (21, 29). As I read and partly extend Barney's characteristics of allegories, the first three variously indicate that allegory pointedly calls attention to its presence; the penultimate characteristic seeks to encapsulate the explicitly philosophical, broadly abstractive, or more loosely conceptual aspect of allegory, even while punning on its more experiential, temporal, diegetic aspect; and the final characteristic gestures simultaneously at the self-reflexive, cultural, and sociopolitical engagements of allegory.

If judgment is comparative, and definition differential, as appears to be our human lot, then Barney's brief treatment of boundary cases is immensely suggestive. It not merely invites but asks insistently for examination of allegory within a context that includes related types of writings. Since Barney believes that allegories require stories, he sees an emblem or triumph as, at best, "a stilled moment in a moving narrative" (29). Pictures and tableaux vivants, even if mobilized, may imply a narrative or be based on one, but this is not the same as being one; to which I would add, this is also not the same as being so purely visual as to be independent of language in conception and reception. When teaching allegory, I therefore extend Barney's examples of boundary cases to writings that verge on but differ from allegory and supplement these with pictures, anything from an emblem to a painting to a cartoon. The similarities and differences provoke lively, sustained discussion. Again, judgment requires comparison and difference, and students respond energetically to this fact.

Van Dyke's theorized argument is somewhat more recent and considerably more linguistic than Barney's. Within a complex whole, which assumes a narrative or dramatic mode, she defines allegory as "a *synthesis* of deictic and nondeictic generic codes"—that is, as time-bound and timeless, particular and universal, concrete and abstract, natural and emblematic, real and Real (40; my emphasis). Such a theorized synthesis opposes any parallel-levels theory of allegory but does not deny the critically engaging strains and tensions of actually achieving one. Although I do not teach Barney, Van Dyke, or even Cicero directly outside specialized, upper-level undergraduate courses and graduate courses, their ideas more broadly inform both the conception of the courses in which I teach Langland's poem and sometimes the actual teaching.

In the undergraduate survey, whose relevant portion currently ranges from *Beowulf* through Shakespeare and seems to me vital to a wider appreciation of Langland's poem, the texts I have paired with parts of *Piers Plowman* have varied according to changes in successive editions of *The Norton Anthology of English Literature*. Collectively, they are fairly typical of the possibilities and limitations of such anthologized texts. With respect to characterization, the pilgrims in Chaucer's General Prologue (for example, the Friar and the Pardoner) invite thematic, historical, and formal comparison with those on the field of folk in *Piers Plowman*, and the sermon in the Pardoner's Tale offers similar comparative possibilities with the confessions of Langland's Seven Deadly Sins or more broadly with Reason's sermon in the *visio* (5.9–59). The play *Everyman* affords another comparative point of reference, both with respect to characterization and to the technology and psychology of confession and penitence. Of course there are larger issues involved in such focused comparisons, such as the changing status of the material world in itself and in relation to a spiritual one, which the limitations of a survey tend to restrict to generalizations if the students are to have the benefit of hands-on contact with a variety of texts. At a chronologically later stage of the survey, the reappearance of the Seven Deadlies in the first book of Edmund Spenser's *Faerie Queene* invites recursive comparison, as does the tormented figure of Spenser's Despair, a possibility to which I return below.

Generically a dream vision, *Piers* is not only comparable to such contemporary visions as *Pearl* or Julian of Norwich's *Showings* but, distinctively, to the first book of *The Faerie Queene*. *Piers* is unique among medieval dream poems in representing a series of dreams, interspersed with inner dreams and waking moments. This is also the structure of the dreaming by Redcrosse in book 1, where the narrator has a comparable tendency to participate in and occasionally to blend with his characters' experiences. One recurrently anthologized dream within a dream of Langland's narrator, Will, depicting the Crucifixion and harrowing of hell, features the figure of the Christ Knight. In a broadly conceived medieval context, both by similarity and contrast, this figure effectively recalls the *Dream of the Rood* and its engagement of a very different warrior society. For a provocatively radical contrast that highlights Langland's handling of the crucial event of Christendom, the conventionally realistic drama of the York *Crucifixion* is effective—shockingly so. (In foregrounding meaningful differences, Mel Gibson's *The Passion of the Christ* [2004] is yet another reverence from another age worth invoking.) Aside from additional representations of Arthurian knights in the Middle Ages—Thomas Malory's *Le Morte d'Arthur* ("The Death of Arthur") offering the obvious candidates—Spenser's first book again provides an extensive opportunity for formal, conceptual, and further cultural comparisons: Spenser's Redcrosse wears the spiritual armor of Ephesians 6.11–17, and his battle with the dragon in the eleventh canto alludes to the harrowing of hell, which Prince Arthur, best of knights, agent of grace, and an evolving symbol like Piers Plowman himself, reenacts more directly and historically (or biblically) in canto eight. Recursive comparisons such as these not only demonstrate, review, clarify, and refine modes of signifying meaning and organizing experience but also function to teach the workings of genre, tradition, and cultural change in imaginative writing much more effectively than merely abstract definitions can.

Boundary cases and thematic connections aside, the purpose for which I most want to use anthologized parts of *Piers Plowman* is to introduce the workings of allegory—the synthesis or attempted synthesis of the real and the Real, the deictic and nondeictic. Here the popularly anthologized portraits of Envy and Glutton are hard to beat. I'm likely to start discussion by asking students whether they have ever thought about what envy is. We then consider whether Langland's is an effective depiction of envy. Before long we are talking about Envy, how he looks—"pale as a sheep's pelt" and "Like a leek that had lain long in the sun" (5.77, 81)—and then noting that what we are reading is a kind of definition in action, or envy humanly expressed.[5] At this point I might introduce a composite lexical definition, such as "a feeling of discontent; ill will because of another's advantages, possessions, and the like, accompanied by a desire to attain them," and ask what is gained by making Envy a combination of such abstraction and a situated person. We follow the development of Envy's feeling, his revelation of how it affects his thinking and behavior more generally, for example, his slide into hypocrisy, bitterness, and loveless self-loathing. Near the end of the sketch, Envy realizes envy's effect—what envy does to you: "For many years I might not eat as a man ought / For envy and ill will are hard to digest. / Is there any sugar or sweet thing to assuage my swelling?" (121–23). Envy has developed ulcers. What Envy as an allegorical character does, not simply what envy abstractly is, is what Envy signifies.

The confession of Glutton works similarly to that of Envy but is even richer, since it is more dialogic and more fully embedded in social life (5.296–384). The character Glutton mixes comfortably with the relatively realistic folk of the tavern—Cissy the seamstress, Tim the tinker, Dave the ditch digger, and a room full of particularized others—and he soon becomes the gluttony of the whole group. From the vivid portrayal of increasingly high spirits to sickening drunkenness to the aching penitence of the morning after, Glutton's vignette offers a lively depiction of medieval low life in the senses both of social class and of morals. In identifiable ways it is at once realistic and Realistic in its development.

From the depiction of Glutton, my method is to follow the bare bones of the *visio* to the utopian impulse of plowing Piers's half acre and its failure in the confrontation, hence paradoxical combination, of Waster with Hunger (6.104–331). Here Hunger, like any good allegorical figure, signifies what he does—indeed, wreak vengeance on work-shirking wasters. But this is not all, for instead of vanishing once vengeance is wreaked, Hunger simply and naturally becomes hungry, and his significance thus breaks loose from a moral function in the poem. He turns out to be not only a correction of sin but also himself a subsequent cause of gluttony, one leading only to rampant inflation, waste, and greed, a cycle of excess and famine. Here again there is much to discuss: the episode presents a multifaceted problem with social, economic, moral, and even philosophical meanings, but, at the same time, whether explicitly or merely implicitly, a revealing instance of the causal logic of allegorical process, which is in many basic ways the backbone of figuration and narrative.

Besides its value for introducing a conception of allegorical process, I find *Piers Plowman* especially useful for laying out the workings of allegorical projection, by which I mean the representation of one character's state of mind or of an aspect of his or her identity in a second character. Here, as with the evolution of the figure of Piers himself, more of Langland's poem is needed than is usually anthologized. This approach therefore applies to more advanced classes, in which a complete edition or translation of *Piers* is on the syllabus. A striking example of allegorical projection occurs when Will the dreamer meets the character Thought and in doing so meets his own thought process, or thinking, in a figure who looks just like him and has been following him around for seven years. The same merging occurs with the dreamer and other abstract figures, such as Imaginatif (reasoning imaginatively), as well as with Will, the faculty, and less simply personified figures, such as Haukyn or even Piers. Throughout *The Faerie Queene* but most conspicuously in its first book, a variety of similar projections occur: for example, with Redcrosse and Sans Joy, Despair, and Contemplation, to mention a representative few (1.5.4–17, 1.9.21–54, 1.10.46–68). Structurally, syntactically, pronominally, and dramatically—all techniques anticipated in *Piers*—Redcrosse becomes indistinguishable from Sans Joy during their ironic battle, under the aegis of Pride, to possess Duessa and the shield of Sans Foy (Faithlessness) (Alpers, *Poetry* 342–43; Anderson, "Redcrosse" 478–79, 484; Anderson, *Growth* 30–33, 36). Later, through the process of dialogue, Redcrosse's perspective increasingly interacts and finally blends with that of the character Contemplation, whose figure is thus redefined as an act of contemplative knowledge (Anderson, *Growth* 44–49). In confronting Despair at another stage of Spenser's poem, Redcrosse faces a character whose appearance insistently recalls his own when he emerges from Orgoglio's dungeon in the preceding canto (1.9.35, 1.8.41). In short, Redcrosse here faces himself. Not surprisingly, the tempter Despair knows all about this knight's earlier failings and cunningly preys on his diseased conscience. Like Spenser's Archimago, he is another expression of the Bible's Old Man who fails to put on the New, as urged in Ephesians 4.22–24. He is also an artist with words, whose figure alludes to that other verbal artist, the Pardoner in Chaucer's tale, and to the Old Man who is a creation (or projection) of the Pardoner's imagination and whose figure, a true boundary case, verges on allegory.[6] This is the kind of allegorical projection, complex yet clear and accessible, found in *Piers Plowman*, where, for a reader, it can serve as a kind of grid, or X-ray version—perceptual, conceptual, and structural—of less openly abstractive and fleshier forms.

On this note, I want to instance a final, more surprising, but still exemplary allegorical projection—perhaps more accurately a descendant of this mode and therefore a boundary case—whose recognition Langland's poem facilitates. This instance occurs in Shakespeare's *King Lear*. While I am persuaded that Spenser knew and responded to *Piers Plowman*, I do not suppose that Shakespeare did, although his having done so is not inconceivable, since three editions and a reprint of the B text of *Piers* were published in the sixteenth century. But when we teach cultural traditions and the content of the form, direct influence is not the primary issue.

Although *King Lear* is not an allegory, it is full of allegorical elements (Anderson, *Reading* 183–200). Conspicuous among these is the role of Fool, a character with only a typical and functional name, who serves as midwife to Lear's folly. Fool, like many an Erasmian and Langlandian predecessor, is a hypostatized thematic word and, from another angle, a verbal kaleidoscope turned round and round until it reveals the fullness and folly of its meaning. In the course of Shakespeare's play, Fool's role develops until it is finally consumed and exceeded by Lear's own greater folly. Elsewhere, I have described much critical commentary on Fool's simply vanishing at the end of act 3 as "a conspiracy of realism [deictic, lowercase *r*] to avoid [this] supremely obvious allegorical meaning" (*Reading* 189). No reader of Langland could miss it.

NOTES

[1]On the tradition of the plowman, see, for example, B. A. Johnson.

[2]The major, noncontemporary author whom Langland is generally thought to have influenced is Edmund Spenser. See Anderson, "Langland, William"; more extensively, Anderson, *Growth.*

[3]For a relevant, extended discussion of metaphor, see Anderson, *Translating* 139–65.

[4]Studies that are admirable in many respects yet troubling in their evident equation of allegory with abstraction are, for example, Wofford; Teskey.

[5]This essays cites *Piers Plowman* in E. Talbot Donaldson's translation (Piers Plowman*: An Alliterative Verse Translation*), which is also available as a Norton Critical Edition (Robertson and Shepherd). For a recent discussion of envy in *Piers Plowman, The Faerie Queene*, and elsewhere, see Anderson, "Satanic Ethos" 139–44.

[6]On the tradition of representing despair, see Snyder; Anderson, "What"; Anderson, *Reading* 61–78, esp. 66–69.

Poetic Anxiety and Popular Culture in *Piers Plowman*

Stephanie Trigg

Piers Plowman is a poem obsessed with authority. In his conversations with his various interlocutors, Will's tone ranges from respectful to curious to querulous as he assesses and revises their various claims to authority. Langland does not fail to turn this scrutiny to his own work when he expresses considerable ambivalence about his vocation as poet and about the ability of poetry to mislead and to distract. At other times he invokes poetry's traditional narrative authority. Among all the voices that clamor to be heard in *Piers Plowman* and among all the professions that appear in the "fair feeld ful of folk . . . / . . . / Werchynge and wandrynge as the world asketh" ("fair field full of folk . . . / . . . / Working and wandering as the world requires"; B.prol.17–19),[1] where do we situate the profession of poet? Is the writing of poetry recognized as work in the Middle Ages?

These are questions that give *Piers Plowman* much of its urgency and passion for modern readers. How can we distinguish Langland's ethical labor as poet from that of the minstrels he is so quick to condemn? Questions about narrative voice and authorial personality are a familiar path into the reading of poetry, and, for Langland, this is a rich vein indeed. It can be a useful point of focus in helping students negotiate a path through the complexities of the theological debates in *Piers Plowman.* While there are many thematic threads that can be tracked through this long and complex poem, the relation between minstrelsy, poetry, and work is one that promises to engage students. The narrator of the poem is always willing to interpose himself and his experiences in the theological and social debates he dramatizes and to measure what he is told against what he has experienced; accordingly, the poem offers many allusions to other kinds of poetry and literature, as it tries to make distinctions between minstrelsy and God's word and to untangle the troubling associations of poetry with light or frivolous entertainment or, worse, laziness. Langland knew that writing was hard work, but he seems unable to say so directly. In this regard, as in many others, the poem proceeds by indirection and dialectic.

The relation between Langland's sprawling alliterative meditations and other forms of popular poetry or song is a subset, as it were, of his larger concerns about the relation between Latin and vernacular knowledge and expression and about the role of "clergy," or learning, in the poem (Somerset, *Clerical Discourse* 24). This latter relation helps us think about the broader matrix of poetic expression in the fourteenth century—across high and popular culture, from Latin to French to English, and from religious to secular (Butterfield 66–69)—and also to ask questions about the representation and nature of popular culture in the poem. (*Popular culture* is perhaps a slightly anachronistic term, but students interested in the history of cultural studies might want to interrogate some of the assumptions about medieval culture in Peter Burke's work, for example.) Critical discussion of poetic register in *Piers Plowman* has tended to focus on Langland's occasional forays into the high style of alliterative court poetry, such as Meed's arrival at Westminster (B.3.9–19), the eloquent metaphysics of Holy Church's discussion of love (B.1.148–58), and the appearance of Jesus before the Crucifixion ("As is the kynde of a knyght that cometh to be dubbed, / To geten hym gilte spores on galoches ycouped" ["As is the nature of a knight that draws near to be dubbed, / To get himself gilt spurs and engraved jousting shoes"; B.18.13–14]), but we may also turn our attention to less elevated stylistic registers that carry traces of medieval popular culture. In particular, Langland seems haunted by the potential affinities between his own poetry and the idle tales, jests, and fantasies of popular entertainment. His allusions to these forms constitute a rich matrix of anxiety about poetry and the role of the poet.

It is tempting to juxtapose the narrative voice of *Piers Plowman* with the variety of narrative voices in Chaucer's poetry. Comparisons are suggestive. How does each poet mask or disguise his own voice when his characters are speaking? To what extent are Langland's concerns about poetry echoed in the Parson's reservations about poetry in Chaucer's prologue to the Parson's Tale or in the relation between Chaucer's parody of both himself and romance poetry in the Tale of Sir Thopas? Despite his self-mockery and his delightfully slippery narrative voice, Chaucer seems more comfortable in the role of the poet than Langland does.

The voice that opens *Piers Plowman* moves through an unlikely mixture of assertion and negation, while the narrator's identity is shrouded, literally, in the mysterious costume of an unholy hermit. Langland's personal voice is notoriously hard to grasp and is not always easily distinguishable from the other voices that crowd and argue their way through the poem (Lawton, "Subject" 4). When we first encounter Will, it is natural to try to identify and analyze (or psychoanalyze) what seems to be a quite personal speaking voice. Yet the first personal pronoun in the prologue often introduces the subjunctive mood or a statement of ignorance or refusal to make further comment. This is particularly evident in Langland's discussion of the minstrels in the prologue:

> And somme chosen chaffare; they cheveden the bettre—
> As it semeth to oure sight that swiche men thryveth;
> And somme murthes to make as mynstralles konne,
> And geten gold with hire glee—synneless, I leeve.
> Ac japeres and jangeleres, Judas children,
> Feynen hem fantasies, and fooles hem maketh,
> And han wit at wille to werken if they sholde.
> That Poul precheth of hem I wol nat preve it here:
> *Qui loquitur turpiloquium* is Luciferes hyne. (B.prol.31–39)
>
> And some made themselves merchants—they managed better,
> As it seems to our sight that such men prosper.
> And some make mirth as minstrels can
> And get gold for their music, guiltless, I think.
> But jokers and word jugglers, Judas' children,
> Invent fantasies to tell about and make fools of themselves,.
> And have whatever wits they need to work if they wanted.
> What Paul preaches of them I don't dare repeat here:
> "Who speaks filthy language" is Lucifer's henchman.

There are a number of questions we could draw out of this passage, and many of its key words could fruitfully be analyzed through the definitions and citations in the *Middle English Dictionary.* The distinction between *mynstralles*, on the one hand, and *japeres* and *jangleres* on the other, is not self-evident. Is lexical and semantic analysis sufficient to understand Langland's use of these words, or do students need to read further in the poem to comprehend the distinction Langland is making here? Langland seems to be opposing "murthes" and "glee" against "fantasies," though he is silent on the nature of either kind of poetry or song's subject matter and gives no indication here of what would be an acceptable "murthe." Students might develop a collective lexicon of words used for poetry and entertainment in medieval literature through their reading in a semester, tracking all these terms—and others—across other medieval poems.

As with many poets, Langland's concerns about art seem connected to concerns about money and payment, another topic with the potential to deepen comparisons between *Piers Plowman* and other medieval poems. In a rather pejorative characterization, minstrelsy as a form of entertainment is clearly framed in this passage by mercantilism, itself the subject of only grudging approval ("As it seems to our sight that such men prosper"). Langland needs to oppose his second category of entertainers to producers of more worthy compositions (does he mean romances? histories?), but he is irresistibly drawn to a second ethical opposition, namely, between poetry or music and work. It is a set of concerns he shares with another London poet, Thomas Hoccleve, who writes autobiographically in his *Compleinte* ("Complaint") and *La Male Regle* ("The Ill-Ruled Life") about the different kinds of writing he does: his professional writing as a clerk in the Office of the Privy Seal and his more personal, confessional writing.

Throughout the meandering course of *Piers Plowman*, Langland subjects his poetic dreamer to a series of interrogations (for example, at C.5) that often return to the question of the poet's own life and work, resulting in a tangle of arguments and distinctions about good and bad minstrelsy and about the nature of clerical service and poetic work, all underpinned by an abiding suspicion of the poetic word. At such moments Langland sometimes sounds overly defensive. At other times the discussion shifts quietly into the allegorical mode, as when the "murye tales" ("merry tales") with which Conscience entertains Patience and Will at the banquet in passus 13 are glossed as the Penitential Psalms (B.13.57).

Students who come to *Piers Plowman* with a background in postmodernism may reflect on the self-referentiality of the poem. They might be invited to track the expressions of anxiety and the direct and indirect statements about poetry and work that thread through the poem. In one of the clearest accusations, Imaginatif berates the poet: "And thow medlest thee with makynge—and myghtest go seye thi Sauter, / And bidde for hem that yyveth thee breed . . ." ("And you meddle with making verse and might go say your Psalter, / And pray for them that provide your bread . . ."; B.12.16–17). The dreamer replies with a quotation from Cato and a reference to various holy men, who ". . . [p]leyden, the parfiter to ben" ("Played to be more perfect"; B.12.24). He defends his "makynge" as a form of solace or comfort but shies away from the conventional, twinned defense of poetry as both comfort or amusement and instruction—the "sentence and . . . solaas" of which Chaucer writes, for example (General Prologue 1.798).[2] Imaginatif continues: ". . . ther are bokes ynowe / To tell men what Dowel is, Dobet and Dobest bothe" (". . . for there are plenty of books / To telle men what Do-Well is, Do-Better and Do-Best both"; B.12.17–18). Throughout the poem Langland expresses considerable doubt about the poetic enterprise, and this particular moment seems also to express an anxiety about originality. We might ask if the poem is describing its own redundancy. James Simpson introduces the paradox:

> Langland's verse is projected from a position of moral urgency which precludes amusement, or which precludes amusement of the standard literary kind, at any rate. It is true that in the course of the poem Langland does seek

> to transform literary entertainment into an extremely playful, intellectually stimulating, spiritual "solace," or entertainment; but he makes this transformation in the light of his awareness that most literary entertainment is, in his view, a waste of time (it is characteristically figures like Sloth who are pictured as being occupied by idle tales. . . . Unlike many poets of the period, Langland associates his kind of poetry with the exploitation of time for spiritual purposes. (Piers 13)

At the same time, such "idle tales" present a lively vision of medieval popular culture and are among the most energetic and dramatic passages in the poem. How, then, does Langland's deep interest in theological and ethical questions accord with his imaginative interest in dramatic and narrative poetry and in the ability of vernacular poetry to realize and explore these issues? Is the poem consistent or inconsistent in its representation of poetic work and the life of poetry?

Langland is repeatedly drawn to the world of popular culture, to the chaotic world of the tavern and the marketplace, where people take untroubled pleasure in poetry and song. These public spaces are often inhabited by the voices of the outsider or the reluctant worker. They are also frequently sites of resistance—or, at least, sites where perspectives other than those of official or hegemonic culture appear. It is also worth recalling in this context that, according to Imaginatif, the angel announced the incarnation equally "to pastours and to poetes" ("To shepherds and sages"; B.12.148); poets are represented here as humble yet privileged outsiders. Comparison with the shepherds in the Wakefield *Second Shepherds' Play* might be instructive here: how do these two different texts represent the juxtaposition of Christian mystery with the everyday life of work?

David Aers draws attention to the way Langland's imagination is often captured by this lively, social world (*Chaucer* 5). This is famously evident in the confessions of the Seven Deadly Sins but also in the condensed ending of the prologue, where the alliterative names of occupations tumble over one another onto the fair field:

> Of all lybbynge laborers lopen forth somme—
> As dykeres and delveres that doon hire dedes ille
> And dryveth forth the longe day with "*Dieu vous save Dame Emme*!"
> Cokes and hire knaves cryden, "Hote pies, hote!
> Goode gees and grys! Go we dyne, go we!"
> Taverners until hem tolden the same:
> "Whit wyn of Oseye and wyn of Gascoigne,
> Of the Ryn and of the Rochel, the roost to defie!"
> —Al this I seigh slepyng, and sevene sythes more. (B.prol.223–31)
>
> Of all living laborers there leapt forth some,
> Such as diggers of ditches that do their jobs badly,

And dawdle away the long day with "God save Dame Emma."
Cooks and their kitchen-boys kept crying, "Hot pies, hot!
Good geese and pork! Let's go and dine!"
Tavern-keepers told them a tale of the same sort:
"White wine of Alsace and wine of Gascony,
Of the Rhine and of La Rochelle, to wash the roast down with."
All this I saw sleeping, and seven times more.

Aers writes that here

> we are shown a mass of self-absorbed social practices in which there is no consciousness of any coherent order, organic unity or social *telos*, let alone a divine one. . . . The poetic conviction communicating this state already encourages us to question the applicability of the leading ideological scheme to the culture Langland inhabits and scrutinizes. . . . (*Chaucer* 5)

Aers's emphasis on Langland's "poetic conviction" points to one of the central paradoxes of the poem: Langland is drawn to experimenting with poetic expression and to exploring and debating the ability of poetry to represent the world, while at the same time he rehearses genuine anxieties about the legitimacy of poetry and its associations with minstrelsy, singing, and "jang[ling]" of various kinds.

In this chaotic scene at the end of the prologue, as the various occupations run forth onto the stage, the social world is given clamorous voice, with the street calls of the vendors and the singing of the laborers. Again, there is ambiguity here about the nature of work. At one level we are told that the laborers are lazy, that they do their work badly and sing songs all day, yet we are shown an energetic crowd "leaping" forward and "driving" the day along with their song. Similarly, the vendors' cries compete with each other in an irresistible cacophony.

This passage is a rich source for the study of medieval popular culture and daily life in London. Who might Dame Emma be? Later in the poem Haukyn refers to an Emma of Shoreditch, who may be a witch (B.13.340). Are these two related? J. A. W. Bennett suggests there is an allusion in the prologue to the queen of King Canute, citing a reference to "the deeds of Emma" sung by a minstrel at St. Swithun's Winchester in 1338 (Queen Emma was "falsely accused of unchastity, and survived the ordeal of walking on red-hot ploughshares"; Piers 103). In any event, Langland gives us a glimpse of popular culture—a snatch of verse or a brief allusion—even though the singing workers are those who "do their jobs badly": singing is a sign of laziness, like the "How trolly lolly!" of those who sit and sing during the plowing of the half acre in passus B.6.116. Comparison with some of the political or historical lyrics that conjure a comparable world of work and recreation is instructive here; for example, "The Blacksmiths" or "London

Lickpenny" (Pearsall, *Chaucer* 399; Dean, *Medieval English Political Writings* 222–25). The poetry of Hoccleve, also set in London, makes an interesting comparison here too.

In the confession of the sins, one of the first things we learn about Sloth, apart from the fact that he can hardly open his eyes, is the opposition of what he does and doesn't know:

> I kan noght parfitly my *Paternoster* as the preest it syngeth,
> But I kan rymes of Robyn Hood and Randolf Erl of Chestre,
> Ac neither of Oure Lord ne of Oure Lady the leeste that evere was maked.
>
> . . . .
>
> I am ocupied ech a day, halyday and oother,
> With ydel tales at the ale and outherwhile in chirches (B.5.395–97, 403–04)
>
> I can't say my Paternoster perfectly as the priest sings it,
> But I know rhymes of Robin Hood and Randolph Earl of Chester,
> But neither of our Lord nor our Lady the least that was ever made.
>
> . . . .
>
> I'm occupied every day, holy days and others,
> With idle tales over ale and at other times in church (B.5.394–96, 402–03)

The ease of this oppositional structure can be problematic for Langland and for his readers. Satire of this kind, like the estates satire of the prologue, slips easily into the familiar binary oppositions between good and bad, positive and negative, holy and secular, so that tales of Robin Hood and the Earl of Chester are easily identified as "idle tales." And yet on closer scrutiny the text rehearses a number of paradoxes. Sloth tells and hears idle tales but is "occupied each day" with this activity; the vocabulary of work is irresistible in describing the intensity with which Sloth does not work. In this regard, the description of Sloth prefigures the encounter with Haukyn in passus 13.

Langland's reference to "rhymes of Robin Hood" as the typical entertainments of folk who neglect their devotions is the earliest such allusion to a tradition of popular literature about the outlaw, though its testimony needs to be read carefully. Bennett cites *Dives et Pauper*, an early fifteenth-century text that similarly speaks of those who would rather "heryn a tale or a song of robyn hode or of sum ribaudry than to here masse or matyns" ("hear a tale or a song of Robin Hood or of some ribaldry than to hear mass or matins"; Bennett, Piers 177; my trans.). The issues are complex, though. Bennett also cites Thomas Chaloner's translation of Erasmus's *Praise of Folie*, condemning fools who "praise a rime of Robyn Hode for as excellent a makyng as Troilus of Chaucer" ("praise a poem about Robin Hood as being as excellent a composition as Chaucer's *Troilus*"; Bennett, Piers

177; my trans.). Yet this is a different argument altogether about literary quality, establishing a hierarchical opposition between an anonymous "rime" and the courtly work of a named author. To establish a consistent discursive hierarchy in Langland's views of poets, minstrels, and idlers, we must acknowledge the contradictory ideas about poetry and vernacular literature in circulation at this time. There is every reason to expect that Langland expresses as much variety and ambiguity on this topic as Chaucer does—for example, in the prologue to the Parson's Tale, where all poetry, whether alliterative or rhyming, is held of little account; and in his Retraction, where only the works on secular topics are recalled.

At other points in the poem, and in other versions, Langland examines the nature of the work he does as a minor cleric, especially in the famous so-called autobiographical addition to the C text, in which Langland presents himself as lazy and makes the excuse that he is too tall to work in the fields. He is chastised by Reason and bid to do something more useful than saying masses for benefactors and donors:

> . . . an ydel man thow semest,
> A spendour that spene mot or a spille-tyme,
> Or beggest thy bylyue aboute at men hacches
> Or faytest vppon Frydayes or feste-dayes in churches,
> The whiche is lollarne lyf, that lytel is preysed
> There ryhtfulnesse rewardeth ryht as men deserueth. (C.5.27–32)[3]

> . . . For you seem an idler,
> A compulsive big-spender or waster of time,
> Or do you beg for a living at men's doorways
> Or freeload on Fridays and feast days in churches,
> Which is a loller's life that wins little praise
> Where righteousness rewards men just as they deserve.

Langland replies that he was put to school at an early age and that he never found any life he liked better "but in this longe clothes" ("except in these long robes"; C.5.41). He describes the tools of his trade: "The lomes that Y labore with and lyflode deserue / Is *pater-noster* and my prymer, *placebo* and *dirige*, / And my sauter som tyme and my seuene psalmes" ("The tools of my trade and means of support / Are *pater noster* and my primer, *placebo* and *dirige* [first words of the antiphons for the Office of the Dead at vespers and matins], / And sometimes my psalter and my seven psalms"; C.5.45–47). The "*pater-noster*" of which Sloth is ignorant is associated here with the minimal, perfunctory performance of clerical duties of an unbeneficed priest. Here again the hierarchy of discourses is hardly straightforward, as Langland seeks to untangle these conflicting impulses: to live well, to express his convictions, to use the vernacular to make sense of theological debates for laypeople, to experiment with alliterative poetry, to give expression to characters like the Sins, and to earn an honest living.

Among many other points in the poem where Langland struggles to define the role of poetry and his own place in the world, there is one more scene worth examining closely here. Passus 13 of the B text offers the most sustained discussion of the minstrel's life, in Haukyn, one of the poem's most problematic figures, who drives one of the major changes in the direction of the poem's narrative, in the dreamer's fourth vision. Conscience has invited the dreamer and Patience to a great feast, though they are seated at a side table, far from Clergy and the guest of honor, the "doctour on the heighe dees" ("Doctor on the high dais"; B.13.61). When Patience is finally invited to speak after dinner, his enigmatic praise of "kynde love" ("natural love"; B.13.151) and of the patient love of one's enemies attracts only abuse from the learned friar: "'It is but a dido,' quod this doctour, 'a disours tale!'" ("'It's just a joke,' said this Doctor, 'a jester's story'"; B.13.173). The friar takes Conscience and Clergy aside and asks them to dismiss Patience as a lying pilgrim. Nevertheless, it becomes clear that Patience appears here as a kind of model minstrel, an after-dinner speaker who truly can both entertain and feed the guests. Is Langland finally offering us a model of good minstrelsy, even one that is characteristically oblique? A possible comparison here might be with the narrative poem *Sir Orfeo*, which presents a model of harping and minstrelsy that is entirely virtuous and the sign of a great king.

After the dinner Conscience, Patience, and the dreamer encounter Haukyn, or Activa Vita, a minstrel who claims to hate idleness, thus introducing another complication to the ideas about minstrels and work established so far in the poem (B.13.222–313). Indeed, Haukyn confuses the matter further in his first few lines of speech, a typically dense Langlandian cluster of semantic allusions and associations. He introduces himself as a minstrel and as a "wafrer," a wafer-seller (B.13.227). In their editions of the poem, A. V. C. Schmidt and Derek Pearsall both comment on the close associations of the two occupations—wafer-sellers, like the "[s]yngeres with harpes, baudes, wafereres" in Chaucer's Pardoner's Tale ("singers with harps, prostitutes, wafer sellers"; 6.479), seem to have combined their trade with "low popular entertaining" (Schmidt, Vision 462 [note to lines 225–27]; Pearsall, Piers 259 [note to line 198])—but *wafres* could be either eucharistic wafers for "godes gestes" ("God's guests"; that is, communicants; C.15.198) or "fancy cakes, as sold in public places" (Pearsall, Piers 259 [note to line 198]). Haukyn seems also to associate his *wafres* with everyday bread (B.13.263–70), alluding to the scarcity of bread in London in 1370. For A. C. Spearing, this is an associative cluster that links the Haukyn episode to the encounter between Piers and Hunger in passus 6 ("Development" 244–48), but for our purposes it is another indication of the extraordinary mobility of signs and associations in Langland's poem and of the difficulty students face in untangling the meaning of specific signs or occupations, especially around this vexed question of the role of poetry. Haukyn is a minstrel, but a hopeless one who cannot lie to make men laugh, tell stories, or play an instrument or dance or fart to amuse an audience at a feast. Nor is he capable of God's minstrelsy, in the performance of his devotions or the suffering of patient poverty. Haukyn's way of life is less virtuous avoidance of idleness and more an imperfect version of the active life, so easily stained and weighed down, like Haukyn's filthy coat, with worldly cares and preoccupations (Maguire 98). Like the Seven Deadly Sins, Haukyn is completely enveloped in, but also perversely energized by, worldly affairs. And in Nicholas Watson's reading, Haukyn, for all his failures, remains "a hopeful object of the poem's pastoral concern" ("*Piers*" 118).

Toward the end of passus 13 Langland seems to address his readers directly, in his own voice, on the problem of sloth. Once again, this vice is characterized as the willingness to hear "wordes of murthe" from "an harlotes tonge" ("words of mirth" from "a ribald's tongue"; B.13.418, 416), but it is contrasted with the idea that rich people should welcome the poor, "the which ben Goddes minstrales" ("who shall be God's minstrels"; B.13.440), to their feasts:

> Forthi I rede yow riche [th]at reveles whan ye maketh,
> For to solace youre soules, swiche minstrales to have—
> The povere for a fool sage sittynge at th[i] table,
> And a lered man to lere thee what Oure Lord suffred
> For to save thi soule fram Sathan thyn enemy,
> And fithele thee, withoute flateryinge, of Good Friday the storye
> (B.13.442–47)

> Therefore I remind you rich men, when you make your revels,
> To solace your souls have such minstrels:
> A poor person for a fool-sage placed at your table,
> And a learned man from whom to learn what our Lord suffered
> To save your soul from Satan your enemy,
> And without flattering fiddle for you Good Friday's story (B.13.441–46)

Simpson comments, "Instead of simply rejecting the practice of listening to minstrels at feasts, Langland characteristically transforms it" (Piers 152). He argues that Langland "preserves the idea of a public poetry, addressed to the powerful, designed to move and convert them" (153). I find it hard to be certain, however, that this idea of public poetry is a literal one. It seems to me that Langland is using the vocabulary of minstrelsy here allegorically and that any idea of a public poetry is suggested only indirectly.

I do agree with Simpson, though, about Langland's ability to transform signs and associations: the cluster of ideas and anxieties about poetry, work, and minstrelsy is a wonderful example of Langland's flexible symbolic method. In its richness and in Langland's willingness to rethink earlier formulations and to work through these changes in his poetry, it is comparable to the Meed episode (B.3.9–19), though harder to teach because examples are dispersed throughout the poem.

Langland is clearly exercised by doubt and anxiety about the value of different kinds of poetry, music, and entertainment; about their relation to labor; and about the role of poetry in bringing to life ethical and spiritual questions in narrative fiction. Attention to these questions can give students a subthread to follow as they read the poem as well as sharpen the picture of medieval poetic culture.

NOTES

[1]Quotations from the B text are from Schmidt's edition (Vision). Translations are Donaldson's (in Robertson and Shepherd's edition).

[2]Quotations from Chaucer are from L. D. Benson's *Riverside Chaucer.*

[3]Quotations from the C text are from Pearsall's edition (Piers). Translations are from Economou.

Piers Plowman and Community

Emily Steiner

Piers Plowman is a poem committed to social reform. It draws liberally from that great genre of medieval correction, estates satire, just as Chaucer humorously does in the General Prologue to *The Canterbury Tales*. Indeed, comparing Chaucer's and Langland's prologues can be a useful exercise for students struggling with *Piers Plowman*'s idiosyncratic and often abrupt treatment of medieval genres (Mann, *Chaucer*; Cooper "Langland's and Chaucer's Prologues"; Justice, "Genres"). Medieval estates satire assumes that if each person performed the tasks and shunned the vices that pertain to his or her station, life on earth would begin to reflect the laws of Christian charity, and humankind might even pull itself back from the brink of apocalypse. This assumption looms large in *Piers Plowman*, realized most dramatically in the prologue, in which the dreamer sets out to describe "alle manere of men" ("all kinds of people"; 18) only to realize that the diversity of human labors—digging, praying, ruling, selling—is inseparable from the propensity to sin: as the dreamer warns, "[t]he mooste meschief on molde is mountynge up faste" ("the greatest evil on earth is rapidly rising"; 67).[1] In order to appreciate the poem's anxiety about social reform and its huge stake in defining community, students might benefit from being briefed on the seven deadly sins as well as on medieval expectations of the apocalypse, which occupied writers for centuries.

I ask students how we, as moderns, think apocalyptically—for example, through environmental activism or our responses to global crises—and how our sense of community reform might depend on the way we envision the future of human societies.

Although Langland's debts to estates satire give some insight into the ways that medieval writers conceived the moral stakes of social life, it is also crucial for students to see that the poem's commitment to reform exceeds the conventions of medieval satire. Its reformist project entails nothing less than a total readjustment of the way people think about their relationships to one another. The poet takes for granted the traditionally structured society of his times, but the poem does contain a continuous chain of thought on the ethics of association—how we should feel and act toward other people, or what here I call community.

Like other medieval "self-help" works, such as the popular penitential poem the *Prick of Conscience* (ca. 1360; Morey)—a short excerpt of which might be used for comparison—*Piers Plowman* teaches us how to be good so we can be saved. Uniquely among such works, *Piers* refuses to offer a coherent step-by-step guide, despite its promising twenty-odd *passus* ("steps"). Instead, it invites its readers to participate in a torturous conversation about what it means to be part of a group: What bonds people to their fellow human beings? How should one identify with other people, and what are the limits to identification? How does class, gender, or belief affect the way human relationships are described? What happens when people discriminate, that is, when they enter into ethical association with some people but not with others? The kinds of questions Langland asks about the formation of community can be productively extended in the classroom to contemporary issues, such as immigration, incarceration, minimum wage, and religious diversity.

In my experience teaching *Piers Plowman*, these questions also enable students to engage with a poet whose learning seems infinite. At the same time, they help make sense of the poem's innovations, by which I mean not simply those places where the poem departs from medieval literary conventions like satire but where it offers up thought experiments about social life. Students can take advantage of the wealth of *Piers* scholarship on fourteenth-century labor relations, medieval theories of poverty, and theologies of the virtuous pagan and of universal salvation, all of which deepen understanding of community in the poem.[2] This scholarship shows that *Piers Plowman* is an experimental poem precisely because it constantly tries to find meaning in its densely wrought historical moment. I am also suggesting, however, that presenting Langland's ideas about community as hypothetical rather than prescriptive allows students to get to the heart of his experimental poetics, and, at the same time, makes his ethical quandaries relevant to modern readers.

One way of introducing students to community in *Piers Plowman* is to have them trace the phrase "blody bretheren" ("blood brothers"), which pops up at significant moments in the poem and forces the poem to speak to the ethical codes of medieval romance. Most students will grasp the concept of blood brothers instinctively: it is one of the primary medievalisms of our culture, ubiquitous in depictions of gangs and fraternities as well as of medieval warfare. In medieval literature and in modern iterations, the concept is aestheticized and romanticized. On the face of it, blood brotherhood seems egalitarian: we may come from different families and backgrounds, but, through this, we are related. But blood brotherhood was originally an aristocratic idea, according to which the near-sacramental fellowship of comrades-in-arms can be substituted for familial ties, because the noble estate is essentially kinship writ large (for example, in a classic scene from Thomas Malory's *Le Morte d'Arthur* ["The Death of Arthur"] Sir Gareth's loyalty to Sir Lancelot surpasses his loyalty to his own brothers). Additionally, from a medieval aristocratic perspective, the ability to identify oneself with another and thus enter into ethical association with that person is itself a noble quality. Simply put, only gentlemen have true fellow feeling, which places them in reciprocal relation with only one another. For example, in Jean Froissart's *Chronicles*, which recounts the Hundred Years' War, nobles are more likely to identify with the plight of foreign enemies than with that of commoners from their own country.

In *Piers Plowman*, "blody bretheren" is supposed to designate a fellowship that supercedes both kinship ties and class identity and brings people of different statuses into ethical and spiritual understanding. Emperor Trajan, in passus 11, issues the boldest statement in this regard, and it pays for students to examine his speech in some detail. According to Trajan, Christ's sacrifice on the cross made everyone "bretheren as of oo blood" ("brothers as if of one blood"), leveling the playing field for rich and poor, Jews and gentiles (196–201; cf. Christ's speech in passus 18, which contrasts Trajan's "bretheren of blood" ["blood brotherhood"; 377], a brotherhood of consanguinity, to a "hole bretheren" ["whole brotherhood"; 378] united in Christ both in blood and in baptism). As Trajan explains, moreover, Christ's bloody sacrifice made possible a radical identification among all people, which confers spiritual nobility on those who take part in it. As I point out to students, this is a powerful proposition: when we perform the ethical act of identifying with other people, do we overcome difference by granting high status to all? Can identification in Christ—a fellowship of sacramental blood—truly trump the differences between rich and poor, nobles and churls, Christians and non-Christians, good and bad?

The poem provides plenty of evidence that this proposition might not be tenable because it is nearly impossible, at least rhetorically, to separate Christian fellowship from aristocratic identity. Or, to put this problem in terms of genre, the values of chivalric romance are not easily assimilated to a literature of social reform. A closer look at Trajan's speech, for example, shows that the idea of a blood brotherhood in Christ confirms rather than eliminates differences in wealth and status: "Ac for the beste ben som riche" ("But it is for the best that some are rich"; 11.197). In fact, for Trajan, the disparity between rich and poor, and, by analogy, between Christian and heathen, actually enables the expression of Christian brotherhood: we can identify spiritually with other people because the real differences can never be fully overcome. It would seem that ethical identification depends on the ability to feel like a noble: the ability to recognize nobility in others—that is, to experience fellow feeling in Christ—is evidence of intrinsic nobility.

To develop this idea further, students can compare Longinus's situation to that of the Jews in passus 18. The blind Longinus alone may joust with Christ because, as a knight, he recognizes in Christ a shared aristocratic identity, one that, in this case, results in privileged physical and spiritual intimacy (83–86). By contrast, says Faith, the Jews at the time of Christ failed to recognize Christ's nobility, proving that they were already churls, deserving of their fallen state in a Christian world (78–109). Students are usually sensitive to the poem's anti-Semitism; additionally, I want them to see that, in this passage, Langland is interested not only in casting the Jews out of salvation history but also in using that history to explore the dynamics of ethical association. (Here, I ask students to contrast passus 18 with 15, in which the poet argues that the conversion of Jews and Muslims in his own time is simply a matter of teaching them the Apostles' Creed. This evangelical vision of universal Christianity is further illuminated for students by *The Book of John Mandeville* [ca. 1360], a sensational travelogue in which the narrator reports his conversation with a sultan, who, though Muslim, is peculiarly knowledgeable about Christianity and is therefore considered ripe for conversion [Kohanski and Benson]).

As Longinus's recognition—and the Jews' misrecognition—of Christ show, the creation of community is an interpretative act, and, indeed, Langland's experiments in community can help students see that the difficulty of poetry is not always simply a matter of taste. Toward the end of passus 5, Piers offers to guide the pilgrims to Truth, but his directions are allegorical and his notion of travel steeped in the language of chivalric affinity: those who know how to reach Truth are those who can conceive of spiritual progress as a set of privileged social relations. For modern readers, allegory of this kind can be didactic and plodding. It is eye-opening for students to learn that what is aesthetically boring to them is ethically off-putting for the marginal folk in the passus. (Advanced students might compare this passage with the debate between Lady Reason and the churlish Natural Understanding in Guillaume de Deguileville's *Pèlerinage de la vie humaine* [ca. 1330–50; "The Pilgrimage of the Life of Man"], an important source for Langland [Deguileville].) For the low-born pilgrims in Piers's company, the only way to derive any spiritual benefit from this kind of allegory is to be inducted into the intimacies of aristocratic community—knowing the right password, for example ("telleth hym this tokene" ["give him this sign"; 5.597]) or speaking in affectionate tones as with one's family ("as bretheren [of o wombe]" ["as brothers from the same womb"; 591]). For these folk, Christian fellowship, experienced through the language of aristocratic sensibility, is unimaginable without ties of blood. Several of them complain that they have no kin in Piers's allegorical country. Piers lightly assures them that Mercy and her son live there "sib to alle synfulle" ("related to all sinful people"; 636). A pardoner and prostitute decide to falsify the blood relations of Christian association: the pardoner goes to find his box of indulgences lest he "be noght knowe there" ("be not known there"; 639), and the prostitute pretends to be his sister. Their failure to penetrate the allegory reveals the high stakes of community.

Piers invokes the idea of blood brothers again in the plowing of the half acre in passus 6 but uses it to raise a different question about community: what happens when we define ethical association not by our ability to feel but by the object of our feeling—the laborer or beggar, kinsman or neighbor? The modern counterpart to this question might be, Should our relation to others be conditioned by how we judge their lifestyle? When we give charity, for example, does it matter if the recipient is a single mother with five children or an addict camped out by a convenience store? What is incumbent upon the giver and the recipient? How should the giver feel? How can the giver balance discrimination and compassion?

Langland's project in this passus is to picture Christian community as a stay-at-home pilgrimage on the medieval manor, a laboring community in which everyone has a job to do. As Piers soon discovers, however, a laboring community is a community defined by something other than ethical identification in Christ. Although initially conceived as a lesson in allegorical plowing—we all labor for Truth—the allegory quickly dissolves, and Piers is left to confront a motley crew of workers, some of whom work cheerfully for little pay, some of whom will work only for higher wages (wrongly, in Piers's opinion), and some of whom refuse to work at all, choosing to beg because they are lazy or impaired.

The episode is fascinating for its engagement with fourteenth-century labor issues, specifically those framed by postplague legislation, which tried to support landowners by restraining a newly mobile and increasingly demanding workforce (Middleton, "Acts"; Aers, *Community* 20–72; K. Robertson). Critical to this engagement, however, is the ethical quandary that informs it, which students can best see in Piers's dialogue with Hunger, a fascinating and controversial character (6.199–290). Piers knows that identifying with others is an ethical act: one's conduct toward other people depends upon a prior feeling of connectedness ("[And] it are my blody bretheren for God boughte us all" ["And they are my blood brothers, because God redeemed us all"; 207]). But if common humanity is manifested in individuals who do not share his values, his association with them will inevitably be defined by judgment and discrimination. Hunger advises Piers to give food to all who need it, leaving punishment of the undeserving to God, but, at the same time, to discriminate carefully between workers and shirkers, giving the better food to those deemed worthy.

Students can follow the terms of this ethical debate—whether to identify or discriminate—starting with Piers's testament at the beginning of passus 6, in which he literally writes out of his association those he disapproves of, impersonating God the Judge ("*Deleantur de libro vivencium*—I sholde noght dele with hem"; "*Let them be erased from the book of the living*—I shouldn't deal with them"; 75); proceeding to the crisis on the half acre; and concluding with Truth's pardon in passus 7. In the pardon episode, Langland begins to offer some solutions to Piers's ethical quandary by providing a form, the pardon, with which readers can think simultaneously about who deserves to be saved and how one should relate to others. The pardon shows that those with whom one should identify in Christ—people deemed worthy or unworthy—help create ethical bonds at the very moment that they are excluded from the general fellowship. Merchants are initially excluded from pardon, but Truth sends them a separate document offering them pardon in return for giving alms (7.23–26). (This passage provides a great opportunity to ask students to think about how legal documents and official papers, in general, exclude or include.) Lawyers, too, are included in the pardon only as long as they plead for the poor pro bono, and beggars are included only if incapacitated (64–65). The pardon episode shows that people uneasily assimilated to traditional societal models, like the three estates, help define community, not because they represent the limits of acceptability but because their special legal status throws the ethics of association into relief. (I point out to my students that in these lines the poet showcases his exceptionalist poetics, which attempts to reconcile the conflicting postures of identification and discrimination: all of *X* are included except *Y*, none of *A* are included except *B*, and so forth.) Here I ask students to compare the B text pardon with the revised and expanded pardon in the C text, where the poet reconsiders the problem of ethical association from the perspective of poor neighbors, who suffer even though they are too ashamed to beg and whose bone-tired women deserve special sympathy.

In passus 11 to 14 the poet returns to questions of identification and discrimination, inclusion and exclusion, but from an entirely different perspective. The dreamer, anxious about his own salvation, wonders whether he should place his eggs in the basket of baptism or of good works, and it becomes clear that this basic theological problem leads to different views of community, which students at any level can perceive. Baptism is temporally inclusive and atemporally exclusive: all Christians— all those living after Christ who believe in Christ—enjoy the saving power of his sacrifice. Jews, Saracens, and pagans belonging to a pre-Christian past are not justified through Christ, except for those enlightened few who predicted Christ's birth. By contrast, justification through works is temporally exclusive and atemporally inclusive: those who lived before Christ but performed good works are saved, but those who, in the Christian era, accept Christ but fail to perform works of charity are damned. In passus 10 to 12, this link between theology and community leads the poet to some wonderfully strange analogies, as, for example, when the dreamer compares the baptized Christian's relation to God to that of a runaway churl to his master (11.125–36). This is a great passage to discuss in class, especially if the teacher supplies some background about manorial labor and about unfree and free tenancies (Keen 134–56).

The obvious answer to the dreamer's query is that one needs to be baptized to have a chance of being saved through good works, which no person can ever satisfactorily perform. But I want my students to see that Langland pursues the binary of baptism and works in order to explore an ethical rather than a strictly theological question: not only who will join the community of the saved but also how people can work imaginatively toward the salvation of others. Working imaginatively toward the salvation of others is a hugely ambitious project that requires an intrepid and capacious poetics. In passus 11 and 12 it takes the form of an obsessive meditation on righteous heathens. To help students understand Langland's ethical investment in the righteous heathen, I ask them to read the life of Pope Gregory the Great in the compilation of saints' lives called *The Golden Legend* (Voragine, vol. 3, ch. 27). Gregory is sympathetic to those who occupy temporal or spatial no-man's-lands, such as Trajan, who lived after Christ but before Gregory, and, in Gregory's day, Anglo-Saxon pagans sold as slaves in the Roman marketplace. Langland shares with Gregory the desire to find a bond that transcends the constraints of time and belief. He is especially invested in the "old tyme" ("old time"; 12.235) poets and philosophers, such as Solomon and Aristotle, who represent the community most dear to his heart, the intellectual community of biblical, classical, and medieval authorities who transmitted scholarship on the natural sciences, political theory, and morality. The collective wisdom of these figures was the foundation of medieval scholarship, yet medieval writers consigned most of them (almost definitely) to hell. Pagan writers thus provide an occasion to enter into ethical association with others by attempting, with Gregory, the nearly impossible: as Imaginatif exclaims, "Ac God is so good, I hope that siththe he gaf them wittes / To wissen us weyes therwith . . . / . . . / That God for his grace gyve hir soules reste" ("But God is good, I expect that since he gave them the ability / To show us the (right) paths / That God will, through his grace, give their souls rest"; 12.269–72).

The desire to work imaginatively toward the salvation of others takes on many different forms in the poem. One example that students find especially thorny and provocative is Langland's experiment in ecocriticism in passus 14, where he compares the lives of wild animals with those of humans both rich and poor. In this passus Patience is railing against riches and extols poverty as the only route to salvation. The poet, however, is under pressure to show that by poor he means those with a poor attitude as well as those who involuntarily suffer the pains of material poverty. Yet he returns over and over again to the spiritual benefits of involuntary poverty, because only real poverty is inherently sympathetic. As he shows in passus 6, however, identifying with the poor can be hard work. In passus 14 the poet wonders whether we can redeem our association with the poor by positing an ethical connection between humans and animals.

For most medieval writers, nature constitutes a symbolic field removed from human experience; for this reason it provides a useful handbook of scientific and moral instruction. Students are amazed by the wealth of medieval lore about animals: they can consult the fascinating thirteenth-century encyclopedia by Bartholomaeus Anglicus, *De proprietatibus rerum*, in John Trevisa's readable English transation, *On the Properties of Things* (Seymour et al.) as well as the gorgeously illustrated medieval bestiaries at *The Medieval Bestiary* Web site (bestiary.ca). Medieval treatises tend to depict animals entirely in terms of human consumption, either classifying them as food or moralizing them as examples. Langland follows in this tradition in passus 12, where Imaginatif glosses the peacock, with its brilliant yet useless feathers, as proud rich men who cannot fly to heaven (235–60). By contrast, in passus 11, the dreamer complains that animals have unfairly been given instinct whereas humans have to make due with free will; the implication is that it might be possible after all to identify with the moral condition of beasts (326–43). In three places in passus 14, the poet goes even further, recognizing that because animals and people live in the same time they experience similar deprivations and joys. By comparing these three passages (which are in closer proximity to each other in the C text), students can note a huge shift in the way the poet imagines the relation between men and beasts and a concomitant shift in his thinking about the poor.

The first passage follows the bestiaries by comparing the natural life of animals to the willed actions of human beings: beasts rely on God for their daily sustenance; people should cultivate the same attitude (14.42–47). The second passage departs abruptly from the bestiaries to compare the seasonal life of poor people to that of beasts: just as beasts physically suffer hunger and cold in winter but have joy in summer, so poor people deserve joy in heaven after suffering (like beasts) on earth (111–17). The third passage further capitalizes on this ethical connection between humans and animals in order to distinguish between poor and rich: poor people, says Patience, are even more sympathetic than beasts, because beasts, like the rich, enjoy some pleasure on earth, while the poor suffer hunger even in summertime (157–65). In constructing this unusual set of analogies between humans and beasts, the poet proposes two ideas about community: first, that animals and people experience similar material conditions and therefore have a natural ethical bond; and second, that the demonstrably sympathetic condition of the poor, realized through the analogy with animals, valorizes our ethical association with them. This is another good opportunity to ask students to compare B and C texts. In B, passus 14, right in the middle of his defense of the poor, the poet inserts a startling proviso for the rich; in C, passus 16, he removes this proviso, perhaps to make a better case for the poor.[3]

Students can learn from *Piers Plowman* that community is not simply a fact on the ground, or a historical construction, but an ongoing ethical and poetic challenge. This approach to community in *Piers Plowman* enables students to compare medieval and modern ethical thought and charitable practice. As I suggested at the beginning of this essay, we share something of Langland's feeling that our own communities—families, cities, countries, and world—are in a state of perpetual crisis. The poem lays out ways of understanding these feelings of crisis and how they affect our relationships to other people.

NOTES

[1] This essay quotes from Schmidt's edition of the B text (Vision).

[2] On labor relations, see Middleton, "Acts"; Aers, *Community* 20–72; K. Robertson. On theories of poverty, see Crassons; Aers, "Christ's Humanity"; Pearsall, "Poverty"; Scott. On theologies of the virtuous pagan and universal salvation, see Whatley; Grady, *Representing*; Hill; Watson, "Visions."

[3] On the complex revisions to this passage, see Warner, *Lost History* 15–31.

"Mede Overmaistreth Lawe": Gendered Personification and the Imaginative Power of the Feminine in *Piers Plowman*

Elizabeth Robertson

Because *Piers Plowman* is so encyclopedic in its range and addresses so many urgent fourteenth-century historical issues—from the failures of institutions to protect the abject poor to the turmoil the plague produced for labor practices—gender seems at first glance to be a small aspect of its encompassing reach. The poem's engagement with gender, however, is much more extensive than usually assumed; indeed, as in-depth study of the poem in the classroom reveals, gender is a primary vehicle through which Langland explores his most pressing social and spiritual concerns. The poem, of course, is above all a personification allegory, and it is well known that the meaning of such allegorical poems depends on embodied performance. Less observed, however, is that embodiment is always gendered: assumptions about gender therefore both limit and enhance meaning especially when, as in Langland's complex use of allegory, the embodied dimension of the concept is as important as its allegorical meaning. An understanding of the uses to which Langland puts gender can be achieved in the classroom by consideration of, first, the distinctive ways in which Langland inextricably intertwines the abstract and the embodied in his allegorical technique and, second, how the gender of the characters met by the narrator, Will, shapes his interactions with them as well as their interactions with one another.[1] Finally, the class can study the ways in which the meaning of certain major principles in the poem—mercy, money, the will, the soul, for example—is furthered by the gendered attributes with which they are associated.

Comprehensive study of these topics is hard to achieve, given the difficulty of finding a place for such a long and challenging poem in the usual English literature curriculum in the United States or, with the possible exception of Oxford and Cambridge, in the United Kingdom. The poem's Middle English language and its complex historical and theological contexts are often perceived as difficulties. To counter such perceptions, I assign the Norton Critical Edition of the B text (Robertson and Shepherd), which contains the Middle English text; E. Talbot Donaldson's translation on the facing page; and over forty sources and backgrounds, such as the Statute of Laborers, the Athanasian Creed, court documents on Alice Perrers, excepts from poems such as *Winner and Waster* and *Mankind*, and some classic critical essays written by major Langland scholars. These secondary sources, especially Elizabeth Kirk's essay on gender in *Piers Plowman* written specifically for the edition, can greatly enhance the introduction of gender in the poem. I encourage students to break their likely dependence on the translation, to train themselves to engage fully with the edition's Middle English, and to consult the definitive scholarly edition of the Middle English version of the poem by A. V. C. Schmidt (Vision). I also urge students to acquire James Simpson's indispensable guide, Piers Plowman*: An Introduction to the B-Text*, which provides invaluable summaries of each vision, and to consult the more recent guides by Anna Baldwin and by Emily Steiner. Baldwin's guide is especially aimed at beginners, while Steiner's is intended for more advanced students. Most undergraduate courses allow for classroom study of the self-contained part of the poem, passus 1–7, known as the *visio*, and sometimes add the culminating vision of the crucifixion, in passus 18. While my discussion focuses primarily on those sections, I suggest ways to probe Langland's use of gender further if the curriculum allows students to read the whole poem (feasible at both undergraduate and graduate levels).[2]

Gendered Personification: Passus 1–7

The first seven passus of the poem afford myriad examples for teaching the particular uses to which Langland puts gendered personification allegory. In these opening passus female characters appear at times as figures common in medieval everyday life—for example, "Rose the regratere" ("Rose, the retailer"), married to Covetousness, in passus 5 of the B text (224) and "Beton the brewestere" ("Beton, the brewster"), who lures Gluttony out of his way in passus 5 (296–384), characters who reflect the various work women did in the late medieval period.[3] The vast majority of Langland's female characters, however, are gendered allegorical personifications—and indeed even Langland's more historical characters are themselves freighted with allegorical meaning. Rose and Beton, for example, are associated with proper measurement (here of retail goods and drink), a topic of major concern in the poem that is often brought to the fore through gender. Langland's allegorical method characteristically intertwines literal or historical meaning with abstract allegorical meaning, making it almost impossible to disentangle the two realms, and study of Langland's gendered personifications needs to take account of how they almost always point both to the immediate historical moment and to the abstract.

A productive way to introduce students to the difficult subject of allegory is to begin with a classroom discussion of Langland's representation of the seven deadly sins in passus 5.[4] Most students have encountered the seven deadly sins before, usually in films, and instructors can ask students to list the sins and what they know about them. A clip from Peter Cook and Dudley Moore's film *Bedazzled* (1967) can remind them that the sin of lust, famously portrayed in the film by Raquel Welsh, is almost always personified as female. But Langland's character Luxuria is, surprisingly, personified as male. This violation of gender expectations can initiate a discussion of the nature of gendered personification, with reference to Helen Cooper's classic essay on the topic ("Gender"), and the class can consider the degree to which Langland consciously makes use of gender expectations in his personifications. Cooper explains that many concepts are gendered as they are because their Latin names were grammatically gendered, and some of Langland's characters conform to that convention: Holy Church's gender, for example, is consonant with the grammatical gender of her Latin name, *Ecclesia*. But many of Langland's characters violate the convention. A number of sins, including Lust (*Luxuria*), are assigned the gender opposite that of their Latin name. Gluttony (*Gula*), for instance, is male in Langland's text, yet he exhibits abject behaviors often associated with the feminine.

Asking students to choose one of the sins and to describe how gender contributes to Langland's representation of the sin can help facilitate student engagement. Gluttony, for instance, is a particularly fruitful example, for his feminine excesses can be considered from the point of view of Bakhtin's theory of the grotesque and in terms of Kristevan theories of excess (Bakhtin; Stallybrass; Kristeva). Patricia Parker has shown how the dangers of feminine excess are fundamental to Edmund Spenser's *Faerie Queene*, a poem deeply indebted to *Piers Plowman* (1–66); a class could compare and contrast the role of feminine excess in the two works, with reference to Parker's work. In addition, with the help of James Paxson's work, the class might explore the extent to which Gluttony and indeed all the sins are queered.[5] Finally, the class might consider the implications of Masha Raskolnikov's argument that the dreamer's encounters with female-gendered personifications diminish as the poem progresses.

By far the most fully developed allegorical figure in the poem is Lady Meed, and the function of gender in her representation has been the subject of a rich critical debate. Among the questions that critics raise and that students could discuss are: How does Lady Meed engage contemporary historical matters, such as marriage practices? Why is money gendered female? Does Lady Meed have agency? What kind of reader is Lady Meed? Is there anything good about her? Critical issues generated by Lady Meed will be familiar to students who have previously encountered Chaucer's Wife of Bath, and it can be helpful to compare and contrast the two figures, especially around issues of medieval marriage, feminine reading, and agency. Lady Meed also can be compared with her rival in the poem, Holy Church, in terms of clothing, parentage, and speech.

Lady Meed's extravagant dress recalls Edward III's consort Alice Perrers (whose love of jewelry is illustrated in an excerpt of the *Chronicon Angliae* [Robertson and Shepherd 485]). The degree to which Lady Meed reflects Perrers's corrupt influence on the court has been usefully discussed by Stephanie Trigg. At the same time, Lady Meed's appearance recalls the biblical description of the whore of Babylon (Robertson and Shepherd 372). Examining the poem in relation to these two sources makes clear how Langland intertwines contemporary historical and biblical figures with his personifications.

In reading these passus, in which False and Conscience are competitors for the hand of Lady Meed, it is helpful for students to have some information about late medieval marriage practices, which is available in Tess Tavormina's thorough study, *Kindly Similitude.* Medieval marriages were often scandalously brokered between men whose only concern was the transfer of money; in marriage women lost their legal agency, becoming what was called "covered" women. That female legal agency in marriage may have been more extensive than has been recognized is illustrated in Christopher Cannon's response to Elizabeth Fowler's important study of covered women, and students can consider how this controversy is exhibited in the Lady Meed passages (Cannon, "Rights"; E. Fowler).

Aided by several essays, students can next consider the ways in which gender furthers both the circulation of money in the poem (women have no meaning in themselves but only in terms of their use) and the cultural anxieties produced by the financial upheavals of the late-fourteenth-century war economy (Lees, "Gender"; Murphy; E. Robertson, "Measurement"). Lady Meed's promiscuity is linked to her status as a figure representing money; like money, Lady Meed gains meaning in transaction. Lady Meed's various meanings, from gift to payment to bribe, are clearly delineated in Simpson's guide to the poem (39–60) and in Simpson's comprehensive essay, "Spirituality and Economics in Passus 1–7 of the B-Text."

Once students have considered how Lady Meed's marriage negotiations reflect contemporary historical conditions and how her giving of gifts, rewards, and bribes recall actual historical events (the creation of donor windows [Marks 3–27] or the payment given to the troops [Schmidt, Vision 419–20] in the winter campaign of the Hundred Years' War; the bribing of court officials [Robertson and Shepherd 443]), students might then debate how much agency Lady Meed possesses. Defining the concept of agency—Paul Smith's book *Discerning the Subject* is useful in this regard—allows students to consider moments in which Lady Meed makes her own choices. Her status as a speaking and a reading subject can be explored in the passages that record her direct speech and her unconventional reading practices (3.331–53), and she can be compared with the Wife of Bath in this sense. Both Lady Meed and the Wife of Bath are selective readers: they choose fragments of Latin texts, which they seem to understand imperfectly, to suit their purposes and may well know only those texts. Such reading practices prompt us to consider the historical conditions that shaped female literacy. Under what circumstances might a woman in the period be able to turn the leaf of a book, as Conscience bids Lady Meed to do (3.341)? Did women and men have different access to books? To what extent did clerics enact the same biased selectivity that Lady Meed does?

Finally, the class might consider the ways in which Lady Meed's association with reward in general intersects with other issues in the poem and indeed, as C. David Benson suggests, looks forward to the poem's culminating celebration of a different kind of Lady Meed or reward, that is, salvation as granted by mercy (Benson, "Function"). The poem, on the one hand, casts Lady Meed as dangerous in her feminine excess—she is seductive, indiscriminate, and multiple. She grants rewards to all seekers and, unmarried, remains capable of assuming many possible identities. Furthermore, as the king complains, "mede overmaistreth lawe" ("mede overmasters law"; 4.176). On the other hand, these negative qualities can be seen in a positive light, for God's love, too, is indiscriminate and boundless and God's mercy in granting salvation to sinners overmasters the old law. Students can come to realize that feminine excess is associated in the poem with not only sin, corruption, and the disorder of society but also, perhaps surprisingly, redemption.

For students who are studying *Piers* in a class on dream visions that includes *Pearl*, another useful exercise is to compare Lady Meed and Mercy to the Pearl-Maiden and to explore the degree to which the Pearl-Maiden's status as a female child shapes the lessons she teaches. The Pearl-Maiden and the narrator debate just the issues that Lady Meed and Mercy raise: the nature of deserved or undeserved reward, the destabilizing effect of gifts (in particular, of God's love) that overflow boundaries and defy rational analysis, and the obscure boundary between material and spiritual value.

Will's Interactions with Gendered Personifications and Their Interactions with One Another: Passus 8–20

In the first part of the poem, the *visio*, the narrator observes gendered personifications from a distance, but in the second half, the *vita*, he interacts with them, and the lessons he learns from the allegorical figures he meets are inflected by gender. One of the more challenging figures with whom Will interacts is Anima, whom he meets in two forms and whom he must understand if he is to succeed in gaining salvation. Anima is grammatically gendered female in passus 9, but her gender changes to an ambiguous one in passus 15, as Will's understanding of the faculty develops. Before they consider how gender informs Langland's representation of the soul, students will first need to know something about how the period understood the makeup of the soul, that is, what is called medieval faculty psychology; the contour of that psychology is explained briefly and lucidly in Simpson's guide (97–100; 171–75) and more fully in my essay "Souls That Matter." Anima appears in two sections of the poem, first in passus 9 and later in passus 15 as a figure of ambiguous gender who is introduced obscurely as a "sotyl thinge withal / One withouten tonge and teeth" ("a subtle thing withal, / One without tongue or teeth"; 12–13).

The portrait of Lady Anima in passus 9 is based on conventional courtly images of aristocratic women. Such women were often viewed in the Middle Ages as prized possessions to be hidden and protected. Wit tells the dreamer that Dowel lives in a castle in which Kynde has also enclosed Lady Anima (9.5–10). In this representation, steeped in chivalric topoi, Langland draws on conventional ideas—articulated by Aristotle and reinscribed in commentaries on Genesis—that women are passive and in need of male protection rather than agents in their own right.[6] Langland also gestures to the historical practices that followed these theoretical ideas: women of upper social status were heavily protected by male and female guardians and kept in the inner recesses of houses or castles. On this topic, students might find useful Peter Stallybrass's discussion of medieval and early modern understandings of the female body as itself a building or castle in which the senses are the entryways and chastity the contested precious treasure within. By consulting Roberta Gilchrist's archeological study of gender and castles (109–48) within the context of Stallybrass's explication of this far-reaching trope, students could explore further how Langland's representation of Lady Anima reflects the way buildings were gendered in the period.

The trope of the soul within a guarded castle reflects not only the actual material practices concerning women but also the gendering of the faculties of the soul in literary sources. Paradigmatic works, such as the thirteenth-century Middle English allegory of the soul, *Sawles Warde* ("The Guardianship of the Soul"), describe the soul as a castle governed by Wit, whose unruly wife, Will, if left ungoverned, could lead the household to ruin. Students could compare this allegory's treatment of the soul (available online in translation [Huber and Robertson]) with that of the lady in the castle in passus 9. The class could consider the following question: what is gained by thinking of the soul as feminine.

Having explored the conventional figure of the soul in passus 9, students can then turn to the much more ambiguously gendered Anima in passus 15 (lines 12–40), a figure who foregrounds the arbitrariness of gender attribution. In this more complex vision, the soul speaks from and occupies a multigendered position: the character names itself both Anima and Animus, and it is only when the narrator names the speaker a "he" that its gender becomes clear. Langland uses a range of gender positions in his representation of the soul in passus 15 in order to demonstrate the way different faculties of the soul are made manifest in actions in the world. Does attributing a masculine gender identity to the soul allow it to engage in a wider range of activities than it would were it given a feminine identity? Finally, given that Langland's interest in gender seems to diminish as Will's knowledge of his soul grows, as Raskolnikov suggests, one might consider whether or not Langland holds a view of the disembodied soul as free of gender. It might be argued, then, that gender is not of particular interest to Langland because of his primary interest in the development of the soul.

Will meets allegorical figures and observes them interacting with each other, and, as in the Lady Meed sequence, the relationship he most often represents is marriage. Students need to be introduced to the different models of marriage, from companionate to hierarchical, that Langland introduces in the second half of the poem. In passus 9, in a surprisingly egalitarian view of marriage, he presents Adam and Eve's marriage as one form of Dowel and an ideal upon which all marriages should be based. Perhaps the most prominent feature of Langland's meditation on marriage in passus 9 is his eschewal of the pervasive misogyny of the age. Typically the fall of humankind is blamed on Eve's sin, but Langland presents Adam and Eve as mutual in their sin: "Adam and heo eten the apple" ("Adam and she had eaten the apple"; 124). For Langland, marriage itself springs from mutual consent and functions to bolster society: see the speech that begins "Do-wel in this world is trewe wedded libbyng folk" ("Do-Well in this world is wedded people who live truly"; 110–19). Although Langland acknowledges a feudal practice in which female choices are dictated by paternal choice, at the same time he stresses the ecclesiastically decreed necessity for mutual consent in marriage: "And thus was wedloke y-wrought with a mene persone / First bi the faderes wille and the frendes conseille, / And sytthenes bi assent of hemself as thei two myghte acorde" ("And thus marriage was made with an intermediate person's help / First by the father's will and the friends' counsel, / And then by their own assent as they two might agree"; 117–19). In addition, he condemns marriages motivated by the desire for money or land, concluding, "For no londes but for love loke ye be wedded" ("For no lands but for love look to it that you marry"; 180).

The next section of the poem charts the development of Will's education, and Langland uses marriage to delineate the role each gender plays in the world. In his presentation of the marriage of Study and Wit and that of Clergy and Scripture, Langland seems to revert to a more conventional view of marriage, in which the wife is subordinate to the husband. Students can be encouraged to explore first why Study and Scripture are presented as feminine and, second, why they are presented as subordinate. Steeped in the practices of the medieval university, this section of the poem can nonetheless be brought to life for students, by, first, asking them to describe their own educational development from early childhood to university and, second, introducing them to the medieval origins of their own educational system.

They might, for example, remember the female teachers of their early schooling. While there are more male teachers in primary schools than there used to be, the stern but loving guidance provided by Langland's figure Study would not be unfamiliar to students. Study is gendered female not only because she is grammatically feminine and subordinated to the higher, masculine faculty of Wit, or knowledge, but also because she reflects the status of women as teachers in late medieval England. As Ralph Hanna has shown, women in the Middle Ages often taught primary school but were denied access to training that would allow them to teach at higher levels ("School"). Study harangues Wit in part because early childhood education was understood in the Middle Ages as a harsh disciplinary regime. While Study's mastery of Wit reverses traditional gender positions in marriage, her scolding behavior draws on common misogynistic tropes of the shrewish wife.

The marriage of the male Clergy to the female Scripture also presents a seemingly traditional marriage, where Scripture is passively subservient to the masterful Clergy. But the hierarchical relation between clergy and scripture—in which scripture is confidently passed on to the laity by the clergy—is precisely what is viewed with suspicion by late medieval dissenters such as the Lollards. Is Langland responding here to the contemporary situation and, if so, to what degree does he present such clerical mediation as exemplary or suspect? In addition, one might explore, with the help of Carolyn Dinshaw's influential study of patristic reading practices in which texts are seen to be female (3–27), the extent to which Langland subscribes to this view in his representation of Scripture as a wife.

If the class looks again at the marriages of Wit and Study and of Clergy and Scripture through the lens of the ideal companionate marriage presented in passus 9, it may wish to reconsider the implications of the hierarchies they seem to instantiate. Does Langland criticize Study's bullying of her husband? Does he question the limitation that Scripture's complete subservience to Clergy suggests? Should education be less punitive, and should Clergy exert less control over Scripture?

Feminine Principles: Passus B.18, C.5, and the Feminized Will

Exploring the gendered nature of allegory can also highlight the workings of principles that are coded as feminine in the poem, which can offer important insights into Langland's theological modes and the nature of poetry itself as an occupation in late medieval England.

While Will's conversations with female allegorical figures diminish as the poem progresses, Will witnesses a crucial exchange late in the poem, in passus 18, among the Four Daughters of God—Mercy, Truth, Peace, and Righteousness—and it is here that the poem presents salvation as the result of feminine principles in the world, in particular those of mercy and peace. The debate of the Four Daughters invites two different kinds of classroom engagement. First, students will need some theological background about the terms of the debate, which is available in Simpson's reading guide (206–16). This is a perfect opportunity to introduce students to the rise of feminine affective piety and to the nature of the feminized Christ, which is particularly well articulated by Caroline Bynum in her influential work, *Holy Feast and Holy Fast.* Langland generally avoids depicting the feminized Christ, which is found in much other medieval writing. In their discussion of Christ's death and resurrection, the Four Daughters enact the Anselmian doctrine of redemption, whereby God's sacrifice of his only son for the redemption of mankind responds not to the devil's rights but emanates instead from God's love of mankind. The emphasis on God's love and the love he invites in return forms the ground upon which late medieval feminine affective piety flourishes. To what degree does Langland endorse this movement?

Second, through close analysis of the language of the Four Daughters' debate, students can consider how certain attributes of argumentation—especially the arational and paradoxical—are associated with the feminine. Given that all four of the daughters are feminine, their debate destabilizes assumptions that women are arational and men rational; however, the principles Mercy and Peace represent are enhanced by their gender, and the different forms of argumentation they present (paradox; song and dance) override those of the other two. Should Truth and Righteousness be understood simply as patriarchal daughters? Do Mercy and Peace win the debate? Students might enact the debate in class to become familiar with the particular poetic strategies each character uses, strategies so brilliantly illuminated by Mary Clemente Davlin in her analysis of this passage (*Game* 89–110). Students can also consider the extent to which the poem privileges mercy over justice, as Simpson argues it does (Piers).

Students are now in a position to probe the properties so crucially connected with justice and mercy—sufficiency and excess—and to review the ways in which Langland uses gender to further his analysis of the crucial roles played by measure in the proper functioning of society and in salvation. The poem begins with Holy Church's lesson that God provides human beings with all they need—food, clothing, and shelter—but it goes on to demonstrate the ways in which individuals and institutions violate that sufficiency when some take more than they need. Each of the sins is specifically associated with some violation of aspects of measurement—Covetousness falsely measures bolts of cloth; Gluttony drinks more than his fair share of ale; and Lady Meed, confusingly, offers some payments equal to their merit but also doles out remunerations that exceed just rewards. Lady Meed in some ways prefigures the figure of Mercy in the poem, for Mercy highlights another aspect of Lady Meed, God's reward of salvation, which emanates from God's boundless love. Female allegorical figures thus illuminate the nature of proper measurement throughout the poem (E. Robertson, "Measurement").

Finally, students can explore the various gender positions occupied in the poem by Will. Begin by having students list his most obvious masculine and feminine attributes (these categories, of course, are always already socially constructed). Will appears to be conventionally masculine: he is married and has a wife, Kit, and a daughter, Calotte. He is able to travel freely around the countryside and engage interlocutors in every major institution, even in those that traditionally denied women access, such as friaries and the university. Despite these clear signals of Will's masculinity, the will was traditionally gendered female. While the protagonist's name may simply represent the masculine name William (perhaps a reference to the author's own name), at the same time, will represents a faculty of the soul often associated with the feminine, as opposed to the faculty of the soul often personified as masculine, reason. Does Langland privilege this more feminized principle in his representation of the progress of the soul?

In addition, Will, as a poet, is engaged in work not expected of a masculine laborer. Through reading the so-called autobiographical passage from the C text of the poem (Robertson and Shepherd 363–66) as well as the Statute of Laborers themselves (428–30), students can learn that writing poetry might have been understood in the period as an occupation not fitting with acceptable forms of masculine work. Will is not identifiably disabled, but he claims to be physically unsuited for physical labor—both too weak and too tall. Although he sings songs for the souls of the dead, he is not a member of the clergy, a peasant laborer, or a land-owning aristocrat. Like the invisible labor of the widow who raises children, cleans clothes, and prepares food, so Will's work as a poet is uncategorizable under the Statute of Laborers. In passus 12, Imaginatif criticizes him as one who "medlest the with makynges" ("you meddle with making verse"; 16). Students can consider the extent to which Will's activities as a poet fit or exceed expectations for traditionally gendered labor.[7]

The class might conclude by speculating whether or not aspects of poems themselves might be coded as feminine. The poetry that Will, as character and poet, produces, that emanates from the will as much as from reason, can be aligned with arational processes found in aspects of verse. The capacity of this poetry to envision and to break traditional boundaries of knowledge through affective rather than rational effects has qualities in common with the very activities in which both Lady Meed and Mercy engage. Davlin has shown how the poetry of Mercy's speech, with its emphasis on paradox and on song, challenges the more rational arguments by Truth and Righteousness.[8] These and other nonsemantic elements of Langland's verse, such as the effects produced by alliteration, contribute to these other ways of knowing. Yet the poem is also often satirical, argumentative, and steeped in the discourses and dialectics of academic theology, forms of expression that emerge from masculine education. Like Lady Meed, Langland's poetry is multiple, exploring many possibilities, sometimes contradictory ones, at once. And like Mercy, Langland's verse overflows boundaries and envisions possibilities outside law. Even in his versification, Langland, like Lady Meed and Mercy, overmasters law. Langland's poetics, as an emanation of the will rather than of reason, may itself be gendered.

Paying attention to the gendered aspects of personification allegory not only uncovers actual historical conditions, theological commonplaces, and pedagogical practices in the Middle Ages but also exposes how all these arenas are shaped by gender constructs that are at times troubling and at times liberating. Comprehensive study of this great poem, inside or outside the classroom, can reveal how fundamental gender is to Langland's visionary understanding of past, present, and future social formations.

NOTES

I am grateful to Jeffrey Robinson, Karen Robertson, and Thomas Goodmann for helpful editorial comments on this essay and especially to Kate Crassons for her perspicacious and wide-ranging response.

[1] A. C. Spearing has rightly queried the ways in which our assumptions about narrators in nineteenth- and twentieth-century texts have shaped the way we understand the speakers of medieval texts. It's worthwhile to caution students about how these assumptions can lead to misinterpretations of medieval texts. See A. C. Spearing, *Textual Subjectivity* and *Medieval Autographies*.

[2] I also lead a thriving *Piers Plowman* reading group, which is open on a voluntary basis to University of Glasgow students of all levels and from any discipline as well as to teaching staff and interested members of the public: it has been meeting weekly for eight years. I recommend this as a way for a medium-sized group to delve deeply into the poem.

[3] Quotations and translations from the poem are from the Norton Critical Edition (Robertson and Shepherd). Langland's representation of women at work might be usefully brought into conversation with what is known historically about women and work in the Middle Ages: see J. M. Bennett; McIntosh. For a response to Bennett, see Hanna, "Brewing Trouble."

[4] On teaching allegory, see Judith H. Anderson's essay in this volume.

[5] In addition to Paxson, see Raskolnikov 168–96. Paxson's essay and Raskolnikov's chapter are among the few sustained queer readings of *Piers Plowman*, though the poem repeatedly queers expectations of all kinds.

[6] For a succinct introduction to these Aristotelian ideas, see Maclean.

[7] On gendered labor, see J. M. Bennett.

[8] Davlin's illuminating reading of the speeches (*Game* 89–110) is a model of close reading well suited for classroom use.

Translation Matters

Thomas A. Goodmann

> In its first phase, the translator's activity is no different from that of a reader or a critic: each reading is a translation, and each criticism is, or begins as, an interpretation.
>
> —Octavio Paz, *Traducción: Literatura y Literalidad*

> Traddutore, traditore. (Translator, traitor.)
>
> —Traditional

The translator, of course, is not a traitor but an advocate for the source, an ally to readers who live outside so many languages, so many texts. A translation of a demanding Middle English text such as *Piers Plowman* eliminates one of the obstracles to including the poem in course syllabi. There are practical reasons to assign a translation. If an instructor wants students to have some experience of the thought-world of *Piers Plowman*, she places her students on safe ground with one or more of the available translations. Students will certainly cover the poem, or parts of it, more rapidly in present-day English than Middle English, which allows inclusion of Langland in a course containing other texts.

Translation was a significant part of Langland's multilingual moment, and it is constituent of the texture of his poetry, too, worthy of considerable attention as one of its modes. In this essay I cite currently available translations, offer ideas for their critical study in comparative analytical essays, and propose some exercises in creative translation. In doing so I invite reflection on the idea of translation itself as a subject of *Piers Plowman*, one with intellectual and pedagogical ripples.

Available Translations and Selected Passages

Instructors teaching *Piers Plowman* in translation may choose from four translations of the B text (Donaldson, Piers Plowman*: An Alliterative Verse Translation*; Goodridge; Schmidt, Piers Plowman*: A New Translation of the B-Text*; Sutton) and one of the C text (Economou).[1] Students may read the entire poem in translation and then study a few episodes or passus in Middle English. Reading a translation prior to reading in Middle English helps students gain an overview of the many episodes in B and C and their many differences. Some episodes most frequently chosen for close study include the B or C prologue, often read in comparison with the General Prologue of *The Canterbury Tales*; the Deadly Sins (B.5; C.6–7); and the passion and life of Christ (B.18–19; C.20–21).

Likewise, a translation may serve as an ancillary reading, assigned (or recommended) to support study of the poem in Middle English, as Kathryn Kerby-Fulton suggests in her essay in this volume on teaching the C text. The Norton Critical Edition (Robertson and Shepherd), with its facing-page text of the Donaldson verse translation, is convenient for such a purpose; I have also taught A. V. C. Schmidt's edition of the B text alongside his prose translation thereof (Schmidt, Vision; Schmidt, Piers Plowman*: A New Translation*). Some of my students appreciate the prose translation because it offers an experience closer to that of reading a novel than does reading verse.

Reading translations can also give advanced undergraduates or graduate students a sense of how Langland changed his poem in revision. Such studies might begin with readings from the B and C texts in translation, then take up critical claims for their order of composition, and finally examine samples of subsequent conflation by scribes who produced conjoint texts. Or students might read Míċeál Vaughan's edition of the A text, which contains just eighty-six pages of Middle English text, and then read part or all of B or C in translation.

Comparative Analysis of Translations and of Transcriptions

In the conventional and relatively passive uses of translations, instructors and students rely on the competence of the translator to gain a sense of important themes, figures, and topics in the B or C texts. As time and interest allow, working with translations can provide an overview of the B or C texts, support selective, introductory study of the Middle English text and its language, or support close study of the entire poem in Middle English. Like all translations, those currently available provide access to a text that requires quite a lot of time to reach a certain level of comfort with its language and with its complex currents of thought.

For all that these translations are more than sufficient, they are nonetheless marked by differences in form, syntax, and diction, of course, that offer opportunities to think about translation itself for students at any nearly any level. Different renditions provide comparative examples of any passage from the poem; the translators' varying choices are evident in the first four lines of the B text prologue, here compared with Schmidt's Middle English text:

> In a somer seson, whan softe was the sonne
> I shoop me into shroudes as I a sheep were,
> In habite as an heremite unholy of werkes,
> Wente wide in this world wondres to here. (Schmidt, Vision)

> In a summer season when the sun was mild
> I clad myself in clothes as I'd become a sheep;

In the habit of a hermit unholy of works
Walked wide in this world, watching for wonders.
(Donaldson, Piers Plowman*: An Alliterative Verse Translation*)

One summer time, when the sun was mild, I dressed myself in sheepskin clothing, the habit of a hermit of unholy life, and wandered abroad in this world, listening out for its strange and wonderful events.
(Schmidt, Piers Plowman*: A New Translation*)

One summer season, when the sun was warm, I rigged myself out in shaggy woolen clothes, as if I were a shepherd; and in the garb of an easy-living hermit I set out to roam far and wide through the world, hoping to hear of marvels.
(Goodridge)

While Donaldson's verse translation and Schmidt's prose translation have the same word counts—Goodridge's translation uses more words—several differences are worth exploring with students. A quick review of the Middle English shows that Donaldson's verse translation is somewhat closer to the original than the prose versions, while the more expansive syntax both of Schmidt and of Goodridge avoids potential confusion for first-time readers by revising locutions such as Donaldson's, "as I'd become a sheep." Similarly, all three translators undo the inversion of the phrase, "whan softe was the sonne." Donaldson offers, line by line, much of the alliterative flavor of the Middle English, yet Schmidt also communicates some sense of the same: summer, sun; habit, hermit, unholy; wandered, world, wonderful. There is less alliteration in Goodridge's translation, which offers the most colloquial and most free version of the three.

Arthur Burrell's translation, from 1912, offers these opening lines with a striking presentation of midline caesura, while retaining syntactic inversions:

In a summer season,   when soft was the sun,
In rough cloth I robed me,   as I a shepherd were,
In habit like a hermit   in his works unholy
And through the wide world I went, wonders to hear.

Marking the caesura in this way opens a door to questions about Langland's line and the alliterative poetry of the time more generally; students may read *Sir Gawain and the Green Knight* for comparison.[2] D. Attwater and R. Attwater's verse translation of the B text, from 1957, likewise strongly marks the caesura with spacing and a medial point:

In a summer season · when soft was the sun,
I clothed myself in a cloak as I a shepherd were,
Habit like a hermit's · unholy in works,
And went wide in the world · wonders to hear.

The Attwaters elide any caesura in the second line and move the alliterative to the first position in the third line, eliminating the unstressed syllables of the Middle English line while curiously attaching the adjective "unholy" to the possessive "hermit's." Terence Tiller's B text rendition, meanwhile, is both expansively fluent in its syntax and fulsome in its alliteration:

> One summer season, when the sun was soothing,
> I shrouded myself in a shaggy sheepskin coat;
> Thus habited like a hermit of unholy life,
> I walked into the wide world to hear of wonders.

Retaining "wide" from the source, Tiller transfers it from adverb ("went wyde") to adjective ("wide world"), retaining its alliterative presence while changing its original sense from how the speaker goes in the world to what the world is like.[3] Peter Sutton's translation avoids the archaic reflexive construction, repeating Tiller's descriptor "shaggy," while doubling Tiller's "wide":

> One summer season when the sun was still soft,
> I set off like a sheep in a shaggy woolen smock,
> The unholy habit of a wandering hermit,
> And went seeking wonders in the wide, wide world.

While it preserves alliteration, Sutton's rendering is in a modern idiom, closer to prose compared with other verse translations: "*Quite* weary with walking I wanted to rest," Sutton continues (7; my emphasis), while ending the poem, "[Conscience] groaned then for Grace, and I gradually awoke" (20.387), creating a less dramatic reading of "gradde after grace" (Schmidt, Vision 20.387) in the final lines than that of other translators (cf. "And then he cried out loud for Grace until I began to awake" [Economou 22.386]; "His final plea was a piercing cry for Grace. It rang on in my ears, till I awoke [. . .]" [Schmidt, Piers Plowman*: A New Translation* 254]).

While a translation of Langland is rarely a primary source in my teaching, no matter which translation we use to support reading the Middle English text, we look to at least one other rendition to ask the following questions: What differences do we see—and what difference do they make? What is gained and lost by the choice of this word or phrase, of verse over prose, and vice versa? Whichever translation is used, it is easy to provide students with a few parallel passages from other translators, and it is a short step further to ask students to compare, in a short written assignment, a few lines of the Middle English B text with two (or more) translations of the same lines. Such an essay will raise students' awareness of Langland's language and may serve to introduce questions about the practice and the art of translation (it can also offer instructors some early indication of students' analytical and expressive abilities). What do students make of the differences among "clad myself," "dressed myself," and "rigged myself out" for the reflexive "shope me"? What are the distinctive effects of "[w]alked wide," "wandered abroad," and "set out to roam far and wide" for "[w]ent wyde"? Or of "watching" and "listening out" and "hoping to hear" for "to here"? (And how does the speaker hope to "hear" wonders, anyway, as Ralph Hanna inquires of his students in his essay in this volume?) What about Goodridge's increase in word count? Are translators supposed to remain as "faithful" ("traddutore") as possible to the original in as many respects as possible? How many? Which ones are most important for this poem?[4]

It is easy to find Burrell's translation in a used copy or a library (it's also available as a reprint from the University of Toronto Libraries); a brief passage from it may be shared in class on screen or in a handout. The upshot of such explorations is often a common sense among class members that no translation is, or can be, perfectly accurate, or fully faithful to what each of us hears as the music of the source. And of course, with Langland, we are addressing a relatively simple act of translation from an earlier stage of the language, if also from a dialect area outside the London English that importantly shaped our own language. I often share a quick image of more challenging translations that run across entirely different language and writing systems, in which the unavoidable losses are all the more apparent, such as what may not be translated from T'ang era calligraphic styles, as well as the distinctive visual negotiation of reading vertical columns and of reading from right to left.

The inherently imperfect craft of translation is part of what I want my students to learn, but my objectives are multiple and fluid and, with Middle English sources, never really innocent. Intending no disrespect to the estimable efforts of Langland's translators, I want my students to become critical readers of translations, so that they may become more tempted to taste the apples from the trees of the poems themselves.[5] All things considered, Middle English—even Langland's Middle English—offers pretty low-hanging fruit in a world of linguistic variety and difference. The remarks from the translators themselves on translating the poems serve such critical reading (Goodridge 19–22; Donaldson, Piers Plowman*: An Alliterative Verse Translation* xv–xvi; Economou xxiii–xviii; Schmidt, Piers Plowman*: A New Translation* xli–xliii). And if students can come to some terms with Langland's Middle English, reading that of Chaucer seems quite easy by comparison; I often read the two poets together in the same course.[6]

Following examples of such differences among translations, I introduce digital images from *Piers Plowman* manuscripts and have students work in small groups to transcribe and compare a passage as recorded in two manuscripts and by two hands.[7] This simple exercise allows us to clarify some terms that, I have found, are often unfamiliar to students, including *manuscript*, *codex*, *edition*, and *translation*. Time and interests shape how far down the corridor of codicology and paleography we may wander; the point is to expose students to the many efforts and decisions necessary to bring a text across to an early modern and to a modern mass readership: transcribing, collating, editing, as well as translating in the traditional sense.

Literal Translation, Literary Transformation, Translation as Trope

Another exercise, which may be adjusted in length, is to ask students to explore the differences in writing verse and prose by rewriting a passage from the Middle English verse of the poem (A, B, or C versions) into Middle English prose word order and to write briefly about the differences, an assignment that will deepen their sense of grammar, morphology, syntax, idiom, and verse. Still another option is to have students translate a passage from Middle English into present-day English alliterative verse—the degree of exactitude being both part of the challenge and a subject for discussion—and then write briefly about the challenges.[8] Following the example of Carl Conrad, one of my Latin teachers, I ask students to write two translations: the first, as literal a rendering as possible; the second, a more idiomatic and potentially more free version that attempts to bring across some of the aural and figural aspects of the source. This too is an exercise easy to pursue across a single line or a longer passage. While the opening lines of the poem, for example, are pretty straightforward in sense, they are also easier than much of the poem insofar as they are narrative, whereas much of the poem is not. Consider, for example, the more idiomatic dismissal by the Doctor of Divinity of what Patience says at the Feast of Patience: "'This is a *dido,*' quod this doctour, 'a dysores tale!'" (Pearsall, Piers C.15.170). A possible translation is "'This is old as Dido,' said this Doctor, 'a ditty-singer's tale.'"[9] Students could be assigned multiple examples, including significantly more difficult ones.

Translation is one among the poem's many interests and anxieties, informing both the sense that laypeople dabble ignorantly in learned debate (Schmidt, Vision 10.103–16) and the view that those who ought to know Latin—including Will himself (1.140–41) but also contemporary clergy—do not. Translation into English is part of the fabric of the poem, as Langland cites, in part or in full, a number of Latin quotations drawn from scripture, hymns, and other sources (Alford, Piers Plowman*: A Guide*). In the B text, passus 18, for instance, the four sisters, Mercy, Truth, Righteousness, and Peace, debate the fate of souls in hell and subsequently witness the harrowing, after which Peace concludes by citing Alain de Lille:

> *Clarior est solito post maxima nebula phebus; Post*
> *inimicicias clarior est amor.*
>
> "After sharpe shoures," quod Pees, "moste shene is the sonne;
> Is no weder warmer than after watery cloudes;

Ne no love levere, ne lever frendes,
Than after werre and wo whan Love and pees be maistres."
(Robertson and Shepherd 18.409–12)

As a rule the sun is brighter after the biggest cloud; After hostilities love is brighter.
"After sharp showers," said Peace, "the sun shines brightest;
No weather is warmer than after watery clouds;
Nor any love lovelier, or more loving friends,
Than after war and woe when Love and peace are masters."
(Donaldson 18.409–12)

Such quotations raise a number of points for discussion, including the imagined primary audience for the poems, which would recognize such Latinity as a sign of authority, as well as other audiences that are assumed to need a translation thereof. What might Langland mean in using both languages? (It is surely different from Chaucer's Nun's Priest's Tale, where the rooster renders "*Mulier est hominis confusio*"—"Woman is man's ruin"—as "Womman is mannes joye and al his blis"—"Woman is man's joy and all his bliss" [L. D. Benson, *Riverside Chaucer* 7.3164, 3166]). The English alliteratives, and the expansion, including personification, lend a homely air of folk wisdom to the Latin maxim. There is also the practical issue for modern translators. Presenting this whole passage (and many similar ones) in present-day English is convenient for readers but levels the dual-language topography of the text: the translator once again a traitor, if unavoidably. Schmidt prints the translated quotation as verse in his prose translation and notes the source in an endnote, while Donaldson (among others) prints the quotation in italics to suggest its otherness and Latinity, citing the source in a footnote.

Formal and Cultural Translation Efforts

A more elastic and expansive sort of translation exercise is to present an episode as a short dramatic exercise.[10] Another topic for discussion, small group work, and a brief writing exercise is to translate the cultural terms and figures of the poem by casting various episodes in Langland and in, say, Dante, with contemporary figures from our own time for the field of folk, Lady Meed, Haukyn (Activa Vita), and the residents of various descending circles of hell. Who would be apt for drowsy, dreamy Will? Piers? Gluttony? the Deadly Sins? Lady Meed? Haukyn? the Samaritan? What types of social groups and professions would you locate in a modern field of folk? And what might you substitute for the field as an inclusive social space? (Might such a space now be digital?) Such an exercise can easily turn frivolous, but it has potential for discussing choices that indicate some of our interpretive investments. In order to draw an approximation of, say, the Cat in twenty-first-century cultural terms (prol. 146–208), we will need to understand something of the political dramas of Edward III's later years and those of the young Richard. The exercise of translating the cultural and historical terms and figures from Langland's poetry and period to those of our own is very much in the spirit of medieval translating, wherein writers routinely modernized (we would say *medievalized*) classical narrative materials, bringing them across to their own times and terms.

By such *passus* ("steps"), then, students may move toward deeper engagement with the subject of translation, as it has been understood in the medieval and the postmedieval periods. None of these pedagogical options are exclusive of one another: reading a little or a lot of Langland in Middle or in present-day English; asking students to try their hand at literal verse or prose translation or to attempt a freer cultural adaptation of an episode or exchange, including visual sources, if they choose; inviting them to use hip-hop idioms to translate Langland's often pungent and powerful alliterative lines. I routinely use a translation alongside the Middle English text, exploring ideas about translation as a critical and creative method for engaging Langland's poetry—and much other poetry too.[11]

"Traddutore, traditore"

Every translation is an interpretation, certainly, just as every interpretation—every reading—is a translation. Every time we sit with our students and ask, "What might this mean and how might we know that this reading is plausible?," we are asking them to engage in chains of translation: from manuscripts to transliteration to edition; from one historical phase of a language to a successive stage; from one language to another; from reader to reader, student to teacher, and round and round again. It is only in failing to keep the inquiry open and moving that we risk betraying the text or our students.

NOTES

[1] A modern translation of A, by Francis Delores Covella, SC, published in 1992, is out of print.

[2] On pedagogical approaches to Langland's line and meter, see Ian Cornelius's essay in this volume.

[3] It is yet another small step to look at the C text's expansion of line 4, as well as its spelling differences from the B text, as presented in Huntington Library MS Hm 143: "In a somur sesoun whan softe was the sonne / Y shope me into shroudes as Y a shep were; / In abite as an heremite vnholy of werkes / Wente forth in the world wondres to here, / And say many selles and selkouthe thynges" (Pearsall, Piers C.prol.1–5). George Economou translates these lines thus: "In a summer season when the sun shone softly / I wrapped myself in

woolens as if I were a sheep; / In a hermit's habit, unholy in his works. / I went out into the world to hear wonders / And to see many strange and seldom-known things."

[4] Translation studies, with a large literature in many languages, presents a subject beyond the scope of this essay and likely outside the primary aims of anyone teaching Langland. But, for interested students, a few works may serve as an introduction, including the volumes edited by M. Baker and by Venuti. On translation in the European Middle Ages, see Beer; Ríkharðsdóttir. On translation in later medieval Britain, see Warren. See also Cooper, "Translation."

[5] See Kathryn Kerby-Fulton's essay in this volume, on teaching the C text, which describes an essay assignment that is a critique of a translation of the poem. For a more severe assessment of modern translations, see Beidler, "Chaucer."

[6] On teaching a comparative reading of the prologues of Langland and Chaucer, see especially the essays by Clopper and Cornelius in this volume. Those by Davlin, Galloway, Hanna, Lawton, Robertson, Steiner, and Trigg also suggest ways to compare Chaucer with Langland.

[7] The Bodleian Library's Web site offers many images of Langland manuscripts, from Bodleian Library MS Douce 104, a C text; selected pages from Bodleian 851, containing the Z text; Digby 102; Digby 145; Digby 171; and MS. Eng. Poet.a.1, the so-called Vernon Manuscript. Two useful texts for introducing students to the study of medieval manuscript books are Clemens and Graham; Kerby-Fulton et al.

[8] See Cornelius's essay in this volume, on teaching Langland's meter and verse.

[9] Economou translates using a consistent contemporary figure, while ceding the terms used by Langland's Doctor: "This is an old routine," said this doctor, "an entertainer's line!"

[10] See Galloway's essay in this volume for an example of this technique. See also Beidler, "Teaching."

[11] Roy Liuzza's edition and translation of *Beowulf* makes such comparative studies easy, as his appendix E (212–31) includes twenty-four translations of the so-called Coast Guard's speech from the past two hundred years, from that of Sharon Turner (1805) to that of Seamus Heaney (2000). See also Liuzza's "*Beowulf* in Translation."

CURRICULAR CONTEXTS

Falling in Love with *Piers Plowman*

Mary Clemente Davlin

Piers Plowman has finally been recognized as one of the masterpieces of English literature and is being taught in person and online in survey courses, in medieval period and devotional literature courses, occasionally in a course of its own, and sometimes in workshops, lectures, and retreats. I have had the privilege of teaching it in most of these settings. Depending on the type of course, the amount of time allotted to the poem varies, as do its language (Middle English or translation) and the parts of the text considered. A single lecture or a non-academic weekend workshop will be highly selective, usually thematic and in translation. In a British literature survey course I allot about a week to passus 18, the most accessible and clearly structured unit within the poem, using the Norton edition, which has E. Talbot Donaldson's translation and the Middle English on facing pages (Robertson and Shepherd, cited here for both text and translation). In a medieval literature course and in a *Piers Plowman* course, I use either A. V. C. Schmidt's edition of the B text in Middle English (Vision) or the Norton, accompanied by Anna Baldwin's *Guidebook to* Piers Plowman. In the medieval literature course, or in a course in devotional literature, vernacular theology, or religious writing, we read the prologue, passus 1 and 5, parts of 11, all of 18, and parts of 19 and 20, over five weeks. For a course in devotional literature that allows only a little time for *Piers*, one might use my *Journey into Love*, perhaps supplementing it with xeroxed passages of the poem in Middle English. A whole semester devoted to *Piers Plowman* allows reading the entire text in present-day English and at least the prologue and passus 1–6 and 16–20 in Middle English as well. For any of these courses, the Internet provides the opportunity for online teaching as well as bibliography and related material, especially at the Web site of the International *Piers Plowman* Society (www.piersplowman.org).

Adults interested in spirituality or religion, like those who have taken an interest in Julian of Norwich, make up a potential audience for *Piers Plowman* beyond that of college students interested in literature. Yet the existence of this great spiritual text is all but unknown outside circles of medievalists. In the last few years I have had the pleasure of introducing groups of people to parts of *Piers* in weekend workshops and retreats. I begin with a brief explanation of the poem; when it was written; its Christian, biblical, and liturgical nature; and why it is attractive to many people today. I choose a theme, translate pertinent passages into modern English, and xerox them. (*Journey into Love* could alternatively be used for such groups or for courses in the history of spirituality.) At each meeting we read and discuss together several passages, and readers relate them to their own experience and to other texts they have read. When we did such a workshop during Holy Week, I selected passages about the Eucharist; passages about the passion and crucifixion; all of passus 18, including the harrowing of hell by the light; and passages about the resurrection. Because the workshop was held at the Dominican motherhouse in Sinsinawa, Wisconsin, we were able to attend Holy Week services before and after talking about the particular passages pertinent to each service. Of course, the most dramatic experience was reading about the harrowing of hell after participating in the service of light on the vigil of Easter.

I have discovered that the poem is attractive to readers of various ages and backgrounds because of its beauty; its concern with issues that are important to us today; its unique structure; its strong, "pregnant" language (Spearing, "Development" 252); its range of tone from farce to sublimity, from earthly to divine; its comprehensive view of human life; its sense of God—biblical, liturgical, deeply personal, but grand; and the fact that Langland is the only narrative poet before Milton to give God a voice (Davlin, *Place*). Readers seem to enjoy the idea that no one yet claims to understand the poem perfectly and that it is thus open to their interpretation. In reading it, many are surprised to learn that the Middle Ages were more complex and sophisticated than they previously thought, finding in Langland a poet who values nature, grapples with what we would call psychology, and attacks prejudices. They discover that Christianity has many faces, since Langland does not belong to the affective tradition, which they may know from Chaucer, lyrics, and artworks of the period, but to an older, objective tradition. Looking at what the Internet offers about *Piers Plowman* makes readers realize that this old text is of great interest to many people today.

This is not to say that *Piers Plowman* is easy for any reader. Those meeting it for the first time need help especially with the structure, wordplay, genre, satire, and vocabulary, even if they have read Chaucer. I like to begin by presenting the narrative as the story of Will, the protagonist, who sets out seeking adventure as a young man and falls into dreams that become his education and carry him to old age. We discuss how dreams are often vehicles for insight in medieval dream visions. At the beginning and end of *Piers Plowman*, Will's dreams show him the world in which he lives; in the middle, they narrow to his own interior life in a section (passus 8–15) that I compare to students' lives in college, as Will comes to know his own thought, intelligence, and other mental faculties. Whether Will is meant to be a person or an allegorical personification, he is a subjectivity, a character, foolish, selfish at times, an observer occasionally involved in action. He wants to find *treuthe* ("truth"), then *fals* ("falsity"), then Dowel (the knowledge of what it is to "do well"), then Piers the Plowman, yet he is often unwilling to accept good advice and acts as a tourist rather than as a pilgrim for most of the poem. What finally changes him and enables him to find what he has been searching for? This question is answered in passus 16 and 19, especially the climactic passus 18, where Will enters into the public worship of the Christian Lent and Holy Week and comes to see Christ as savior. Yet the poem does not end there; unlike the *Divine Comedy*, it returns to the sufferings and corruption of this world in Will's own time, ending as Will hears Conscience cry out to God on his way to find Piers the Plowman.

In this first reading, attention needs to be paid to structure. Diagrams of the poem, like that in Margaret Williams's translation (21) or in John Burrow's *Langland's Fictions* (20), or verbal analyses like Joseph Wittig's (*William Langland* 15–53) or Mary Carruthers's (*Search* 7) are helpful for both teachers and students. In either an in-person or an online class, instructors may ask each student to graph or sketch Will's progress through the poem—the plot—on the three levels of waking, sleeping, and dream-within-dream. Sharing sketches leads to discussion of the ways in which the poem is circular or cyclical and its use of several kinds of time: calendar time in Will's life story, cyclical annual time in the liturgical cycle, historical time leading to an apocalypse. John Lawlor suggests another way to look at structure: "The method of the poet . . . is not so much to develop an argument as to make us undergo its development" (Piers Plowman*: An Essay* 11). He shows that while Will thinks of his experience as a search for God, the poem shows that God is searching for Will as well. Another aspect of structure is genre (see Bloomfield; Justice, "Genres"). While this is a difficult subject, it offers the opportunity for students to grasp what allegory is or may be as well as how lyric may enter into narrative.

What will the typical class period or online discussion be like? Study questions will facilitate understanding of the text: for example, a search for oppositions in passus 1 (truth versus falsity, comfort versus care) can lead to good discussion. If this is a medieval literature course, it is useful to ask students to compare and contrast *Piers* to other texts they have read. If the text is being read principally in Middle English, tips on translating and on difficult words before a reading and short translation quizzes after it will encourage careful translation.

Thorough discussion of a few passages in Middle English that illustrate wordplay will alert students to the need for careful, close reading. Dramatization of small sections will point out Langland's descriptive powers and humor. Later, students or pairs of students might report to the class on key critical articles, inviting discussion. Teaching *Piers* online, whether wholly or in a hybrid course, demands study questions that require not only general knowledge that students can relate to the reading but also actual reading and understanding of the text in relation to theory or structure and connections among parts of the poem. All these should lead to online discussion by students and teacher.[1]

For many students and scholars, thematic study of the poem is enriching, and students may be encouraged to look for themes that interest them to serve as the basis of a final project or a report to the class. This may begin with an event or object in the poem, such as written documents (like the pardon and letters) or domiciles (like the tower, the dungeon, the heart); with an idea (like pardon); with a character and his or her meaning (like Meed, Book, or Piers); with clothing (for instance, in the prologue, the confession, or the Haukyn episode); with a social situation, like poverty, the status of women, marriage (see Tavormina), or anti-Semitism; with a pattern, like mistakes made by characters or relations between teachers and Will as a student; or with a key word. Making students aware early on that the poem contains material relevant to their own interests or majors is especially helpful. For example, those studying gerontology might explore passus 19–20, about Will's old age and that of his wife. Students of education or psychology might find, especially in passus 8–16, an interesting study of the mind, its faculties, and the process of learning. English majors see expertise in description and concreteness in passus 5, use of puns in passus 1, mastery of sound and rhythm and tenderness of expression throughout and can compare Langland's satire with Chaucer's in the prologues to *Piers* and to the *Canterbury Tales*. History majors can learn about Ricardian politics and social history in the prologue. Students in theology or pastoral studies learn about what the mysteries of Christianity meant to a brilliant fourteenth-century Catholic. Economists find out about fourteenth-century attitudes toward poverty.

Even if this first reading is in translation, it is essential for students to be introduced to at least a few passages in Middle English in order to understand its richness, which is inevitably lost in translation. The poet uses the polyvalence of certain key words, like *treuthe*, *love*, *kynde*, *werk*, to say several things at once and to relate several levels of meaning (Davlin, *Game*). For example, in passus 1, Holy Church tells Will that

> Ac tho that worche wel, as holi writt telleth,
> And enden, as I ere seide, in Treuthe that is the best
> Mowe be siker that her soule shal wende to Hevene
> Ther Treuthe is in Trinitee, and troneth hem alle.

> But those who wish to work well, as holy words direct,
> And who end, as I said earlier, in Truth that is best
> May be certain that their souls will ascend to Heaven
> Where Truth is in Trinity, bestowing thrones on all who come. (1.130–33)[2]

The repetition of "truth" within three lines is obvious, and in the second use, it just as obviously means God, truth in the tower. But what, in line 131, does it mean to "end . . . in truth"? To end in a state of integrity? To remain faithful to the end? To have the moral virtue of honest fidelity? Or could it mean to end in God? Three times in the B text—at passus 1, line 86; passus 5, line 486b, and passus 9, line 65a—the poem quotes 1 John 4.8 and 4.16: "One who abides in love abides in God and God in that person" (Alford, Piers 35, 50, 60). The poet is thus capable of imagining someone good actually living (and therefore ending) in God. One can argue about the relative merits of these interpretations, and a translator (though not a reader) has to choose one or the other. But reading the Middle English, aware of the various meanings of "treuthe," one can also see connections among these meanings. How does one live in God if not by being "trewe"? Does the poet believe that a life of virtue is based upon a close relationship with God? Langland uses repetition and punning to cause the alert reader to relate various meanings in a single word. This is a rich field for in-person or online classroom discussion.

The same sort of wordplay marks the use of the word *kynde* ("nature"; "kind") throughout the poem. C. S. Lewis's essay on the word *kind* is a useful introduction to the richness of the word even in our own times, and anyone who has studied *King Lear* will be familiar with the notion that kindness is natural while unkindness is unnatural or monstrous (*Studies* 24–33). Will describes his meeting with Kynde in passus 11, lines 327–68, in perhaps the most beautiful nature poetry written before the nineteenth century, nature comprising the whole world that surrounds us—birds, beasts, and flowers. Yet in passus 18, *kynde* has a different meaning, a philosophical and theological one: "And after God auntrede hymself, and toke Adames kynde" ("And afterward God offered himself, and took Adam's nature"; 222); God takes on Adam's nature, human nature, in the incarnation. In the same passus, Christ plays on the word *kynde* with two other meanings: "For I were an unkynde kynge but I my kynde holpe" ("For I'd be an unkind king unless I gave my kin help"; 398), which is to say, it would be unloving and unnatural for Christ to not help his kin, those who share his human nature. Also, since Christ is believed to have two natures, human and divine, he surely also means that he would be an unnatural king, one who fails to follow his own divine nature. Students can learn to notice and discuss resonances of many meanings as they encounter the word *kynde* and Langland's economy and artfulness in the way the meanings relate to one another. All these meanings are also relevant to the meanings of the phrase *kynde knowing* that appears throughout the poem.

An easy exercise that helps students understand such polyvalent words is to find a photo or short video that illustrates a word's meanings. For instance, family pictures might illustrate *kynde*: one can see family likeness in the faces, as the members are bound by kinship; thus, they are the same kind of people. If the family shows affection, the photo may also illustrate their kindness. A series of photos or videos might suggest *treuthe*, one showing a person speaking the truth, another acting honestly, another promising fidelity. Dictionary exercises reinforce this understanding of language. A Bible dictionary will explain the Hebrew names for God, including *emet*, meaning "that which has been put to the test and has revealed itself to be solid" (Guillet 35), a root meaning of *treuthe*. The *Middle English Dictionary* or the *Oxford English Dictionary* will give the various fourteenth-century meanings of *treuthe* and other key words on which Langland plays. Even a few passages read in Middle English against the background of such exercises will open students to an awareness of the possibilities of language and the need to read the poem with alertness to potential puns.

Readers need to develop an awareness that characters in *Piers Plowman* lie, make mistakes, and even deceive themselves, so their words cannot always be taken at face value or as the words of the author (W. E. Rogers). For instance, in the debate of the Four Daughters of God, in passus 18, Righteousness is certain that no humans will be saved: ". . . I, Rightwisnesse, recorde thus with Treuth / That her peyne be perpetuel and no preyere hem helpe" ("I, Righteousness, record this with Truth, / That their pain should be perpetual and no prayer should help them"; 199–200). Yet later Christ declares that Righteousness's opinion is erroneous. The poem is, in other words, a dramatic text (W. E. Rogers 22–24). As David Lawton has pointed out, characters in the poem are not always people but sometimes allegorical personifications or other kinds of subjectivities ("Subject").[3] However, like people, they can be analyzed through their words, styles, and physical descriptions. Lady Holy Church and Lady Meed make a classic study in contrasts, which could profitably be dramatized by students in person or online. The Seven Deadly Sins and Haukyn, Actif Man, also present a range of emotion from broad satirical humor to pathos and lend themselves to dramatic representation.

Piers Plowman is remarkable for its investigation of the great mysteries of the Christian faith, such as the Trinity, the incarnation, the sacraments, the nature of the Church, the indwelling of the Holy Spirit. These are mysteries precisely because they cannot be explained or understood logically. Each includes two seemingly incompatible truths: for example, God is one but there are three persons in God; Christ is God and man. Unlike the affective poets and painters of his time, Langland unfailingly insists on both truths at the same time, requiring the mind to go deeper into the mystery rather than accepting an easy explanation. So, for example, in the description of Christ's death in passus 18, names and actions demand the reader's awareness of both his divinity and humanity: "'*Consummatum est*,' quod Cryst and comsed forto swowe, / Pitousliche and pale as a prisoun that deyeth. / The Lord of Lyf and of Lighte tho leyed his eyen togideres" ("'*Consummatum est*,' said Christ and started to swoon, / Piteously and pale like a prisoner dying. / The Lord of Life and of Light then laid his eyelids together"; 57–59). The phrases "started to swoon," "[p]iteously and pale like a prisoner dying," and "then laid his eyelids together" are full of pathos for a young man dying. They would seem to express the affective mode of religious poetry, stressing Jesus's suffering humanity. Yet the names "Cryst" (the Messiah) and "Lord of Lyf and of Lighte" insist on the divinity and power of the one dying and the essential mystery of God's death. Underscoring these oppositions is typical of Langland's method for leading the reader into the Christian mysteries.

Besides developing skill in close reading of the text, including its wordplay, structure, and dramatic quality, students should learn, and perhaps report to the class, about the political, social, liturgical, artistic, and biblical matters that affected and were affected by the poem. Notes in the *Penn Commentary* (Barney, *Penn Commentary*; Galloway, *Penn Commentary*) and in standard editions of the poem (Skeat; J. A. W. Bennett, Piers; Pearsall, Piers; Schmidt, Vision), commentaries in John Alford's *Companion*, Baldwin's *Guidebook,* James Simpson's Piers Plowman: *An Introduction*, and David Aers's *Beyond Reformation?* will give a good introduction to political and theological satire, especially in the prologue and passus 1–3. A number of recent articles on poverty in *Piers Plowman*—by Aers ("Justice"), Denise Baker, Janet Coleman, Christopher Dyer ("*Piers*"), Margaret Kim, Elizabeth Kirk ("Langland's Plowman"), Derek Pearsall ("Poverty"), Geoffrey Shepherd, and Nicolette Zeeman ("Condition")—and Anne M. Scott's book will give insight into social conditions. Pictures of a fourteenth-century tithe barn, built so much like a fortress or a cathedral (Sitwell 62; Davlin, *Place* 129–31), will clarify the meaning of the barn of Unity, or Holy Church, in passus 19–20. If the course is offered in the spring, students can undertake some primary research into the liturgical context of passus 18 by attending an Easter vigil service in a local church and comparing it to the entrance of the light into hell (18.124, 263–403) and by studying the liturgical songs sung in churches on Palm Sunday (18.6–9). The confession scene (passus 5.9–59) has similarities to a present-day communal reconciliation service that a student might observe in a local church. Students interested in the Bible can use Alford's Piers Plowman*: A Guide to the Quotations*, Michael Kuczynski's book on the psalms, and *The Blackwell Companion to the Bible in English Literature* (Mason et al.) to explore how *Piers Plowman* interweaves the Bible with its English narrative, each text clarifying the other.

Not all of *Piers Plowman* is visual, but some sections, like the prologue, the Meed episode (passus 2–3), the confession of the sins (passus 5.62–477), and the coming of Antichrist (passus 19–20), are filled with graphic descriptions including colors, smells, human postures, costumes, and other physical elements. These too can be represented dramatically or drawn by students and compared with marginal illustrations in medieval manuscripts, as shown, for instance, in Lilian Randall's book on images in manuscripts. Representations of manuscript images are available online, and extensive use of them is called for here. Students might look to medieval art for scenes (crucifixions, for example) that are similar to Langland's descriptions. At first, they may think that all crucifixion scenes are alike, but contrasting pathetic affective examples with works of Duccio or Fra Angelico, for example, will enable them to see great variation.

Some students might be interested in the increasing body of knowledge and conjecture on who Langland was and where he lived and worked.[4] Others might be interested in Langland's form of alliterative verse (Turville-Petre, *Alliterative Revival*; Lawton, "Style"), in the number and condition of early manuscripts, and in the number of versions of the poem.

It is important for advanced literary students to become familiar with criticism from various theoretical perspectives, such as stylistics, formalism, feminism, Marxism, queer and gender theory, thematic or structural analysis, and various interdisciplinary approaches such as "animal studies, environmental studies, and object-oriented criticism" (Davis and Steiner 2). Supplemental articles or books may be assigned to explicate a difficult or especially interesting passage in *Piers* and to display the use of a particular theory; the Norton edition contains essays and excerpts that are useful in this regard (Robertson and Shepherd). New work on the poem may be discovered in recent programs of the International Congress on Medieval Studies, in Kalamazoo, and the International Medieval Congress, in Leeds, and in the annual bibliography published in the *Yearbook of Langland Studies*. Undergraduates as well can now be exposed to manuscripts and manuscript study through the Internet, photocopies, and the *Piers Plowman Electronic Archive* (Knowles and Stinson), which "has helped make *Piers Plowman* accessible to the digital age" (Davis and Steiner 2). In addition, a trip to a nearby research library can be arranged to allow undergraduates in-person access to medieval manuscripts.

Some students will want to compare experiences described in the poem to their own experiences—their awareness of corruption in government, society, or church; their discovery of God; their experience of old age or pain—their own or someone else's. (Elizabeth Salter has called *Piers* "a seismograph of universal pain" [*Fourteenth-Century English Poetry* 112]). Others may want to compare or contrast it with other literature. For example, the protagonist of Graham Greene's *Honorary Consul* struggles, as Will does, with how a person can "[l]erne to love" ("[l]earn to love"; *Piers* 20.208). The episode in the land of longing (passus 11), in which Will is distracted from his spiritual quest by fleshly desires, may recall a similar episode in James Joyce's *Portrait of the Artist as a Young Man*. A music student might choose to analyze the interpretation of the poem in Andrew Gant's chorale "The Vision of Piers Plowman."

In my experience teaching *Piers Plowman*, people are delighted with its beauty and relevance. If we select passages that please, puzzle, or excite them, our audience (whether made up of students or not) will catch our fascination and make it their own.

NOTES

[1]I am grateful to Ellen McManus, of the Department of English, Dominican University, for these ideas.

[2]Quotations and translations of the poem come from the Norton Critical Edition (Robertson and Shepherd).

[3]On personifications in the poem, see also Griffiths.

[4]See, for example, J. A. W. Bennett, "Chaucer's Contemporary"; Kane, Piers Plowman*: The Evidence*; Hanna, *William Langland*; Matheson. Photographs of Great Malvern also give students a sense of Langland's origins.

Teaching *Piers Plowman* in Interdisciplinary Courses

Richard K. Emmerson

Like many medievalists trained in English, I have taught *Piers Plowman* in a variety of literature courses at both undergraduate and graduate levels. These include surveys of medieval literature, where I like to juxtapose the poem's opening to Chaucer's *General Prologue*; undergraduate seminars focusing on Langland and the alliterative tradition and on *Piers Plowman* and dream visions; and a topically organized graduate seminar titled Chaucer and the Crisis of Late Medieval England for master's students in English with precious little background in medieval literature. In over forty years in the classroom, however, I have found teaching the poem in interdisciplinary courses to be the most challenging and in some ways the most rewarding setting. This essay describes two interdisciplinary graduate courses for students not primarily in English programs in which *Piers Plowman* played a key role, either as the culmination or as the foundation of the course.

The course in which the poem culminated a semester of study was offered for the Divinity School at Harvard University while I served as executive director of the Medieval Academy of America. The Apocalyptic Imagination in the Middle Ages enrolled fourteen graduate students from Harvard's art history, classics, English, and history departments as well as from its Divinity School and from the theology programs at Boston College and Boston University. Needless to say, these were smart students with diverse backgrounds, although most shared a strong interest in the Middle Ages. Nevertheless, only one (the sole graduate student in English) had previously read *Piers Plowman*, although most were familiar with other major literary works such as Chaucer's *Canterbury Tales*. I mention the composition of the class because I believe strongly that concern for audience is as important for effective teaching as it is for effective writing.

The course objective was to study the influence of the Book of Revelation (the biblical Apocalypse) on the literary, religious, and visual culture of the Middle Ages. Students would read the biblical book and be introduced to major exegetical approaches to its interpretation during the Middle Ages, but the focus was less on Revelation itself as on the many varied ways in which it influenced medieval culture. Students would study a wide range of verbal and visual texts produced over a thousand-year span throughout Europe, including commentaries and histories, sermons and saints' lives, eschatological plays and visionary poetry, illustrated Apocalypse manuscripts and early printed books, and sculpture and stained glass. In addition to extensive weekly readings on medieval art, eschatology, religious and social history, and literature, students were assigned readings from *The Apocalypse in the Middle Ages*, which I edited with Bernard McGinn, and from McGinn's anthology *Visions of the End: Apocalyptic Traditions in the Middle Ages*, both of which are available as reasonably priced paperbacks. The relatively short excerpts anthologized in McGinn's *Visions* were supplemented by much longer assigned readings from the Bible, Augustine's *City of God*, two plays available in paperback translations—the twelfth-century Latin *Ludus de Antichristo* ("Play of Antichrist") and the fourteenth-century French *Jour du Jugement* ("Day of Judgment")—Hildegard of Bingen's *Scivias*, Bonaventure's *Life of Francis*, Dante's *Divine Comedy*, and *Piers Plowman*, which held its own in this impressive company.

Students worked on extensive seminar papers, of course, and I was pleased by the variety of topics they selected and by the quality of their research and writing. Each student was also required to report on a major work of scholarship. These reports, integrated topically and historically into the chronologically organized syllabus, included books studying the full range of medieval apocalypticism, such as David Burr's *Olivi's Peaceable Kingdom: A Reading of the Apocalypse Commentary*; my coauthored book with Ronald B. Herzman, *The Apocalyptic Imagination in Medieval Literature*; Andrew Gow's *The Red Jews: Antisemitism in an Apocalyptic Age, 1200–1600*; Robert Lerner's *The Powers of Prophecy: The Cedar of Lebanon Vision from the Mongol Onslaught to the Dawn of the Enlightenment*; Suzanne Lewis's *Reading Images: Narrative Discourse and Reception in the Thirteenth-Century Illuminated Apocalypse*; Bernard McGinn's *The Calabrian Abbot: Joachim of Fiore in the History of Western Thought*; and Rosemary Muir Wright's *Art and Antichrist in Medieval Europe*.

Piers Plowman provided an excellent culmination for the course. Supplementary reading for the seminar meeting included *Pearl*—as a contemporary apocalyptic counterpoint to *Piers*—and two essays, Penn Szittya's "Domesday Books: The Apocalypse in Medieval English Literary Culture" and my "'Or Yernen to Rede Redels?': *Piers Plowman* and Prophecy." As it happened, two students gave reports on scholarship that proved relevant for the discussion: Curtis Bostick's *The Antichrist and the Lollards: Apocalypticism in Late Medieval and Reformation England* and Barbara Nolan's still useful *The Gothic Visionary Perspective*, which includes chapters on illustrated Apocalypse manuscripts, Dante, and *Pearl*. These reports helped situate the apocalyptic eschatology of *Piers Plowman* between earlier, more orthodox visionary traditions and contemporary heterodox polemical apocalypticism. No student had selected that day's other option for a book report, Kathryn Kerby-Fulton's *Reformist Apocalypticism and* Piers Plowman, so I summarized its argument. The ensuing discussion worked well, since students had earlier read *Scivias* and could assess the connections Kerby-Fulton draws between Hildegard and Langland.

One result of placing *Piers Plowman* in such a course is that students can appreciate not only its rich complexity but also the way it seamlessly weaves together so many strands of religious and intellectual thought that are crucial to the medieval apocalyptic imagination. Another advantage of such a seminar is that it introduces the poem to the next generation of medievalists working in disciplines where they may not have otherwise studied *Piers Plowman.* As one future church historian remarked, "I can't believe I could have become a historian of the medieval church and not have read this stunning poem!" Of course, a potential danger in such a thematically designed seminar is that *Piers Plowman* (and, indeed, all of the assigned primary texts) would be reduced to just another example of the overriding theme. For this reason I assigned the poem in the Donaldson translation (Piers Plowman*: An Alliterative Verse Translation*) to ensure that students would read the entire poem and thus appreciate it as a work of literature in its own right. I was delighted by student responses to the poem and the results of the course. Although class discussion not surprisingly focused on the concluding two passus, the poem's opening image of contemporary society perched between heaven and hell, the contrast between Lady Meed and Holy Church, the confession of the deadly sins and the tearing of the pardon, Dowel's interiorized visions, and the poem's restructuring of salvation history were read through an apocalyptic lens that provided a remarkably sharp perspective and led to many insights into both the poem and the semester's topic. I had decided to teach *Piers* because I wanted students to know the poem and its vernacular appropriation of medieval apocalypticism; what I had not expected was the extent to which the poem would provide a capstone for the entire course.

When I went to Florida State University to chair the Department of Art History, my teaching focused primarily on visual texts, particularly medieval illustrated manuscripts. But because my contract required that I teach a course each summer, when there are few art history students in residence, I developed interdisciplinary courses designed to attract students from other departments, such as Medieval Art and Drama. Twice I taught Medieval London, a course for upper-level undergraduates and graduate students, which looked at the role of London and its environs as a cultural center during the later Middle Ages and in which *Piers Plowman* played a significant role. Interdisciplinary in approach and subject matter, the course was designed to study the representation and influence of London in works of art, architecture, history, and poetry. It focused on the age of Richard II and included study of the Wilton Diptych, Westminster Abbey, Westminster Palace, stained glass and sculpture, illustrated manuscripts, civic performances, chronicles, and selections from the poetry of Geoffrey Chaucer, John Gower, Thomas Hoccleve, William Langland, and John Lydgate. Discussions centered on the literary and visual arts in relation to social (e.g., Black Death, Great Rising of 1381), political (e.g., overthrow of Richard II), and religious (e.g., apocalypticism, heresy) events and movements.

Summer courses at Florida State are compressed into six weeks, meeting for three hours twice a week, so the assigned readings were not as extensive as they would have been during a regular academic semester. Nevertheless, the reading was demanding, selected to complement a course structured along topical rather than chronological criteria. For example, the topic Two Cities, Their Saints, and Their Churches introduced the Westminster-London pairing by studying the manuscript of the Anglo-Norman *Life of Saint Edward the Confessor* ("Life") on the one hand and *St. Erkenwald* on the other. Assigned readings included Ruth Nissé's excellent "'A coroun ful riche': The Rule of History in *St. Erkenwald*" and Caroline M. Barron and Marie-Hélène Rousseau's "Cathedral, City, and State." For that class meeting students reported on Paul Binski's *Westminster Abbey and the Plantagenets: Kingship and the Representation of Power, 1200–1400*, which combines a detailed study of architecture and decoration with a meticulously researched analysis of the abbey's political and religious significance for the city, king, and realm.

Since the course was officially housed within art history, it placed much more emphasis on visual materials than did the apocalypticism course at Harvard. Since I did not want individual classes to focus on a single discipline (today, history; tomorrow, poetry; next week, art), each meeting mixed attention to visual and verbal texts. During the first few weeks, topics were highly focused and included Trilingual London, which analyzed, for example, the *Holkham Bible Picture Book* and William Rothwell's "The Trilingual England of Geoffrey Chaucer"; Royal London, which studied the Wilton Diptych, Westminster Hall, and Michael J. Bennett's "The Court of Richard II and the Promotion of Literature"; and Civic London, which examined several of the impressive publications of the Museum of London Archaeology Service,[1] as well as Thomas Hoccleve's poetry and John Lydgate's mummings.[2] I defined London rather broadly, influenced by Marion Turner's wonderful essay "Greater London," and I added social, political, and religious topics such as Plague and the Iconography of Death, Revolt and Revolution, and Religious Anxiety and Heresy. One topic, Saints and Pilgrims, was designed to extend London's environs to Canterbury (so we could study the Becket Windows[3] as well as Chaucer) and to Bury St. Edmunds (so we could study the facsimile of Lydgate's *Life of St. Edmund, King and Martyr* as well as the Croxton *Play of the Sacrament*).

During the past twenty years or so I have come to worry that students read fewer and fewer books, relying for their research instead on articles available through *JSTOR* and other databases and, increasingly it would seem, on *Wikipedia*. To counter this trend, I ask students in all my courses to present critical reports on important books; the reports should connect the books' arguments to the seminar's readings and topics. Although some at first are resistant, students generally like working their way through a chunky book and are proud to command the scholarship, even if they may be intimidated by the length of the reading, the detailed footnotes, and, more alarmingly, the assignment to summarize so much research in a twenty-minute report. The exercise forces students to condense an extended argument into what is essential. Books suggested for reports in the Medieval London course included Michael Bennett's *Richard II and the Revolution of 1399*, Sylvia Federico's *New Troy: Fantasies of Empire in the Late Middle Ages*, Dillian Gordon's *Making and Meaning: The Wilton Diptych*, Barbara Hanawalt's *Growing Up in Medieval London: The Experience of Childhood in History*, Ralph Hanna's *London Literature, 1300–1380*, Steven Justice's *Writing and Rebellion: England in 1381*, Ethan Knapp's *The Bureaucratic Muse: Thomas Hoccleve and the Literature of Late Medieval England*, Shannon McSheffrey's *Marriage, Sex, and Civic Culture in Late Medieval London*, Anne Rudloff Stanton's *The Queen Mary Psalter: A Study of Affect and Audience*, and Paul Strohm's *England's Empty Throne: Usurpation and the Language of Legitimation, 1399–1422.*

Unlike the Harvard apocalypticism course, which culminated with a discussion of *Piers Plowman*, the Medieval London course began with the poem and integrated it into discussions of many topics. The poem was the only textbook students were required to purchase, an indication of its centrality to the course (other readings were available from library reserve or through the course's *BlackBoard* site). As with the Harvard course, I assigned a translation, to ensure that students read the entire poem quickly, since they needed to have a sense of the whole rather early in the course. This time I chose George Economou's version of the C text, which contains the famous autobiographical passage in passus 5, where Will describes his life with Kit in Cornhill. This was my first time teaching C, and the results were enjoyable. Since one never knows a topic better than when teaching it, the decision gave me a genuine appreciation for C, and in the future I expect to return to this version of the poem. The Economou translation is particularly readable, making *Piers Plowman* accessible to the students, only two of whom (neither of them English majors) had read it before. This accessibility was important for the success of the course, because we spent the first three-hour class period discussing the poem without the aid of any secondary reading. I wanted students to form their own opinions about *Piers*, to ask questions uninfluenced by scholar-experts, and especially to describe their impressions of medieval London based on the poem. After this intense beginning, we returned to *Piers* repeatedly throughout the summer: for example, when we discussed trilingualism or the Great Rising of 1381 or apocalypticism and heresy. I was also delighted to note that students alluded to the poem in unexpected ways while commenting on other topics that in my initial planning I had not connected to *Piers*, such as London buildings, manuscripts, and historical texts.

The energetic poetry of *Piers Plowman* and its ear for the abundant variety of medieval London's voices—ranging from the court at Westminster to the back alleys radiating from around St. Paul's—are well known to medievalists, but it was encouraging to see how students were quickly fascinated by the poem and how it became a touchstone for medieval London life. I had hoped something like this would happen, but what surprised me was the extent to which *Piers Plowman* helped visualize medieval London. In *Personification in* Piers Plowman, Lavinia Griffiths comments that Langland was reluctant "to engage in the verbal drawing of elaborate speaking pictures" and that as a result "there are few clearly-memorable images" in the poem (53). When the poem is studied within the visual as well as literary and historical contexts of London, however, those images start to take real shape. To help students get a better sense of the poem's visuality, I also asked them to read C. David Benson's *Public* Piers Plowman, particularly the essays "Public Art: Parish Wall Paintings" (157–201) and "Public Life: London Civic Practices" (203–45). Also very helpful for placing Langland within the vibrant life of late-fourteenth-century London is Derek Pearsall's "Langland's London." By the end of the course, students understood Pearsall's opening comment that "London remains, in epitome, the problem that the poem does not solve" (186).

After I became dean of liberal arts at Manhattan College in New York, I missed teaching, needed a break from mind-numbing committees, and wanted to interact with students in nonadministrative ways. I introduced a course called Monasticism and the Arts as an option to meet the college's Catholic studies requirement not only for students in arts and sciences but also those in business, education, and engineering. It surveyed the ways in which monasticism was represented in and influenced medieval art, both visual and literary. Ranging from Saint Anthony and the desert fathers through Francis and Dominic, the course studied a wide range of manuscript illustrations, mosaics, sculptures, and frescoes. It also read several hagiographic texts, such as the lives of Saints Martin, Benedict, and Cuthbert, as well as Hrotsvitha's plays, Herrard of Hohenburg's *Hortus deliciarum* ("Garden of Delights"), Hildegard of Bingen's *Scivias*, Bonaventure's *Life of Francis* and, of course, *Piers Plowman.* I was amazed by not only how little students knew about their Catholic heritage but also how much they enjoyed these often challenging texts and the ways in which they problematize this heritage. After studying the Franciscans and Dominicans and the beautiful works of art they inspired, students engaged the antifraternal responses of contemporaries that were powerfully set forth in Langland's vigorous alliterative lines. I was delighted to see how well undergraduates responded to the poem, which regularly inspired some of the best class discussions. As one student wrote in a course evaluation, "*Piers Plowman* rocks!"

My experience teaching *Piers Plowman* has been remarkably varied, involving courses at all levels of the curriculum, from sophomore surveys to graduate seminars. Teaching the poem in interdisciplinary courses has shown me that it can inform a wide variety of medieval topics, that it is flexible enough to be the basis for thematically organized surveys as well as focused seminars, and that it appeals to students in many disciplines, including art history, English, history, and religious studies. *Piers Plowman* is a remarkable poem that deserves a central place in the humanities curriculum and should not be restricted to students of medieval English literature. I hope the success of the interdisciplinary courses described in this essay will inspire other teachers to include *Piers Plowman* in a variety of courses. Students will be challenged, but they will be greatly rewarded, and their teachers will not be disappointed.

This essay has focused on the contributions *Piers Plowman* makes to interdisciplinary courses. On the one hand, such courses most certainly should not replace sustained engagement with the poem in advanced undergraduate and graduate seminars, but, on the other hand, they provide a way to introduce the poem to many students otherwise unlikely to read *Piers Plowman*. Interdisciplinary teaching presents real challenges, though. Students need to be shown how to interpret a work of art, focusing, for example, on design as well as iconographic features; similar attention to the formal elements of dramatic, narrative, and poetic texts is essential, which students tend to read as documents. Since students often lack historical knowledge, it is critical to contextualize *Piers Plowman* carefully. Students must understand the historical change that occurred between the creation of the brilliant Assisi fresco cycle, usually attributed to Giotto, in the early fourteenth century and the poem's representation of mendicancy in the late fourteenth century. Detailed, if necessarily brief, lectures on patronage, regional attitudes, and relevant intellectual and social history are crucial. Interdisciplinary courses do provide their own contexts, though. By the time students in a graduate seminar on apocalypticism reach *Piers Plowman* on the syllabus, it isn't necessary to give background on the figure of Antichrist. The biggest challenge, though, is to resist the temptation for the poem to become yet another example of the course's theme. If *Piers Plowman* cannot be read in its entirety, selections must be read carefully and, most important, as poetry. By respecting its artistry and Langland's unique vision of Antichrist, London, or antifraternalism, we can teach *Piers Plowman* as a poem for our time that helps make the Middle Ages relevant to a new generation of students.

NOTES

[1] In particular, see Schofield.

[2] Students were thoroughly engaged by Claire Sponsler's "Alien Nation: London's Aliens and Lydgate's Mummings for the Mercers and Goldsmiths."

[3] Students read Anne F. Harris's "Pilgrimage, Performance, and Stained Glass at Canterbury Cathedral."

Teaching the Play of *Piers Plowman*

Andrew Galloway

In fall 2001, the historian Paul Hyams and I, an English teacher, cotaught an undergraduate class at Cornell University that sought to merge teaching English literature with history, from the twelfth to the end of the fourteenth century, with *Piers Plowman* as a long finale. When Paul suggested we produce a medieval play at the end of the class—which had alternated literary with historical sources and assignments, week by week and assignment by assignment—I proposed a dramatic reading of passus 18 of the B text. I assumed others had tried this, but I was unaware of the long and sometimes distinguished tradition of producing parts or versions of *Piers Plowman*. I also did not suspect how much a dramatic realization might achieve over our usual pedagogical focus, contextualization, and interpretation.

It might seem strange to demote interpretation, especially since *Piers Plowman* often seems full of puzzles: allegorical, verbal, ethical, economic, textual, social, and outright riddling—all deserving and requiring so much reconsideration and background that these matters, rather than the performative interest of any section or speech, seem to demand first consideration. In fact, in the regular class term we followed the usual priorities. Performing the play of *Piers Plowman* was carried out outside required class discussions and assignments, at a public celebration of readings in various medieval materials established by Cornell's Medieval Studies Program, before a wider public than the class. At the time, I had not sought to learn if *Piers Plowman* had been dramatically performed before, but of course it had and has continued to be. Two polished productions I am now aware of include *The Vision of William Concerning Piers the Plowman*, produced by the Joculatores Oxonienses and directed by Meg Twycross, in 1974, at Oxford's University Church of St. Mary the Virgin, which selected a series of moments and scenes from the *visio* up through the pardon; a photograph of this production shows a dapper Conscience (Lister Matheson) and an alluring Meed (Sarah Carpenter) in what may be the high end of modern dramatic performances of the poem (fig. 1). In 2012 Peter Sutton and Stephanie Connell presented a dramatic reading of *William Langland: Poet and Dreamer* at the Autumn in Malvern Festival, which drew from selections from across the entire poem (from Peter Sutton's translation) but embedded those into an original framing, amid "William and Kit's reminiscences about his life while they were waiting in Purgatory for Saint Peter with his keys."[1]

Ours was by no means as polished or professional a production as either of these, as a stray photograph of the Flagellation of Christ shows (fig. 2). And any such attempt can seem festive superfluency for a class. But there are reasons to believe that this is where encountering *Piers Plowman* should begin, and

Figure 1. Conscience (Lister Matheson) and Lady Meed (Sarah Carpenter). *The Vision of William Concerning Piers the Plowman*, produced by Joculatores Oxonienses and directed by Meg Twycross, University Church of St. Mary the Virgin, Oxford, 14–18 May 1974. Photo by permission of Sarah Carpenter and of M. Teresa Tavormina for the estate of Lister Matheson.

where it might regularly return, in order to grapple with and appreciate aspects of the poem that remain closed to textual and thematic parsing. Of course we all know there are indications that medieval literature was often read aloud in its own time, although just as often the evidence suggests medieval idealizations of this for various purposes. Few public readings of a medieval poem are more elegantly imagined than in the early-fifteenth-century manuscript of *Troilus and Criseyde*, Cambridge University, Corpus Christi College Ms. 61, whose frontispiece shows an idealized but identifiable image of Chaucer—dead at least a decade by then—at a pulpit before an equally idealized, languidly inattentive courtly audience of (the long-deposed) Richard II, in a semi-Petronian scene of various distractions, while what seems to be Criseyde's ancient exchange is decorously enacted behind them.[2] But *Troilus and Criseyde* also calls attention to its readers, and its own written letters, "Loo, next this vers" (1.399). We know nothing of the earliest readings of *Piers Plowman*, any more than we do those of *Troilus and Criseyde*. But whereas scholars have long emphasized the many genres *Piers Plowman* synthesizes (Morton Bloomfield seminally identified

Figure 2. Christ (Eric Shuler) and Satan (Paul Hyams) in Cornell University's English and history class production of *Piers Plowman*'s Crucifixion passus, 8 Dec. 2001. Photograph by Curtis Jirsa.

six, with three "literary" and three "religious" genres, from "dialogue" to "sermon" [10]), its generic and formal variety can also be traced much more directly than most poetry by Chaucer to genres with some theatrical or performative presence in late medieval England, especially in the London region. Those theatrical genres range from the royal entry (prologue), to courtroom debate (passus 2–4), to confession (passus 5), to labor strikes (passus 6), to academic quodlibetal debate (passus 8–12), to feast-day plays and banquets in guild halls (passus 13), not to mention sermons and the innumerable plays of the Passion that lie behind the Crucifixion scene (passus 18). Grammar, commentary, and exegesis all have their place in situating *Piers Plowman*, but even those were often assisted by or conducted in oral performance. Although London lacked city-sponsored cycle drama, just outside London in Clerkenwell sacred drama was staged from the 1380s, and in forms that lasted for several days like those on the Continent rather than only a single day like the other English civic cycle drama (Lancashire 54–62). If we recognize *Piers Plowman*'s concentrations of legal language and lore, we should also consider how much debates were part of legal education and holiday celebration in the lawyers' inns, located at the northwestern edge of London's wall. Renaissance London drama emerged as much from these as from religious drama: an *interludium* ("interlude") is mentioned at Furnivall's Inn in 1412; the first English tragedy, the oratorical *Gorboduc* (1562), by Thomas Norton and Thomas Sackville, was written by and for members of the Inner Temple (Nelson and Elliot 1: xvii–xxviii, 3; 2: 624–751).

Beyond direct uses of or parallels to such local performative forms and traditions, *Piers Plowman* mentions a wide range of performative genres, albeit usually disparagingly: from musical farting, harping, tumbling, joke telling, and other forms of minstrel entertainment (13.229–34), to riddling contests (13.135–85), wrestling (14.244), and prize fighting and tournaments of all kinds (15.164–65)—the last two popular in London (Lancashire 55, 63). Often the performative genres mentioned in the poem (such as the guessing game about the price of a cloak in Gluttony's tavern [5.320–27]) seem simpler than the self-consciously ironic or allegorized versions of them redeployed there. But instances outside the poem could feature some of the same complexities as their evocations in the poem. The idea of disguised knights fighting in tournaments in passus 18 parallels a motif of French romances (Clifton), but disguised combatants were also regular parts of London tournaments in the mid- and later fourteenth century. A tournament in 1362 involved challengers dressed as the Seven Deadly Sins; more pointedly political, King Edward III and his knights arrived to a London tournament in 1359 dressed as the London mayor and the city's aldermen (Lancashire 63–64), merging compliment and challenge to London's infamous sense of its independent prestige.

The realization of any dramatic text depends, of course, on the general and particular contexts of the production, but late medieval drama often calls attention to its present production more clearly than drama in other periods. As

Sharon Aronson-Lehavi argues, late medieval English religious drama invites and implicitly theorizes the importance of presentism in religious drama's meanings and bodily experiences while staging events based on distant sacred history. Aronson-Lehavi focuses on the York Play of the Crucifixion, whose capacity for such dramatic "eventfulness"—a "performative emphasis not only on the character but also on the bodies and identities of the performers" (112)—she finds the period itself able to recognize and exploit, in spite of the risk of blasphemy and skepticism about the distant reality of sacred history and its miracles. These views by a theorist of drama might be applied to what *Piers Plowman* also presents. Key figures, from Will to Piers the Plowman, change roles and adopt new identities in ways that imply a degree of theatricality to both allegorized ideas and their social affiliates. A dramatic reading of *Piers Plowman* makes bodily and immediate both the effort to express meaningful ideas to (generally hostile) listeners and the mutations of entities and what they mean. With all its local specificities and points of tacit topical recognition (like having a demanding teacher such as Paul Hyams play Satan attacking a crucified student, as in fig. 2), dramatic reenactment brings attention all the more to the poem's continual subtexts of attention to circumstances and social assumptions, through which the poem tends to multiply rather than settle its initial questions. It seems no coincidence that not only the author's own repeated revisions but also all the surviving copies of this poem are highly varied and full of signs of how scribes participated in its re-creation.[3]

Performing the play of *Piers Plowman* became for us another way to ask some of the questions that concerned our class, including how one might think history and literature together. By choosing to stage a famously historical stretch of Langland's long, difficult narrative poem that semester, which began with the shock of 9/11 and was filled with the mesmerizing horror of continuously televised war—rather than, for instance, *The Second Shepherds' Play* (which we had also read)—we approached that intersection between history and literature by experiencing *Piers*'s restless ethical and social thought and debate as a more productive kind of action than what might have been possible through adventure, heroic combat, erotic love, or indeed any plot that seemed to offer smoother resolutions or a sense of finished interpretations.

As Bloomfield long ago pertinently observed, "Will is 'both in and out of the game,' a spectator and an actor in almost evenly divided roles" (15); in remaking the poem with living actors, the split between the narrator as past historical agent (or at least immediate witness) and as present raconteur was evident in the inevitable decision to split this role between Will and narrator. This separation, however clear at the beginning if the narrator functions as a kind of chorus while Will experiences his dream, is both complicated and elided at the end, when Will, after crawling to the cross while the narrator describes that action, upstages and supplants the narrator by becoming responsible for recounting the

Crucifixion story and its meaning to his wife and daughter in the passus's final lines. He briefly becomes more of a narrator reframing the experience as well as more of a historical agent tied directly to visionary experience and to a present social world. That last is a world of routinized institutional practice, formalized by the sort of prayers and general assertions that any churchgoing medieval Christian might regularly hear, a sharp contrast to the immediately preceding vision itself. But the proximity of the narrator's direct vision of the harrowing of hell, as if, like the legends of Dante, he were still smoking from his passage through the inferno, charges his ordinary final prayers with extraordinary force: "May no grisly goost glide there it shadweth!" (18.433; "may no grisly spirit glide in [God's] shadow").[4] It is both a letdown and an extraordinarily metadramatic moment (Galloway, "Intellectual Pregnancy" 146–47).

Perhaps because of this final moment, William Rogers calls the entire passus a "critique" of drama, since "drama . . . calls for, and receives, resolution. But for a life in progress, there is as yet no resolution. The patriarchs and prophets go to heaven with Jesus. The Daughters of God compose their differences. But the dreamer is left with a life still full of loose ends, a life still in the process of creeping to the Cross" (263–64). Yet as Aronson-Lehavi's focus shows, medieval religious drama likewise does not offer such tidy resolutions or formally separate its sacred past from contemporary social and religious practices.[5] Even amid Will's unfinished pursuit of understanding and being understood, the waking coda in passus 18 shows him supplanting the role of the narrator, emphasizing and redefining the nature of who is authorized to teach or judge (that continual ignition point in the poem) while pointing to the problem of the connection between the poet's persona and the poem's narrator, its sacred history and its pressingly topical concerns, its action in the world and its telling of its tale.

The distance yet connection between Langland's persona and narrator has motivated critical discussions of *Piers Plowman* from the early twentieth-century authorship controversy through the most sophisticated recent discussions.[6] But less scholarly readers of *Piers Plowman* are likely not to focus on this issue as keenly as they do on, for instance, Chaucer's often ironic shifts into and out of claims of directly experiencing and recording tales or private love laments. When one performs *Piers Plowman* or sees it performed, especially the end of passus 18, the historicity of both the present, retrospective narrator and the dreamer of these visions is simultaneously if somewhat paradoxically affirmed. A poem obsessed with beginnings (see D. Vance Smith) leads finally to direct experience of Christianity's origins, just as the final passus looks toward the Christian world's end. Yet the poet's willingness to use his narrator to fulfill a major goal of medieval Christian meditation and mysticism—participation in the Crucifixion—does not lead to a fuller detachment from the present world and society (as is often true in mystical accounts). Instead, this return to origins evokes the sense that everything could and does change depending on the next argument one encounters or the next experience one has. What Jesus himself learns by experience as a fellow human being matters to his understanding of pain and bondage in hell, just as it matters how adroitly Jesus can argue with Lucifer to free (some of) the souls in hell. The weight of history is invoked at every step of the poem's encounter with the Crucifixion and the harrowing of hell, but the outcome at every step seems undetermined, a matter of fresh experiences and new trials, continuing an emphasis begun in passus 1 with Holy Church's sermon on trying all things to learn what truth is.[7]

This effect in the Crucifixion passus is difficult to account for, although many scholars and students have responded to that passus as a cathartic turning point, when deep divisions between ideas and action, divisions epitomized by the narrator's reductively literalized search for Dowel, seem to resolve. Utterly predictable though the passus's broad historical narrative must be, it seems to shake off the dead weight of doctrine and retellings of sacred history with which Will is constantly bombarded, even more fully entering the present world than the poem's prologue does, whose vision culminates with the unjudged and unjudgeable hubbub of London tradespeople's street cries (prol. 217–31). Even more than the prologue but paralleling its immediacy and sense of existential choice, in the Crucifixion passus experience matters, for making history as well as gaining understanding.

That effect is enhanced by performing the Crucifixion passus, in which large riddles of social identity, ethical consistency, and the match or mismatch between past and present history are entered even through small puzzles, encountered first as practical problems. One is the amorphous identity and value of crowds. In passus 18 the crowd broadly considered is made up of Jews; as elsewhere in medieval writing, they constitute a quintessentially urban group. Their role in the poem as urbanites might be compared to that of ancient Jews of Jerusalem in the second-most-popular alliterative poem of this period, the sensationally violent *Siege of Jerusalem* (Galloway, "Alliterative Poetry"). The casting and staging of the crowds in passus 18 bring out, however, the paradoxical or shifting nature of this poem's anti-Judaism and the problem of defining the identity and ethical standing of urban mobs in general. Is the group of "olde folk" singing "Hosanna" (18.8) the same as "Olde Jewes of Jerusalem" who sing "*Benedictus qui venit in nomine Domini*" ("Blessed is he who cometh in the name of the Lord"; 18.17a)? Are these also the "muche peple" ("many people"; 18.36) who cry condemnations of Jesus and are in turn somberly told by Faith that they, as the forefathers of all modern Jews, can no longer own property or pursue any legitimate profession but must "al barayne be and usurie usen" ("be all barren and live by usury"; 18.106)? In a dramatic production, a visually indicated separation between the pious "olde folk" or "Olde Jewes" and the less identifiable rabble of "muche peple" seems demanded, if one had more resources than we had.

Our merging of them was required by a small cast, just six students. But should those subidentities of Jewish crowds in fact be distinguished? At one moment the urban Jewish community might be heard uttering pious hymns, at another it issues calls for violence. How can one judge these or other crowds, and with what precision? For a later-fourteenth-century readership or audience, mobs of any kind might be hard to distinguish securely, like the London urban factions that clashed in major riots between the populist and elitist mayors during the 1370s and 1380s, not to mention the often confused violence of the 1381 Rebellion.[8] In general, medieval Christian culture was all too ready to conglomerate Jews of any kind and any period, perhaps driven by defensive awareness of Christianity's secondary and dependent historical status on Judaism (Narin van Court). That dependency is here tacitly reversed by displaying the Jews' primal sin and their subsequent permanent penalty. Their mob action is punished with collective disenfranchisement, in legal language that makes the scene a transparent window between the immediate, late medieval present and the ancient past: "Youre fraunchyse, that fre was, fallen is in thraldom" ("your legal standing of freedom has fallen into serfdom") Faith declares to the Jews (18.103). This declaration, stripping rights of civil freedom from Jews forever, makes them serfs (as they were officially considered throughout medieval England), albeit bound to no lord but the king. Many Christians would know the terms of this status well, even in late-fourteenth-century England, from which the Jews had been expelled a century before *Piers Plowman* was written; for serfdom and freedom were basic categories of social identity through the fourteenth century, here made into a condition that is not (as usual) inherited through family lineage but instead imposed as a new role. The rapid decline through the fourteenth century in numbers of those considered serfs—from two million to perhaps half that, and by the end of the following century just a few thousand—suggests that a sense of malleable, performative identity touched even this fundamental notion (Bailey, *Decline* 4–5, 34–35, 62–63). Passus 18 enacts, among other things, the reverse transformation: entry into serfdom, simultaneous with entry into a single subaltern identity. In the course of the poem's action, the various Jewish groups and individuals, at first vaguely distinguishable as sagely old or brashly and violently young, are conglomerated by Faith's judgment into a single mass of serfs.

Individual transformations of identity are pivotal elsewhere in the poem, and thus as inherently performative elsewhere. Meed, who begins as a defiantly vibrant debater, is reduced by Conscience's definitions of her as mere worldly and unmerited reward into what the "moost commune of that court" ("majority of the commons of that court") call a "hore" (4.166), sent to prison and not to reappear in person again (Galloway, *Penn Commentary* 328)—although the quiet winking and following of her by the lawyers and petty officials show that the principle of unearned earthly reward is even harder to contain once it has lost its vivid personification, in spite of the king's complacent triumph at the end of the scene in passus 4. Even Conscience will be reduced by the end of the poem to vagrancy and yearning or despair, a victim of the gradual deprivations of all the learning, courtly support, and rhetorical confidence that are so visible in his debut with Lady Meed, and sartorially evident in the 1974 production by the Joculatores Oxonienses of that initial debate (fig. 1). How might Conscience be portrayed if the scene continued to the end of the poem? Throughout *Piers Plowman* identity is as radically performative as the ideas and interpretations that the dreamer and the narrator posit.

Coinciding with 9/11 and the mobilization of American military power against increasingly wider Islamic regions and populations, the class in which we performed the play of *Piers Plowman* lost some focus on and sensitivities to the poem but gained others. The violence of the Jewish mob in the poem was evident—captured in our production by Hyams himself rendering a blow to Christ's head (fig. 2)—but so was the indiscriminate nature of their punishment. Beyond the Jews, the shifting loyalties and identities of such extras convey a sense of the city as crowd, by which the increasing isolation of Will is all the more demarcated. We (and our students) might recall the prologue and wonder how this rabble of Jews compares to the folk in the field, the street peddlers of London, or the mass of pious but unreflective pilgrims who "thrungen togideres, / Cride upward to Crist and to his clene moder" ("thronged together, / Cried upward to Christ and to his pure mother"; 5.510–11) but also "blustreden forth as beestes over baches and hilles" ("blundered forth like beasts over banks and hills"; 5.514), as fallible and divisive as the crowd collected by Piers the Plowman to plow his half acre.

The same question in another form emerges in dramatizing who was freed from hell. It was neither practical nor desirable for us to separate the sinister crowd condemned by Faith from the later crowds of Jewish patriarchs and prophets in hell, who are kept imprisoned until some unknown number of them are led to salvation by Christ (18.401–07). Practicalities might force anyone to do as we did: use the same group of actors to represent the crowd both legally condemned and eternally saved. This small problem captures a wider one: neither the human narrator nor the demonic guardians can see who is "led forth" to salvation: "Astroth and al the route hidden him in hernes; / They dorste noght loke on Oure Lord, the leste of hem alle, / But leten hym lede forth what hym liked and lete what hym liste" ("Ashtoreth and all the gang hid themselves in corners; / They dared not look at our Lord, the least of them all, / But let him lead away what he liked and leave what he wished"; 18.405–07). The devils' and narrator's blindness at this crucial moment might well be emphasized dramatically by some effects of concealment or glaring lights (or torches) to make this last crowd scene invisible. Even without special effects, any production forces one to confront the poem's profound uncertainty of who will be chosen.

This question haunts the poem, from the uncertain list closing the prologue (217–31) to Holy Church's elusive promises (1.79–84) to the massive doubts of the pardon (7.144–81) to the frequent recursion to Psalm 14 (King James Version 15), "Domine, quis habitabit?" ("Lord, who will dwell in [your tabernacle]?"; Galloway, *Penn Commentary* 46, 241–44) to Will's own agony of "wheither I were chose or noght chose" ("whether I was chosen or not chosen"; 11.117), this last the closest moment in the poem to a Puritan crisis of faith, like that which John Bunyan describes in *Grace Abounding.* The identity of those saved in passus 18 resists both dramatic realization and readerly understanding, but drama makes the problem clearer. The audience (or readers) and the demons are blinded and filled with doubt, and the present witnesses, including the poet-narrator, cannot name or see who leaves hell to ascend with Christ. Our production rendered this moment by raising a white sheet to conceal the entire crowd, among whom Christ chose the unknown few.

A class spent moving back and forth between historical and literary writings from post-conquest England heightens the sense of all historical and literary narratives as contingent performances. Reading the treatment of William the Conqueror in the Peterborough Chronicle and again in the chronicle of Orderic Vitalis, and both of these against Geoffrey of Monmouth's portrayal of the golden age of pre-Saxon Britain, raises questions about whose purposes and which values are served by any historical narrative, whether it recounts contemporary or ancient events. So too, reading the debate poem of *The Owl and the Nightingale* next to the vivid remaking of the world of Arthur and its destruction by the Saxons in other twelfth- and thirteenth-century conceptions such as those by Wace and Layamon, shows how national and all identities are shaped by dialogue and confrontation. In a similar way, reading *Pearl* and *Sir Gawain and the Green Knight* next to Jean Froissart's *Chronicle*, including consideration of Froissart's view of 1381 and his transformation of the *Life of the Black Prince* by the Chandos Herald, allows a perspective on how judgments shape but also are challenged by historical or quasi-historical medieval narratives. The presentation of the explosively factional world of London politics and society in Thomas Favent's narrative of the Merciless Parliament of 1388 (Galloway, "History") followed by selections from *Piers Plowman* and then by *The Second Shepherds' Play* raises similar questions about the contingent and often paradoxical moral and social categories in these medieval narratives, in some respects more clearly than is possible when encountering modern narratives of our own times, which so readily dominate our thinking especially, though not only, at times of crisis.

Even carefully reading and discussing historical and literary materials like these (and I have just outlined our course syllabus) does not enact *Piers Plowman*'s imperative of learning as doing as directly and engagingly as a dramatic reading or full dramatization of some of this idea-riven but deeply experiential poem. Performance, in raw amateur or highly professional forms, helps us encounter the poem's obsession with learning by experience, in a way that interpretation alone cannot—for undergraduates or anyone else. God himself, as

Peace says in passus 18, "took Adames kynde / To wite what he hath suffred in thre sondry places, / Bothe in hevene and in erthe—and now til helle he thenketh, / To wite what alle wo is, that woot of alle joye" ("took Adam's nature, / To see what he had suffered in three separate places, / Both in Heaven and on earth, and now he heads for hell, / To learn what all woe is like who has learned of all joy"; 221–24). How else than as a radical theory of performance—an immersive incarnation of "total acting" (Aronson-Lehavi 115–24)—are we to see this idea of improvisatory, disguised, but wholly and alertly present divinity, re-creating the most predictable moment of medieval Christian history? Humanity's ever-unknown claims to salvation may be on trial here, but rather than solve that riddle, Peace simply explains that God also needs to learn by doing, by inhabiting and reinterpreting his role in new circumstances and new theaters, including ours.

NOTES

[1]Personal correspondence with Mr. Sutton. A professionally trained actor, director, and playwright, Sutton regularly presents dramatic readings of sections from his translation of the poem, as he also did at the International *Piers Plowman* Society meeting in Seattle, 25 July 2015. See http://www.petersutton.eu/index.php.

[2]The image is reproduced on the site *Parker Library on the Web* (parkerweb.stanford.edu/parker/actions/thumbnail_view.do?size=basic&ms_no=61&page=1V). On the audience depicted in the frontispiece, see especially Pearsall, "*Troilus* Frontispiece." For more recent discussion of the image that traces Chaucer's pulpit to Genius's in images in the *Roman de la Rose*, see Joyce Coleman.

[3]See Fletcher for a meditation on the poem's ethically performative nature; and Kane, "Text," for its extraordinary textual variation.

[4]Citations of Piers are to A. V. C. Schmidt's edition of the B text (Schmidt, Vision), which, along with Donaldson's translation, we ordered for the class (here I occasionally adapt Donaldson's translation). The dramatic reading was performed, with some effort, in Middle English.

[5]See also Galloway, "Imagining" 211–15, 235.

[6]Kane offers a foundational framework for the modern, post-authorship-controversy terms of the question ("Autobiographical Fallacy"). Middleton has revisited the issue, with increasingly wide implications for the poem's participation in its social context ("Idea"; "Acts"), and it remains central in Wittig's disagreement with Middleton (Wittig, "'Culture Wars'"). See also Spearing, *Textual Subjectivity*, for an argument that medieval texts do not presuppose the idea of a narrator unless and only when one is explicitly indicated.

[7]For this theme in Holy Church's sermon and elsewhere in the poem, see Galloway, *Penn Commentary* 180–84.

[8]See Nightingale, 228–319, for one sequence of volatile events and riots in late-fourteenth-century London. For medieval notions of crowds and mobs, see Galloway, "Communities."

Going Forth in the World: *Piers Plowman* and Service Learning

Kate Crassons

> Thoroughgoing ignorance about the ways of others is largely a privilege of the powerful.
>
> —Kwame Anthony Appiah, *Cosmopolitanism*

Piers Plowman is a poem haunted by the subject of poverty. Langland's work, as numerous critics have shown, makes an important literary intervention into an urgent cultural debate about the ethical status of poverty and of the poor.[1] Langland thus emerges as a central voice among late medieval writers, lawmakers, and theologians who vigorously interrogate the meaning of poverty by asking, most fundamentally, Is poverty a sign of perfection suffered in sacred imitation of Christ? Or is it a mark of wretchedness, idleness, and sin?[2] Langland's preoccupation with these questions grew in intensity over the course of his poetic career. The new material that he added to the C text of *Piers Plowman* in passus 5 (lines 1–108) and 9 (lines 70–161) deals with poverty as it is experienced by a dizzying assortment of people.[3] These people range from the working poor, single mothers, holy hermits, and lunatic lollers—people suffering from a kind of sanctified mental illness—to figures whose moral status is questionable at best. This latter group includes another category of lollers, those who are able to work yet refuse to, as well as, among others, beggars with bags, idlers, minstrels, and Will himself, the narrator of *Piers Plowman*, who wanders throughout the poem as a mendicant not affiliated with any official ecclesiological body. Through these and other figures Langland probes the epistemological complexities of poverty. He questions again and again how we can come to know the real presence of need, especially when some beggars are inclined to claim it falsely while the true poor, deserving of help, hide their neediness and bear it with patience.

Langland's concern with poverty as something that is difficult to discern stems from larger ethical questions also central to the poem's social and theological visions: What are our obligations to our fellow human beings and particularly to those who are most vulnerable? Should Christians give charity to anyone who asks, as Jesus commands in Luke 6, or should Christians practice discriminate almsgiving, seeking to prevent fraud and to ensure that charitable resources are directed only to those truly in need?[4] The ethical stakes of such questions were particularly high in the Middle Ages. One has to think only of the parable of Dives and Lazarus in Luke 16 or of the Last Judgment as imagined in Matthew 25—texts central to the vast medieval literature on poverty and charity. In both Gospel passages the failure to give to those in need leads directly to damnation. To deny or neglect a person in poverty is to reject Christ himself.

While concern for salvation is unlikely to be the core issue in modern discussions of poverty, *Piers Plowman*'s expansive meditations on the subject nonetheless remain relevant to the exploration of poverty as a phenomenon that persists in our world today. In a senior seminar that I teach on poverty from the Middle Ages to the present, *Piers Plowman* functions as a seminal text for enabling students to approach poverty in its fullest complexity. In addition to studying poverty through literature, students in this course also engage in service learning, a pedagogical strategy that makes work in the community an essential part of the learning experience.[5] This essay offers my reflections on the intellectual and ethical value of combining service learning with the study of poverty in *Piers Plowman*. I argue that performing community service helps my students overcome the medieval otherness of *Piers Plowman*, a dense and historically allusive poem. Interacting with community members over the course of the semester gives them a sense of the real urgency of the poem's primary obsessions and educational models. And, in turn, reading *Piers Plowman* proves to be crucial in minimizing the otherness of the local community. My students' engagement with the intricacies and allegorical modes of the text helps them find a way into the daunting task of exploring poverty through their interactions with strangers. The poem provides them with important perspectives on the complexities of poverty not only in the medieval period but in their own community as well.

Before exploring the intellectual dynamics of pairing *Piers Plowman* with service learning, I give a brief overview of the course and explain my rationale for teaching Langland's poem in conjunction with work in the community. As an examination of poverty through literature, the course features texts ranging from the Bible and Franciscan writings to George Orwell's novels and *Nickel and Dimed*, Barbara Ehrenreich's best-selling exposé of the working poor in modern America. *Piers Plowman* lies at the heart of the course, and we spend several weeks studying the C text, which features Langland's most elaborate ruminations on poverty. Since students in this course are not likely to have experience with Middle English beyond perhaps Chaucer's *Canterbury Tales*, I use George Economou's translation of the poem.[6] I supplement this text with the critical apparatus in Derek Pearsall's Middle English edition, Piers Plowman*: A New Annotated Edition of the C-Text*, which features substantive notes that are indispensible in contextualizing the poem for readers unfamiliar with its historical and theological milieu.

Piers Plowman is worth sustained attention in my course because the poem models for students how to approach poverty as a densely complicated issue, one that transcends historical and disciplinary boundaries. For example, Langland's involved poetic processes are instrumental in revealing poverty as a force that is both an economic designation and a form of representation that articulates claims of need in highly flexible ways.[7] With its focus on both economic necessity and the affective dimensions of the human will, the poem, furthermore, helps students approach poverty as a material reality and as an emotional or psychological experience. And, finally, *Piers Plowman*'s historically situated reflections make students more attentive to the cultural continuities and differences that shape poverty as a phenomenon in today's world.

If Langland's text offers students a model for how to think about poverty, the service learning aspect of the course also can be said to draw on Langland's approach to poverty: working with people in the local community highlights how poverty is a question of ethical responsibility and social relations. The course's intellectual and ethical vision demands that students acknowledge poverty as a lived experience, as something present beyond the classroom walls, and indeed there are a number of organizations serving the poor adjacent to Lehigh's campus. Despite its presence in the local community, poverty is a condition that remains largely invisible to most students, who tend to spend their time on campus. Taking my course thus requires a change of habit for typical Lehigh undergraduates, demanding, to quote Anthony Appiah, that they confront "the ways of others" about whom they are largely ignorant (xviii).

In this sense, my course aims to translate Appiah's important political and ethical lesson into pedagogical practice. Both the topic of the course and its service learning method aim to challenge the insularity that can inadvertently characterize the educational experience at an elite, private university. The assigned texts, and *Piers Plowman* in particular, expose students to unfamiliar social, economic, and religious models central to life in a distant world. The content of the course, in conjunction with service learning, also facilitates students' exploration of poverty as a condition with multiple causes, meanings, and manifestations. In focusing on Langland's poem and other early texts while also requiring work in the community, the seminar challenges students to confront simultaneously the otherness of the medieval past and the otherness of economic difference.

Because there is no service learning coordinator at my university, in planning for the course I visited and carefully assessed a number of agencies near campus that serve the poor. My goal was to have students work in three different places, enabling them to see poverty as a complex and variable experience.[8] Specifically, I tried to select organizations that might benefit from the particular skill sets of my students. I also tried to prioritize organizations that would benefit my students in terms of pedagogical opportunities. To this end, I attempted to evaluate the organizations' willingness and ability to partner with my class and to spend their valuable time talking with us about their specific functions and challenges. Furthermore, I tried to foreground organizations that would offer occasions of interaction between my students and people in the community.

The result of these investigations was a partnership with a local soup kitchen and homeless shelter, a Head Start classroom, and an after-school homework club for children in low-income families. Students are required to complete twenty hours of work at these organizations over the course of the semester. I require students initially to work in all three organizations but encourage them to narrow their focus to one place in order to develop a stronger connection with a specific community group. While fulfilling the requirement has not been a problem thus far, I monitor students' service hours with sign-in sheets held by supervisors at each organization, and students write weekly journal entries reflecting on their experiences in the community. I do not assign specific topics, but I sometimes call attention to a provocative quotation or issue from class discussion to encourage students to make concrete connections between the assigned reading and their experiences in the community. Because the journals are so important in bridging the gap between the students' service work in the community and their intellectual work in the classroom, I devote some class meetings solely to discussing their journals and experiences in the community. On these days I guide the discussion with reference to the texts under study; conversely, on days devoted to discussing texts I attempt to draw on their community experiences where appropriate.[9]

Among the assigned texts in the course *Piers Plowman* proves particularly effective in engaging students with the realities of poverty in their own campus community. As they read the poem they catalog the many types of poverty Langland addresses. We discuss the poem's seemingly limitless desire to taxonomize the poor and explore our own reliance on categories and stereotypes for thinking about poor people in today's world. We also consider the various ethical motivations for such schemes of social characterization, thinking in particular about the lures of epistemological clarity and the obstacles—both practical and moral—confounding such a goal. The poetic process of *Piers Plowman* becomes an important part of this conversation. Given that the text makes no commitment to sustaining narrative development, I encourage my students to find other means of orientation within such a potentially perplexing poem. We thus attend to Langland's dialectical style, noting, for example, how the personifications Recklessness and Patience pursue the merits of voluntary poverty while Free Will (Liberum Arbitrium) and later Need himself go on to criticize the ethics and viability of willed indigence, especially as practiced by the friars. In reading assignments focused on small sections of the poem and in frequent writing assignments on particular passages, students quickly learn that their preconceived notions about poverty hardly do justice to the sheer complexity of the subject as Langland pursues it. In *Piers Plowman* poverty is not something that can be readily defined, summed up, or approached from a single ideological perspective.

This realization comes to inform students' interactions with members of the community, particularly at a local soup kitchen and homeless shelter. My desire is for students to move beyond simplistic conceptions of the poor as either victims of the system or slackers seeking a handout.[10] I also want my students to think about the ethical liabilities of the community service they are undertaking. It would be easy for them to imagine themselves, rather reductively, as either benevolent angels of charity or exploitative subcultural tourists.[11] I urge my class to approach their time in the community much as *Piers Plowman* approaches the subject of poverty—to recognize its capaciousness and complexity while also being cognizant of the potential risks in rendering judgments about their fellow people. To learn from their experiences in the community and to approach their service work with ethical sensitivity, my students aim to translate *Piers Plowman*'s dialectical exploration of poverty into lived experience.

This is, of course, not an easy or perfectly executable task, and my students are certainly daunted by the prospect of going to unfamiliar places, though only blocks from campus, to interact with the homeless and needy. The poem, however, offers a means to bridge this cultural gap. This is perhaps not surprising, given literary texts' ability to engender habits of empathy. Martha Nussbaum, for example, has argued that literature and, more particularly, realist novels can stimulate compassion in readers who confront an issue like poverty—an issue that "is in a way common and close at hand—but which is often, in its significant strangeness, the object of profound ignorance and emotional refusal" (10). Appiah has made a similar argument about literature, insisting that "conversations across boundaries of identity . . . begin with the sort of imaginative engagement you get when you read a novel . . ." (85).[12] Both critics focus on novels in highlighting the ethical and affective power of literary texts. For Nussbaum in particular, it is the novel's highly developed and concrete mode of characterization that inspires empathy, allowing readers to "experience what happens to [the characters] as from their point of view" (66).

But where lies the pedagogical and ethical potential of Langland's allegorical poem, which tends to eschew the detailed, realistic portraits of individual characters that Nussbaum finds so powerful? Certainly, the novel is not the only literary form that generates empathy, and I would argue that, especially when it comes to poverty, Langland's allegorical abstractions can foster identification across great social divides. Personification allegory operates by turning particular states, feelings, and faculties into abstract figurations. In *Piers Plowman*, the use of personification allegory challenges the notion of a purely individual identity and creates the opportunity for identification not limited by a reader's singular experiences and desires. By isolating and abstracting various conditions, allegorical figures in the poem make those conditions universal and therefore potentially meaningful to all human beings. This sense of connection is clear in my students' study of personifications such as Need and Patience, but it is the figure of Hunger that proves most useful in helping my class apprehend the challenges of poverty in the modern world. After reading about Hunger in *Piers Plowman* and understanding how it personifies an abstract sensation and a repressive economic strategy, students are able to perform their work in the soup kitchen with greater ethical sensitivity, political awareness, and intellectual intensity.

In the figure of Hunger Langland blends a historically specific account of political conflict with the potentially universal experience of being hungry. The politicized aspects of Hunger, as critics have demonstrated, offer commentary on the charged economic situation that developed in postplague England (Aers, *Community* 20–72; Kim). The plague and its great demographic collapse brought about an acute labor shortage, and agrarian workers found themselves newly positioned to take advantage of increased mobility and high wages.[13] Employers and landowners, not surprisingly, reacted critically to these changed socioeconomic relations, and throughout the second half of the fourteenth century Parliament issued labor legislation primarily aimed at capping wages at preplague levels.[14] These laws, interestingly, also cast mobile workers as idlers and able-bodied beggars, figures who closely resemble the wasters of passus 8. In the poem, Hunger's "statute" resolves postplague labor conflicts much more efficiently than the laws do (8.342). He gets people to work obediently for mere subsistence. After Hunger's arrival, "There was no lad living that wouldn't bow to Piers / To be his faithful servant though he had no more / Than food for his labor and his gift at noon" (8.194–96). Hunger thus emerges, at least initially, as a political and economic remedy for Piers; he proves highly effective at controlling wasters, who refuse work and fake disability to live in idleness sustained by the plowman's hard-won alms.

When students learn about the historical and ideological conflicts central to the half-acre episode, they understand, through attention to the allegorical figure, how the experience of hunger entails so much more than not having enough to eat. In the poem "Sir" Hunger displays his power, compelling people to work "for fear of death" (8.202). Hunger is the function of a repressive political strategy that seeks to maintain the economic supremacy of the elite at the expense of workers' rights, agency, and advancement. This historically specific representation of Hunger informs students' speculation on hunger as a force prompting people in their own community to seek food from a soup kitchen. In their journals they ask some pointed questions: Does the hunger of people in the community have structural roots, like it so clearly does in the half-acre episode? And, if so, how might an individual's experience of hunger signal a larger systemic problem? What, in short, are the causes of hunger in our own community?

In the half-acre episode, Piers ultimately comes to recognize Hunger's practical and ethical limitations as a force for controlling workers. Even as the plowman benefits from Hunger's effects on the wasters, he nonetheless has misgivings about Hunger in the same moment that the figure makes his effects felt. Through its representation of Hunger as a physical sensation, the poem makes it possible to see poverty outside a specific historical perspective. To explore these other dimensions of the personification, I ask my students to read carefully the passage describing Hunger's arrival and to think about something that might otherwise seem obvious: what it feels like to be hungry. Students quickly notice the physicality of Hunger and his violent treatment of his victims:

> Hunger in haste then grabbed Waster around the belly
> And hugged him so tight his eyes watered.
> He battered the Breton about his cheeks
> So that he looked like a lantern the rest of his life,
> And he so beat both of them up he nearly busted their guts
> Had not Piers with a peas-loaf called him off. (8.171–76)

In this account Hunger emerges swiftly and bears incredible force. Those who suffer Hunger's effects feel as though they have been physically beaten: their eyes water, their wombs ache, and their distended stomachs feel about to burst. These dehumanizing physical effects are underscored by the Bretoner whose hollow cheeks give him the appearance of a lantern.

By focusing narrowly on the primal experience of severe hunger, students can step back momentarily from the ideological positions, fears, and assumptions about the poor that the poem engages in this scene. In describing its dire effects, the poem explores hunger as a potentially universal feeling—something that anyone in any time or place could experience in a profoundly physical way. In this manner the poem once again leads students to consider the experience of hunger by people in their own community: What are the people at the soup kitchen feeling as they wait in line for food? Do they experience physical pain as a result of being hungry? How would it feel, my students ask, if they themselves were the ones in the food line? These meditations on hunger as a universal vulnerability almost inevitably lead students back to the systemic causes of hunger and poverty in the local community. Langland's sophisticated use of personification allegory enables students to traverse these different aspects of hunger so fluidly. Their attention to the poem's formal dynamics helps them apprehend the intricate dynamics of poverty not only as the experience of individual people but as a consequence of larger historical and political structures.

While the study of *Piers Plowman* is clearly instrumental in making students' service activities pedagogically valuable, I also find the reverse to be true—that their service activities enhance their understanding of the poem. By reading the poem and performing service work, the class does not simply learn about the complexities of poverty in the Middle Ages and in the present day. Rather, they experience a pedagogical practice that allows them to internalize the urgency of some of *Piers Plowman*'s most central concerns. For example, students learn powerful lessons about the formation of community: they identify and interrogate social boundaries; get to know many different kinds of people; and, after getting more comfortable in the community agencies, express surprise at not having been aware of these places before taking the course.

Langland similarly explores the challenges of attaining social unity, especially given the increasing fluidity of communities in the half century following the plague. Part of Langland's passion in writing about poverty stems from the sense of obligation he feels toward all Christians, possibly even to those said to waste community resources. This compassion is evident in Piers's growing suspicion of Hunger's coercive policies, a suspicion that leads him to wonder if it is right to expose his fellow Christians—his "blood brothers"—to such abuse (8.217). The poem's anxious concern for the poor can also be seen in passus 9, which considers the various groups of people covered by Piers's pardon. While the half-acre scene first presents hunger as the result of refusing to labor, passus 9 acknowledges that the working poor also experience need. Langland writes movingly of "poor folk in hovels" who work relentlessly but who nonetheless can barely feed their children or provide for themselves (9.72). Such people "wak[e] up nights / To rise on the bedside to rock the cradle, / Also to card and comb wool, to patch and wash, / To rub flax and reel yarn and to peel rushes. . . ." (9.78–81). Yet still "their children . . . cry out for food. / And they themselves also suffer much hunger . . ." (9.76–77).

This form of poverty still exists, and students encounter it when groundskeepers and other uniformed workers from the university come to the soup kitchen for lunch. In getting to know such people as their own needy neighbors, students grasp firsthand the ethical urgency of Langland's concern for the working poor. In their journals and in class discussion they ask heated questions that evoke both the compassion in passus 9 and Piers's earlier anxieties about his blood brothers. The moral stakes of the poem's reflections on poverty and charity come alive as students wonder what they and their university owe to those in their own community who work full-time, perhaps at multiple jobs, yet still do not have enough to eat.

The students' experience in the community also makes tangible their reflections on the proper organization of resources and the possible causes of hunger—other concerns central to *Piers Plowman*'s exploration of poverty. Passionately foregrounding the sacrament of penance as a means of promoting justice, *Piers Plowman* repeatedly issues the command *redde quod debes*—"render what you owe." This penitential call has relevance to modern readers of the poem, for it urges us to acknowledge that we have obligations to our fellow people and to examine how our habits affect others. Langland's exploration of the sins conveys this message in a profound way, particularly for students who find themselves drawn to the infamous figure of Glutton, a personification who spends the day drinking and then throwing up after finding himself drawn into a tavern on his way to church. While it is not difficult to appreciate how this figure offers a warning about the personal consequences of overindulgence, the students' work in the community enables them to perceive the social dimensions of gluttony with particular acuteness. As they witness the realities of hunger almost daily in their service, Glutton's vomit becomes a glaring symbol of social and moral corruption: to waste food is to abuse one's neighbor and increase someone else's hunger. Because we have been shaped to some degree by the modern culture of capitalist consumption, it can be difficult for any of us to recognize the immediate social implications of gluttony. These implications, though, are central to *Piers Plowman*'s ethic of community, and students come to apprehend them readily, questioning how they and society at large might be complicit in creating hardships that other people suffer.

There are also times when my students experience firsthand the poem's strenuous desire to fix the boundaries of community and to render transparent the true meaning of need. On one occasion my class encountered a couple of their fellow college students eating lunch at the soup kitchen after their fraternity had been kicked off campus. Finding themselves without a meal plan, the students took advantage of the center's open policy in order to get a free meal. Perhaps unsurprisingly, my class was angered at such behavior and argued that the fraternity members were not in dire need but had other networks of support available to them. My students' reactions to these freeloaders resonated in particular with *Piers Plowman*'s impassioned debates about discriminate versus indiscriminate charity. While students generally think that a soup kitchen's open policy is essential to affirming the dignity of the poor and making them feel welcome, the fraternity brothers' enjoyment of the center's generosity provoked moral outrage, conjuring a modern-day image of Langland's "beggars with bags" (9.98).

In addition to internalizing the ethical urgency motivating Langland's treatment of poverty and charity, the students' experiences in the community also replicate the process of learning that takes place in *Piers Plowman* itself. At its beginning *Piers Plowman* presents us with a pilgrim seeking knowledge through dream visions, interior meditations, and exchanges with various interlocutors. In these modes Will frequently encounters people he does not know, and his interactions with them prove to be crucial in his search for an ethical life. By combining their reading of *Piers Plowman* with work in social agencies, my students experience a pedagogical practice not unlike Will's own education. While they serve people in the community, they are in turn served by that community, which proves to be a valuable resource in their exploration of an ethical life. Danielle Allen has theorized this form of pedagogy, writing that "[s]trangers feed the human desire to learn" (166).

Though *Piers Plowman* expresses fears about strangers and the communal effects of anonymity, the poem is not resistant to the pedagogical model Allen describes. As a dense and massively learned text, it certainly displays a commitment to traditional modes of academic training, but Will's status as an outsider emphasizes his detachment from clerical institutions. When he does pursue seemingly academic forms of knowledge, Langland casts this pursuit as allegory in the form of personal encounters with strangers. For example, Will happens upon Study, the wrathful wife of Wit, and, pleased by Will's humility, she eventually refers him to her cousin Clergy. His meeting with Clergy leads to brief instruction by Scripture, who challenges Will's mental capacity and provokes in him an intellectual crisis. In these exchanges, Will encounters figures without having any prior knowledge of them or special aptitude for their teaching. Furthermore, in the larger poem, Langland repeatedly stresses the strangeness of the interlocutors Will meets. For example, Will does not initially know or recognize the figures of Holy Church, Thought, Imaginatif, Free Will, or Hope. This process of learning is thus one of engagement and interaction, but it is also destabilizing in its insistence that Will must talk to strangers.

Both the poem and my students' experiences make clear that this pedagogy entails great challenges. Will's search for knowledge at times feels frustratingly endless, and he must negotiate the teachings of numerous figures whose compelling ethical theories are articulated with varying degrees of authority and sometimes with misguided intentions. This proves to be a difficult process, and we find Will at different occasions yielding up his quest for knowledge in utter despair (Zeeman, Piers). After his meeting with Study, for example, we are told that Will "wept for woe and anger at her words" only to be "swept away" into "the land of longing" (11.167, 169, 170). Such emotions are not unknown to my students, whose encounters in serving the community are also sometimes frustrating, uncomfortable, or hard to bear. When they perceive injustice, it is challenging for them and me to channel their anger into a pedagogically useful arena. Furthermore, their experiences in the community are always unpredictable, and students sometimes have to contend with unfriendly or aggressive people who seem to revel in making them uncomfortable.

Despite some unpleasant experiences, community service is ultimately edifying for my students, both personally and in their study of *Piers Plowman*. The admittedly difficult experience of talking to strangers is crucial to modeling an ethical pedagogy central to *Piers Plowman*. For my students, as for Will, learning is an act of wandering wide in the world as much as a matter of reading and writing. This act is neither predictable nor painless, but it offers what Langland might see as an essential education, one that has the potential to develop in students broader habits of knowing, patience, and humility. Praised in *Piers Plowman* itself, such virtues make students better readers of the poem as they struggle with its historical alterity, narrative dissonance, and initially peculiar ethical obsessions.

Students' experience in the world makes *Piers Plowman* a more readable and rewarding poem, while the text likewise makes students better readers of the world. *Piers Plowman* can foster habits of empathy, allowing students to engage with the otherness of both a distant past and a socially divided present. Its allegorical representation of potentially universal conditions draws on historical specificity yet also transgresses personal, cultural, and social boundaries that might otherwise limit students' abilities to become effective knowers of the world. Finally, *Piers Plowman*'s commitment to complexity is perhaps both the poem's greatest challenge to students and its greatest gift. Whether one studies poverty or another pressing social issue, *Piers Plowman* deserves to be taught in the undergraduate classroom, for it models an intellectual and ethical sensitivity that will serve students in their pursuits long after leaving college.

NOTES

[1]There is a massive critical literature on Langland's treatment of poverty. In addition to numerous articles on the figures of Hunger and Need, see Aers, "*Piers Plowman* and Problems"; Aers, *Community* 20–72; Aers, *Sanctifying Signs* 99–156; Clopper; Crassons 208–318; Middleton, "Acts"; Pearsall, "Poverty"; Scase, Piers 47–119; Scott; Shepherd; Szittya, *Antifraternal Tradition* 247–87.

[2]On debates about the meaning of poverty in late medieval England, see Moisa; Aers, *Community* 20–72; Crassons 1–20.

[3]Middleton, "Acts," argues that the opening of passus 5 represents Langland's final additions to the poem.

[4]On medieval debates about the practice of almsgiving, see Mollat 134; Rubin 68–74; Aers, *Community* 23–24; Tierney, *Medieval Poor Law* 54–64; Tierney, "Decretalists."

[5]Service learning can be defined as "a teaching and learning strategy that integrates meaningful community service with instruction and reflection to enrich the learning experience, teach civic responsibility, and strengthen communities." See the *National Service-Learning Clearinghouse* Web site for this definition and other helpful resources on service learning (gsn.nylc.org/clearinghouse).

[6]All quotations of the poem in this essay are from Economou's translation.

[7]For a discussion of poverty as a social phenomenon that entails issues of representation and interpretation, see Aers, *Sanctifying Signs* 99–156; Crassons 49–67; Fradenburg.

[8]There is a wealth of useful resources for developing service learning courses. The *National Service-Learning Clearinghouse* (gsn.nylc.org/clearinghouse) offers the best centralized collection of these materials, including bibliographies, sample syllabi, and faculty tool kits for employing service learning in higher education.

[9]Because the journals are so integral in the course, I grade them on students' efforts to analyze their work in the community with respect to the course content.

[10]For a recent study that seeks to complicate these conceptions of the poor, see Shipler.

[11]The practice of critical service learning offers a way of redressing some of the ethical difficulties of service learning. Such difficulties arise especially when service learning is

understood as a means of enhancing students' preprofessional skills through unambiguously charitable work. Making service learning itself an explicit part of our critical conversations, the students and I reflect on the power dynamics inherent in service learning relationships. Furthermore, by performing sustained service work, the students have the opportunity to make meaningful connections in the community and to develop a set of shared concerns. The course also links community service to issues of social justice, and, through the various literary works we read, we discuss poverty as both a personal experience and a systemic social problem. On the problematic power differential in service learning and ways to overcome it, see Mitchell; Clark; T. L. Lewis.

[12]Appiah defines *conversation* as a term that not only refers to "literal talk" but also serves "as a metaphor for engagement with the experience and ideas of others" (85).

[13]See Hatcher and Miller 29; Postan 27–39; Dyer, *Making* 268, 271–72, 357–58; Bolton 214–15, 238–41.

[14]See Aers, *Community* 20–72; Dyer, *Making* 282–85, 290, 315, 319; Middleton, "Acts"; Rubin 31–33; K. Robertson 13–50.

Giving Priority to the A Version of *Piers Plowman*

Míċeál F. Vaughan

We have more than fifty witnesses to distinct versions of the poem(s) titled *Piers Plowman* from the later fourteenth to the sixteenth century. Such variation is not, of course, unusual in the dynamic textual world of medieval manuscripts, but to local variation of scribal texts *Piers Plowman* adds the more substantial diversity of distinct versions. As a result, scholars and readers must not only wrestle with unstable, not demonstrably authorial texts but also decide whether or not it is possible, or proper, to speak about *Piers* as if it were a single work.

In this regard, the condition of *Piers Plowman*, and of many scribal texts more generally, is not altogether dissimilar from what we find in modern digital textuality. Are the texts that appear (and disappear and reappear) on our computer screens and phones stable, and do they bear some trustworthy authority? A similar, healthy skepticism about stability and authority should also inform responses to the variability of texts in a manuscript culture—and even in the culture of early printing. Who is the author and what is the authority of a crowd-sourced *Wikipedia* entry? We describe such texts as open, subject to "communal authorship" of a sort not completely alien to the scribal producers of the manuscript copies and printed editions of *Piers Plowman* (Simpson, "Power" 147).[1]

The existence of three distinct versions of the poems we call by the single name *Piers Plowman* has been for the most part uncontroversial among scholars of late medieval English literature: even those who disagreed about whether they were the work of a single author or of two or more remained content with

W. W. Skeat's so-called Langland myth and with his chronological sequencing of the three versions he named A, B, and C.[2] In the last few decades, however, a number of scholars have raised objections not merely to the traditional ordering but even to whether or not a fourth version (Z) should be added to the sequence (Rigg and Brewer). Even if the number and order of the versions cannot be agreed on, we would do well to resist speaking as though there were a single poetic referent for *Piers Plowman*.[3]

This is not the place to adjudicate the issues of authorship nor those involved in the recent debate over the chronological sequence of A and B.[4] This essay aims at a rather more modest goal: to advance a case for the literary and pedagogical priority of A over the other versions of *Piers Plowman*. But the recent controversy over the number and chronology of the versions may well attract renewed, and deserved, attention to the A version, which has too often been ignored on the principle that it was an abandoned, superseded early version of the poem. Since the B version remains for most readers definitive in discussions of *Piers Plowman*, its relation to A is a crucial one, particularly since the ordering of the versions has been thrown into question.[5]

Reading A from the perspective of the later and ostensibly more complete B, as most readers do, however, significantly devalues the A version, itself a coherent text worthy of serious attention. Seen as the superseded first draft of the poem, A has been lodged in a marginal position by modern criticism. This is unfair to its achievement as one of the earliest works of the alliterative revival (Turville-Petre, *Alliterative Revival*). After all, *Piers* A is virtually the only text from that fourteenth-century movement that survives in a large number of copies, in multiple versions, which attests to its popularity and wide influence. And the variety of those versions and copies underscores the poem's continued appeal and diverse reception during almost two centuries following its first appearance. *Piers* A, then, provides not only an important near-contemporary witness to the political and social unrest in the middle of the fourteenth century but also a standard against which to assess the continuing anxieties produced by the serious divisions during the reign of Richard II and beyond.

To approach A, therefore, only as an antecedent (or derivative) of B inevitably generates various forms of misprision. It really is necessary, as David Fowler insisted for decades, to read A on its own terms, as a distinct version (Piers the Plowman 4–9, 205; Introduction 36–37). And while my own view of those terms may differ from my late colleague's, I nonetheless wholeheartedly agree with his underlying principles: the A version of *Piers* is a worthy and distinctive poem, a witness to a poet of powerful social vision and moral judgment who inaugurated a distinctive literary tradition of political and social critique that continues in a number of strands at least to the sixteenth century (Hudson, "Epilogue"; Barr).

From the inferred historical references in the text, most scholars would assign the composition of *Piers* A to the period between 1362 and 1374, which lies within the last two decades of Edward III's fifty-year reign (1327–77) and an important phase of the Hundred Years' War: the truce concluded in 1360 was in many respects the pinnacle of England's good fortune; a decade later the tide had turned and England's gains were receding. The economic and institutional effects—both secular and ecclesiastical—of the black death (ca. 1348–50) still shaped major facets in English society. The dotage of Edward III and the machinations of his mistress Alice Perrers—possibly a suggestive exemplar for Lady Meed (Trigg)—were generating unrest and uncertainty among the lords and the people; and, after the composition of the A version, the death of Edward's heir, the Black Prince, in 1376 and the coronation of Edward's young grandson Richard when the king died in 1377 did little to settle the internecine squabbles of powerful princes and magnates. (Such concerns clearly affected a number of B's revisions of A's opening dreams.)

But even if *Piers* A were to turn out not to be the earliest surviving version of the poem (and of the literary tradition of Piers the Plowman), there remain a number of attractive reasons to use it in the undergraduate classroom. Its relatively short length and clear literary structure, combined with the energy and variety of its sociopolitical engagement, enhances the poem's appeal for relative newcomers to medieval English literature. Further, its accomplished use of personification allegory, its complicated sense(s) of ending, its well-articulated and strongly debated points of view, and even the textual issues raised by the continuation in passus 12 all provide occasions for literary, textual, historical, and moral questions that will sustain the interest of more advanced readers. (And this is to leave aside entirely the contested matter of authorship.)

Many of these elements in the A version, some of them quite distinctive, get buried in discussions of the more capacious, and less easily digestible, longer versions. By sheer number of lines, the center of interest in B and C is elsewhere than in their revisions to A's first two dreams. The extended length militates against readers' giving the earlier parts of *Piers Plowman* the attention they deserve, and their public concerns can be marginalized as setting the stage for the more interior, personal journey of the narrator-dreamer that takes up the bulk of the B-continuation, to use David Fowler's term for passus 11–20 (Piers the Plowman). Furthermore, nothing essential is lost by first reading *Piers* in the A version: its form and content are easily comprehended by newcomers, and its appeal might even motivate readers to take up B or C for serious and informed study at a later date. After an attentive reading of A, students are more prepared not only to compare closely how the B-continuation redefines and redirects A's *vita* but also to undertake a subtler, more careful analysis of the local, detailed effects of B's changes to A's three dreams.

As interesting as the dreams and debates in the B-continuation and in C's revision of the expanded B version are, their distinctively personal, psychospiritual inwardness and conceptual complexity are neither as accessible nor as stirring as the more public, outward, and sociopolitical concerns raised by A and vitally extended in B's revisions of A's actions in its opening dreams. In A, problems with secular and ecclesiastical institutions appear, if not always in black and white, at least in primary colors. Lovers of the later versions may lament the absence from A of the lively fable of the rat parliament at the end of B's prologue and of the narrator's moving *apologia* at the beginning of passus 5 of C. But fewer would feel the loss of the subtler difficulties of the "inward journey" (Wittig, "*Piers Plowman* B") involving, say, Imaginatif or Anima; or of the scholastic hairsplitting found in terminological distinctions, such as those involving *mede* and *mercede*, and in disputes about the salvation of the heathen (Grady, *Representing*), however indicative they are of later medieval thought and controversy; or of the lengthy, liturgically grounded journey into biblical history in the later passus (Vaughan, "Liturgical Perspectives"). Important as these are for the revised visions and versions of *Piers*, they do not readily engage most beginning students and can challenge the attention of even advanced readers.

To begin with the practical matter of the A version's compact size: its roughly 2,600 lines (including passus 12) allow it to fit more easily than the considerably longer B or C (each about 7,300 lines) in a medieval English survey course without unbalancing the syllabus. A is barely longer than *Sir Gawain and the Green Knight* or the General Prologue together with the Knight's Tale of *The Canterbury Tales*, allowing for Chaucer's shorter lines. Furthermore, none of the three dreams in A is much longer than Chaucer's Miller's Tale and Reeve's Tale combined. Unlike the longer versions, with *Piers* A students and teachers are not pushed to rush through the poem at the expense of closer reading of the opening dreams. An instructor can discuss an entire text rather than depend on excerpts or an otherwise truncated text of B such as J. A. W. Bennett's admirable edition of its first eight passus (Piers Plowman). And *Piers* A rewards such attention: its rich array of lively characters and of wordplay and humor can be appreciated more fully when they are not made to serve as the introduction to the more extensive geography of the longer versions.

The overall structure of A is considerably clearer than that of the B-continuation or its C revision. The dreams of A present three quite distinct actions, each with its own coherent, if episodic, structure. Each takes up a compact set of concerns and presents them by means of its own dramatis personae. While there are narratorial commentaries and transitional narratives to join the dreams, in A the insistence on following the development of the central narrator-dreamer is less prominent than in the B-continuation. The dreamer's world and maturing appreciation of its complexities are the main concern; the internal faculties of understanding and their limits become the important focus of the B-continuation and redirect the journey inward, toward epistemological, psychological, and spiritual considerations relatively unexamined in the first two dreams in A, and only initiated at a fairly elementary level in the A *vita*. In discussing the B poet's process of reorienting the A *vita*, Elizabeth D. Kirk well characterized it as carrying out "the B poet's modulation from A's story of private defeat to his own universal drama" (*Dream Thought* 127). But this drama is achieved at some cost to the immediacy and accessibility of the public matters in A's more direct account.

A couple of the literary and textual features of *Piers* A are further inducements for selecting it for the undergraduate classroom. The dream vision as a literary form can be traced back to biblical and classical times, but there is no clear antecedent for *Piers*'s combining a series of separate dreams by a single narrrator-dreamer in a continuous sequence (Burrow, *Langland's Fictions* 6–27, 113–18). This sequence should invite readers to consider point of view and to distinguish carefully among the dreamer, narrator, and author in *Piers Plowman*. Readers of the B version will more or less routinely refer to the narrator-dreamer, the *I* of *Piers Plowman*, as Will (or Wil or Wille), and point to the signature in B, at line 152 of passus 15, as justification for this (Kane, Piers Plowman*: The Evidence*). Many extend that reference further, to the putative author William Langland. But the narrator-dreamer in A is not explicitly called Will—at least not until the end of the partially suspect passus 12, at lines 86, 96, and 100 (Middleton, "Making"; Warner, "John But"). The three earlier references to Wille, all in the second dream of the *visio* (5.43–44, 6.73–74, 8.42–44), refer to him in the third person. If they refer to the dreamer, they do so in a strangely oblique fashion; elsewhere, the narrator-dreamer uses the first person when he unambiguously refers to himself (e.g., prol. 1–16, 1.2, 1.10, 2.1–14, 5.3–10, 8.91, 8.149–85, 9.1–22, 9.49–69, 9.103–16). There is no obvious reason why he would shift the point of view in his own narrative here and alternately speak of himself in the first and third persons. Consequently, unless we take as authorial the colophon, *Explicit hic Visio Willelmi de Petro de Ploughman* (*Here ends the Vision of William concerning Piers the Plowman*), which variably connects the *visio* and the *vita* in a number of A manuscripts, we are not required to name the narrator-dreamer as Will until the problematic last lines of passus 12.[6]

Aside from the last two instances in passus 12, then, there is nothing in A that requires us to take the name of the author as Will (or William Langland), and indeed there is nothing in the *visio* that would invite us to assign that name to the narrator-dreamer. Nor, for that matter, is his identification with the author crucial to the meaning of various episodes in *Piers* A. Giving students the opportunity to consider these relations, and even the status—authorial, scribal, multiscribal—of passus 12, will stimulate their critical thinking and provide a ready point of connection to the familiar world of digital texts while encouraging them to reflect on exactly what authority texts on the Internet have—or ought to have. It can also provide a pertinent occasion to raise issues about medieval texts and the identity, frequently anonymous and often multiple, of their author(s), features that immediately raise questions about the kind of authority the texts may have. Furthermore, considering passus 12 as an addition (by whomever) opens the door to reflections on the long-lasting *Piers Plowman* tradition and what appears to be a more general late medieval fondness for continuations and sequels—a fondness that also underwrites current patterns of Hollywood movie production and the appeal of later director's cuts of earlier successful versions, which are equivalent to critical editions of authorial texts, excising the accretions made in the earlier production.

Even more immediately, perhaps, the status of passus 12 introduces the question of whether or not what we call *Piers* A is a complete text and whether or not the end of passus 11 has a sense of an ending. While it has become commonplace to talk of the A version as unfinished or incomplete, this is arguably the result of readers' and critics' familiarity with the longer versions. There were, no doubt, some similar views of the poem's ending with passus 11 in the fourteenth century. Otherwise there probably would not have been the addition of passus 12 in at least three manuscripts, nor four manuscripts in which passus 11 of A is followed by C's passus 11 (beginning around line 295) through passus 22, nor the B-continuation. All of these sequels to *Piers* A attest to at least some contemporaries' sense of the poem's open-endedness and the absence of satisfying closure at the end of passus 11. Yet some scribes and readers considered the work complete at the end of passus 11. A few scribes of A reinforced the sense of an ending with additions at the close of passus 11. But they can hardly be said to have created an ending for something that was not otherwise concluded. A comparison of the ending of passus 11 with that of the A *visio* (passus 8) reveals an acceptably formal attempt at closure (Fowler, Introduction 30), and the ending of A at passus 11 is no more or less open than the conclusion of B and C. We accept the closure of B and C at least in part because there is nothing more offered by contemporary witnesses. With A, however, we do not have such silence, and we surmise that A is unfinished, incomplete, broken off because the poet or others continued the series of dreams that compose A. But a reader of *Piers* A who is neither committed to a presumption of unitary authorship nor burdened by familiarity with the longer versions—in other words, a fresh reader of *Piers Plowman*—may well agree, even after investigating the issues raised by point of view and passus 12, that "[t]here is a sense of ending in the last lines of A.11 . . ." (Kane, Piers Plowman*: The Evidence* 188). After all, in the surviving manuscripts of *Piers* A no scribe supplied a line like that found in the margin of the Hengwrt Manuscript at the end of Chaucer's Cook's Tale: "Of this Cokes tale maked Chaucer na moore" ("Chaucer composed no more of this Cook's tale"; fol. 57v; Ruggiers 224–25; my trans.). And some *Piers* A scribes indeed punctuated their copies with forceful assertions of closure: for example, the scribe of the later-fifteenth-century MS Douce 323, who followed the last line of A, passus 11, with "[n]ow of þis litel book y haue makyd an ende / Goddis blessyng mote he haue þat drinke wil me sende / Explicit liber petri plouman" ("I have now finished copying this little book / May God bless anyone who will send me a drink / Here ends the book of Piers Plowman"; my trans. [see Vaughan, "Ending(s)" 237]).

Finally, for those with historical, or new-historicist, leanings, *Piers* A provides a veritable treasure trove.[7] Prominent in A, but perhaps somewhat lost in B and C, is how the disagreement between Theology and Holy Church over the genealogy and character of Lady Meed points to a core ambiguity in the poem's view of such authorities. While we hear the dreamer (for example, at the end of passus 8, lines 149–85) echoing the views of Holy Church from the end of passus 1 (lines 149–61), in the waking scene that follows at the beginning of passus 9—the prologue to the *vita*, which significantly echoes the wandering, uncertain condition of the narrator-dreamer at the beginning of the *visio*—he engages in formal disputation with the two Franciscan friars he meets. Where does truth (or Truth) reside in these moments of debate? When the dreamer rejects learning at the end of passus 11, has he again earned Holy Church's earlier sobriquet "dotede daffe" ("ignorant fool"; 1.120; my trans.) or have we arrived at a crucial realization that neither the dreamer nor his dreamed or waking interlocutors provide clear, final answers to his many questions? Does this, in turn, lead us to look at the disagreement between Holy Church and Theology with fresh eyes and hesitate before acceding to the authority of Holy Church?

Such questions are not necessarily disingenuous or heretical, nor are they the product of an ideological stance grounded on skepticism about single authorship. Even if complete, *Piers* A challenges easy interpretation. That is the mark of an important literary work, an importance validated in its own era by its influence on the many continuations and revisions of its text. The appeal of *Piers* A does not derive entirely from what was produced later in the tradition the text initiated, but its reception provides unambiguous testimony of its importance to contemporaries. The vibrant, modern critical tradition of medieval English studies would do well to consider its attractions and challenges. A good place to begin rereading the many poems we call *Piers Plowman* is to introduce the A version in our undergraduate classrooms.

NOTES

[1] I am, of course, displacing Simpson's idea of "communal authorship" to the scribal arena of manuscript production; his phrase refers to the internal dynamics of the poem with its competing personified forces of will and reason within a "complex set of potentially conflicting [psychological] powers" ("Power" 157) that ultimately resolve into a "common will" (154, 164–65) "whereby the poem's authorship ideally becomes its readership" (154).

[2] See Benson, *Public* xii–xv, 3–42, for the definition and history of the "Langland myth." See also C. Brewer; Simpson, "Power"; Warner, *Myth.*

[3] The five manuscripts that conjoin A and C may also qualify as a distinct text of the poem, as perhaps do the three conjoint CAB manuscripts; the two distinct branches of the

B version likewise attest to different stages in the text's transmission. Among other anomalous texts of *Piers* is the unique conflation of ABC in Huntington MS 114. An accessible and trustworthy account of the various texts is Kane, "Text." My own edition of the A version (Vaughan, Piers) is based on Rawlinson Poetry MS 137 (Ra), the sole witness to the complete passus 12. This essay cites the A version in my edition unless otherwise indicated.

[4]In raising questions about the order of A and B, Anne Hudson also queried whether B and C might have been independent revisions of an earlier version ("Variable Text" 60). More substantive arguments for reversing the A-B order are found in Mann, "Power"; and in Bowers, "*Piers Plowman*'s William Langland." Mann draws on an earlier essay (Meroney). The critical reactions to these arguments have forcefully reasserted the traditional chronological order: see Traugott Lawler's response to Bowers's essay ("Response") and his more extensive, later response to Mann's ("Reply"). See also Kane, "Open Letter." For recent questions about the relation of the B and C versions, see Warner, *Lost History* 40–61.

[5]Considering in particular the current ending(s) of the A version, we may well remain unconvinced that A descended from B. The argument for B-to-A ordering largely derives from the late dating of A manuscripts and from differences in local, selected passages of the poems rather than from a fuller consideration of the poems' larger structures and emphases. On the endings of A, see Vaughan, "Ending(s)"; see also Thomas Prendergast's essay in this volume.

[6]Unless otherwise noted, translations from the A text are from Covella. The colophon quoted here is in the form of the explicit in Cambridge, Trinity College, MS R.3.14 (T). Variants appear in other manuscripts: London, British Library, MS Harley 6041 (H^2); Liverpool, University Library, MS F.4.8 (Ch); Oxford, Bodleian Library, MS Rawlinson Poetry 137 (Ra); Oxford, University College, MS 45 (U); and New York, Pierpont Morgan Library, MS M 818 (J). I omit the last line of passus 9 from this inventory of references to Will, since there is no such reference in my edition of the line, which reads "Here his wil wolde I wite" ("I'd like to know what he wants now"; my trans.), where other editions have, following MS T, "Here is wil wolde wyte" ("Will, here, wants to know").

[7]Benson's *Public* Piers Plowman opens up a number of interesting topics of this sort (e.g., 43–75), many drawn from the sections that B and C derive from A.

The Pedagogy of an Oppressed Text: The C Version of *Piers Plowman*

Kathryn Kerby-Fulton

C. S. Lewis once wrote that Langland could "hardly make his poetry into a poem" (*Allegory* 161).[1] Langlandians are both justly offended and justly amused by Lewis's impenetrability on this point, but at least some of this impatience with the loose structure of *Piers* would have been mitigated if Lewis had had access to a good C text. Skeat's was the only scholarly edition available in his day, and Skeat had used Phillipps MS 8231 (now Huntington Library HM 137) as his base C text.[2] As Elizabeth Salter and Derek Pearsall wrote when they produced the first modern edition of C in 1967, "[Skeat's C] was based on a bad manuscript, a sophisticated recension by an interfering scribe, and the pedantry and verbosity which have long been laid to the charge of the C Text poet are in fact partly the responsibility of this scribe" (1–2). The "interfering scribe" obscured a text that I think Lewis would have thought more highly of than he did of the B text: Lewis prized what Northrop Frye called "poetry of product" more than "poetry of process,"[3] and in the C text Langland comes closer to a poetry of product than in any of his texts. To put it quite simply, C is smoother, less chaotic, tighter, and more purposeful than B. It is eminently teachable and makes a wonderful introduction to *Piers Plowman* for undergraduates. For the same reason that one would introduce James Joyce's longer fiction to undergraduates with *Ulysses* rather than *Finnegan's Wake*, I teach C to first-time readers of *Piers*. No text of *Piers* is polished in the sense that, for instance, *Pearl* is. But C's shape and trajectory are clearer than those of earlier versions, and, most important, it is the poet's last surviving word.[4] If Langland had lived to be the age of Abraham, he'd still have been revising his poem, and we'd likely have exhausted all the letters of the alphabet to label his versions. But C is the most finished work we've got.

This essay is divided into two sections: the first on how to teach the C text and the second on why. Those not interested in the nuts and bolts of syllabi and course titles may wish to focus on the second section, which is the literary argument for teaching C as a brilliant revision of B.

How to Teach the C Text: Approaches for Undergraduates and Graduates

When I teach *Piers* to undergraduates, I teach C with supplemental extracts from B and from A to show the high points of Langland's lifelong revisionary struggle. I order Derek Pearsall's original language edition for the class, and that is the text we work from daily, although I order George Economou's translation as an optional text (though we never use it in class, it usually sells out). I also provide a lengthy handout summarizing the C text in detail, a kind of vade mecum with certain passages highlighted—the ones that students must know to make sense of the poem and to prepare for the translation and commentary tests. Students who feel swamped are invited to read the translation through once to grasp the larger structure and storyline (in so far as Langland deigns to offer one). Then in class we work through Pearsall's C text from beginning to end, mainly going over the key passages in the set readings for each week. I teach the C text over six or seven weeks, and roughly every two weeks students write a test on the next group of passus (these are divided into thematic units with titles that make sense to students, e.g., The Marriage of Lady Meed or The Plowing of the Half Acre). On the tests students choose from three or four substantial quotations of about 30–40 lines each, all selected from the highlighted passages on the summary. During the fifty-minute test students translate the chosen passage and write a literary commentary on it, using any combination of close reading, thematic, historical, or cultural contextualizations they wish. It works very well. By the time they have done their fourth test, they have written about at least four key passages drawn from across the poem in its original language and have studied many more in preparation. I normally teach *Piers* to undergraduates in a course called Major Alliterative Poets, in which it is followed by *Pearl* and by *Gawain*, also taught in the original language and using the same model of translation and commentary tests. (The *Pearl* and *Gawain* tests differ from the *Piers* tests only in that the list of passages students must study is shorter, and they are allowed to consult a glossary during the test for a few items of more difficult vocabulary). These three texts compose the entire course, and the last assignment is a detailed critique of one of the published translations of any of the three poems. This assignment is, perhaps surprisingly, always a success, and students emerge from the course with a healthy respect for the limitations of literary translation. As one student said, reading the translation of the poem now felt to her like seeing a Disney animation of a great novel.

As we proceed through the C text, I provide handouts of key passages from both A and B. For instance, at C.11.298 we discuss the ending of the A text and compare its final pages with their counterparts in B and C, asking why A ends abruptly at just this spot and what enabled Langland to continue in the B-C tradition. The issues that exercise the dreamer here of course involve salvation of non-Christians and radical questioning of God's justice. No matter what their background, students respond with passion to these themes and to the puzzle of A's abrupt ending. With graduate students, one can go into much more detail about the poem's revision process; I also give them an assignment asking them to reconstruct all the variants of a passage of their choice from the Athlone editions (Kane, Piers Plowman*: The A Version*; Kane and Donaldson; Russell and Kane) and to evaluate the editors' emendations. This ensures that they understand how variants in any literary text actually work (even advanced students often do not) and some of the unique and famous editorial challenges *Piers* presents to the larger field of textual criticism. Nonmedievalist graduate students can be invited to compare these with the equally famous editorial challenges in Shakespeare and Joyce.

I teach *Piers* in graduate courses with titles such as Medieval Interiorities and Modern Readers: Historical and Formalist Approaches; Langland, Chaucer, and Literary London: Formalist, Historicist, and Material Culture Approaches; London Reading Circles and the Rise of the Ricardian Poetry: From New Historicism to Cultural History; The Long Fourteenth Century and the Rise of English; The Alliterative Revival: From Early Middle English Origins to the Great Fourteenth-Century Poets; and Books under Suspicion: Censorship and Tolerance in Medieval English Literature. The last course even works surprisingly well at the undergraduate level, emphasizing issues concerning the history of biblical translation and religious dissent still relevant today.

Why Teach the C Text? Langland's Last Revisions and Their Impact

To teach Langland's revisions to undergraduates I often use the "Appendix: Major Additions, Omissions, and Transpositions of Material in the C Version" from Economou's C translation (161–62), which can be photocopied for the class. This list allows students to see at a glance how Langland achieved the smoother structure of C through many of the major omissions and transpositions. The major B passages I hand out in photocopies for comparison with C are selections from the prologue, the tearing of the pardon (B.7.119–43), and Imaginatif's dressing down of Will about writing poetry (B.12.16–54). The B passages from passus 7 and 12 were creatively reworked by Langland into C passages of equal fame: Imaginatif's attack was reincarnated into C's so-called autobiographical passage (5.1–108), and the excised pardon episode was reworked into Langland's charismatic additions on radical poverty, "lunatic lollars" (9.105–39) and the apostolic life (C.9). Speculation on why Langland removed the pardon episode always generates great classroom discussion. Reading the account in the C text first, students are often surprised to learn about the pardon episode, because quite clearly it didn't fit Langland's larger purpose in C. The poem is actually *more* subversive without it: in C nothing undermines Piers's own sturdy defense of and belief in the pardon from Truth (the pardon itself a highly contentious, bold document in which Langland makes room for social groups not yet accepted into the Church's salvational schema), but one that Langland stuck by even in his final version (Kerby-Fulton, "Confronting"). With its progressive social inclusiveness—as when merchants weep for joy at their estate's acceptance, albeit just in a marginal gloss to the pardon (9.22–42)—and direct communication between Truth and Piers (9.1), the underlying message is that no priest is needed to mediate between God and humankind. In C the priest comes off as a literal-minded annoyance, but not as a figure capable of inducing Piers to destroy the very document of salvational emancipation for all social classes, even those at the time excluded in canon law.

Approaching the poem at its key revisionary moments reveals that in Langland nothing is ever truly excised. Instead of lamenting the disappearance of the pardon scene from C, one can be awed not only by the excision's dignifying of Piers's power but also by Langland's striking new additions to the passus. In the pardon, the poet had briefly gestured toward the charismatic voluntary poverty Piers vows to adopt. In C the gesture becomes a tour de force: among various holy paupers of passus C.9, we now have the prophetic "lunatic lollars," and Langland's new attempt to portray Piers's B-text conversion to the apostolic life by representing it among the mentally, psychologically, and materially disadvantaged on the street in everyday life. If one teaches B, one can bring in part of passus 9 of C for isolated consideration (as J. F. Goodridge did in his Appendix B [260–61]), but doing so misses the larger context of the massive and magisterial addition running from lines 61 to 281 of C.9. The addition lifts the pardon from a religious document in B to a religiosocialist manifesto in C and includes a lengthy discussion on begging, labor, and illicit hermits and other itinerants, both lay and clerical. It contains what may be the first ever discussion in English of single-parent families headed by women scraping out a meager living in destitute households. These women take their place in the passage alongside the poignant lunatic lollars, and amid a searching discussion of whether to give to street beggars, all capped off by a vivid—indeed vicious—indictment of the social injustice permitted by simoniac bishops, who are likened to guard dogs refusing to bark at thieves.

Taking students from the short pardon scene of B to the rainbow of new issues and poetry in passus 9 of C is a pleasure and a superb example of how C can be both leaner and fuller, and even more sparkling as a socioreligious poem. Medieval reader response, moreover, shows that the C additions could be popular: this section, along with the only extant passage that shows "the poet in his working clothes," as Derek Pearsall puts it ("'Ilchester' Manuscript" 192), has unfinished lines containing almost no alliteration (C.prol.106–17) that were apparently leaked to the public early (Kerby-Fulton et al. 70–79). The Ilchester Manuscript pushes the new passus 9 addition right up to the front of the poem. Its scribe (Scribe D), a man from Langland's own dialect area, even skillfully fixed the defective alliteration of the leaked prologue passage. One need not take undergraduates through the minutiae of such textual discoveries, but the evidence they provide that some of Langland's C revisions were a hot-ticket item is certainly intelligible to students. Even more pertinent to the classroom is the Douce illustrator's crowding of passus 9 in particular with numerous illustrations. The seventy-three color images in the Douce manuscript offer the only extant cycle of *Piers* illustrations and are a great tool for teaching the poem; one of the huge bonuses of teaching C is being able to follow the text through the cycle.[5]

The other major topic I teach in relation to revision issues is Langland's apparent political restraint in C: for example, the scaling back of the momentary lunatic goliard passage of the B prologue (lunacy, however, as we have just seen, is given a much stronger hand to play in the passus 9 addition to C) and the apparent new social conservatism of passus 5's diatribe against the buying of religious office or knighthood. This is a good opportunity to have students read the John Ball letters and discuss the Rising of 1381. Despite B's modern reputation as a left-wing political poem, it contains nothing as socially powerful as the C additions on voluntary and involuntary poverty (see also the other huge addition in praise of poverty at C.12.153–13.100) or the addition to C on why marrying for love rather than money is so important (C.10.254–69). Other passages unique to C make for empathetic reading and good student discussion: for instance, the rebellious role given to Recklessness in C, where he takes over the dreamer's persona for a lengthy stretch and asks the challenging and impish questions to which orthodox Christian doctrine leaves itself open. Important evidence of Langland's ultimate views about the role of Piers in the poem is the addition of lines 138–48 of passus 15, described by Pearsall's note as follows: "C here cuts through the riddles of the B text, and some complex redefinitions of the three lives, sweeping all aside in a demonstration of the ruthlessness of perfect love: 'Love your enemies' (Matt. 5:44, Luke 6:27), the revolutionary core of the Sermon on the Mount." So often we as Langlandians fixate on obvious differences between B and C, like those discussed above as well as Langland's sporadic late preferences for Latinate over vernacular names—Haukyn becoming Activa Vita, for example, or the entirely new character in C given the unmusical name Liberum Arbitrium (Free Will). These names, however, were clearly not dull to Langland's contemporaries: the Douce manuscript portrays Liberum Arbitrium (fol. 74) as a beautiful, buff young squire in the courtly love tradition and Activa Vita (fol. 69) as the most alert and poignant of the working poor. But for a modern audience, too, what C does time and again is "cut through" the obscurities or prolixities of B to powerful clarities.

An apt metaphor for teaching *Piers Plowman* from C would be studying the biography or oeuvre of a famous adult and bringing forward writings or snapshots from his childhood or early prime. The child is father of the man, and we learn so much about the poem's past from A and B. But how many of us would want to be remembered by the *penultimate* draft of our magnum opus? Scholars can argue the different merits of the texts, as they do, for instance, of Wordsworth's lifelong revisions to *The Prelude*, but to me a much better analogy for Langland's versions might be Chaucer's F and G texts of the prologue to *The Legend of Good Women*. In them a contemporary Middle English poet struggles with political, personal, and patronage issues, creating the kind of "rolling revision" that leaves editors attached to the fixities of print culture reeling. The *Riverside Chaucer* prints the F and G texts in parallel, and no serious critic of the *Legend* would ignore either version. That, I think, is what we, as responsible teachers of Langland, must ultimately insist upon. And we will need a more textually comprehensive textbook than the recent Norton Critical Edition, which contains only B (Robertson and Shepherd). The C text, with its sleeker trajectory, is a more graspable narrative for beginners and is available in Derek Pearsall's beautiful 2008 glossed edition of his 1978 edition. And we live in hope of the publication of a parallel multitext edition of C affordable for students.[6] They, too, deserve to know the poet's final wishes.

NOTES

[1]On Lewis's attitude toward Langland, see my "Standing on Lewis's Shoulders: Some Reflections on C.S. Lewis's Stance as a Critic of Medieval Literature."

[2]Skeat was apparently influenced by the clarity of the hand and extensive program of rubrication in HM 137 (2: xix–xxiv). For sample images online, see "HM 137."

[3]See Stingle.

[4]This is a point that Derek Pearsall has made consistently in both his editions of the C text: "Being the author's latest revision, it presumably represents his latest thinking and therefore, *a priori*, what he is entitled to ask to be remembered by" (Piers 3).

[5]For color images of the full cycle in Oxford, Bodleian Library, MS Douce 104, see bodley30.bodley.ox.ac.uk:8180/luna/servlet/view/search/what/MS.%20Douce%20104?q=Douce%20104. See also Pearsall and Scott. For interpretive discussions, see Kerby-Fulton and Despres.

[6]A. V. C. Schmidt's parallel-text edition is highly informative but unlikely to be affordable for most students.

Appendix 1: A Student Introduction to the Language of the C Text

Axton Crolley

The language in the C text of William Langland's *Piers Plowman* can be strikingly different from present-day English and even from Chaucer's English. The manuscript on which Pearsall's annotated edition, Piers Plowman*: A New Annotated Edition of the C-Text*, is based is written in a South West Midlands dialect, which frequently varies from Chaucer's London dialect. This introduction provides students with the basic knowledge necessary to smoothly read Pearsall's edition. Since difficult lines in the poem are explained in its footnotes and annotations, this guide provides only a rudimentary working knowledge of the most pressing grammatical and lexical issues. No specific linguistic knowledge is assumed, only high-school-level familiarity with a European language.

Pronunciation and Spelling. Reading Langland's text aloud is the key to comprehending it. The letters *i*, *e*, *a*, *o*, *u* are usually pronounced closer to the Spanish or French pronunciations. Normally, *i* sounds like the vowel in American English *beat*, *e* like that in *bait*, *a* like in *bot*, *o* like in *boat*, and *u* like in *boot*. All consonants are pronounced, even when clustered together like in *knowe* (pronounced *kuh-no*). Sometimes *gg* is pronounced like the *y* in *year*, for example, in Middle English *segge* ("say"). The letter *y* sometimes interchanges with the letter *i*, for example, *mornyng* ("morning"). The letters *v* and *u* can interchange, for example *vp* ("up") and *haue* ("have"). If you are using an edition of Pearsall's text from before 2008, you will encounter the characters þ (called "thorn" and pronounced like *th*) and ȝ (called "yogh" and pronounced like the first sound in *year*).

Nouns. Plural nouns normally end in *-es*, as in *thynges* ("things"). Possessive nouns also end in *-es*, as in *goddes loue* ("God's love").

Adjectives. Sometimes, but not always, adjectives have an *-e* on the end, as in *gode seyntes* ("good saints"), especially if the noun is plural.

Personal Pronouns. This chart shows how some pronouns differ in present-day English and Middle English:

PRESENT-DAY ENGLISH	MIDDLE ENGLISH
he, his, him	*his, him/hem/hym*
she, her	*she/scho, here*
it	*hit/it*
they, their, them	*thei, here, hem/hym*
you, your	*thow, thee, thin*
you (pl.), *your*	*ye, yow, yowre*

Reflexive Pronouns. Middle English sometimes does not use reflexive pronouns, such as *myself, himself,* and *themselves*, where present-day English would, for example, *in preiers and penaunces potten hem mony* ("to prayers and penance many put themselves") or *Y shope me into shroudes* ("I dressed myself in garments").

Verbs. Verbs change form depending on the subject of the sentence. Here are the present tense forms for "to sing," again comparing present-day English to Middle English:

PRESENT-DAY ENGLISH	MIDDLE ENGLISH
to sing (infinitive)	(*to*) *singen*
I sing (first person)	*I sing*(*e*)
you sing (second person)	*singest*
she sings, he sings (third person)	*singeth*
they sing, we sing (plural)	*singeth, singen*

Similar endings can appear in the past tense as well, and the past tense is indicated by either an *-ed* suffix (as in *placed*) or by vowel change (as in *sang*). Some words that today form past tenses with *-ed* (*help* → *helped*) in Langland's language changed their vowel to form the past tense (*help* → *yholpe*).

Contractions. Certain phrases can be contracted, like in *haddestow* ("had thou"). Usually these end in *-tow*.

Word Order. Langland's word order frequently differs from that of present-day English, as in *what he do sholde* ("what he should do"). Sometimes Langland doesn't use relative pronouns like *that* or *which* in the way present-day English would, as in *and sethe he radde religioun here reule to holde* ("and afterwards he counseled those of religious orders to hold to their rule"). Similarly, sometimes Langland doesn't use prepositions where present-day English would, as in *wo is hym that* ("woe is to him that").

Trouble Words. The following word forms appear frequently in the text. Use this glossary, based on Pearsall's, to aid in reading.

ac but

anon, anoen at once

ar before

artow art thou, are you

bad commanded, ordered

ben, beth are

biful happened

can know, be able

comune common people, community

couthe, coude could

fele many

forthy therefore

gome man

kyne kind

halde hold, consider

han have

hele health, spiritual health

lacke to slander, to blame

lat allow, let

lede man

lele true

lifelode livelihood, sustenance

luste to desire

leue believe

mo more

moste greatest

myhte might

nere (ne + were) were not

parfay indeed

quod said

rede advise

reuthe pity

segg man

seigh, sei, say, sigh saw

selcouthe strange, rare

selde seldom

siker, sikerliche safe, certain

sith since, after

shrive, shrove hear, make confession

spede succeed

soth, soeth true

swythe very, greatly

tene to harm, to trouble

wende go, turn

wit, wyt wisdom, intelligence

witterly, witterlyche for certain, truly

woet, wot knows

uch, uche each

lewed unlearned

licam, **lycame** body

mette dreamed

me me, myself; also one, as in "one can say that"

Y I

yede went

yeve give

yut still, yet

Appendix 2: A Sketch of the Clerical Orders

Lawrence M. Clopper

In the Middle Ages there was no church with a capital *C*. It would be more accurate to say the church was made up of communities that were cooperative, resistant to oversight of various kinds, intent on defining their own political and ideological positions, and, consequently, self-defining. A simple test to reveal differences within the larger body of the church would be to ask the kinds of questions that a medieval person might ask and had to resolve before entering a clerical order: Do I want to be a secular cleric or a monk or a friar? If a monk, do I want to be a Benedictine or a Cistercian? If a friar, do I want to be a Franciscan or a Dominican? Or do I just want to be a simple parish priest? The conditions for answering this series of questions might depend on how one saw the mission of an order: What is their way of life? What is the degree of poverty? Is the order contemplative or active or some combination of the two? And, undoubtedly, there are many other questions. This line of inquiry highlights the differences among the various orders but especially how potential candidates imagine the occupation of each. In making a choice the candidates define themselves by committing to the order to which they are drawn.

Langland has a clear understanding of what different clerical orders were to do, how they were related to one another, and how they ought to be provisioned. His is a rather austere view of these matters, and thus we can see his project, *Piers Plowman*, as a reformist text. Langland criticizes clergy members for their failings no matter what status or occupation they have. Some of these clerical failures are repeated throughout the text: simony; absenteeism, especially in order to go to London or another large city where the clerical market is more profitable; the concern for money, especially the selling of services for personal profit; the taking of secular positions in the government; the violation of the office to which one was called; and the failure to provide an example of that which one teaches or preaches.

Table 1 is an attempt to give some idea of how the medieval church was theoretically structured. The first distinction is that between secular and regular clergy. *Secular* comes from *saeculum* (the world) because these clerics deal directly with the laity; thus, they are in the world, as opposed to monks, who ideally have withdrawn from the world. Both monks and friars are called regular clerics because they vow themselves to observe a *regula* ("rule"). There were also some mixing of these categories: canons, whether regular or secular, performed functions similar to those of the secular clergy.

The table's middle column shows the secular hierarchy. At the top is the pope, who claimed in his role to be the direct descendent of St. Peter, Christ's disciple and supposedly the first pope. The cardinals, just below, elect a pope, a moment of superiority, but are subordinate to him after the election. The papal *curia* ("court") was made up of the cardinals and other officials who administered clerical and other matters within the purview of the papacy.

Moving outward from Rome to the whole of Christendom, we notice that Northern Europe is carved up into archbishoprics and bishoprics. A *cathedra* ("bishop's seat"), the center of a bishop's authority, is located in a cathedral.

Table 1. The Secular Clergy

REGULAR CLERGY	SECULAR HIERARCHY	FRIARS AND MENDICANTS
	Pope	
Benedictines (rule c. 540)	Cardinals	Dominicans (black friars); established 1216
	Archbishops Canterbury, York	Franciscans (friars minor); rule 1223
Cluniacs (founded 909; reformed Benedictine Rule)	Bishops (dioceses, sees)	Augustinian (Austin) friars; formed by the pope in 1256 from various hermit orders
Cistercians (white monks); founded 1098; reformed Benedictine Rule	Regular canons (black canons)	
	Secular canons	Carmelites; founded as a strict eremitical order in Palestine c. 1195; later reorganized in Europe as a mendicant order
	Deans	
Carthusians; founded 1084; created their own rule 1133	Archdeacons	Crutched friars; often thought to be friars though they were canons regular
	Parish priests or vicars	
	Possible associates: curates, chaplains, deacons, subdeacons, clergy in minor orders, acolytes, etc.	
	Unattached to hierarchy:	
	Hermits and anchorites (private rules)	
	Pardoners (sent by the pope or bishop)	

Bishops are administrators, but they also see that the necessary clerical obligations are carried out, preach the central doctrines of the church, provide a moral example for all men, and see to the needs of the poor. The bishops were believed to have descended from the apostles (Acts 4:32–35). There were two archbishoprics in England, Canterbury and York, and fifteen bishoprics. Canterbury was a monastic and York a secular cathedral. Of the remaining fifteen, six were monastic (Durham, Ely, Norwich, Rochester, Winchester, and Worcester) and eight secular (Bath and Wells, Chichester, Lichfield, Exeter, Hereford, Lincoln, London, and Salisbury). Carlisle was a house of regular canons.

A bishop, who had to be in orders before election, might be named by the cathedral community or be seated by papal provision (private appointment) or by nomination of the king. A bishop who was a secular cleric, therefore, might be enthroned in a monastic cathedral, or, frequently in the fourteenth century, might be a person from the university or royal service. Episcopal rights and duties reside in the office of the bishop no matter whether the person in the office was present or absent and despite what he did or did not do. This is a crucial distinction because it is not the person of the bishop who authorizes and performs necessary rituals but the office mediated through the person of the bishop. The bishop alone was able to administer the sacrament of ordination by which clerics below him were instituted in their positions. When he ordained a priest, he also gave title to him, provisions sufficient to maintain the person and his church as well as legal appointment to the benefice. In addition, ordination conferred the power to celebrate the Mass and to hear confession and offer absolution, except for major offenses reserved by the bishop. The bishop alone had the right to preach doctrine unless he personally relinquished it to others, for example, to itinerant friars.

During the reforms of the twelfth century monks were put out of many of their monasteries for failing to observe the life to which they had vowed themselves. They were replaced by regular canons or secular clerics. The heads of secular communities were deans; their function was to see that the cathedral and its clergy operated properly. Monastic houses, whether cathedral or monastery, were overseen by an abbot or his deputy, the prior.

Between the bishop at the top and the parish priest at the bottom were numerous positions that are difficult to sort into a simple hierarchy because of differences of office and obligation, relation to institutions within the church, as well as positions and duties of representatives of the bishop: canons, regular or secular; deans; subdeans; archdeacons; and subdeacons, each of whom was attached to a territory or to a specific community, such as monastery, cathedral, or collegiate or parish church. At the bottom of this hierarchy is the parish priest. In order to say Mass, he would require persons in minor orders such as acolytes, who may have been laypeople. Langland does not refer to these lesser persons specifically, but he may have represented the persona he created as someone in minor orders; these do not require a vow of chastity.[1] A parish priest or parson is the holder of an ecclesiastical benefice (appointment to a clerical position) who has full possession of its rights and use of its property. In some parishes the priest might transfer his obligations and sacramental functions to a representative, a vicar, who was paid a part of the priest's stipend. In larger parishes there may also have been a curator, a person who has cure of souls, that is, someone who hears confession, dictates some form of restitution for sins committed, and grants absolution to the contrite. The curator may be a person who is resident, a priest or vicar, or, in the case of friars appointed by a bishop, itinerant.

At the bottom of the clerical orders there was some fluidity between laypeople and clerics; the parson or vicar might have glebe land attached to the church either as separate fields or as strips in the common fields. The parish priest, therefore, might perform the same manual labor, plowing and sowing, as did his lay parishioners.

At the lowest level of or outside this hierarchy were hermits and anchorites, who live according to private rules created by the person or in conjunction with an adviser. These people might be under jurisdiction of a sponsor or a proximate cleric.

Loosely tied to the hierarchy are pardoners, who are frequently mentioned in *Piers* and other works from the period. Pardoners were apparently notorious, as in Chaucer's Pardoner and his tale. Supposedly, they were licensed by the pope or bishop, perhaps under the royal seal, but had no immediate overseers to control their actions even though they might be attached in some way to a hospital, especially that of St. John of Jerusalem. The pardoner was a seller of pardons or indulgences, the income from which was supposed to go to the hospital but all or most of which went into his own pocket. They often claimed to be clerics with the authority to absolve sin, but they did not have such authority because they were laymen, clerics in lower orders, or some other quasi cleric. In any event, a bishop's bull (Schmidt, Vision, B.prol.69, 73) did not authorize anyone to grant absolution, only to travel in the jurisdiction to raise money.

The left column of table 1 shows the various monastic orders and the right column shows the mendicants who belonged to the begging orders, that is, those allowed to live by begging rather than by or in addition to laboring. The monastic orders usually were not subordinate to the secular hierarchy because they were instituted by individuals—either patrons or groups of individuals of like mind—consequently, they had no institutional or jurisdictional relation to the pope or other authorities even though the pope, bishop, patron, or the community itself might claim to be the overseer of the community with the right to name bishops (if a cathedral), abbots, priors, and others to their offices and to discipline those within the community. Monks vowed obedience, chastity, and poverty and vowed to adhere to the Rule of Saint Benedict, established in the sixth century.

The monastic orders experienced a cycle of establishment; lapse in observance, especially with regard to poverty and manual labor; and the institution of a reformed order. The Benedictine order (black monks), the earliest, was reformed as the order of Cluny (Cluniacs). The Cistercians (white monks), centered at Citeaux, seceded from the Cluniac order to found a reformed order according to strict Benedictine principles. The Carthusians were monastics who developed their own rule in order to establish communities devoted to prayer and contemplation.

Nunneries were foundations of or attached to the male orders. Most nunneries in England were Benedictine or Cistercian. The Franciscan and Dominican orders had few nunneries in England. In general the rule for nuns was modeled on that for monks, except that many of the rigors of a rule were softened on the grounds that women were frailer than men, as was frequently asserted in the period. Nuns usually were subject to the male houses attached to them because, among other things, they required a priest to say Mass and provide the sacraments, practices that were forbidden to women.

Lateran IV, held in 1215 under Innocent III, was possibly the most significant council before the end of the Middle Ages. It dealt with numerous issues across a broad span of activities, from the reformation of the papal curia to the crusades to the battle against heresy. Two canons are important for the present discussion: one laid down what the laity were to be instructed in and when and how they were to confess their sins and receive the sacrament, and a second forbade the formation of new orders, required the reformation of existing ones, and forced all these to accept one of the traditional rules: that of St. Benedict or that of St. Augustine. Within a few years the papacy saw that two new orders, Dominican and Franciscan, could be used to aid the parish clergy in fulfilling the obligations of the first canon. Later in the thirteenth century a variety of smaller orders were combined into one—Augustinian (or Austin) friars—or accepted a mendicant rule that had been in process before Lateran IV, that of the Carmelites. The Carmelites were an enclosed contemplative order. The Augustinian friars followed the Franciscans and Dominicans into villages, towns, and cities after leaving their hermitages in order to proselytize and offer services that had traditionally been performed by parish priests. These four orders are referred to as papal orders since the papacy authorized them. The mendicant orders, therefore, were outside the secular hierarchy and regulated themselves but were subject, in some situations, to the head of the secular hierarchy, the pope.

Even though Langland refers at times to the four orders of friars, he is primarily interested in the Franciscans and Dominicans. In the C text, however, he refers several times to the five orders (8.191, 9.344, 15.80). The most likely candidates for the fifth are the so-called Crutched friars, who were regular canons. The name refers to their practice of carrying crucifixes in their hands or having ones sewn on their garments. They worked chiefly in hospitals.

In 1214 the Castilian priest Dominic decided to found a special order to combat heresy. He adopted the Rule of Saint Augustine, which he had observed as a canon, and reinforced it with the stricter customs of the Premonstratensian canons. Dominicans were called black friars, because of the color of their outer garment; friars preachers; or members of the Order of Preachers. They were also frequently characterized, both favorably and unfavorably, as the *canes domini* (the dogs of God), a play on the Latin name *Dominicanes*, because they pursued the enemies of God.

Francis of Assisi, the son of a well-to-do Italian merchant and his Provençal wife, gave up his worldly life after serving as a soldier. The formation of the Franciscan order, whose members were also known as the gray friars, took an entirely different path, partly because of Francis's charisma and his practice of abject poverty and because he had the support of Hugolino, Bishop of Ostia, who later became Pope Gregory IX (1227–41). Hugolino helped with the creation of the Franciscan Rule of 1223 and, as pope, built the basilica at Assisi to hold Francis's body in 1228 and quickly canonized Francis as saint the same year. Francis was reluctant to create an order with a traditional rule but was persuaded to create one that included some of his wording and thoughts in addition to more formal parts of the rule such as liturgical obligations. By the time the rule was finalized Francis's group of mostly laymen had begun to attract great numbers of priests and educated scholars, an eventuality that altered the Franciscan mission. Shortly after the rule's confirmation, the papacy saw that the Franciscans could perform a function similar to that of the Dominicans—preaching. Both orders established schools for training brothers to preach. In addition, both became major intellectual forces within the universities of Oxford and Paris, incurring the wrath of the secular and monastic clerics who had formerly controlled those institutions. At times they also came into conflict with parish clergy because the papacy had granted the mendicants three privileges, two of which were traditionally assigned to the parish priest: cure of souls and right of sepulture (burial); the third, preaching, had to be authorized by the bishop.

NOTE

[1]See the first inner dream (Schmidt, Vision B.11.6–404) and the C text *apologia* (C.5). See also discussion in Donaldson, Piers Plowman*: The C-Text* 199–226.

NOTES ON CONTRIBUTORS

Judith H. Anderson is Chancellor's Professor Emeritus at Indiana University and author of seven books, including *The Growth of a Personal Voice:* Piers Plowman *and* The Faerie Queene; *Reading the Allegorical Intertext: Chaucer, Spenser, Shakespeare, Milton*; *Light and Death: Figuration in Spenser, Kepler, Donne, Milton*, and *Spenser's Narrative Figuration of Women in* The Faerie Queene. She is also coeditor of five volumes, including Piers Plowman*: An Alliterative Verse Translation*, translated by E. Talbot Donaldson.

C. David Benson has taught at several universities and published books and articles on various medieval subjects, especially Middle English poetry. He has a soft spot for his book on Chaucer's *Troilus and Criseyde*, but he is most proud of his book on Langland, *Public* Piers Plowman.

Gina Brandolino is a lecturer in the Department of English and the Sweetland Center for Writing at the University of Michigan. Though trained as a medievalist, she teaches courses on a wide range of topics, including horror, comics, social class, and medieval literature. She has published articles on pedagogy and Middle English literature in *Pedagogy: Critical Approaches to Teaching Literature, Language, Composition, and Culture* and *Studies in Medieval and Renaissance Teaching.*

Lawrence M. Clopper (1941–2014) taught at Indiana University, Bloomington, from 1969 until his retirement in 2005. He edited *The Dramatic Records of Chester, 1399–1642* in the Records of Early English Drama series (1979). He is the author of *Songs of Rechelesnesse: Langland and the Franciscans* (1997) and of *Drama, Play, and Game: English Festive Culture in the Medieval and Early Modern Period* (2001), which was awarded the 2002 David Bevington Award from the Medieval and Renaissance Drama Society for the best new book on early drama. He published over forty articles in scholarly journals, including essays addressing each of the poems by the anonymous author of *Sir Gawain and the Green Knight*, as well as formative essays on medieval romance, drama, and Langland. His work garnered support from the National Endowment of Humanities, the American Council of Learned Societies, and the American Philosophical Society; among others awards, he was recognized with a Guggenheim Fellowship.

Ian Cornelius is Edward Surtz, S.J., Associate Professor at Loyola University Chicago. He is the author of *Reconstructing Alliterative Verse: The Pursuit of a Medieval Meter* (2017) and of essays and articles published in the *Journal of English and Germanic Philology*, *Medium Ævum*, *New Medieval Literatures*, *Representations*, and the *Oxford History of Classical Reception in English Literature.*

Kate Crassons is associate professor of English at Lehigh University and the current director of Lehigh University Press. Her first book is *The Claims of Poverty: Literature, Culture, and Ideology in Late Medieval England* (2010). She is currently working on a monograph tentatively titled *Signs of Wonder: Faith, Ethics, and Epistemology in Medieval and Early Modern England* and a book for general readers in the field of disability studies.

Axton Crolley received an MA in medieval studies from the University of Notre Dame in 2016, an MPhil in Anglo-Saxon, Norse, and Celtic from the University of Cambridge in 2014, and a BA in linguistics from the University of South Carolina in 2013. He is currently a JD candidate at the University of South Carolina School of Law.

Mary Clemente Davlin, OP (1929–2017) was professor emerita of English at Dominican University. She is the author of three books about *Piers Plowman*, including *A Game of Heuene: Word Play and the Meaning of* Piers Plowman B (1989), *The Place of God in* Piers Plowman *and Medieval Art* (2001), and *A Journey into Love: Meditating with the Medieval Poem* Piers Plowman (2008), as well as many articles and videos about medieval literature. Her most recent essay is "Style and Stylistics in the Work of Charles Muscatine: A Retrospect," in *The Chaucer Review* (2018).

Richard K. Emmerson is visiting distinguished professor of art history at Florida State University and formerly president of the Consortium for Teaching the Middle Ages, executive director of the Medieval Academy of America, and editor of *Speculum*. He has published more than fifty articles studying medieval apocalypticism, drama, illustrated manuscripts, and visionary poetry, and seven books, including *Approaches to Teaching Medieval English Drama* and *Apocalypse Illuminated: The Visual Exegesis of Revelation in Medieval Illustrated Manuscripts*. A fellow of the Medieval Academy, in 2009 he received its Award for Excellence in Teaching Medieval Studies.

Andrew Galloway is professor of English at Cornell, where he has twice served as acting chair of the English Department and twice directed the Medieval Studies Program. His books include *The Penn Commentary on* Piers Plowman, *Volume 1* (2006), *Medieval Literature and Culture* (2006), and many edited volumes, including, with Andrew Cole, *The Cambridge Companion to* Piers Plowman (2014). He has published nearly one hundred essays, chapters, and encyclopedia entries on the intellectual and social contexts of medieval English poetry from *Beowulf* to *Piers Plowman*, Chaucer, and Lydgate, as well as on medieval history writing, textual criticism, and the medievalism of William Cullen Bryant.

Thomas A. Goodmann is associate professor of English at the University of Miami, where he teaches courses on Old and Middle English literature, including Chaucer and Langland; Old Icelandic-Norse language and literature; Continental romance; and Arthur. He has published essays on John Wycliffe and on teaching *Piers Plowman* and serves as president of TEAMS: Teaching Association for Medieval Studies (2015–19). He is executive director of the New Chaucer Society.

Ralph Hanna is professor of palaeography, emeritus, at Keble College, Oxford University. His most recent large publication is *The Penn Commentary on* Piers Plowman, *Volume 2*. Lately he has spent much time examining unpublished materials associated with Beryl Smalley's "classicizing friars."

Madonna J. Hettinger holds the inaugural appointment as the Lawrence Stanley Professor of Medieval History at the College of Wooster, where she teaches on the environmental history of the Middle Ages, epidemics in history, the impact of the black death in Tuscan communities, and the performance of gender in the Renaissance. Her essay "Unbounded Affection: The Complex Lives of 'Simple' Peasants in Late Medieval England" appeared in

The Ties That Bind: Festschrift in Honor of Barbara A. Hanawalt (2010). She is currently researching the cultural exchange produced by overland travel from the twelfth through the fourteenth centuries, with special emphasis on pilgrims, envoys, and traders.

Sarah A. Kelen is dean of undergraduate programs and professor of English at Nebraska Wesleyan University. Her research focuses on Middle English literature and early modern medievalism. She is the author of *Langland's Early Modern Identities* (2007) and the editor of *Renaissance Retrospections: Tudor Views of the Middle Ages* (2013). She is currently working on a book about metaphors of nationalism in early modern linguistic historiography.

Kathryn Kerby-Fulton holds an endowed chair at the University of Notre Dame. Her books include *Reformist Apocalypticism and* Piers Plowman (1990), which won the John Nicholas Brown Prize from the Medieval Academy of America; *Iconography and the Professional Reader: The Politics of Book Production in the Douce Piers Plowman*, with Denise Despres (1999); *Books under Suspicion: Censorship and Tolerance of Revelatory Writing in Late Medieval England* (2006), which won the Haskins Gold Medal from the Medieval Academy; and *Opening Medieval English Manuscripts: Literary and Visual Approaches*, with Maidie Hilmo and Linda Olson (2012). She is preparing to publish *The Clerical Proletariat and the Rise of Medieval English Literature.*

David Lawton is professor of English and religious studies at Washington University in St. Louis. He was executive director of the New Chaucer Society from 2002 to 2012 and is editor of *The Norton Chaucer* (forthcoming). He has published widely on Chaucer, Langland, and other medieval writers, as well as on blasphemy and the Bible. His most recent book is *Voice in Later Medieval English Literature: Public Interiorities* (2017).

Thomas A. Prendergast is professor of English at the College of Wooster. His most recent books include *Affective Medievalism: Love, Abjection, and Discontent*, with Stephanie Trigg (2018); *Poetical Dust: Poets' Corner and the Making of Britain* (2015); and a collection of essays, edited with Jessica Rosenfeld, entitled *Chaucer and the Subversion of Form* (2018).

Elizabeth Robertson is professor and chair of English language at the University of Glasgow. With Jane Burns and Roberta Krueger, she cofounded the Society for Medieval Feminist Scholarship. She has edited books of essays and published articles on gender and religion in Middle English writings in journals such as *Studies in the Age of Chaucer* and *Speculum*. She is the author of *Early English Devotional Prose and the Female Audience* and is currently completing *Chaucerian Consent: Women, Religion, and Subjection in Late Medieval England.* She is also the coeditor, with Emily Huber, of *The Katherine Group* and, with Stephen Shepherd, of the *Norton Critical Edition of* Piers Plowman.

William E. Rogers is Bennette E. Geer Professor of Literature Emeritus at Furman University, where he taught from 1974 to 2010. He is the author of *Interpretation in* Piers Plowman (2002) and *Interpreting Interpretation: Textual Hermeneutics as an Ascetic Discipline* (1994).

Emily Steiner is professor of English at the University of Pennsylvania and recipient of several teaching awards, including the Christian R. and Mary F. Lindback Award for Distinguished Teaching (2016). She is the author of *Documentary Culture and the Making of*

Medieval English Literature (2003) and *Reading* Piers Plowman (2013), among other works. She tweets about *Piers Plowman* and other medieval topics at Piers@Penn.

Stephanie Trigg is Redmond Barry Distinguished Professor in English Literature at the University of Melbourne. She is also currently a chief investigator with the Australian Research Council Centre of Excellence for the History of Emotions. Her most recent book is *Shame and Honor: A Vulgar History of the Order of the Garter* (2012), and she coedited two special issues of *Postmedieval: A Journal of Medieval Cultural Studies* (2016 and 2017).

Míċeál F. Vaughan is professor emeritus at the University of Washington, Seattle, since 2015. He has been studying, teaching, and writing on *Piers Plowman* for more than four decades, first studying the B version for his PhD at Cornell and later turning his attention to the A version. He is the editor of Piers Plowman*: The A Version* (2011) and a forthcoming edition of MS Rawlinson poet. 137 for the *Piers Plowman Electronic Archive*. He is working on a book about the transmission and reception of Chaucer's Retractions.

Lawrence Warner is reader in medieval English Literature at King's College London, and the author of *The Myth of* Piers Plowman*: Constructing a Medieval Literary Archive* (2014), which received the 2016 Beatrice White Prize from the English Association for outstanding scholarly work in the field of English literature before 1590. He is also the author of *The Lost History of* Piers Plowman*: The Earliest Transmission of Langland's Work* (2011) and has served as director of the International *Piers Plowman* Society from 2013 to 2017 and as coeditor of *The Yearbook of Langland Studies* from 2004 to 2012.

Nicholas Watson is Henry B. and Anne M. Cabot Professor of English Literature at Harvard University. He is the author of *Richard Rolle and the Invention of Authority* (1991); *The Idea of the Vernacular: An Anthology of Middle English Literary Theory, 1280–1520*, with Jocelyn Wogan-Browne et al. (1999); *Writings of Julian of Norwich: A Vision Showed to a Devout Woman and A Revelation of Love*, with Jacqueline Jenkins (2005); *John of Morigny's Liber florum celestis doctrine / The Flowers of Heavenly Teaching*, with Claire Fanger (2015); and some fifty articles on Middle English and other topics. His current projects include *Vernacular Theology Before the English Reformation: Balaam's Ass*, *Vernacular Theology before the English Reformation, Volume 2: The Mystical Ark*; and, with Claire Fanger, a translation of John of Morigny's *Liber florum*.

WORKS CITED

Abrams, M. H., general editor. *The Norton Anthology of English Literature.* 3rd ed., vol. 1, W. W. Norton, 1974.

Adams, Robert. *Langland and the Rokele Family: The Gentry Background to* Piers Plowman. Four Courts Press, 2013.

———. "The Rokeles: An Index for a 'Langland' Family History." Cole and Galloway, pp. 85–96.

Aers, David. *Beyond Reformation? An Essay on William Langland's* Piers Plowman *and the End of Constantinian Christianity.* U of Notre Dame P, 2015.

———. *Chaucer, Langland, and the Creative Imagination.* Routledge / Kegan Paul, 1980.

———. "Christ's Humanity and *Piers Plowman*: Contexts and Political Implications." *Yearbook of Langland Studies*, vol. 8, 1994, pp. 107–25.

———. *Community, Gender, and Individual Identity: English Writing, 1360–1430.* Routledge, 1988.

———. "Justice and Wage-Labor after the Black Death: Some Perplexities for William Langland." *The Work of Work: Servitude, Slavery, and Labor in Medieval England*, edited by Allen Frantzen and Douglas Moffat, Cruithne Press, 1994, pp. 164–190.

———. "*Piers Plowman* and Problems in the Perception of Poverty: A Culture in Transition." *Leeds Studies in English*, vol. 14, 1983, pp. 5–25.

———. *Salvation and Sin: Augustine, Langland, and Fourteenth-Century Theology.* U of Notre Dame P, 2009.

———. *Sanctifying Signs: Making Christian Tradition in Late Medieval England.* U of Notre Dame P, 2004.

Agamben, Giorgio. *Remnants of Auschwitz: The Witness and the Archive.* Translated by Daniel Heller-Roazen, Zone Books, 1999.

Alford, John A., editor. *A Companion to* Piers Plowman. U of California P, 1988.

———. "The Idea of Reason in *Piers Plowman*." Kennedy et al., pp. 199–215.

———. "Langland's Learning." *Yearbook of Langland Studies*, vol. 9, 1995, pp. 1–17.

———. Piers Plowman*: A Guide to the Quotations.* Arizona Center for Medieval and Renaissance Studies, 1992.

———. "The Role of the Quotations in *Piers Plowman*." *Speculum*, vol. 52, 1977, pp. 80–99.

Allen, Danielle. *Talking to Strangers: Anxieties of Citizenship since Brown v. Board of Education.* U of Chicago P, 2004.

Allen, Judson Boyce. Conference paper. Medieval Association of the Pacific Annual Conference, January 1982, Claremont Colleges, CA.

———. *The Ethical Poetic of the Later Middle Ages: A Decorum of Convenient Distinction.* U of Toronto P, 1982.

———. "Langland's Reading and Writing: *Detractor* and the Pardon Passus." *Speculum*, vol. 59, 1984, pp. 342–62.

Alpers, Paul J. *The Poetry of* The Faerie Queene. Princeton UP, 1967.

Amtower, Laurel, and Jacqueline Vanhoutte, editors. *A Companion to Chaucer and His Contemporaries: Texts and Contexts*. Broadview Press, 2009.

Anderson, Judith H. *The Growth of a Personal Voice:* Piers Plowman *and* The Faerie Queene. Yale UP, 1976.

———. "Langland, William." *The Spenser Encyclopedia*, edited by A. C. Hamilton et al., U of Toronto P, 1990, pp. 425–26.

———. *Reading the Allegorical Intertext: Chaucer, Spenser, Shakespeare, Milton*. Fordham UP, 2008.

———. "Redcrosse and the Descent into Hell." *ELH*, vol. 36, 1969, pp. 470–92.

———. "Satanic Ethos and Envy: The Origin of Evil and Death in *Paradise Lost*." *Milton Studies*, vol. 51, 2010, pp. 137–64.

———. *Translating Investments: Metaphor and the Dynamic of Cultural Change in Tudor-Stuart England*. Fordham UP, 2005.

———. "What I Really Teach When I'm Teaching Spenser." *Pedagogy*, vol. 3, 2003, pp. 177–83.

Appiah, Kwame Anthony. *Cosmopolitanism: Ethics in a World of Strangers*. Norton, 2006.

Aronson-Lehavi, Sharon. *Street Scenes: Late Medieval Acting and Performance*. Palgrave Macmillan, 2011.

Astell, Ann. *Political Allegory in Late Medieval England*. Cornell UP, 1999.

Attwater, D., and R. Attwater, translators. *The Book Concerning Piers the Plowman, Translated into Modern English Verse*. Everyman, 1957.

Bailey, Mark. *The Decline of Serfdom in Late Medieval England: From Bondage to Freedom*. Boydell Press, 2014.

———. "Peasant Welfare in England, 1290–1348." *Economic History Review*, vol. 51, no. 2, 1998, pp. 223–51.

Baker, Denise. "From Plowing to Penitence: *Piers Plowman* and Fourteenth-Century Theology." *Speculum*, vol. 55, 1980, pp. 715–25.

Baker, Mona, editor. *Routledge Encyclopedia of Translation Studies*. Routledge, 2001.

Bakhtin, M. M. *Rabelais and His World*. Translated by Helene Iswolsky, Indiana UP, 1984.

Baldwin, Anna. *A Guidebook to* Piers Plowman. Palgrave Macmillan, 2007.

Bale, John. *Illustrium maioris Britannia scriptorum . . . summarium*. [Ipswich], 1548. Reprint, Theodoricum Plataenum, 1549.

———. *Scriptorum Illustriu[m] maioris Brytanniae quam nunc Angliam & Scotiam uocant Catalogus. . . .* Ioannis Oporinus, 1557.

Barney, Stephen A. *Allegories of History, Allegories of Love*. Archon, 1979.

———, editor. *The Penn Commentary on* Piers Plowman*: Volume 5; C Passus 20–22; B Passus 18–20*. U of Pennsylvania P, 2006.

Barr, Helen. *The* Piers Plowman *Tradition: A Critical Edition of* Pierce the Ploughman's Crede, Richard the Redeless, Mum and the Sothsegger, *and* The Crowned King. Charles E. Tuttle / J. M. Dent, 1993.

Barron, Caroline M., and Marie-Hélène Rousseau. "Cathedral, City, and State." *St. Paul's: The Cathedral Church of London, 604–2004*, edited by Derek Keene et al., Yale UP, 2004, pp. 33–44.

Beer, Jeanette, editor. *Translation Theory and Practice in the Middle Ages*. Medieval Institute Publications, 1997.

Beidler, Peter G. "Chaucer and the Trots: What to Do about Those Modern English Translations." *The Chaucer Review*, vol. 19, no. 4, 1985, pp. 290–301.

———. "Teaching Chaucer as Drama: The Garden Scene in the Shipman's Tale." *Exemplaria*, vol. 8, no. 2, 1996, pp. 485–93.

Bennett, J. A. W. "Chaucer's Contemporary." Hussey, pp. 310–25.

———, editor. Piers Plowman*: The Prologue and Passus I–VII of the B-Text*. Oxford UP, 1972.

———, editor. *The Vision of Pierce Plowman, now fyrste imprinted by Roberte Crowley . . . Anno Domini 1505*. Paradine Press, 1976. Facsimile.

Bennett, Judith M. *Ale, Beer, and Brewsters in England: Women's Work in a Changing World, 1300–1600*. Oxford UP, 1996.

Bennett, Michael J. "The Court of Richard II and the Promotion of Literature." Hanawalt, *Chaucer's England*, pp. 3–20.

———. *Richard II and the Revolution of 1399*. Sutton, 1999.

Benson, C. David. "The Function of Lady Meed in Piers Plowman." *English Studies*, vol. 61, no. 3, June 1980, pp. 193–205.

———. *Public* Piers Plowman*: Modern Scholarship and Late Medieval English Culture*. Penn State UP, 2005.

Benson, C. David, and Lynne S. Blanchfield. *The Manuscripts of* Piers Plowman*: The B-Version*. D. S. Brewer, 1997.

Benson, Larry D., general editor. *The Riverside Chaucer*. 3rd ed., Houghton Mifflin, 1987.

Berger, Thomas. "Opening Titles Miscreate: Some Observations on the Titling of Shakespeare's Plays." *The Margins of the Text*, edited by David C. Greetham, U of Michigan P, 1997, pp. 155–72.

Bernard, G. W. *The Late Medieval English Church: Vitality and Vulnerability before the Break with Rome*. Yale UP, 2012.

Binski, Paul. *Westminster Abbey and the Plantagenets: Kingship and the Representation of Power, 1200–1400*. Yale UP, 1995.

Black, Joseph, et al., editors. *The Broadview Anthology of British Literature*. 2nd ed., Broadview Press, 2009.

Blanch, Robert J., editor. *Style and Symbolism in* Piers Plowman. U of Tennessee P, 1969.

Bloomfield, Morton. Piers Plowman *as a Fourteenth-Century Apocalypse*. Rutgers UP, [1961].

Bolton, J. L. *The Medieval English Economy, 1150–1500*. J. M. Dent, 1980.

Bostick, Curtis. *The Antichrist and the Lollards: Apocalypticism in Late Medieval and Reformation England*. Brill, 1998.

Bowers, John M. *Chaucer and Langland: The Antagonistic Tradition*. U of Notre Dame P, 2007.

———. *The Crisis of Will in* Piers Plowman. Catholic U of America P, 1986.

———. "*Piers Plowman*'s William Langland: Editing the Text, Writing the Author's Life." *Yearbook of Langland Studies*, vol. 9, 1995, pp. 65–90.

Brewer, Charlotte. *Editing* Piers Plowman*: The Evolution of the Text*. Cambridge UP, 1996.

Brewer, Charlotte, and A. G. Rigg, editors. Piers Plowman*: A Facsimile of the Z-Text in Bodleian Library, Oxford, MS Bodley 851*. Cambridge UP, 1994.

Brewer, Derek, editor. *Studies in the Vernon Manuscript*. D. S. Brewer, 1990.

Brink, Susan. "Modern Puberty." *Los Angeles Times*, 21 Jan. 2008, articles.latimes .com/2008/jan/21/health/he-puberty21.

Brown, Peter, editor. *A Companion to Medieval English Literature and Culture, c. 1350–c. 1500*. Blackwell, 2007.

Burke, Peter. *Popular Culture in Early Modern Europe*. 3rd ed., Ashgate Publishing, 2009.

Burr, David. *Olivi's Peaceable Kingdom: A Reading of the Apocalypse Commentary*. U of Pennsylvania P, 1993.

Burrell, Arthur, translator. *Piers Plowman: The Vision of a People's Christ*. J. M. Dent and Sons / E. P. Dutton, 1912.

Burrow, John A. "Autobiographical Poetry in the Middle Ages: The Case of Thomas Hoccleve." *Proceedings of the British Academy*, vol. 68, 1982, pp. 389–410.

———. *Essays on Medieval Literature*. Oxford UP, 1984.

———. "Langland *nel Mezzo del Cammin*." *Medieval Studies for J. A. W. Bennett*, edited by P. L. Heyworth, Clarendon Press, 1981, pp. 21–41.

———. *Langland's Fictions*. Oxford UP, 1993.

Burrow, John A., and Thorlac Turville-Petre. *The Piers Plowman Electronic Archive, Vol. 9: The B-Version Archetype*. *Piers Plowman Electronic Archive*, Society for Early English and Norse Electronic Texts, 2014, piers.chass.ncsu.edu/texts/Bx. SEENET Series A.12.

Butterfield, Ardis. *The Familiar Enemy: Chaucer, Language, and Nation in the Hundred Years War*. Oxford UP, 2009.

Bynum, Caroline. *Holy Feast and Holy Fast: The Religious Significance of Food to Medieval Women*. U of California P, 1987.

Calabrese, Michael. *An Introduction to* Piers Plowman. UP of Florida, 2016.

Camargo, Martin. "Chaucer and the Oxford Renaissance of Anglo-Latin Rhetoric." *Studies in the Age of Chaucer*, vol. 34, 2012, pp. 173–207.

Cannon, Christopher. *Middle English Literature*. Polity, 2008.

———. "The Rights of Medieval English Women: Crime and the Issue of Representation." Hanawalt and Wallace, pp. 156–85.

"The Canterbury Tales." *Treasures in Full: Caxton's Chaucer*, The British Library, www.bl.uk/treasures/caxton/canterbury.html.

Carruthers, Mary. *The Book of Memory*. 2nd ed., Cambridge UP, 2008.

———. *The Search for St. Truth: A Study of Meaning in* Piers Plowman. Northwestern UP, 1973.

Certeau, Michel de. *The Writing of History*. Translated by Tom Conley, Columbia UP, 1985.

Chamberlin, John S. "What Makes *Piers Plowman* So Hard to Read?" *Style*, vol. 23, no. 1, Spring 1989, pp. 32–48.

Chambers, R. W., et al., editors. Piers Plowman*: The Huntington Library Manuscript (HM 143) Reproduced in Photostat*. The Huntington Library, 1936.

Cicero. *De oratore*. Edited by G. P. Goold, translated by E. W. Sutton, completed by H. Rackam, Heinemann, 1988. 2 vols.

Clark, Caroline. "Changing Places: Theorizing Space and Power Dynamics in Service Learning." *Service Learning in Higher Education*, edited by Dan W. Butin, Palgrave Macmillan, 2005, pp. 71–87.

Clemens, Raymond, and Timothy Graham. *Introduction to Manuscript Studies*. Cornell UP, 2007.

Clifton, Nicole. "The Romance Convention of the Disguised Duel and the Climax of *Piers Plowman*." *Yearbook of Langland Studies*, vol. 7, 1993, pp. 123–28.

Clopper, Lawrence M. *"Songes of Rechelesnesse": Langland and the Franciscans*. U of Michigan P, 1997.

Coghill, Nevill. "The Pardon of *Piers Plowman*." *The Collected Papers of Nevill Coghill*, edited by Douglas Gray, Harvester Press, 1988, pp. 137–98. Originally published in *Proceedings of the British Academy*, vol. 30, 1946, pp. 303–57.

Colaianne, A. J. Piers Plowman*: An Annotated Bibliography of Editions and Criticism, 1550–1977*. Garland Publishing, 1978.

Cole, Andrew. *Literature and Heresy in the Age of Chaucer*. Cambridge UP, 2008.

Cole, Andrew, and Andrew Galloway, editors. *The Cambridge Companion to* Piers Plowman. Cambridge UP, 2014.

Coleman, Janet. "Property and Poverty." *The Cambridge History of Medieval Political Thought, c. 350–c. 1450*, edited by J. H. Burns, Cambridge UP, 1988, pp. 607–48.

Coleman, Joyce. "Where Chaucer Got His Pulpit: Audience and Intervisuality in the *Troilus and Criseyde* Frontispiece." *Studies in the Age of Chaucer*, vol. 32, 2010, pp. 103–28.

Coleman-Jensen, Alisha, et al. "Household Food Security in the United States in 2016." *United States Department of Agriculture Economic Research Service*, 2017, www.ers.usda.gov/publications/pub-details/?pubid=84972.

Collette, Carolyn P., and Harold Garrett-Goodyear, editors. *The Later Middle Ages: A Sourcebook*. Palgrave Macmillan, 2010.

Cook, William R., and Ronald B. Herzman, editors. *The Medieval World View: An Introduction*. 3rd ed., Oxford UP, 2011.

Cooper, Helen. "Gender and Personification in *Piers Plowman*." *Yearbook of Langland Studies*, vol. 5, 1991, pp. 31–48.

———. "Langland's and Chaucer's Prologues." *Yearbook of Langland Studies*, vol. 1, 1987, pp. 71–81.

———. "Translation and Adaptation." Corrie, pp. 166–87.

Copeland, Rita. "Pathos and Pastoralism: Aristotle's *Rhetoric* in Medieval England." *Speculum*, vol. 89, 2014, pp. 96–127.

———. *Rhetoric, Hermeneutics and Translation in the Middle Ages: Academic Traditions and Vernacular Texts*. Cambridge UP, 1991.

Cornelius, Ian. *Reconstructing Alliterative Verse: The Pursuit of a Medieval Meter*. Cambridge UP, 2017.

"Corpus Christi College MS. 201." *Early Manuscripts at Oxford University*, image.ox.ac.uk/show?collection=corpus&manuscript=ms201.

Corrie, Marilyn, editor. *A Concise Companion to Middle English Literature*. Wiley, 2009.

Covella, Francis Dolores, SC, translator. Piers Plowman*: The A-Text: An Alliterative Verse Translation*. Introduction and notes by David C. Fowler, Center for Medieval and Renaissance Studies, 1992. Medieval and Renaissance Text and Studies.

Crane, Susan. "The Writing Lesson of 1381." Hanawalt, *Chaucer's England*, pp. 201–22.

Crassons, Kate. *The Claims of Poverty: Literature, Culture, and Ideology in Late Medieval England*. U of Notre Dame P, 2010.

Crowley, Robert, editor. *The Vision of Pierce Plowman*. London, 1550.

———, editor. *The Vision of Pierce Plowman*. 2nd ed., London, 1550.

Cummings, Brian. "Reformed Literature and Literature Reformed." Wallace, *Cambridge History*, pp. 821–51.

Cummings, Brian, and James Simpson, editors. *Cultural Reformations: Medieval and Renaissance in Literary History*. Oxford UP, 2010.

Damrosch, David, general editor. *The Longman Anthology of British Literature*. 4th ed., vol. 1, Pearson, 2010.

Dante. *Divina Commedia*. *Princeton Dante Project*, etcweb.princeton.edu/dante/index.html.

Darnton, Robert. *The Great Cat Massacre and Other Episodes in French Cultural History*. Random House, 1985.

Davidson, Clifford, editor. "Play Five, The Fall." *The York Corpus Christi Plays*. Medieval Institute Publications, 2011. *TEAMS: Middle English Text Series*, University of Rochester, d.lib.rochester.edu/teams/text/davidson-play-5-the-fall.

———, editor. *A Tretise of Miraclis Pleyinge*. Medieval Institute Publications, 1993.

Davis, Rebecca, and Emily Steiner. "Commentary." *Yearbook of Langland Studies*, vol. 28, 2014, pp. 1–2.

Davlin, Mary Clemente. *A Game of Heuene: Word Play and the Meaning of* Piers Plowman *B*. D. S. Brewer, 1989. *Piers Plowman* Studies 7.

———. *A Journey into Love: Meditating with the Medieval Poem* Piers Plowman. Marymount Institute Press, 2008.

———. *The Place of God in* Piers Plowman *and Medieval Art*. Ashgate Publishing, 2001.

Dean, James M. *Medieval English Political Writings*. Medieval Institute Publications, 1996. TEAMS Middle English Texts Series.

———, editor. *Six Ecclesiastical Satires*. Medieval Institute Publications, 1991.

Deguileville, Guillaume de. *The Pilgrimage of the Life of Man*. Translated by John Lydgate. *Corpus of Middle English Prose and Verse*, University of Michigan Library, 2006, quod.lib.umich.edu/cgi/t/text/text-idx?c=cme;cc=cme;view=toc;idno=AJT8111.0001.001.

De Man, Paul. *Blindness and Insight: Essays in the Rhetoric of Contemporary Criticism*. U of Minnesota P, 1971.

DiMarco, Vincent. Piers Plowman*: A Reference Guide*. G. K. Hall, 1982.

Dinshaw, Carolyn. *Chaucer's Sexual Poetics*. U of Wisconsin P, 1989.

Dobson, R. B. *The Peasants' Revolt of 1381*. MacMillan, 1983.

Donaldson, E. Talbot, translator. Piers Plowman*: An Alliterative Verse Translation*. Edited, introduced, and annotated by Elizabeth D. Kirk and Judith H. Anderson, W. W. Norton, 1990.

———. Piers Plowman*: The C-Text and Its Poet*. Yale UP, 1949.

Doyle, A. I., editor. *The Vernon Manuscript: A Facsimile of Bodleian Library, Oxford, MS Eng. poet.a.1*. D. S. Brewer, 1987.

Doyle, A. I., and Malcolm Parkes. "The Production of Copies of the *Canterbury Tales* and the *Confessio Amantis* in the Early Fifteenth Century." *Medieval Scribes, Manuscripts, and Libraries: Essays Presented to N. R. Ker*, edited by V. J. Scattergood and Andrew G. Watson, Scolar, 1978, pp. 163–210.

Duby, Georges. *The Three Orders: Feudal Society Imagined*. Translated by Arthur Goldhammer, Chicago UP, 1980.

Duffy, Eamon. *The Stripping of the Altars: Traditional Religion in England, c. 1400–c. 1580*. 1992. 2nd ed., Yale UP, 2005.

Dunning, T. P. Piers Plowman*: An Interpretation of the A-Text*. Longmans, Green, 1937.

Dyas, Dee. *Pilgrimage in Medieval English Literature, 700–1500*. D. S. Brewer, 2001.

Dyer, Christopher. *Making a Living in the Middle Ages: The People of Britain, 850–1520*. Yale UP, 2002.

———. "*Piers Plowman* and Plowmen: A Historical Perspective." *Yearbook of Langland Studies*, vol. 8, 1994, pp. 155–76.

Economou, George, translator. *William Langland's* Piers Plowman*: The C Version; A Verse Translation*. U of Pennsylvania P, 1996.

Emmerson, Richard K. "'Or Yernen to Rede Redels?': *Piers Plowman* and Prophecy." *Yearbook of Langland Studies*, vol. 7, 1993, pp. 27–76.

Emmerson, Richard K., and Ronald B. Herzman. *The Apocalyptic Imagination in Medieval Literature*. U of Pennsylvania P, 1992.

Emmerson, Richard K., and Bernard McGinn, editors. *The Apocalypse in the Middle Ages*. Cornell UP, 1992.

Fan, Jessie X., et al. "Household Food Expenditure Patterns: A Cluster Analysis." *Monthly Labor Review*, vol. 130, no. 4, Apr. 2007, pp. 38–51. *Bureau of Labor Statistics*, www.bls.gov/opub/mlr/2007/04/art3full.pdf.

Federico, Sylvia. *New Troy: Fantasies of Empire in the Late Middle Ages*. U of Minnesota P, 2003.

Fletcher, Alan. "The Essential (Ephemeral) William Langland: Textual Revision as Ethical Process in *Piers Plowman*." *Yearbook of Langland Studies*, vol. 15, 2002, pp. 61–84.

Fowler, David. Introduction. Covella, pp. 1–37.

———. Piers the Plowman*: Literary Relations of the A and B Texts*. U of Washington P, 1962.

Fowler, Elizabeth. "Civil Death and the Maiden: Agency and the Conditions of Contract in *Piers Plowman*." *Speculum*, vol. 70, 1995, pp. 760–92.

Fradenburg, Louise O. "Needful Things." Hanawalt and Wallace, pp. 49–67.

Frank, Robert Worth, Jr. Piers Plowman *and the Scheme of Salvation*. Yale UP, 1957.

Freccero, John. "The Significance of *Terza Rima*." *Dante: The Poetics of Conversion*, edited by Rachel Jacoff, Harvard UP, 1986, pp. 258–71.

Galloway, Andrew. "Alliterative Poetry in Old Jerusalem: The *Siege of Jerusalem* and Its Sources." *Medieval Alliterative Poetry: Essays in Honour of Thorlac Turville-Petre*, edited by J. A. Burrow and Hoyt N. Duggan, Four Courts Press, 2010, pp. 85–106.

———, editor. *The Cambridge Companion to Medieval English Culture*. Cambridge UP, 2011.

———. "Communities, Crowd Theory, and Mob Theory in Late-Fourteenth-Century English History Writing and Poetry." *Mobs: An Interdisciplinary Inquiry*, edited by Leonard Michael Koff and Nancy van Deusen, Brill, 2011, pp. 141–64.

———, editor and translator. "History or Narration Concerning the Manner and Form of the Miraculous Parliament at Westminster in the Year 1386, in the Tenth Year of the Reign of King Richard the Second after the Conquest, Declared by Thomas Favent, Clerk." *The Letter of the Law: Legal Practice and Literary Production in Medieval England*, edited by Emily Steiner and Candace Barrington, Cornell UP, 2002, pp. 231–52.

———. "Imagining the Literary in Medieval English." *Imagining Medieval English: Concepts of Language, 500–1500*, edited by Tim Machan, Cambridge UP, 2016, pp. 210–37.

———. "Intellectual Pregnancy, Metaphysical Femininity, and the Social Doctrine of the Trinity in *Piers Plowman*." *Yearbook of Langland Studies*, vol. 12, 1998, pp. 117–52.

———, editor. *The Penn Commentary on* Piers Plowman*: Volume 1; C Prologue—Passus 4; B Prologue—Passus 4, A Prologue—Passus 4*. U of Pennsylvania P, 2006.

Gant, Andrew. "The Vision of Piers Plowman." Three Choirs Festival, 2002.

Gascoigne, George. *The Steel Glas*. *The English Poets*, edited by Thomas Humphry Ward, Macmillan, 1880. *Bartleby.com*, 2013, www.bartleby.com/337.

Geertz, Clifford. *The Interpretation of Cultures: Selected Essays*. Basic Books, 1973.

Gilchrist, Roberta. *Gender and Archeology: Contesting the Past*. Routledge, 1999.

Gillespie, Vincent. "'[S]he do the police in different voices': Pastiche, Ventriloquism, and Parody in Julian of Norwich." *A Companion to Julian of Norwich*, edited by Liz Herbert McAvoy, D. S. Brewer, 2008, pp. 192–207.

———. "Vernacular Theology." Strohm, *Middle English*, pp. 401–20.

Godden, Malcolm. *The Making of* Piers Plowman. Longman, 1990.

Goldie, Matthew Boyd. *Middle English Literature: A Historical Sourcebook*. Wiley-Blackwell, 2003.

Goodmann, Thomas A. "Why *Not* Teach Langland?" *Studies in Medieval and Renaissance Teaching*, vol. 21, no. 1, Spring 2014, pp. 9–22.

Goodridge, J. F., translator. *Piers the Ploughman*. 1959. Revised ed., Penguin Books, 1966.

Gordon, Dillian. *Making and Meaning: The Wilton Diptych*. National Gallery, 1993.

Gow, Andrew. *The Red Jews: Antisemitism in an Apocalyptic Age, 1200–1600*. Brill, 1995.

Gradon, Pamela. "Langland and the Ideology of Dissent." *Proceedings of the British Academy* vol. 66, 1980, pp. 179–205.

Grady, Frank. "*Piers Plowman*, *St. Erkenwald*, and the Rule of Exceptional Salvations." *Yearbook of Langland Studies*, vol. 6, 1992, pp. 61–86.

———. *Representing Righteous Heathens in Late Medieval England*. Palgrave Macmillan, 2005.

Graff, Gerald. *Beyond the Culture Wars: How Teaching the Conflicts Can Revitalize American Higher Education*. W. W. Norton, 1993.

Green, Richard Firth. *A Crisis of Truth: Literature and Law in Ricardian England*. U of Pennsylvania P, 1999.

———. "John Ball's Letters: Literary History and Historical Literature." Hanawalt, *Chaucer's England*, pp. 176–200.

Greenblatt, Stephen, general editor. *The Norton Anthology of English Literature*. 9th ed., vol. 1, W. W. Norton, 2012.

———, general editor. *The Norton Shakespeare: Based on the Oxford Edition*. 2nd ed., W. W. Norton, 1997.

Griffiths, Lavinia. *Personification in* Piers Plowman. D. S. Brewer, 1985.

Guillet, Jacques. *Themes of the Bible*. Translated by Albert J. LaMothe, Jr. U of Notre Dame P, 1960.

Habermas, Jürgen. "An Awareness of What Is Missing." *An Awareness of What Is Missing: Faith and Reason in a Post-secular Age*, by Habermas et al., translated by Ciaran Cronin, Polity Press, 2010, pp. 15–23.

Hadju, David. *The Ten-Cent Plague: The Great Comic-Book Scare and How It Changed America*. Farrar, Straus, and Giroux, 2008.

Hailey, R. Carter. "Robert Crowley and the Editing of *Piers Plowman* (1550)." *Yearbook of Langland Studies*, vol. 21, 2007, pp. 143–70.

Halmi, Nicholas. "Coleridge on Allegory and Symbol." *The Oxford Handbook of Samuel Taylor Coleridge*, edited by Frederick Burwick, Oxford UP, 2009, pp. 345–58.

Hanawalt, Barbara, editor. *Chaucer's England: Literature in Historical Context.* U of Minnesota P, 1992.

———. *Growing Up in Medieval London: The Experience of Childhood in History.* Oxford UP, 1993.

———. *The Ties That Bound: Peasant Families in Medieval England.* Oxford UP, 1989.

Hanawalt, Barbara, and David Wallace, editors. *Medieval Crime and Social Control.* U of Minnesota P, 1999.

Hanna, Ralph. "Alliterative Poetry." Wallace, *Cambridge History*, pp. 488–512.

———. "Brewing Trouble: On Literature and History—and Alewives." *Bodies and Disciplines: Intersections of Literature and History in Fifteenth-Century England*, edited by Barbara A. Hanawalt and David Wallace, U of Minnesota P, 1996, pp. 1–18.

———. *London Literature, 1300–1380.* Cambridge UP, 2005.

———. "School and Scorn: Gender in *Piers Plowman*." *New Medieval Literatures*, vol. 3, 1999, pp. 213–27.

———. "The Versions and Revisions of *Piers Plowman*." Cole and Galloway, pp. 33–49.

———. *William Langland.* Ashgate Publishing, 1993. Vol. 3 of *Authors of the Middle Ages, English Writers of the Late Middle Ages.*

Harris, Anne F. "Pilgrimage, Performance, and Stained Glass at Canterbury Cathedral." *Art and Architecture of Late Medieval Pilgrimage in Northern Europe and the British Isles*, edited by Sarah Blick and Rita Tekippe, Brill, 2005, pp. 243–81.

Harwood, Britton J. Piers Plowman *and the Problem of Belief.* U of Toronto P, 1995.

Hass, Andrew, et al., editors. *The Oxford Companion to Literature and Theology.* Oxford UP, 2007.

Hatcher, John, and Edward Miller. *Medieval England: Rural Society and Economic Change, 1086–1348.* Longman, 1978.

Hewett-Smith, Kathleen, editor. *William Langland's* Piers Plowman*: A Book of Essays.* Routledge, 2001.

Hill, Thomas. "Universal Salvation and Its Literary Context in *Piers Plowman* B.18." *Yearbook of Langland Studies*, vol. 5, 1991, pp. 65–76.

Hilton, Rodney. *Bond Men Made Free: Medieval Peasant Movements and the English Rising of 1381.* 1973. 2nd ed., Routledge, 2003.

"HM 114." *Guide to Medieval and Renaissance Manuscripts in the Huntington Library*, encoded by Sharon K. Goetz, Henry E. Huntington Library and Art Gallery, 2003, bancroft.berkeley.edu/digitalscriptorium/huntington/HM114.html.

"HM 137." *Guide to Medieval and Renaissance Manuscripts in the Huntington Library*, encoded by Sharon K. Goetz, Henry E. Huntington Library and Art Gallery, 2003, bancroft.berkeley.edu/digitalscriptorium/huntington/HM137.html.

"HM 143." *Guide to Medieval and Renaissance Manuscripts in the Huntington Library*, encoded by Sharon K. Goetz, Henry E. Huntington Library and Art Gallery, 2003, bancroft.berkeley.edu/digitalscriptorium/huntington/HM143.html.

Horobin, Simon. "Adam Pinkhurst, Geoffrey Chaucer, and the Hengwrt Manuscript of the *Canterbury Tales*." *Chaucer Review*, vol. 44, 2010, pp. 351–67.

Huber, Emily Rebekah, and Elizabeth Robertson, editors. *The Katherine Group (MS Bodley 34)*. Medieval Institute Publications, 2007. *TEAMS: Middle English Text Series*, University of Rochester, d.lib.rochester.edu/teams/publication/huber-and-robertson-the-katherine-group.

Hudson, Anne. "Epilogue." Alford, *Companion*, pp. 251–66.

———. "*Piers Plowman* and the Peasants' Revolt: A Problem Revisited." *Yearbook of Langland Studies*, vol. 8, 1994, pp. 85–106.

———. *The Premature Reformation: Wycliffite Texts and Lollard History*. Oxford UP, 1988.

———. "The Variable Text." *Crux and Controversy in Middle English Textual Criticism*, edited by A. J. Minnis and Charlotte Brewer, D. S. Brewer, 1992, pp. 49–60.

Hussey, S. S., editor. Piers Plowman*: Critical Approaches*. Methuen Publishing, 1969.

Johnson, Barbara A. *Reading* Piers Plowman *and* The Pilgrim's Progress. Southern Illinois UP, 1992.

Johnson, Eleanor. *Practicing Literary Theory in the Middle Ages: Ethics and the Mixed Form in Chaucer, Gower, Usk, and Hoccleve*. U of Chicago P, 2013.

Jones, Mike Rodman. *Radical Pastoral, 1381–1594: Appropriation and the Writing of Religious Controversy*. Ashgate Publishing, 2011.

Jordan, William Chester. *The Great Famine, Northern Europe in the Fourteenth Century*. Princeton UP, 1996.

Justice, Steven. "The Genres of *Piers Plowman*." *Viator*, vol. 19, 1988, pp. 291–306.

———. *Writing and Rebellion: England in 1381*. U of California P, 1994.

Justice, Steven, and Kathryn Kerby-Fulton, editors. *Written Work: Langland, Labor, and Authorship*. U of Pennsylvania P, 1997.

Kane, George. "The Autobiographical Fallacy in Chaucer and Langland Studies." Kane, *Chaucer and Langland*, pp. 1–14.

———. *Chaucer and Langland: Historical and Textual Approaches*. U of California P, 1989.

———. "Langland, William." *Oxford Dictionary of National Biography*. Oxford UP, 2004–16, www.oxforddnb.com/view/article/16021?docPos=1.

———. "An Open Letter to Jill Mann about the Sequence of the Versions of *Piers Plowman*." *Yearbook of Langland Studies*, vol. 13, 1999, pp. 7–34.

———, editor. Piers Plowman*: Glossary; Will's Visions of Piers Plowman, Do-Well, Do-Better, and Do-Best*. Athlone Press, 2005.

———, editor. Piers Plowman*: The A Version; Will's Visions of Piers Plowman and Do-Well*. 1960. 2nd ed., Athlone Press, 1988.

———. Piers Plowman*: The Evidence for Authorship*. Athlone Press, 1965.

———. "Reading *Piers Plowman*." *Yearbook of Langland Studies*, vol. 8, 1994, pp. 1–20.

———. "Some Fourteenth-Century 'Political' Poems." *Medieval English Religious and Ethical Literature: Essays in Honour of G. H. Russell*, edited by Gregory Kratzmann and James Simpson, Boydell and Brewer, 1987, pp. 82–91.

———. "The Text." Alford, *Companion*, pp. 175–200.

Kane, George, and E. Talbot Donaldson, editors. Piers Plowman*: The B Version.* 1975. Athlone Press, 1988.

Keen, Maurice. *England in the Later Middle Ages*. 2nd ed., Routledge, 2003.

Kelen, Sarah A. *Langland's Early Modern Identities*. Palgrave Macmillan, 2007.

———. "Which Middle Ages? Literature Anthologies and Critical Ideologies." *Literature Compass*, vol. 1, 2004, pp. 1–6. *Wiley Online Library*, doi: 10.1111/j.1741-4113.2004.00030.x.

Kennedy, Edward D., et al., editors. *Medieval English Studies Presented to George Kane.* D. S. Brewer, 1988.

Kerby-Fulton, Kathryn. *Books under Suspicion: Censorship and Tolerance of Revelatory Writing in Late Medieval England.* U of Notre Dame P, 2011.

———. "Confronting the Scribe-Poet Binary: The Case of the Z Text of *Piers Plowman* and the Evidence of London Reading Circles." *New Directions in Medieval Manuscript Studies: Essays in Honour of Derek Pearsall*, edited by Kerby-Fulton et al., U of Notre Dame P, 2014, pp. 489–515.

———. "*Piers Plowman*." Wallace, *Cambridge History*, pp. 513–38.

———. *Reformist Apocalypticism and* Piers Plowman. Cambridge UP, 1990.

———. "Standing on Lewis's Shoulders: Some Reflections on C. S. Lewis's Stance as a Critic of Medieval Literature." *Studies in Medievalism*, vol. 3, 1991, pp. 257–78.

Kerby-Fulton, Kathryn, and Denise L. Despres. *Iconography and the Professional Reader: The Politics of Book Production in the Douce* Piers Plowman. U of Minnesota P, 1998.

Kerby-Fulton, Kathryn, et al. *Opening Up Middle English Manuscripts*. Cornell UP, 2012.

Kim, Margaret. "Hunger, Need, and the Politics of Poverty in *Piers Plowman*." *Yearbook of Langland Studies*, vol. 16, 2002, pp. 131–68.

King, John N. "Robert Crowley's Editions of *Piers Plowman*: A Tudor Apocalypse." *Modern Philology*, vol. 73, 1976, pp. 342–52.

Kirk, Elizabeth. *The Dream Thought of* Piers Plowman. Yale UP, 1972.

———. "Langland's Plowman and the Re-Creation of Fourteenth-Century Religious Metaphor." *Yearbook of Langland Studies*, vol. 2, 1988, pp. 1–21.

Kirchhoff, Sue. "Surplus U.S. Food Supplies Dry Up." *ABCNews*, abcnews.go.com/Business/story?id=4770135&page=1.

Kline, Daniel T., editor. *The Medieval British Literature Handbook*. Bloomsbury Academic, 2009.

Knapp, Ethan. *The Bureaucratic Muse: Thomas Hoccleve and the Literature of Late Medieval England.* Pennsylvania State UP, 2001.

Knott, Thomas A., and David C. Fowler, editors. Piers the Plowman*: A Critical Edition of the A-Version*. Johns Hopkins UP, 1952.

Knowles, Jim, and Timothy Stinson. "The *Piers Plowman* Electronic Archive on the Web: An Introduction." *Yearbook of Langland Studies*, vol. 28, 2014, pp. 225–38.

Kohanski, Tamarah, and C. David Benson, editors. *The Book of John Mandeville*. Medieval Institute Publications, 2012. *TEAMS: Middle English Text Series*, University of Rochester, d.lib.rochester.edu/teams/publication/kohanski-and-benson-the-book-of-john-mandeville.

Kristeva, Julia. *The Powers of Horror: An Essay in Abjection*. Columbia UP, 1982.

Krochalis, Jeanne, and Edward Peters, editors. *The World of* Piers Plowman. U of Pennsylvania P, 1975. The Middle Ages Series.

Kruger, Steven. "Dialogue, Debate, and Dream Vision." Scanlon, *Cambridge Companion*, pp. 71–82.

Kuczynski, Michael P. *Prophetic Song: The Psalms as Moral Discourse in Late Medieval England*. U of Pennsylvania P, 1995. Middle Ages Series.

Kuskin, William. *Recursive Origins: Writing at the Transition to Modernity*. U of Notre Dame P, 2013.

Lancashire, Anne. *London Civic Theatre: City Drama and Pageantry from Roman Times to 1558*. Cambridge UP, 2002.

Lawler, Traugott. "The Pardon Formula in *Piers Plowman*: Its Ubiquity, Its Binary Shape, Its Silent Middle Term." *Yearbook of Langland Studies*, vol. 14, 2000, pp. 117–52.

———, editor. *The Penn Commentary on* Piers Plowman*, Volume 4: C Passus 15–19; B Passus 13–17*. U of Pennsylvania P, 2018.

———. "A Reply to Jill Mann: Reaffirming the Traditional Relation between the A and B Versions of *Piers Plowman*." *Yearbook of Langland Studies*, vol. 10, 1996, pp. 145–80.

———. "Response to John Bowers, '*Piers Plowman*'s William Langland: Editing the Text, Writing the Author's Life.'" *Yearbook of Langland Studies*, vol. 9, 1995, pp. 94–98.

Lawlor, John. "The Imaginative Unity of *Piers Plowman*." *The Review of English Studies*, new series, vol. 8, no. 30, 1957, pp. 113–26.

———. Piers Plowman*: An Essay in Criticism*. Edward Arnold, 1962.

Lawton, David. "English Literary Voices, 1350–1500." Galloway, *Cambridge Companion*, pp. 237–58.

———. "The Style of *Piers Plowman*." Alford, *Companion*, pp. 223–50.

———. "The Subject of *Piers Plowman*." *Yearbook of Langland Studies*, vol. 1, 1987, pp. 1–30.

———. *Voice in Later Medieval English Literature: Public Interiorities*. Oxford UP, 2017.

Lees, Clare A. *The Cambridge History of Early Medieval English Literature*. Cambridge UP, 2012.

———. "Gender and Exchange in *Piers Plowman*." *Class and Gender in Early English Literature: Intersections*, edited by Britton H. Harwood and Gillian R. Overing, Indiana UP, 1994, pp. 112–30.

Lerer, Seth. *Boethius and Dialogue*. Princeton UP, 1985.

———. *Chaucer and His Readers: Imagining the Author in Late Medieval England*. Princeton UP, 1993.

Lerner, Robert. *The Powers of Prophecy: The Cedar of Lebanon Vision from the Mongol Onslaught to the Dawn of the Enlightenment.* U of California P, 1983.

Levine, Caroline. *Forms: Whole, Rhythm, Hierarchy, Network.* Princeton UP, 2015.

Lewis, C. S. *The Allegory of Love.* Oxford UP, 1958.

———. *Studies in Words.* Cambridge UP, 1960.

Lewis, Suzanne. *Reading Images: Narrative Discourse and Reception in the Thirteenth-Century Illuminated Apocalypse.* Cambridge UP, 1995.

Lewis, Tammy L. "Service Learning for Social Change? Lessons from a Liberal Arts College." *Teaching Sociology*, vol. 32, 2004, pp. 94–108.

"The Life of St. Edward the Confessor (MS Ee.3.59)." *University of Cambridge Digital Library*, cudl.lib.cam.ac.uk/view/MS-EE-00003-00059/1.

Liuzza, Roy M., editor and translator. Beowulf: *A New Verse Translation.* Broadview Press, 1999.

———. "*Beowulf* in Translation: Problems and Possibilities." Ramsey, pp. 23–40.

Lydgate, John. *Life of St. Edmund, King and Martyr.* Edited by A. S. G. Edwards, British Library, 2004.

Machan, Tim William. "Early Modern Middle English." *Caxton's Trace: Studies in the History of English Printing*, edited by William Kuskin, U of Notre Dame P, 2006, pp. 299–322.

Maclean, Ian. *The Renaissance Notion of Woman: A Study in the Fortunes of Scholasticism and Medical Science in European intellectual Life.* Cambridge UP, 1980.

Maguire, Stella. "The Significance of Haukyn, *Activa Vita*, in *Piers Plowman*." *The Review of English Studies*, old series, vol. 25, 1949, pp. 97–109.

Mandell, Laura, and Rita Raley. *Anthologies and Miscellanies.* 4 Nov. 2002, oldsite .english.ucsb.edu/faculty/rraley/research/anthologies.

Mann, Jill. *Chaucer and Medieval Estates Satire.* Cambridge UP, 1973.

———. *Langland and Allegory.* Medieval Institute Publications, 1992. Vol. 2 of The Morton W. Bloomfield Lectures on Medieval English Literature.

———. "The Power of the Alphabet: A Reassessment of the Relation between the A and B Versions of Piers Plowman." *Yearbook of Langland Studies*, vol. 8, 1994, pp. 21–50.

"Manuscript Images from Bodleian MS Douce 104: 'C-Text' of William Langland's *Piers Plowman*, 1427." *Luminarium: Anthology of English Literature*, 2010, www.luminarium.org/medlit/msdouce104.htm.

Marks, Richard. *Stained Glass in England during the Middle Ages.* Routledge, 2003.

Marshall, Claire. *William Langland:* Piers Plowman. Northcote House Publishers, 2001. Writers and Their Work.

Martin, Priscilla. Piers Plowman*: The Tower and the Field.* Macmillan, 1979.

Mason, Emma, et al., editors. *The Blackwell Companion to the Bible in English Literature.* Blackwell, 2009.

Matheson, Lister. Review of *William Langland* by Ralph Hanna. *Yearbook of Langland Studies*, vol. 8, 1994, p. 193.

Matsushita, Tomonori. *A Glossarial Concordance to William Langland's* The Vision of Piers Plowman*: The A-Text*. Shohakusha Publishing, 2009.

———, editor. *A Glossarial Concordance to William Langland's* The Vision of Piers Plowman*: The B-Text*. Olms-Weidman, 1997–2009. 3 vols.

———, editor. Piers Plowman*: The A Text, A Facsimile of the Society of Antiquaries of London MS 687*. Senshu UP, 2007.

———, editor. Piers Plowman*: The A Text, A Facsimile of Trinity College, Cambridge MS R.3.14*. Senshu UP, 2010.

———, editor. Piers Plowman*: The A Version, Facsimiles of the Twenty Manuscripts with Their Diplomatic Texts*. Senshu UP, 2008. 3 vols.

———, editor. Piers Plowman*: The Z Version, A Facsimile of Bodleian Library, Oxford MS Bodley 851*. Senshu UP, 2008.

———, editor. The Vision of Piers Plowman*: The C Text; A Facsimile of Huntington Library, San Marino, MS HM 143*. Senshu UP, 2010.

———, editor. *William Langland's* The Vision of Piers Plowman*: The B-Text, A Facsimile of Trinity College, Cambridge MS B.15.17*. Senshu UP, 2010. Senshu Studies in Language and Culture 10.

McGinn, Bernard. *The Calabrian Abbot: Joachim of Fiore in the History of Western Thought*. Macmillan, 1985.

———, editor. *Visions of the End: Apocalyptic Traditions in the Middle Ages*. Rev. ed., Columbia UP, 1998.

McIntosh, Marjorie. *Working Women in English Society, 1300–1620*. Cambridge UP, 2005.

McKisack, May. *The Fourteenth Century, 1307–1399*. Oxford UP, 1959.

McLeod, Susan. "The Tearing of the Pardon in *Piers Plowman*." *Philological Quarterly*, vol. 56, 1977, pp. 14–17.

McSheffrey, Shannon. *Marriage, Sex, and Civic Culture in Late Medieval London*. U of Pennsylvania P, 2006.

Meroney, Howard. "The Live and Death of Longe Wille." *ELH*, vol. 17, 1950, pp. 1–35.

Middle English Dictionary. Edited by H. Kurath et al., Regents of the University of Michigan, 1964–2001.

"Middle English Text Series Texts Online." *TEAMS: Middle English Text Series*, University of Rochester, d.lib.rochester.edu/teams/text-online.

Middleton, Anne. "Acts of Vagrancy: The C Version 'Autobiography' and the Statute of 1388." Justice and Kerby-Fulton, pp. 208–317.

———. *Chaucer, Langland, and Fourteenth-Century Literary History*. Edited by Steven Justice, Routledge, 2013. Variorum Collected Studies Series.

———. "The Critical Tradition." Alford, *Companion*, pp. 1–25.

———. "XVIII. *Piers Plowman*." *A Manual of the Writings in Middle English, 1050–1500*, edited by Albert E. Hartung, vol. 7, Yale UP, 1986, pp. 2211–34, 2417–43.

———. "The Idea of Public Poetry in the Reign of Richard II." *Speculum*, vol. 53, 1978, pp. 94–114.

———. "An Introduction: The Critical Heritage." Alford, *Companion*, pp. 1–25.

———. "Making a Good End: John But as a Reader of *Piers Plowman*." Kennedy et al., pp. 243–66.

———. "Narration and the Invention of Experience: Episodic Form in *Piers Plowman*." *The Wisdom of Poetry: Essays in Early English Literature in Honor of Morton W. Bloomfield*, edited by Larry D. Benson and Siegfried Wenzel, Medieval Institute Publications, 1982, pp. 91–122.

———. "William Langland's 'Kynde Name': Authorial Signature and Social Identity in Late Fourteenth-Century England." *Literary Practice and Social Change in Britain, 1380–1530*, edited by Lee Patterson, U of California P, 1990, pp. 15–82.

Miller, Mark. *Philosophical Chaucer: Love, Sex, and Agency in the Canterbury Tales*. Cambridge UP, 2009.

Minnis, A. J. *Medieval Theory of Authorship*. 2nd ed., U of Pennsylvania P, 1984.

Mitchell, Tania D. "Traditional vs. Critical Service-Learning: Engaging the Literature to Differentiate Two Models." *Michigan Journal of Community Service Learning*, vol. 14, no. 2, Spring 2008, pp. 50–65.

Moisa, Maria. "Fourteenth-Century Preachers' Views of the Poor: Class or Status Group?" *Culture, Ideology and Politics*, edited by Ralph Samuel and Gareth Stedman Jones, Routledge / Kegan Paul, 1982, pp. 160–75.

Mollat, Michel. *The Poor in the Middle Ages*. Translated by Arthur Goldhammer, Yale UP, 1986.

Mooney, Linne R. "Chaucer's Scribe." *Speculum*, vol. 81, 2006, pp. 97–138.

Morey, James H., editor. *The Prick of Conscience*. Medieval Institute Publications, 2012. *TEAMS: Middle English Text Series*, University of Rochester, d.lib.rochester.edu/teams/publication/morey-prik-of-conscience.

Murphy, Colette. "Lady Holy Church and Meed the Maid: Re-envisioning Female Personifications in *Piers Plowman*." *Feminist Readings in Middle English Literature*, edited by Ruth Evans and Lesley Johnson, Routledge, 1994, pp. 140–64.

Narin van Court, Elisa. "The Hermeneutics of Supersession: The Revision of the Jews from the B to the C text of *Piers Plowman*." *Yearbook of Langland Studies*, vol. 10, 1996, pp. 43–87.

Nelson, Alan H., and John R. Elliott, Jr., editors. *Inns of Court*. Boydell and Brewer, 2010. Records of Early English Drama. 3 vols.

Nightingale, Pamela. *A Medieval Mercantile Community: The Grocers' Company and the Politics and Trade of London, 1000–1485*. Yale UP, 1995.

Nissé, Ruth. "'A coroun ful riche': The Rule of History in *St. Erkenwald*." *ELH*, vol. 65, 1998, pp. 277–95.

Nolan, Barbara. *The Gothic Visionary Perspective*. Princeton UP, 1977.

Nolan, E. Peter. "Beyond Macaronic: Embedded Latin in Dante and Langland." *Acta Conventus Neo-Latini Bononiensis: Proceedings of the Fourth International Congress of Neo-Latin Studies*, edited by R. J. Schoeck, Medieval and Renaissance Texts and Studies, 1985, pp. 539–48.

Nussbaum, Martha. *Poetic Justice: The Literary Imagination and Public Life*. Beacon Press, 1995.

The Oxford English Dictionary. Edited by John Simpson and Edmund Weiner, 2nd ed., Clarendon Press, 1989.

Parker, Patricia. *Literary Fat Ladies: Rhetoric, Gender, Property*. Methuen, 1987.

Patterson, Lee. "The Logic of Textual Criticism and the Way of Genius: The Kane-Donaldson *Piers Plowman* in Historical Perspective." *Negotiating the Past: The Historical Understanding of Medieval Literature*, by Patterson, U of Wisconsin P, 1987, pp. 77–113.

Paxson, James J. "Gender Personified, Personification Gendered, and the Body Figuralized in *Piers Plowman*." *Yearbook of Langland Studies*, vol. 12, 1998, pp. 65–96.

Pearsall, Derek, editor. *An Annotated Critical Bibliography of Langland*. U of Michigan P, 1990.

———, editor. *Chaucer to Spenser: An Anthology of Writings in English, 1375–1575*. Wiley-Blackwell, 1998.

———. "The 'Ilchester' Manuscript of *Piers Plowman*." *Neuphilologische Mitteilungen*, vol. 82, no. 2, 1981, pp. 181–93.

———. "Langland's London." Justice and Kerby-Fulton, pp. 185–207.

———, editor. Piers Plowman*: A New Annotated Edition of the C-Text*. 1978. Revised ed., U of Exeter P, 2008.

———. "*Piers Plowman* Forty Years On." *Langland, the Mystics and the Medieval English Religious Tradition: Essays in Honor of S. S. Hussey*, edited by Helen Phillips, D. S. Brewer, 1990, pp. 1–9.

———. "Poverty and Poor People in *Piers Plowman*." Kennedy et al., pp. 167–85.

———. "The *Troilus* Frontispiece and Chaucer's Audience." *Yearbook of English Studies*, vol. 7, 1977, pp. 68–74.

Pearsall, Derek, and Kathleen L. Scott, editors. Piers Plowman*: A Facsimile of Bodleian Library, Oxford, MS Douce 104*. D. S. Brewer, 1992.

Pearsall, Derek, and Duncan Wu, editors. *Poetry from Chaucer to Spenser: Based on* Chaucer to Spenser: An Anthology of Writings in English, 1375–1575. Wiley-Blackwell, 2002.

Peirce, Charles Sanders. *Collected Papers of Charles S. Peirce*. Edited by Charles Hartshorne and Paul Weiss, Harvard UP, 1931–35. 6 vols.

Petrarch. *The Secret*. Edited by Carol E. Quillen, Bedford / St. Martin's, 2003.

Postan, M. M. *The Medieval Economy and Society: An Economic History of Britain in the Middle Ages*. Weidenfeld and Nicolson, 1972.

Proust, Marcel. *À la recherche du temps perdu*. Edited by Jean-Yves Tadié, Gallimard, 1999.

Puttenham, George. *The Arte of English Poesie*. Edited by Edward Arber, Alex. Murray and Son, 1869. *Google Books*, books.google.com/books/about/The_Arte_of_English_Poesie.html?id=_h7N5cx2QyoC.

Raabe, Pamela. *Imitating God: The Allegory of Faith in* Piers Plowman *B*. U of Georgia P, 1990.

Ramsey, Mary K., editor. Beowulf *in Our Time: Teaching* Beowulf *in Translation. Old English Newsletter Subsidia*, vol. 31, Medieval Institute Publications, 2002.

Randall, Lilian. *Images in the Margins of Gothic Manuscripts*. U of California P, 1966.

Raskolnikov, Masha. *Body against Soul: Gender and* Sowlehele *in Middle English Allegory*. Ohio State UP, 2009.

Rigg, A. G., and Charlotte Brewer, editors. Piers Plowman*: The Z Version*. Pontifical Institute of Mediaeval Studies, 1983. Studies and Texts 59.

Ríkharđsdóttir, Sif. *Medieval Translations and Cultural Discourse: The Movement of Texts in England, France and Scandinavia*. D. S. Brewer, 2012.

Roan, Shari. "Some Girls' Puberty Age Still Falling, Study Suggests." *Los Angeles Times*, 8 Aug. 2010, articles.latimes.com/2010/aug/08/science/la-sci-puberty-20100809.

Robertson, D. W., Jr. *A Preface to Chaucer*. Princeton UP, 1962.

Robertson, D. W., Jr., and Bernard F. Huppé. Piers Plowman *and Scriptural Tradition*. Princeton UP, 1951.

Robertson, Elizabeth. "Measurement and the 'Feminine' in *Piers Plowman*: A Response to Recent Studies of Langland and Gender." Hewett-Smith, pp. 167–94.

———. "Souls that Matter: The Gendering of the Soul in *Piers Plowman*." *Mindful Spirit in Late Medieval Literature: Essays in Honor of Elizabeth D. Kirk*, edited by Bonnie Wheeler, Palgrave Macmillan, 2006, pp. 165–86.

Robertson, Elizabeth, and Stephen H. A. Shepherd, editors. *Piers Plowman*. W. W. Norton, 2006. Norton Critical Editions.

Robertson, Kellie. *The Laborer's Two Bodies: Literary and Legal Productions in Britain, 1350–1500*. Palgrave Macmillan, 2005.

Rogers, Owen, printer. *The vision of Pierce Plowman, newlye imprynted after the authours olde copy, with a brefe summary of the principall matters set before every part called Passus. . . .* London, 1561.

Rogers, William Elford. *Interpretation in* Piers Plowman. Catholic U of America P, 2002.

Rothwell, William. "The Trilingual England of Geoffrey Chaucer." *Studies in the Age of Chaucer*, vol. 16, 1994, pp. 45–67.

Rubin, Miri. *Charity and Community in Medieval Cambridge*. Cambridge UP, 1987.

Rudd, Gillian. *Managing Language in* Piers Plowman. D. S. Brewer, 1994.

Ruggiers, Paul G., editor. The Canterbury Tales*: A Facsimile and Transcription of the Hengwrt Manuscript with Variants from the Ellesmere Manuscript*. U of Oklahoma P, 1979.

Russell, George, and George Kane, editors. *Piers Plowman: The C Version*. Athlone Press, 1997.

Salter, Elizabeth. *Fourteenth-Century English Poetry*. Clarendon Press, 1983.

———. Piers Plowman*: An Introduction*. Basil Blackwell, 1962.

Salter, Elizabeth, and Derek Pearsall, editors. Piers Plowman*: Selections from the C-Text*. Edward Arnold, 1967. York Medieval Texts.

Saunders, Corinne, editor. *A Companion to Medieval Poetry*. Wiley-Blackwell, 2007.

Scala, Elizabeth. Review of *Shakespeare in the Middle Ages*, edited by Curtis Perry and John Watkins. *The Medieval Review*, Indiana U, 2010, scholarworks.iu.edu/journals/index.php/tmr/article/view/17035/23153.

Scanlon, Larry, editor. *The Cambridge Companion to Medieval English Literature, 1100–1500*. Cambridge UP, 2009.

Scase, Wendy. "*Dauy Dycars Dreame* and Robert Crowley's Prints of *Piers Plowman*." *Yearbook of Langland Studies*, vol. 21, 2007, pp. 171–98.

———, editor. *A Facsimile Edition of the Vernon Manuscript: A Literary Hoard from Medieval England*. Software by Nick Kennedy, Bodleian Library / University of Oxford, 2011. DVD-ROM.

———, editor. *The Making of the Vernon Manuscript: The Production and Contexts of Oxford, Bodleian Library, MS Eng. poet.a.1*. Brepols, 2013.

———. Piers Plowman *and the New Anticlericalism*. 1989. Cambridge UP, 2007.

Schless, Howard H. "The Backgrounds of Allegory: Langland and Dante." *Yearbook of Langland Studies*, vol. 5, 1991, pp. 129–42.

Schmidt, A. V. C. *The Clerkly Maker: Langland's Poetic Art*. D. S. Brewer, 1987.

———. *Earthly Honest Things: Collected Essays on* Piers Plowman. Cambridge Scholars Publishing, 2012.

———, translator. Piers Plowman*: A New Translation of the B-Text*. Oxford UP, 1992.

———, editor. Piers Plowman*: A Parallel-Text Edition of the A, B, C, and Z Versions*. Vol. 1, Longman, 1995.

———, editor. Piers Plowman*: A Parallel-Text Edition of the A, B, C, and Z Versions*. Vol. 2, Medieval Institute Publications, 2008.

———, editor. Piers Plowman*: A Parallel-Text Edition of the A, B, C, and Z Versions*. 2nd rev. ed., Medieval Institute Publications, 2011. 2 vols.

———, editor. The Vision of Piers Plowman*: A Critical Edition Based on Trinity College Cambridge MS. B.15.17*. 1978. 2nd ed., J. M. Dent / Charles E. Tuttle, 1995. Everyman Library.

Schofield, John. *Holy Trinity Priory, Aldgate, City of London: An Archaeological Reconstruction and History*. Museum of London Archaeology Service, 2005.

Schott, Christine. "Marginalia in *Piers Plowman*." *Rare Book School*, 2014, rarebookschool.org/2014/fellowships/rbs-uva/plowman.html.

Scott, Anne M. Piers Plowman *and the Poor*. Four Courts Press, 2004.

Seymour, M. C., et al., editors. On the Properties of Things, *John Trevisa's Translation of Bartholomaeus Anglicus,* De Proprietatibus Rerum*: A Critical Text*, Clarendon Press, 1975–1988. 3 vols.

Shepherd, Geoffrey. "Poverty in *Piers Plowman*." *Social Relations and Ideas: Essays in Honour of R. H. Hilton*, edited by T. H. Aston et al., Cambridge UP, 1983, pp. 169–89.

Shesgreen, Sean. "Canonizing the Canonizer: A Short History of *The Norton Anthology of English Literature*." *Critical Inquiry*, vol. 35, no. 2, 2009, pp. 293–318.

Shipler, David. *The Working Poor: Invisible in America.* Alfred A. Knopf, 2004.

Simpson, James. *Burning to Read: English Fundamentalism and Its Reformation Opponents.* Harvard UP, 2007.

———. "Desire and the Scriptural Text: Will as Reader in *Piers Plowman*." *Criticism and Dissent in the Middle Ages*, edited by Rita Copeland, Oxford UP, 1995, pp. 215–43.

———. "From Reason to Affective Knowledge: Modes of Thought and Poetic Form in *Piers Plowman*." *Medium Ævum*, vol. 55, 1986, pp. 1–23.

———. Piers Plowman*: An Introduction to the B-Text.* 1990. 2nd rev. ed., Liverpool UP, 2007. Exeter Medieval Texts and Studies.

———. "The Power of Impropriety: Authorial Naming in *Piers Plowman*." Hewett-Smith, pp. 145–65.

———. "Spirituality and Economics in Passus 1–7 of the B-Text." *Yearbook of Langland Studies*, vol. 1, 1987, pp. 83–103.

Sitwell, Sacheverell. *Monks, Nuns, and Monasteries.* Holt, Rinehart, and Winston, 1965.

Skeat, W. W. "An Essay on Alliterative Poetry." *Bishop Percy's Folio Manuscript*, edited by J. W. Hales and F. J. Furnivall, vol. 3, N. Trübner, 1867–68, pp. xi–xxxix.

———, editor. *The Vision of William Concerning Piers the Plowman in Three Parallel Texts: Together with Richard the Redeless.* 1886. Oxford UP, 1986. 2 vols.

Smith, D. Vance. *The Book of the Incipit: Beginnings in the Fourteenth Century.* U of Minnesota P, 2001.

Smith, Paul. *Discerning the Subject.* U of Minnesota P, 1988.

Snyder, Susan. "The Left Hand of God: Despair in Medieval and Renaissance Tradition." *Studies in the Renaissance*, vol. 12, 1965, pp. 18–59.

Somerset, Fiona. "'Al þe comonys with o voys atonys': Multilingual Latin and Vernacular Voice in *Piers Plowman*." *Yearbook of Langland Studies*, vol. 19, 2005, pp. 107–36.

———. *Clerical Discourse and Lay Audience in Late Medieval England.* Cambridge UP, 1998.

Spearing, A. C. "The Development of a Theme in *Piers Plowman*." *The Review of English Studies*, vol. 11, 1960, pp. 241–53.

———. "Langland's Poetry: Some Notes in Critical Analysis." *Leeds Studies in English*, vol. 14, 1983, pp. 182–95.

———. *Medieval Autographies: The "I" of the Text.* U of Notre Dame P, 2012.

———. *Textual Subjectivity: The Encoding of Subjectivity in Medieval Narratives and Lyrics.* Oxford UP, 2005.

Sponsler, Claire. "Alien Nation: London's Aliens and Lydgate's Mummings for the Mercers and Goldsmiths." *The Postcolonial Middle Ages*, edited by Jeffrey Jerome Cohen, St. Martin's Press, 2000, pp. 229–42.

Stallybrass, Peter. "Patriarchal Territories: The Body Enclosed." *Rewriting the Renaissance: The Discourses of Sexual Difference in Early Modern Europe*, edited by Margaret Ferguson et al., U of Chicago P, 1986, pp. 123–42.

Stanton, Anne Rudloff. *The Queen Mary Psalter: A Study of Affect and Audience.* American Philosophical Society, 2001.

Steiner, Emily. *Documentary Culture and the Making of Medieval English Literature.* Cambridge UP, 2003. Cambridge Studies in Medieval Literature.

———. *Reading* Piers Plowman. Cambridge UP, 2013. Reading Writers and Their Work.

Stingle, Richard. "Frye, Northrup." *The Johns Hopkins Guide to Literary Theory and Criticism*, edited by Michael Groden et al., 2005–12, litguide.press.jhu.edu.

Stock, Brian. *The Implications of Literacy: Written Language and Models of Interpretation in the Eleventh and Twelfth Centuries.* Princeton UP, 1983.

Strohm, Paul. *England's Empty Throne: Usurpation and the Language of Legitimation, 1399–1422.* Yale UP, 1998.

———, editor. *Middle English.* Oxford UP, 2007. Oxford Twenty-First Century Approaches to Literature.

Sutton, Peter, translator. Piers Plowman*: A Modern Verse Translation.* McFarland, 2014.

Szittya, Penn R. *The Antifraternal Tradition in Middle English Literature.* Princeton UP, 1986.

———. "Domesday Books: The Apocalypse in Medieval English Literary Culture." Emmerson and McGinn, pp. 374–97.

Tadié, Jean-Yves. *Marcel Proust: A Life.* Translated by Euan Cameron, Viking Books, 2000.

Tavormina, Teresa M. *Kindly Similitude: Marriage and Family in* Piers Plowman. D. S. Brewer, 1995.

Taylor, John, et al., editors and translators. *The St. Albans Chronicle: The* Chronica Maiora *of Thomas Walsingham: Volume 1, 1376–1394.* Clarendon Press, 2003.

Teskey, Gordon. *Allegory and Violence.* Cornell UP, 1996.

Thrupp, Sylvia. *The Merchant Class of Medieval London.* U of Michigan P, 1948.

Tierney, Brian. "The Decretalists and the 'Deserving Poor.'" *Comparative Studies in Society and History*, vol. 1, no. 4, 1959, pp. 360–73.

———. *Medieval Poor Law: A Sketch of Canonical Theory and Its Application in England.* U of California P, 1959.

Tiller, Terence, translator. The Vision of Piers Plowman *by William Langland.* British Broadcasting Company, 1981.

Tiller, Terence, and J. R. R. Tolkien, translators. *William Langland's* Piers Plowman *with* Sir Gawain and the Green Knight, Pearl, *and* Sir Orfeo *(anon.).* Everyman's Library, 2001.

Todorov, Tzvetan. *The Fantastic: A Structural Approach to a Literary Genre.* Cornell UP, 1973.

Trapp, J. B., et al., editors. *Middle English Literature.* 2nd ed., Oxford UP, 2002. Vol. 1 of *Oxford Anthology of English Literature.*

Treharne, Elaine, editor. *E-Medieval: Teaching, Research, and the Net.* With Orietta Da Rold. Special issue of *Literature Compass*, vol. 9, no. 12, 2012.

———, editor. *Old and Middle English, c. 890–c. 1450: An Anthology.* 3rd ed., Wiley-Blackwell, 2009.

Treharne, Elaine, and Greg Walker, editors. *The Oxford Handbook of Medieval Literature in English*. Oxford UP, 2010.

Trigg, Stephanie. "The Traffic in Medieval Women: Alice Perrers, Feminist Criticism, and *Piers Plowman*." *Yearbook of Langland Studies*, vol. 12, 1998, pp. 5–30.

Turner, Marion. "Greater London." *Chaucer and the City*, edited by Ardis Butterfield, D. S. Brewer, 2006, pp. 25–40.

———, editor. *A Handbook of Middle English Studies*. Wiley-Blackwell, 2013.

Turville-Petre, Thorlac. *The Alliterative Revival*. Rowman and Littlefield, 1977.

———. *Reading Middle English Literature: An Introduction*. Wiley, 2006.

Van Dyke, Carolynn. *The Fiction of Truth: Structures of Meaning in Narrative and Dramatic Allegory*. Cornell UP, 1985.

Vaughan, Míċeál F. "The Ending(s) of *Piers Plowman*." Vaughan, *Suche Werkis*, pp. 211–41.

———. "The Liturgical Perspectives of *Piers Plowman B*, XVI–XIX." *Studies in Medieval and Renaissance History*, new series, vol. 3, 1980, pp. 87–155.

———, editor. Piers Plowman*: The A Version*. Johns Hopkins UP, 2011.

———, editor. *Suche Werkis to Werche: Essays on* Piers Plowman *in Honor of David C. Fowler*. Michigan State UP, 1993.

Venuti, Lawrence, editor. *The Translation Studies Reader*. Routledge, 1999.

Vickers, Nancy. "Seeing Is Believing: Gregory, Trajan, and Dante's Art." *Dante Studies*, vol. 101, 1983, pp. 67–85.

The Vision of William Concerning Piers the Plowman. Directed by Meg Twycross, Joculatores Oxonienses, 14–18 May 1974, University Church of St. Mary the Virgin, Oxford.

Voragine, Jacobus de. *The Golden Legend*. Translated by William Caxton. *Internet Medieval Sourcebook*, Fordham University, sourcebooks.fordham.edu/basis/golden legend/index.asp.

Walker, Greg. "The Textual Archaeology of the *Plowman's Tale*." *Studies in Late Medieval Literature and Early Renaissance Texts in Honour of John Scattergood*, edited by Anne Marie D'Arcy and Alan J. Fletcher, Four Courts Press, 2005, pp. 375–401.

Wallace, David. "Assessing the New Author: Commentary on Dante." *Medieval Literary Theory and Criticism, c. 1100–c. 1375: The Commentary Tradition*, edited by A. J. Minnis and A. B. Scott, with the assistance of David Wallace, revised ed., Clarendon Press, 1991, pp. 439–58.

———, editor. *The Cambridge History of Medieval English Literature*. Cambridge UP, 2002.

———, editor. *Europe: A Literary History, 1348–1418*. Oxford UP, 2016.

Warner, Lawrence. "John But and the Other Works That Will Wrought (*Piers Plowman* A XII 101–02)." *Notes and Queries*, new series, vol. 52, 2005, pp. 13–18.

———. *The Lost History of* Piers Plowman*: The Earliest Transmission of Langland's Work*. U of Pennsylvania P, 2011.

———. *The Myth of* Piers Plowman*: Constructing a Medieval Literary Archive.* Cambridge UP, 2014.

———. "Plowman Traditions in Late Medieval and Early Modern Writing." Cole and Galloway, pp. 198–213.

———. "Scribes, Misattributed: Hoccleve and Pinkhurst." *Studies in the Age of Chaucer*, vol. 37, 2015, pp. 55–100.

———. "The Vision of Piers Plowman, Said to Be Wrote by Chaucer: Leland's *Petri Aratoris Fabula* and Its Descendants Revisited." *Chaucer Review*, vol. 48, 2013, pp. 113–28.

Warren, Michelle R. "Translation." Strohm, *Middle English*, pp. 51–67.

Watson, Nicholas. "Chaucer and Langland." Hass et al., pp. 363–89.

———. "*Piers Plowman*, Pastoral Theology, and Spiritual Perfectionism: Hawkyn's Cloak and Patience's *Pater Noster.*" *Yearbook of Langland Studies*, vol. 21, 2007, pp. 83–118.

———. "Visions of Inclusion: Universal Salvation and Vernacular Theology in Pre-Reformation England." *Journal of Medieval and Early Modern Studies*, vol. 27, no. 2, 1997, pp. 145–88.

Weinstein, Simcha. *Up, Up, and Oy Vey: How Jewish History, Culture, and Values Shaped the Comic Book Superhero.* Barricade Books, 2009.

Whatley, Gordon. "The Uses of Hagiography: The Legend of Pope Gregory and the Emperor Trajan in the Middle Ages." *Viator*, vol. 15, 1984, pp. 25–63.

Whitaker, T. D., editor. *Visio Willi de Petro Ploughman Item Visiones ejusdem de Dowel, Dobet, et Dobest.* Murray, 1813.

William Langland: Poet and Dreamer. Performance by Peter Sutton and Stephanie Connell, 2012, Autumn in Malvern Festival, Malvern, England.

"William Langland's *Piers Plowman* at the Kelly Writers House." *PennSound*, University of Pennsylvania, 2007, writing.upenn.edu/pennsound/x/Piers-Plowman.php.

Williams, Margaret, RSCJ, translator. Piers the Plowman *by William Langland.* Random House, 1971.

Wittig, Joseph S. "'Culture Wars' and the Persona in *Piers Plowman.*" *Yearbook of Langland Studies*, vol. 15, 2001, pp. 167–95.

———. "*Piers Plowman* B, Passus IX–XII: Elements in the Design of the Inward Journey." *Traditio*, vol. 28, 1972, pp. 211–80.

———. Piers Plowman*: Concordance.* Athlone Press, 2001.

———. *William Langland Revisited.* Twayne Publishers, 1997. Twayne's English Author Series.

Wofford, Susanne. "Britomart's Petrarchan Lament: Allegory and Narrative in *The Faerie Queene.*" *Comparative Literature*, vol. 39, 1987, pp. 28–57.

Wright, Rosemary Muir. *Art and Antichrist in Medieval Europe.* Manchester UP, 1995.

Wright, T., editor. *The Vision and the Creed of Piers Ploughman, newly imprinted.* Pickering, 1832. 2 vols.

———. *The Vision and the Creed of Piers Plowman, newly imprinted.* Pickering, 1842. Rev. ed., 1856. 2 vols.

Zeeman, Nicolette. "The Condition of *Kynde*." *Medieval Literature and Historical Inquiry: Essays in Honour of Derek Pearsall*, edited by David Aers, Boydell and Brewer, 2000, pp. 1–30.

———. Piers Plowman *and the Medieval Discourse of Desire.* Cambridge UP, 2009.

———. "*Piers Plowman* in Theory." Cole and Galloway, pp. 214–29.

Zumthor, Paul. *Introduction à la poésie orale.* Seuil, 1983.

———. *Oral Poetry: An Introduction.* Translated by Kathy Murphy-Judy, U of Minnesota P, 1990.

———. "Pour une poétique de la voix." *Poétique*, vol. 40, 1979, pp. 514–24.

INDEX